Development control

£39.99

The Natural and Built Environment series

Editors: Professor Michael J. Bruton, The Residuary Body for Wales
Professor John Glasson, Oxford Brookes University

Development control

PRINCIPLES AND PRACTICE

Keith Thomas

Spon Press
Taylor & Francis Group

LONDON AND NEW YORK

First published in 1997 by UCL Press

Reprinted 2004
By Routledge
2 Park Square, Milton Park,
Abingdon, Oxon, OX14 4RN

Transferred to Digital Printing 2004

Routledge is an imprint of the Taylor and Francis Group, an informa business

British Library Cataloguing-in-Publication Data
A CIP catalogue record for this book is available from the British Library.

Library of Congress Cataloging-in-Publication Data are available

ISBN 10: 1-85728-626-X (cased)
ISBN 10: 1-85728-627-8 (limp)

ISBN 13: 978-1-85728-626-7 (cased)
ISBN 13: 978-1-85728-627-4 (limp)

Printed and bound in Great Britain by
TJI Digital, Padstow, Cornwall

To my friendly and frenetic colleagues in
the School of Planning, Oxford Brookes University

Contents

8 Conflict and controversy 223

9 The future 265

Preface

This book on development control was written to fill a perceived gap in the market for books on the environment. Town and country planning activity is one way in which society seeks to control its surroundings. Other controls include environmental health and building regulations. Town and country planning as practised in the UK may be divided into three major activities: plan-making which provides a vision of how an area might be in the future, taking initiatives such as new town building and the redevelopment of old town centres and last but not least development control.

But what is development control? Whenever a prospective developer wants to build something substantial or change the use of a building, permission – planning permission – is sought from the local council. The local council is usually the democratically elected district council. The council may grant or refuse permission in line with their plan. What they are doing is controlling development. The development may be relatively small scale such as a house extension or changing a large house into a hotel or large scale such as building a large factory. In each case common problems will arise, for example what will the development look like? Will there be enough parking and can the road network take the strain? And will the factory or hotel be noisy?

As the population has become wealthier and home and car ownership has increased, it has become much more sensitive about developments in its area. There is now widespread concern about green issues and whether we are wantonly destroying our environment on which we all depend. Recent rapid increases in car usage and atmospheric pollution in the 1990s have particularly heightened awareness.

Surprisingly there is no book on development control in the UK which takes an overview of this important environmental safeguard although there are some on specialist aspects. It is the purpose of this book to fill this gap. It has been developed from courses on development control at Oxford Brookes University and is based on an earlier simpler book *An introduction to development control* (Thomas 1994). This was written for lay readers and students coming to development control for the first time.

The present readership is likely to be students of town and country planning, estate management, architecture and cognate subjects such as civil engineering, landscape, geography, law, economics, politics and sociology. It will also interest general readers who want a deeper understanding of environmental issues and controls. The book is not intended as a guide for householders on how to obtain planning permission (see DOE Mar 1996, Dijksman 1992, Willman for the Consumers Association 1990) nor is it a guide to planning law (see Grant, continuing, Alder 1989, Morgan & Nott 1995, Casely-Hayford 1995) nor as a reference book for planning practitioners (See Holt, continuing). Each of these has its merits: some are very focused and specialist, for example Alder on development control law. Others such as Holt on development control practice are large-scale works. In this case it runs to three volumes and a million words.

The author's intention is to provide an overview of the subject in the round to bring out the principles involved in development control illuminated by examples taken from practice. As the subject matter is wide ranging the book is not exhaustive, although the author hopes that the main subject areas have been covered.

It is assumed readers will have some knowledge of town and country planning. To make reading as easy as possible the author has used the following formula where it is relevant for each subject area: background, description, comment and argument. The reader will rapidly become aware that argument is very important in this subject area.

A glossary and short notes appendix deals with some technical definitions and covers some of the subjects not covered in the main text. A further appendix deals with development control in the Celtic lands. However, as the principles and practice are generally the same throughout the UK English sources are normally quoted.

Every effort has been made to be accurate and up-to-date as far as spring 1996 with some later entries. However, readers should always refer to original sources where necessary. Although the main principles of development control have remained unchanged for half a century, there is a constant stream of adjustments and improvements to the system in the light of practice and political change.

Acknowledgements

I would like to acknowledge the unstinting help of my colleagues Bob Bixby, Roy Darke, Jane Darke, John Glasson, Philip Grover, Roddy Macdonald, Roger Mason and Joe Weston, who have commented on parts of the text.

I would also like to acknowledge the longstanding help given to me by Catherine Tranmer, the planning subject librarian at Oxford Brookes University.

I must wholeheartedly thank my wife, Tonie, for typing and helping to prepare the text for publication.

Thanks are also due to Roger Jones for editorial and production assistance.

Finally, I gratefully acknowledge permission from the authors and the Royal Town Planning Institute for the use of copyright material in Tables 5.1 and 6.10.

Abbreviations

DoE, WO, SOED/SODD, DoE (NI), UK
Department of the Environment (for England), Welsh Office, Scottish Office Environment Department/Scottish Office Development Department and the Department of the Environment for Northern Ireland. These are central government agencies responsible for oversight of the development control system in the constituent countries of the United Kingdom (UK). Where (S) is inserted in an abbreviation, it refers to Scotland.

GDO, GPDO and GDPO
General Development Order 1988, General Permitted Development Order 1995 and General Development Procedure Order 1995. These important statutory instruments lay down in general terms various categories of development which do and do not require planning permission and associated matters. The GDO 1988 was superseded by the GPDO and GDPO in 1995.

LPA
Local planning authority. Local planning authorities in Britain are normally democratically elected district councils. In Northern Ireland central government is the local planning authority. In London they are the London Boroughs. For limited purposes shire counties in England, but not metropolitan counties, may be LPAs. They prepare development plans and are responsible for nearly all day-to-day development control work, which is the subject of this book.

PPG, MPG, RPG and NPPG, PAN
Planning Policy Guidance notes, Mineral Planning Guidance notes, Regional Planning Guidance notes in England and National Planning Policy Guidelines and Planning Advice Notes in Scotland. In Wales, English and Welsh PPGs were superseded by Planning Guidance (Wales) with effect from Spring 1996: Technical Advice Notes (TANs) were awaited for Wales in 1996. These publications contain central government policy and technical advice on the preparation of development plans and the operation of the development control system.

UCO
Use Classes Order. The UCO 1987, another statutory instrument, lays down which changes of use of land and buildings require planning permission.

CHAPTER 1
Introduction

Introduction

> Planning as an activity is widely recognized as a legitimate and valued aspect
> of public policy. General understanding of development control is far more
> advanced than of development plans and their purposes. (McCarthy et al.
> 1995: vi)

The quotation above is from an investigative survey carried out at the instigation
of the Department of the Environment. It established that in the 1990s the activity
of development control was recognized by the public as valued by them. However, there was a long-held contrary view.

> Development control, the term used in Britain to define the system of issuing
> permits for land-use development, has been for the most part a vilified process. Although the nadir of its fortunes has passed – the low point seems
> to have been somewhere between 1980 and 1985 – to British ears the term
> rings with overtones of bureaucratic time-wasting and negativism. From
> within the planning profession, too, development control has not always
> been seen in a favourable light. For long the Cinderella of the profession,
> as several commentators have described it, until the 1980s it tended to attract
> less qualified staff and to be associated with drudgery. The smart thing for
> new recruits to the profession was forward planning . . . . Some of that at
> least has changed; there is nothing now to suggest that development control
> staff have fewer qualifications than their colleagues who prepare plans, and
> development control has for some time been recognized as no less intellectually challenging than plan-making. Yet, even today, planning literature
> has rather less to say about the control of development than it does about
> plan-making and policy (Booth 1996: 1).

Development control in the UK, as it is practised in the 1990s, came into being
as a result of powers contained in the Town and Country Planning Acts 1947,
which became operative in 1948. After half a century it has come of age as a
very important professional activity, both to the public at large and to the

1

professions closely associated with the built environment (McCarthy et al. 1995). The planning of towns, of which development control is part, is a very ancient activity. For example, classical Greek and Roman towns were often laid out in a systematic way. Examples exist from a wide range of cultures from China to Europe and independently in pre-Columbian America. The need to plan towns, and the country, seems to be deeply imbedded in the human psyche. Towns are still with us that were laid out for defensive purposes, the aggrandizement of the powerful, to reflect social and economic divisions in society, as acts of philanthropy, and for religious reasons.

Modern town planning in the UK sprang partly from the need to solve the problems of squalor brought on by rapid urbanization in the nineteenth century and partly to cope with rebuilding war-damaged cities after the Second World War. At that time there was a coalition of interests. In part, planning was seen as an arm of the welfare state, concerned in particular with better housing, better working conditions, slum clearance and better health. Planning in a wider sense, rather than *laissez-faire* capitalism, was necessary for the successful conclusion of the war effort. In part, planning was promoted by those concerned with the countryside. The protection from development of good agricultural land for food production has been a longstanding theme, as has the protection of the beauty of the countryside from urban sprawl. Another strand has been the "city beautiful movement": development is a form of public art. This background is enlarged upon in Chapter 6 (see Ashworth 1954, Cherry 1974, Booth 1996.)

The importance of development control can be considered in two other ways. First, about a half of all annual investment in the UK is in "land, buildings and works". This amounts to about one tenth of the gross national product. Experience has shown that it is vital that these assets are well managed. Much, but not all of this development investment passes through the development control system for a decision as to whether it should be allowed or not. Each year about half a million planning applications for development are processed. They fluctuate with the trade cycle. For example, in England in 1988–9 there were 683000 applications, but in 1992–3 only 464000; that is a fall of about a third in quite a short period (DoE annual, Thomas 1995). These fluctuations can bear heavily on the workloads of local councils. Secondly, development control is the largest single identifiable activity carried out by local authority planning departments. In a survey of planning staff in England and Wales in 1991, development control occupied 26 per cent of the relevant workforce; next were development plans at 13 per cent, management at 7 per cent and appeals at nearly 5 per cent (Local Government Management Board & RTPI 1992: 32). Each of the other activities, arguably and possibly associated with development control (e.g. enforcement nearly 3%) occupied less than 5 per cent of the workforce. Advising clients on planning applications and appeals is also a major part of the work of private planning consultants.

The content of this book has been circumscribed by the availability of the literature. As Booth has implied above, the literature is not as comprehensive as one might hope. No original research has been undertaken here by the author. Reliance has been on published sources. Much day-to-day knowledge of the practice of development control is locked inside the heads of development controllers, developers and other related professionals and councillors. Unless they report it or it is extracted through research, it remains there.

As development control as currently practised is highly dependent on statutory powers, a key starting point is the Town and Country Planning Act 1990 and the Planning and Compensation Act 1991 and subsidiary legislation, especially the General Permitted Development Order 1995 and the Use Classes Order 1987. The legislative background is described in Chapter 3. As practice is very much guided by other central government guidance, one must look next to Circulars and Planning Policy Guidance Notes (PPGs). They not only give government policy on how development plan and development control issues should be approached but also the background considerations, of which one needs to be aware to understand the issues. Apart from these, central government publishes other statements of their position, such as good practice guides, and also sponsors research, which is frequently used in the text. However, the literature mentioned so far has been produced in the 1980s and early 1990s by a right-wing government enjoying an almost unprecedented fourth term of office. Clearly, it had an explicit free-market deregulatory agenda: guidance and their research programme are shaped by this. The critical reader should therefore always be asking what would change if a government of another persuasion were in power. It must be remembered that, on the other hand, many local governments who effectively make most of the day-to-day development control decisions are of quite different persuasions.

Apart from central government sources, there is a range of other bodies and individuals that produce literature which has been incorporated in the text, much of it critical of the way the development control system works and how it might be altered and improved. Two major sources are academic and professional books and journals, some of which might be described as research based and others practice based. Research may be for the purposes of practice or into practice itself. It is based on the science and social science tradition that sets up a hypothesis or hunch about reality, which is investigated by systematically collecting and sifting evidence that seeks to prove or disprove it by rational argument. Professional literature, if it can be distinguished from academic literature, is written more from the author's day-to-day experience as he sees it. It is no less valuable. It may consist of letters to the press or short commentaries. Besides these sources, there is literature produced by environmental pressure groups with particular axes to grind. Of course, planning literature comes not only from those engaged in mainline planning and development control but also from other disciplines, for example law and architecture.

Considered in rather a different way, changes in the principles and practice of development control can come about in at least three structured ways, each of which results in considerable literature:

- As a result of draft policy guidance issued for consultation on the basis of

3

information received. Where improvements in the system are sought, central government often issues draft guidance to other government bodies, academics, professional associations and pressure groups for comment. Comments are considered that lead to modifications before definitive guidance is issued.

- As a result of formal inquiry into particularly fraught situations. Experts and others are invited to submit evidence. It is sifted, and recommendations are made to government for action.
- As a result of specifically sponsored research in the scientific tradition. Projects are set up with a brief from government to investigate particular issues. They are usually carried out by private consultants or academics. Recommendations are made to government for action.

The resulting literature may be ephemeral and/or difficult to locate and access.

Before briefly describing the structure of the book, a description of the structure of the development control system is offered. Coming to the subject from outside for the first time can be very confusing. I therefore offer some structuring devices to aid understanding. They all overlap and interact. Development control is a very wide-ranging subject and can embrace all human endeavour as far as it is expressed in the use of land:

- *Substance and procedure* Development control is concerned with the real substance of development, for example the colour of a building or the width of a road. It is also concerned with a rational and legal procedure – a bureaucratic paper chase – by which decisions are made. In practice, substance and procedure are inseparable.
- *Scale* Development control operates at widely different scales. At a humble level it may be concerned with the type of bricks or tiles used in a building. At the other end of the scale it could deal with an international airport extension. The customary scales of operation are: site level, local or district level, strategic or county or regional level, national level and international level. Many planning applications are small-scale householder applications (see Appendix III).
- *Professional disciplines* It is in the nature of the building industry that many professionals are involved, all with their own perspectives. These include architects, landscape architects, surveyors, civil engineers, lawyers, financial experts and others, including politicians and administrators. The role of the planning profession is to ensure that what is built fits into the environment in an orderly way.
- *Activities in adapted spaces* Planners are concerned with four basic types of human activity and the buildings and spaces that accommodate them: workspaces, such as factories and schools; residential buildings, such as houses and residential institutions; and leisure facilities, such as playing fields and theatres. Transport is the fourth activity, which physically connects the other three, for example by road. Development control is not only concerned with new buildings but also with new activities in old buildings.

Consider the parking implications of changing a house to an office. Moreover, these activities interact: substantial new housing leads to an increased demand for new shops, schools and road space.

The structure of the book is as follows. Chapter 1 introduces the subject and deals particularly with the purposes and characteristics of development control. Chapter 2 is concerned with the town and country planning system and sets development control in its wider context. Chapter 3 outlines the legal basis and deals inter alia with planning application procedures. The reader will become aware that the legal basis is complex. Chapter 4 on simplifying development control is somewhat of a diversion. It may be left until later, although it follows logically from Chapter 3. It contains arguments as to where the boundaries of development control should lie. Chapter 5 describes the factors taken into account when planning permission is granted or refused, with an emphasis on this crucial decision. Chapter 6 deals with the substantive subject matter of most applications: siting, design, external appearance, access and landscaping. Chapter 7 is something of a potpourri, ranging from the relatively nice to the relatively naughty in development control terms: conservation, the countryside, advertisements, minerals and hazardous uses. Each is a special topic deserving special treatment. Chapters 8 and 9 stand somewhat apart. I have sought throughout to intersperse the text with the arguments that surround development control issues. Chapter 8 has, perhaps idiosyncratically, topics not hitherto touched on, which lend themselves to debate, for example development control and land values. Chapter 9 looks to the future by examining three topics considered important in the mid-1990s: quality in the environment, sustainability, and the ramifications of international influences.

At this stage I would like to enter three caveats or warnings. First, the book is not exhaustive. I have taken a range of subjects pursuing them to different depths. Sometimes there is little more than discussion and comment but in other cases arguments and research are reported in more depth. This is partly dictated by the literature available and partly by the need to keep the length of the book manageable. The latter has been ameliorated by a Glossary and short notes Appendix. Secondly, principles have been exemplified by drawing on a variety of scales and activities in adapted spaces. It has not proved possible to do this in a systematic way so that all scales and activities are dealt with. Thirdly, there is the matter of development control case studies. I considered the introduction of "boxed case studies", that is boxed insertions in the text in which individual planning applications are described and analyzed by way of illustration (see Ratcliffe & Stubbs 1996, which included case studies). Many of these are available elsewhere: a selection is given in Appendix II.

The purposes and characteristics of development control

The purposes of development control

The purposes of the development control system are part of the wider purposes of town and country planning. The purposes of town and country planning are part of the wider purposes of environmental control dealt with in Chapter 2. At the highest level of generalization the purpose of the development control system is to ensure efficient and effective land use in the public interest. As far as it is possible to separate them, we can disaggregate this general purpose into "people purposes" and "property purposes".

People purposes

A prime people purpose is to satisfy the social and economic aspirations of the citizenry as far as they are expressed through land use. Thus, the decision-makers in the development control system will normally react positively to proposals to develop, whether it be a large factory or a "granny flat". However, there may be good planning reasons why development should be refused.

As people – owners, occupiers and users – have varied aims and objectives, their use of land and buildings may involve conflict between them (e.g. a potentially noisy factory next to housing). A major purpose of development control is to resolve conflict. A subordinate purpose, in a democratic society, is democratic involvement and accountability. This involves elected representatives in central government, which sets the general framework for conflict resolution by statute and regulation, and locally elected councillors, who effectively make most development control decisions. In coming to their decisions, they consult other parties such as highway authorities, neighbours and civic societies. One of the purposes of the development control system is to facilitate public participation, which we hope results in better decisions and the consensus of interested parties. Neighbour protection is a rather separate people purpose. The public interest mentioned above is a wide term. It is dealt with in this chapter below. Development control decisions are designed to protect the public generally and not to protect the interest of one group rather than another. However, in the exercise of development control powers, owners and others do look to the planning system to protect them. For example, if a householder is concerned about loss of privacy from a neighbouring house extension, the local planning authority (LPA) may require one wall of the extension to be windowless to prevent overlooking. A further people purpose relates to equity and fairness. Major applications for development often come from the wealthy and powerful. It is an important purpose of the development control system to ensure that other interests are catered for. For example, in allowing a superstore, the LPA may insist on the inclusion of a bus lay-by to help those without cars.

Property purposes

Turning now to property purposes, as far as they are separable from people purposes, a prime purpose is the coordination of investment in land and buildings. Land and buildings are in many ownerships, but each plot and each activity forms part of a working system, a working whole. In making development control decisions, the LPA has to ensure as far as possible that developments in one part of the system are not grossly out of synchronization with others. It is particularly important that road and sewerage infrastructure is of adequate capacity and that public open space, say, is of adequate standard to cater for new developments.

Proposed development may be new building or an adaptation of existing development. A particular purpose of the development control system in the UK is the conservation of the heritage, whether it be the countryside, natural resources or older buildings, and the integration of new development with the old. As part of this wide purpose there are two further purposes. First, decision-makers must ensure that development works in a functional sense, for example that parking and access arrangements in a new development are quantitatively adequate and are safe. Secondly, they must ensure development is visually pleasing. This fraught issue is dealt with in Chapter 6. Enhancing environmental quality is a purpose embracing both functional and aesthetic considerations. When control decisions are made about development, decision-makers refer to a wide range of guidance documentation and to their own experience and professional expertise (Ch. 5). One purpose of the development control system is to ensure that this supporting information is utilized (especially development plans).

The people and property purposes of development control and the methods of implementation are close and interactive. The purposes are implemented in part by decisions to refuse or grant planning permission and in part by enforcement action against unauthorized development. Thus, one of the purposes of the development control system is to facilitate decision-making by a clear process. Granting planning permission with conditions may positively enhance the environment and it promotes development. Refusal of planning permission and enforcement action prevents development which would harm it. Development control helps to fulfil the vision provided by development plans.

Alder (1989: 12) drew attention to the fact that the Town and Country Planning Act 1971, and apparently later Acts, did not state the purposes for which development control powers may be used. He cited academics and practitioners who couched their goals in general terms such as managing change, enhancing the usefulness of land and buildings for the common good, and solving problems in complex contexts. Planning has no purposes of its own, but is a microcosm of society. He drew attention to underlying traditions and value systems such as utilitarianism, paternalism, utopianism and the protection of property rights.

Booth (1996: ch. 1) saw the purposes of development control from a historical view point. First, he felt that there had been a search for the ideal city, especially from an aesthetic point of view, from the Renaissance onwards. Secondly, building control was seen as a form of social control. Elizabeth I had sought to limit new buildings as a way of preventing the socially restive poor from migrating to London. The third purpose of development control was the control of disease and the promotion of health. Late nineteenth-century working-class housing had much improved layouts for this reason. Fourthly, by the early twentieth century, proactive plans were being produced to control land-use activities in accordance with a strategy, rather than just to regulate buildings. Development control became an activity to promote development. Finally, development control has come to be seen as a means of resolving conflicts between competing landed interests. Developers see development control mechanisms as restricting what they may do, and the wider public castigates the development controllers for not being sufficiently robust in the face of developers.

Characteristics of development control

How can development control be characterized in action on a day-to-day basis; what does it mean to the public at large and to the developer? Many of the characteristics are listed in Figure 1.1. Some relate to physical site considerations and others to non-physical political and administrative matters.

Quite a different characterization of development control is one of tensions and conflict between the opposing concepts and ideas that underlie day-to-day practice. Figure 1.2 summarizes some of these. Indeed, this book is premised on the arguments and polemic involved with development control, rather than a simple description of day-to-day practice and/or how planning permission is obtained. Illustrations of these arguments will be found throughout the book.

This common inheritance and government guidance

At the highest level of generalization the government paper *This common inheritance* (DoE 1990d) laid out the UK government's view on the environment. The paper, like development control, is very wide-ranging. It endorsed the planning system as it has developed so far, as a method of reconciling development and conservation pressures (ibid.: paras 2–7). The government sees itself as setting the framework (e.g. via green belts) in which local authorities can work (ibid.: ch. 6). The government's objectives are admittedly primarily economic:
- economic growth at all levels
- land and premises to provide people with jobs
- housing to meet the needs of all sectors of society
- environmental safety (e.g. against floods and industrial hazards)
- preservation of good agricultural land for food
- safe and efficient transport systems
- access to provide choice and value
- best use of mineral resources.

Figure 1.1 Characteristics of development control.

- Each application for development is unique and each application site is unique. A decision to grant or refuse the proposal takes this uniqueness into account. The decision is not taken by using a standard formula nor a simple set of rules.
- Applications for development vary greatly in size and complexity, from say a house extension to a major city centre redevelopment. Applications may vary from a simple local design issue, such as a new shop front, to strategic issues such as the development of major new settlements.
- The LPA, as decision-maker, uses discretion to cope with uniqueness in coming to a decision. Discretion is used in the factors taken into account in decision-making. Discretion is used in framing the terms of the decision, that is to grant with conditions or refuse with reasons.
- Discretion is constrained by guidance issued at national level and development plan policy usually decided locally.
- The decision to grant or refuse is made by a procedure involving informal discussion between the applicant and the LPA, formal application, technical report on the implications of the application by paid officials, and decision by democratically elected representatives, with the possibility of appeal against the decision.
- Development control is part of the development process by which society builds and maintains the built and natural environment.
- The development control system includes enforcement procedures designed to combat unauthorized development.
- LPAs vary greatly in character from rural districts to large cities, each with a wide variety of development control problems.
- The number of planning applications and LPA workloads varies over the years with the trade cycle. It takes time to make decisions; this is pejoratively called "delay". Development control is reactive: it cannot normally influence the environment where there is no application to develop.
- Development control, as an activity, is synoptic, eclectic and synthesizing. That is, it seeks a wide overview and borrows from many disciplines, focusing on links and relationships between places and activities.
- It seeks to cope with dynamic change in the built environment and safeguard a sustainable future. It therefore involves flexibility in decision-making and uncertainty for the developer.
- It is the most public face of the planning system, involving public consultation. Development control is a public activity.
- Although development control is at first sight concerned with land and buildings, it primarily serves the people who use them. Social, economic and political factors underlie development control decisions. Decisions have distributional or equity effects. Some parties benefit from decisions, but others may be disadvantaged.
- Parties to an application to develop are normally seeking to promote "good development on the ground". Negotiation is involved in the attempt to bring about a win/win situation where parties are seeking compromise in solving conflicts of objectives. Development control is concerned with practical problem solving. It should not be viewed as inevitably resulting in a win/lose outcome.
- Currently, development control in the UK is plan led, but plans are not the only consideration in development control decisions.
- Development control is a positive activity. It is part of the process of continual improvement in the quality of the environment, the attainment of vision and ultimately the fulfilment of ideologies (see Minett 1986).

Figure 1.2 Tension and unresolved conflicts in development control.

Source of tension	Comment
Holistic vs partial	Development control decisions should take "everything into account". Resource constraints mean that only key aspects may be taken into account.
Synthetic vs special interests	In equity, all parties should have their concerns accommodated. In practice the powerful prevail.
Democratic vs autocratic	Although development control practice is democratic, private property interests are not so characterized.
Public vs private	Development control seeks to safeguard the public interest against the private.
Lay vs professional	Key development control decisions are made by lay people on professional advice. Professional advice may be rejected.
Intellect vs values	Development control is a rational process but we are driven by our emotions and values.
Legislation vs anarchy	Rules and regulations may guide development but the size and complexity of the environment means that much (trivial) development is uncontrolled.
Cooperation vs competition	Town development must be coordinated for the town to work as a whole, but a freely competitive market may disrupt this.
Ecology vs economy	Economic growth may destroy our habitat. Both words are derived tellingly from *oikos* (Greek: home).
Local vs regional	Regional and national vision may be compromised by local expediency.
Long term vs short term	The need for immediate solutions may lay up problems for the future.

(I am grateful to Professor Ferenc Vidor of Budapest Technical University for concepts in this figure.)

Other government priorities have conservation as their theme:
- sustaining the character and diversity of the countryside
- reserving high-grade minerals
- defending green belts to prevent sprawl
- maintaining town centres

- revitalizing older urban areas
- improving the amenity of residential development
- conserving the built heritage and encouraging good design and the arts.

Many of these objectives could be objected to economic growth for example, and there seems little mention of equity.

The planning system is seen as providing guidance through Circulars, incentive by designating land for development in development plans, and control that ensures that private developers do not override the public interest and people affected by proposals can have their say. With special reference to development control, it is the LPA's job to decide on applications with the possibilities of appeal where applicants are dissatisfied. In 1990 the government felt on balance that the reconciliation of public and private interests was about right. It voiced concern about delay, demolition of houses, satellite dishes, agricultural buildings, hedgerows and enforcement, nearly all of which have been addressed since. What is controversial at any one time changes as problems are solved and others arise. Continuing problems are energy conservation, environmental impact of large developments, the interface between planning and pollution controls, taking cultivable land for housing, traffic and land use, minerals and land use after mineral extraction, and compensation paid for land acquisition. Special chapters are devoted to integrating agricultural and forestry policy with economic, planning and wider environmental policy (DoE 1990d.: ch. 7). Others deal with towns and cities (ibid.: ch. 8), especially city centres, including design guidance, and with heritage (ibid.: ch. 9).

Surprisingly, none of the key government statements on development control make a clear and explicit statement of the purposes of development control (DoE 1980, DoE 1992c, SOED 1993, 1994a, WO 1996). Purposes are inferred from the purposes of the planning system, which are shown in Figure 1.3.

The development process and development control

The development process is concerned with the stages by which buildings are built. The principal stages are:

1. initiation
2. building
3. disposal.

Planning permission is normally sought towards the end of the initiation stage before building starts. Development control considerations affect the whole process. Development control is a small but vital part of the development process (Ratcliffe & Stubbs 1996: ch. 10).

Development starts when an owner or developer sees the opportunity to use a property to better advantage, say by a minor house extension, or building 300 houses, or changing the use of a house to a shop. Development may not always

Figure 1.3   The purposes of the planning system.

- To balance the protection of the natural and built environment with the pressures of economic and social change (DoE 1980: paras 1 and 17). But compare this with "to maintain and enhance the quality of the natural heritage and built environment" (SOED 1994a: para. 4).
- To set the land-use framework for economic development; encourage economic, social and environmental regeneration (SOED 1994a: paras 4 and 10); to help rebuild the economy (DoE 1980: paras 3 and 11); to provide investment and jobs (WO 1996: para. 4); to conserve the urban environment, bring into use unused land, etc., assist urban regeneration and reduce pressure on **greenfield** sites (WO 1996: para. 5).
- To have concern for making things happen in the right place at the right time (DoE 1980: para. 1; SOED 1994a: para. 3). To provide an adequate and continuous supply of land suitable for development (WO 1996: para. 5). Development plans should give developers certainty about the type of development that will be permitted at a given location (ibid.: para. 8).
- To meet the need for housing (DoE 1980: para. 1). To provide homes (WO 1966: para. 4).
- To protect the green belt, countryside beauty and agricultural land (DoE 1980: para. 4; DoE 1992c: para. 2). To protect the countryside, designated areas, conservation of the landscape, historic sites, natural habitats and agricultural land (WO 1996: para. 5).
- To facilitate public accountability (DoE 1980: para. 10). Decisions best determined locally by LPAs (WO 1996: para. 6).
- To control the exterior appearance of development (DoE 1980: para. 20).
- To secure the efficient and effective development and use of land in the public interest (DoE 1992c: para. 2; SOED 1994a: para. 3; WO 1996: para. 8).
- To resolve conflicts between activities . . . as well as to prevent development that is not acceptable (DoE 1992c: para. 4; SOED 1994a: para. 3).
- To act as a forum for public information, involvement and debate and for consultation (SOED 1994a: paras 3 and 12).
- To be mindful of global, national, regional and local levels (SOED 1994a: para. 4) and to take account of international obligations (DoE 1992c: para. 4).
- To ensure sustainable development living on the Earth's income rather than eroding its capital (DoE 1992c: para. 3; SOED 1994a: para. 5; WO 1996: para. 4).
- To streamline the regulatory framework (SOED 1994a: para. 9). The planning system should be efficient, effective and simple (WO 1996: para. 7).
- To maintain and enhance the quality of the environment (SOED 1994a: para. 11; WO 1996: para. 4).
- However, it is not the function of planning to inhibit competition or regulate for other than planning purposes (DoE 1992c: para. 6; WO 1996: para. 7).
- Applications for development should be allowed in accordance with the development plan unless the proposal would cause demonstrable harm (WO 1996: paras 7 and 8).
- Reasons for the refusal of planning applications must be given or, if granted, contrary to the development plan and the advice of statutory consultees (WO 1996: para. 7).

be for profit, although it often is. Building and land costs are an important consideration.

The initiation stage involves site investigation and housing market research on large schemes, such as a housing development and product market research, for say a factory or shop extension. The market for buildings is usually separate from the market for the products that buildings may produce or sell. Design and costing need to be done and sources of finance arranged. Builders need to be briefed. The initiation stage crucially involves the investigation of the planning status of the proposal. If planning permission cannot be obtained, when in fact it is necessary, then this will abort the project. The proposal may be permitted development (e.g. renewing the roof of a building), in which case planning permission may not be necessary. If planning permission is necessary, then the likelihood of getting it is gauged by informal exploratory discussions with the local planning authority. This is backed by a perusal of national and local planning policies such as planning policy guidance at national level, and development plans and design guides at local level. These matters are dealt with in Chapter 2. On the assumption that planning permission is obtained and building can start, later stages may be affected by conditions attached to the planning permission.

The building stage may be a simple house extension, in which case planning conditions are not likely to be important. However, on large sites, such as a factory estate or mineral working, planning conditions may affect operations. For example, in both cases, wheel-washing equipment might be required to keep public roads clean; the development may be phased across the site over a period of years; trees may need to be fenced and protected; working hours and noise may be restricted.

The disposal and final use of the development may be restricted once the development is complete. Disposal may be by sale or lease, or the developer may use the property himself. In any event, conditions imposed with the planning permission run with the land. Conditions that may affect the development at this stage involve the maintenance of landscaping and restrictions on occupancy (e.g. housing for the elderly). During building and disposal stages, the LPA checks that development has been carried out as approved. If there have been major departures – for example, no agreed landscaping has been planted and maintained or a dangerous unauthorized access has been opened up onto a main road – then the LPA has to decide whether to act. If breaches are minor, it may not. If enforcement action is involved (Ch. 3), unauthorized buildings may have to be demolished.

Theories of development control

Development control is thought to be a day-to-day practical activity and not really a theoretical subject. However, underlying it there are basic ideas and concepts which this section will address. Perhaps "theory" is too grand a word at this stage of the subject's development. Without delving too deeply, a theory is a generalized description about reality which helps explain a situation; such description can be used to infer what might happen in similar situations in future. For example, it may be observed that opening large new shopping centres will adversely affect the business of existing centres. The size of the impact will depend upon their relative size and their distance apart. Armed with appropriate quantitative data

13

on turnover, size and distance, it is then possible to estimate the impact that a proposed shopping development might have on the existing facilities. Theory may range from mere intuitive hunch, through speculation, to well established principles. One may object that "It's all very well in theory but will it work in practice?"; in reply the theorist says: "there is nothing so practical as a good theory". It is difficult to envisage any action such as a development control decision which does not have its basis in ideas in the minds of the parties to the decision. The parties themselves may not have a clear view of the principles on which they are working. The recent development of town planning has been eclectic and synoptic; that is, it borrows from other disciplines and seeks to have an overall embracing view of the problem in hand. Not only is planning synoptic in this sense, but problems are seen from different personal perspectives. The Royal Town Planning Institute was founded by a group of architects, surveyors, civil engineers and lawyers. Or to put it more popularly, imagine a farmer, a developer and an archaeologist are crossing a field; the farmer thinks it is just the place for growing carrots, the developer thinks houses and the archaeologist a dig.

A perusal of planning theory literature (Healey et al. 1982, Paris 1982, Reade 1987, Hague 1991) shows that much of the discussion is at a higher level than development control. That is to say, it is concerned with how the built environment works as a whole and how planning as an activity fits into it. In fact, development control is rarely mentioned. Some theories deal with the rationality of planning and procedures for planning. Others deal with particular perspectives, for example political perspectives, which deal with theories of the state at central and local level, or geographical perspectives, which seek to explain differential development between regions and within cities. Planning theory borrows widely from the social sciences and also from the natural sciences and the arts; for example, quantitative models of traffic flows and philosophical discussion of aesthetics on which this book touches.

One of the boldest attempts to theorize about development control is McLoughlin (1973). He postulated that recent town planning is concerned with desired states expressed in planning schemes consisting of written statements and maps. Planning schemes were concerned primarily with social, economic and strategic policy and secondarily with ensuring that land and building use reflected these policies. Development control is a method of controlling land and building use. Difficulties arise because towns are socially, economically and administratively complex, and change rapidly over time. The land and buildings have many facets varying from aesthetic considerations to traffic safety to the economy of the countryside. Moreover, although land and buildings change slowly, societal values and norms shift over time. The key to understanding is the notion of control itself. Without control, in a *laissez-faire* market, matters would be chaotic, with disorders ensuing, such as slum housing and traffic congestion. "Very obviously we have come to realize the sheer complexity of our perception of urban and social phenomena. We are now prisoners of the realization that everything in the city affects everything else. Modern system theory suggests that the very existence of complex systems logically requires a vast amount of intrinsic control or ordering, organizing processes." He went on to describe the environment as a system, such as the human body or a car, with constituent parts each interacting and forming a working whole. He raised the question whether in fact cities would tend towards chaos without planning control, or whether the city is homeostatic, tending towards a steady state, without apparent control, rather like the human body. He differentiated the city as a system as something to be planned for from the planning system itself, which includes administrative systems such as the development control system. He saw cybernetics (the science of control and information) as a way of understanding and guiding these systems. He cited the principle of requisite variety. This suggests that, in a complex system such as the built and natural environment, the intrinsic controls need to have such variety that they can cope with complexity and be adaptive to changes in the system itself (ibid.: chs 8 and 9). No wonder the development control system is so complicated, with many "bits and bobs".

Within these all-embracing concepts are other ideas. Brotherton (1992) took the view that a theoretical understanding of development control could be developed from an examination of planning application refusal rates at local and central government level on appeal. His study was narrowly focused on explaining the relationship between central government, LPA and the applicant. He was not primarily concerned with controlling the environment in its widest sense. His methods of statistical analyses of planning applications are too complex to explain here. He postulated that a key to understanding development control was that the LPA makes most of the key development control decisions but is influenced by central government policy through Circulars and PPGs, and by the quality of the applications submitted (ibid.: 3). The proportion of applications refused reflects LPA policy stance or strictness (ibid.: 6). Likewise, when central government receives appeals, its dismissal rate reflects its policy stance. His statistical analysis covered a variety of geographical areas from the mid-1970s to the late 1980s for different types of application. Among his conclusions (ibid.: ch. 7) was that, not surprisingly in his view, "while the policy gap may change over time and differ between areas, it always remains small. In large measure therefore central government and LPAs act in concert: central government policy is little different from LPA policy." He then asked the interesting question: "Is development control central government led or LPA led?" He felt at first sight that development control was central government led. It issued Circulars, decided appeals, set the legal framework, and could intervene in locally produced development plans. But on the other hand most applications are granted by LPAs, against which there is no right of appeal (say by third parties) and thus by implication central government supports all approvals. Moreover, as it allows some appeals, it takes a more relaxed view than LPAs. In addition, LPAs determine nearly all applications using their discretion, and central government determines only about 3 per cent where refusal is involved. There is clearly potential for LPAs to pursue policies and practices that are significantly different from those of central government. He was of

15

the view that central government may encourage or constrain, but in essence it followed where LPAs led.

McLoughlin's systems approach was all embracing. Within this wider system, arguably the most important from a development control point of view is the capitalist free-market economic system. It is concerned with the ownership of land and the production and improvement of buildings. It is because the operation of the unfettered free market results in demonstrable harm to property interests that planning exists as a regulatory activity. Harm may be to neighbours, such as loss of privacy by development, or to a wider public, such as road danger, or dereliction after mineral working, or visual intrusion attributable to advertisements. Capitalism has resulted in uneven development between regions and within cities.

Although development rights were nationalized after the Second World War, land and building ownership has remained largely private. Apart from the now widespread owner-occupation of houses, effective ownership of agricultural land and of industrial and commercial buildings is in relatively few hands. Profitmaking is the prime driving force in the production and maintenance of the built environment. Uncontrolled submarkets exist in housing, farms, shops, offices, factories, warehouses, leisure facilities and private vehicles. They are serviced by financial institutions, such as building societies, pension funds and insurance companies, with their own financial imperatives which shape the built environment. Arguably, planning regulation is now the hand-maiden of propertied interests. Development plans give some certainty in risky markets, contrasting with the problems of hope value reported on by Uthwatt (1942). Development control gives some protection against injury by neighbours by preventing unacceptable development and by imposing conditions when planning permission is granted. An understanding of the role of profit and markets is a key to understanding the purpose of development control. The focus of planning has shifted from welfare to property values. The decline of new public planning initiatives has run in parallel, such as new towns and the use of compulsory purchase for redevelopment purposes, to partnerships and new initiatives, such as urban development corporations and Enterprise Zones. In these new initiatives, development control has been taken from traditional local authority hands (see Hague 1984). What is surprising is that development control has not been taken out of the hands of LPAs entirely, whereas further education has. Property interests would perhaps be better served by local quangos of developers, builders and businessmen.

The extent of Thatcherite influences on planning and development control is a moot point. The rhetoric is a bonfire of controls. But what has happened to planning control and planning policy? And what have the policy outcomes been? Urban development corporations have not been very successful at creating development and jobs. They have made a marginal difference in the investment climate and are slow to show results. While central government has sought to impose the planning framework from above, local government has been pursuing its own rather different goals at local level. Conflicting ideologies are at work: conviction politics versus consultation and consensus, and minimal government versus

16

authoritarianism (Allmendinger 1994: vi–ix). The relationship between Thatcherism and development is exemplified in Enterprise Zones and Simplified Planning Zones discussed in Chapter 4.

Development control in the public interest?

"The town and country planning system is designed to regulate the development of land in the public interest" (DoE 1992c: para. 2). "The Chartered Object of the Royal Town Planning Institute is to advance the science and art of town planning for the benefit of the public" (RTPI 1994: 1). But what is the public and what is the public interest? Taylor, from whom this section draws (1994: ch. 5), quoted the work of Schubert and of Sorauf, who described the idea of the public interest as a "conceptual muddle". Ross (1991: 55–7) felt that, as a justification for planning decisions, "the concept is abstract almost to the point of irrelevance" and concluded that "the post-war consensus on the public interest has disintegrated to such an extent that it is vital to demonstrate which interests planning seeks to advance". Maybe it is just rhetoric behind which we hide. Capitalist society is postulated on competition and conflict. Indeed, one of the roles of the development control system is to resolve conflict. Maybe there is no one public interest but many and conflicting ones – many publics with various combinations of interests. On the other hand, although there may be many public interest groups, interests may well coincide and overlap. In fact there may be a core of interests on which we can all agree. Moreover, even within an individual interest group there may be conflicting interests and the group has to judge the benefit and harm that a given line of action might engender.

Taylor (ibid.) drew attention to four aspects of such interest judgements:

- We might readily ascribe to the value of life and a healthy environment, but different groups may make different value judgements about life itself. Consider the religious believer and the atheist.
- Interest judgements are different from moral judgements. Is it right or wrong (see Ch. 8) to earn large profits from speculative land deals?
- But how can we judge or identify a person's interest? New towns, it was argued by town planners after the Second World War, were built in the interests of the future inhabitants. In a democracy, a central tenet is that individuals themselves are the best judges of their interests: hence the growth of public participation in development control (Ch. 8).
- It is not just as individuals that we have interests; individuals have interests as members of groups. We belong to many interest groups in our lifetime. When we are young, prospective housing development may threaten our playing fields and when we are old we may want sheltered housing.

However, maybe there are interests that we all share. For a proposal to be in the public interest it must be in the interests of all and not just be in the interest of a section of the public. "The public at large" or "unspecified individuals" or "members of the public" or "common interest" might be ways of describing this situation. In this context anyone is not everyone: anyone can enjoy a national park but not everyone does, because they prefer to do other things. Moreover, although all may potentially benefit from national parks, it is a matter of fact and degree whether individuals do. **Planning standards** (e.g. visibility splays at road junctions) are in the common interest. Taylor cited negative applications of the common interest, for example forbidding flashing neon lights in the Cotswolds; and positive applications, for example the provision of public open space. But some planning initiatives have distributive effects. For example, green belts may enhance cities and safeguard the environment of owners and occupiers there, but disadvantage the poor trying to obtain housing. Should we therefore abandon green belts as a development control device?

Taylor described two further concepts of the public interest: the Benthamite utilitarian sum of individual interests and the so-described Hegelian holistic conception of the public interest. The former view argues that the public interest is the sum of individual interests and indeed the public interest cannot exist without the individuals who comprise it. Cost–benefit analysis of the alternative sites for a third London airport in the 1970s was an application of this idea in that costs and benefits to many individuals were analyzed and weighed. Notwithstanding the methodological problems of cost–benefit analysis, an airport may be in the public interest but to the disbenefit of those living close by. In the Hegelian approach a nation or society subscribes to some overall ideal or purpose which, it is claimed, is good for society as a whole. Comprehensive redevelopment after the Second World War was seen as building a new world: it was progressive and up-to-date. But limited cognizance was taken of the problems of individuals and firms who were displaced and rehoused.

Taylor (ibid.) concluded his discussion by saying he thought that the public interest in the context of town and country planning should embrace two undeniable spheres of interest. These are: tackling large-scale environmental issues, such as pollution and sustainability, which will determine what happens to life on Earth and secondly the enhancement of the public realm – streets and parks which everyone can use – so that they may be as safe, congenial and beautiful as possible.

Whereas Taylor was concerned with the philosophical concept of the public interest, Hutton (1996) reported how the public interest was applied in day-to-day development-control appeal cases. He found PPG1 (DoE 1992c) confusing. He analyzed appeal decisions: by visual amenity, overlooking, loss of outlook and loss of sunlight and daylight. He was concerned with the distinction between neighbours' private interests and the general public interest, which PPG1 admits may coincide. It was found indeed that no one individual has a right to a view if it is threatened by a development proposal. However, if the quality of the environment is reduced below a generally acceptable level, then he may have such a right. Where there was a loss of an outlook from a public place such as a road,

18

or where the proposal adversely affected a view, then it was likely to be material. Where a proposal may have adversely affected the sunlight, daylight or privacy of just one neighbour, then appeals showed that this was unacceptable, especially if the result was not transient and affected a habitable room. But as with all planning applications there are variations in the outcomes, depending on the merits of the case. Private interest, especially if expressed through objections to a proposal, can thus coincide with the public interest. For a further discussion of these issues in the UK see Chapter 6, and see Chapter 9 for the USA.

Conclusion

This chapter has introduced the subject of development control and drawn attention to its all-embracing character and complexity. The final section has shown that planning and development control are based on a concept – the public interest – which is elusive to define but which nonetheless is a cornerstone of day-to-day decision-making.

The next chapter will set development control in the context of the town and country planning system in the UK.

CHAPTER 2

Development control and the town and country planning system

Introduction: what applicants cope with

The purpose of this chapter is to describe and comment on the system that deals with development control applications. The system has the image of a bureaucratic politicized burden in need of deregulation. Research and commentaries have shown that, by and large, it is accepted as necessary but could be improved (SOED 1994a, McCarthy et al. 1995). The administrative arrangements at central and local government level are outlined and the process of making planning applications is described. Further sections deal with how an application for development is processed and with the various interested parties, called stakeholders, who are involved. Finally, the relationship between development plans and development control is considered. (The role of the public is discussed more fully in Ch. 8.)

As mentioned in Chapter 1, applicants for development have many factors to consider besides planning permission. As many applications are made by householders, it is likely that they will only make one application in a lifetime. More important players can be divided into two groups: those developing for themselves (e.g. Marks & Spencer and their shops) and developers building for others (e.g. national housebuilders selling in the mass market). Important players have to acquire sites, carry out market research, design and cost the development, deal with subcontractors, deal with other statutory controls such as building regulations, organize finance and legal agreements, and dispose of or use the property once finished. Planning and development controls are just two of the many regulatory mechanisms in a complex society and one of the many considerations that applicants have to take into account when contemplating development.

The current system dates from the period 1944–7. It was needed to curb interwar sprawl and deal with slums and war damage. The system of development plans had a major overhaul in the late 1960s (Planning Advisory Group 1965). Local government, one of the main operators of the system, was reorganized in the 1960s and 1970s for the first time in a hundred years; further modifications were made in the 1980s and 1990s. However, the development control system seems to have withstood the test of time, warts and all. It was the subject of a major enquiry in 1975 (Dobry 1975) but has remained largely unaltered since 1947.

Administration

Administrative arrangements

The UK is a unitary state without a written constitution and therefore has no entrenched principles that preserve local powers. The administration of the development control system springs from powers granted by central government to local government. Local government itself is a creature of central government, and the courts ensure that planning decisions are made according to legislation. On a day-to-day basis, development control is a local government function, as it deals with myriad unique individual sites, and decisions need to be made as close as possible to the site to which they relate. Where major strategic issues might be involved, central government reserves the right to call in planning applications for its own decision.

Central government

Although the UK of Great Britain and Northern Ireland is a unitary, rather than a federal, state, for development control purposes, England, Wales, Scotland and Northern Ireland are separate, each with its own ministry for the environment and often with separate government guidance and legislation (Appendix I). "Britain" is used to describe the UK situation generally and English practice is quoted, as often the principles are the same. The DoE has regional offices in England. There is no accountable regional tier of elected government in the UK, although it has long been mooted.

In England and Wales the Secretary of State for the Environment is responsible for planning legislation, the principal Act being the Town and Country Planning Act 1990 (Reference Services 1992; see Fig. 2.1). Guidance is issued in England by the Secretary of State for the Environment and in Wales by the Secretary of State for Wales. In Scotland the principal act is the Town and Country Planning (Scotland) Act 1972. In Northern Ireland, responsibility for planning is with the Department for the Environment for Northern Ireland.

In addition to the four Secretaries of State, other government bodies involved with development control include:

- Regional conferences of planning authorities, which address issues of

Figure 2.1 The planning responsibilities of the Secretary of State (Reference Services 1992; see Appendix I).

- Planning legislation, such as the Town and Country Planning Act 1990, from which many powers are derived
- Subsidiary legislation under the Town and Country Planning Acts, so-called statutory instruments such as the General Permitted Development Order
- Issuing guidance to local authorities and developers, particularly Planning Policy Guidance Notes (PPGs) and Circulars, which are referred to throughout this book
- Calling in planning applications for his own decision because they are of strategic importance or raise important issues of principle, such as building in the green belt
- The Planning Inspectorate, which hears appeals against adverse local development control decisions and handles public inquiries into development plans
- Issuing strategic guidance, particularly Regional Planning Guidance, to be taken into account in preparing development plans
- Calling in development plan proposals for approval where his intervention is necessary.

importance beyond local authority boundaries. Examples are SERPLAN (South Eastern Region Planning Conference) and LPAC (London Planning Advisory Committee), which covers the now abolished Greater London Council area. Similar bodies are likely to be set up in Wales and Scotland following the demise of counties and regions there (WO 1996: para. 13). They are consulted by central government, about issues such as retailing, transport and waste disposal, which are included in regional planning guidance. This guidance eventually filters down to local plan and development control level.

- Central government consultees, for example the Environment Agency, are referred to for advice in their fields of expertise.
- The Secretary of State for National Heritage is responsible for listing **listed buildings** and is often consulted on major proposals in conservation areas. Listed buildings and **conservation areas** have stricter development control criteria applied to them. **English Heritage** is the relevant body in England, Cadw in Wales, and Historic Scotland in Scotland (Ch. 7).
- Special arrangements apply in national parks such as Dartmoor. They have plan-making and development control powers within their areas. They are partly funded by central government and partly by local government (Reference Services 1992: 60–1). They are administered by committees of the relevant county councils (GMA Planning 1994: 75).
- In new towns, being replaced by the Commission for the New Towns, central government had power of direction overruling the LPA (ibid.: 75).
- Urban development corporations set up to revivify rundown inner cities since 1980. These normally have usurped development control powers from local authorities. Only consultation remains, as in London Docklands. However, in Cardiff development control powers have remained with the LPA (ibid.: 75).

Local government

Elected local government authorities make environmental decisions at local level close to the sites where a knowledge of their idiosyncrasies of the sites concerned is necessary for successful decision-making. They are generally arranged in a county, district and parish hierarchy, and are concerned with plan-making, development control and enforcement, depending on their status and powers.

Local authority arrangements were reorganized in the 1990s with the abolition of Welsh counties and Scottish regions and the creation of new unitary authorities separated from shire counties in England. In England, but not the metropolitan counties and the Greater London Council area, shire counties produce structure plans and make limited development control decisions related to waste and minerals. Where unitary authorities were created within counties, county councils lost their responsibilities over the unitary authority area. The unitary authority has the full range of development plan and control functions (i.e. both county and district matters), including minerals and waste planning. The districts in English shire counties make local plans: the unitary authority districts in metropolitan counties make unitary development plans: these districts/boroughs deal with all planning applications in their areas. Powers are available for joint working between local authorities. Planning functions in national parks were unaffected by local government changes in the mid-1990s. From 1997 it was intended that they become independent local planning authorities (DoE 1996b: 2, 4 and Annex). Elsewhere, in Wales and Scotland, districts as unitary authorities make unitary development plans and deal with planning applications. At each level these are generally referred to as local planning authorities (LPA). In some cases further jurisdictions exist below district level. In rural areas English parish councils are normally consulted on applications that affect them. In Scotland and Wales there are comparable community councils. They have no power of decision. In urban areas so-called mini-town halls or area offices may have some development control functions devolved to them (Spawforth 1995: 6).

Within district and county councils, development control powers are normally exercised by the planning committee – one of several committees such as highways, housing or leisure, which match the services authorities might provide. Planning committees are variously named planning and environment, planning and estates, planning and development, or economic development, depending on local emphasis and the combination with other functions. Such planning committees may also have development control subcommittees. Occasionally the full council may take decisions on important planning issues, rather than the planning committee.

The planning committee consists of elected councillors selected from the full council. Decisions on plans and planning applications are therefore essentially political and entail political uncertainty. A change of personnel on the committee, through rotation or election, may make a previously unacceptable application become acceptable. Committees are advised on technical matters by the planning department of the council staffed in part by technical officers. They are likely to be chartered planners, engineers or architects. However, the planning committee is not bound by the advice of officials and may reject it (Zetter et al. 1996). Officers themselves may often grant planning permission in trivial cases through delegated powers. Normally, planning applications are not decided on party political lines, but they may be. Sometimes the council may not make a decision – a deemed refusal against which there is appeal to central government. Councillors are subject to lobbying by constituents and pressure groups. See Chapter 8.

Just as central government issues guidance for local authorities and developers, so local government does for developers. The principal documents are:

- structure plans at county level, which outline in general terms how the county is to be developed in the future; settlement growth policies, including housing, jobs and shopping, are frequently included
- local plans nest within structure plans at district level and give much greater detail than structure plans; they deal with policies for individual sites
- unitary plans are a combination of local and structure plans drawn up by unitary authorities
- subject plans supplement other development plans, e.g. for minerals
- planning, design or development briefs outline how local councils envisage important sites being developed and contain guidance on urban design, access and so on
- councils may resolve to adopt guidance for developers on specific topics, e.g. shop front design.

Further details of development plans (e.g. contents) are given below.

In conclusion, two things must be said. First, for the first-time applicant for planning permission, there does seem to be a confusing array of bodies and documents, not to mention other regulatory jurisdictions such as building regulations. To circumvent this problem, it has been suggested that district councils open "one stop shops", where all necessary advice and permits can be dealt with. This has proved useful in the USA (Thomas 1988c). Secondly, central and local government do not always see eye to eye. Central government may intervene and alter locally proposed plans and call in planning applications taking them out of the hands of LPAs.

Stakeholders

Development control is essentially a local government matter. However, other parties, often called stakeholders or agents, are involved. This section will deal with stakeholders; subsequent sections will deal with the role of development plans.

In a study of housebuilding in central Berkshire, Short et al. (1986) identified the main stakeholders in a set of evolving relationships. They operated a set of

25

rules that in themselves changed as a result of the agents interacting. To a greater or lesser extent the power of the stakeholders has changed over time. Local government was reorganized in the mid-1970s to strengthen it, but Conservative policies after 1979 weakened it, for example by rate capping and attempting to move council housing out of local authority control. The freeing of market forces after that date gave housebuilders much more encouragement (e.g. in DoE 1980).

Particular stakeholders may have others nesting within them. For example, the housebuilder/developer may have to contend with other interests such as land-owners, banks, architects, subcontractors, building societies and eventually occupiers, once development is complete (Short et al. 1986: 39).

The neighbours and the public at large may be divided into individuals with differing views, a residents' association presenting a collective view, or a national group such as the Council for the Protection of Rural England. More formally they may be represented by a parish or community council. Although having no power of decision, they comment on all planning applications in their jurisdiction and thus seek to influence the LPA. Statutory consultees, such as highway author-ities, also have a stake in decisions (see Ch. 8). The LPA is not necessarily unan-imous in its view: councillors may be subject to lobbying and may differ among themselves. Councillors and planning officers may differ (see Ch. 8). The prin-cipal relationships between stakeholders are lobbying, negotiations and formal guidance. In day-to-day practice the relationship between the applicant and the LPA is probably the most significant. This may take the form of preapplication discussion and, in significant developments, negotiations over planning con-ditions and **planning agreements** should planning permission be granted. All stakeholders are aware of formal central government guidance, such as Circulars and PPGs, which permeate and influence the development control system. Lob-bying (i.e. making verbal and written representations) takes place between all the stakeholders. The views of stakeholders in the planning system, including devel-opment control, were reported on by McCarthy et al. (1995) (see Ch. 8).

The strength and frequency of interaction between stakeholders varies. Research by Short on Berkshire showed that housebuilders had frequent contact with district planning officers, only occasionally with elected representatives, and rarely with the Department of the Environment (ibid.: 93). As for pressure on councillors (as part of the planning stakeholding) in coming to planning decisions, 74 per cent of councillors said officers' recommendations were very important, 42 per cent said community group representations were very important, but only 28 per cent said DoE advice was very important or important; indeed, 50 per cent said it was of little or no importance (ibid.: 133).

A characteristic of the Short et al. (1986) description of housing development and Guy's (1994) of retail development is that ultimate occupiers are not usually present at the planning decision stages. They are important stakeholders. Where owner-occupiers are the developers building for themselves, then they can represent their own interests. However, a good deal of shop-, office-, factory- and housebuilding takes place speculatively with unknown future owners and occupiers. Moreover, buildings are longlasting assets. It is one of the jobs of the LPA to safeguard their future interests through the operation of the development control system.

The role of development plans in development control

For the layman, town and country planning would appear to be about plans. But surprisingly McCarthy et al. (1995: iv) found that the general public as a group seemed to know more about the role of development control in the planning system than they did about development plans. They knew generally that, if you wanted to build something, you had to ask the Council: but plans were a bit of a mystery. Although development plans have always been important as a framework for making development control decisions, there is a realization that they are often dated and cannot cover every contingency. Plan coverage is geographically patchy. Resort then has to be made to other guidance such as government Circulars and to the background knowledge that developers, officers and councillors have of other **material considerations** (Ch. 5).

Plan purposes and preparation

As development plans form the principal framework for development control decisions, it is useful at this stage to say something about their purpose and preparation. The main central government guidance documents are: Ministry of Housing and Local Government 1970, DoE 1992b, DoE 1992v, SODD 1996c. The principal contents of plans are given in Figure 2.3.

Plan purposes
The purposes of development plans – structure, local, unitary and subject – are a subset of the purposes of planning (Ch. 1). These are shown in Figure 2.2.

These purposes are uncontroversial and somewhat mechanical. Morgan & Nott (1995: 130) offered a different interpretation: first, the protection of property interests; secondly, in the light of the failure of free market forces, government intervenes to supply the needs of the country in terms of land and property; thirdly, the government can be seen as managing and contributing to ensure that land is used in the general interest; and, finally, government can intervene in the land market by compulsory purchase, ownership, and by constraining the free market in protected areas. That all this has happened with a right-wing government in the 1980s and early 1990s is surprising.

Plan preparation
Plan preparation procedures, which need not detain the reader long, can be looked at in two ways. First, they are a legal process whereby the LPA:

27

Figure 2.2 The purposes of development plans.

- To indicate how an LPA envisages its geographical area developing in the future, bearing in mind social, economic and environmental issues
- To ensure that essential infrastructure is provided (e.g. roads), which the free market in land and buildings does not normally safeguard
- To ensure that plans of different scales and types nest within each other and are compatible (e.g. local plans with structure plans) and with plans of adjacent districts, and reflect national policy guidance
- To coordinate the provision of major developments (e.g. housing and shops)
- To provide a clear framework for development control decisions and guidance to those proposing development
- To provide some certainty to those seeking planning permission and some certainty to owners and occupiers that their amenity will not be upset
- To safeguard the cultural and natural heritage (e.g. by green belts and conservation areas)
- To seek to ensure that the various parts of the environment work in a quantitative sense (e.g. matching housing, jobs and transport facilities) and providing standards (e.g. parking standards)
- To act as promotional documents indicating to developers where (re)development would be encouraged
- To identify locations where it may be necessary for an LPA to take the initiative (e.g. town centre redevelopment), where ultimately compulsory purchase may be necessary to facilitate site assembly and reconstruction
- To indicate to large organizations and firms possible future trends in the locality, so that they can plan and so that their intentions may be fed into land-use planning processes (e.g. provision of educational facilities or large shops)
- To steer development onto land most suited to it (e.g. industry on extensive flat land)
- To safeguard amenity by zoning
- To provide a context for local authorities, developers, landowners, pressure groups and the general public to discuss land-use issues and go some way towards reconciling them through consultation and inquiry procedures
- To mesh with other types of plans (e.g. **transport policies and programmes**)
- To identify in general terms the resources necessary to fulfil a plan
- To provide vision and a sense of place for inhabitants
- To devise policies at an appropriate level of detail: these may include general criteria on the type of conditions that might be used when granting planning permission; requirements for **planning obligations (planning gain)** may also be given; cross reference may be made to supplementary planning guidance (e.g. on shop front design) but not actually be included in a plan
- To identify agencies that might implement parts of a plan
- To provide a benchmark from which negotiations over conditions and planning obligations can be started.

- declares an intention to prepare a plan
- publishes a draft plan
- publishes a final plan
- arranges a public inquiry
- notifies modifications
- eventually adopts the plan.

At most stages there is wide publicity and the opportunity for the public to make representations. Plans are reviewed periodically. Secondly, plan preparation is a practical method of compiling a document – a development plan – providing both a vision of the future and methods of solving land-use problems. Traditionally the stages have been (Roberts 1974):

- survey and studies of the plan area to identify issues
- analysis of issues and objectives and the generation of alternative solutions to problems
- the formulation of the plan
- finally monitoring and review.

The customary contents of plans are shown in Figure 2.3.

The granting of planning permission, largely in line with the development plan policies, is the major way in which the vision of the plan is fulfilled. The continuing monitoring of the implementation of planning permission indicates to the LPA development pressure, the onset of new issues and problems, and whether the vision of the plan is being fulfilled. The conclusions from monitoring are fed into the subsequent round of plan-making and review.

Figure 2.3 Principal contents of development plans (Ministry of Housing and Local Government 1970: 63; DoE 1992b: Section 5; SODD 1996c).

General
- Brief statement on component documents
- Area of plan and its structure
- National and subnational framework
- General aims, strategies and policies for the area
- Subarea details

Subjects of the plan
- Population
- Employment, income and the local economy
- Resources, including the natural heritage
- Housing
- Industry and commerce
- Transportation
- Shopping
- Education
- Other social and community issues
- Tourism, recreation and leisure
- Conservation, townscape and landscape
- Utilities, including energy
- Other, e.g. minerals and waste

Other
- Conflict of policies
- Phasing
- Development control policies

Problems associated with the role of plans in development control

The use of development plans is not without problems as far as development control is concerned:

- They may be outdated and may not reflect current economic and social realities.
- Structure plans and local plans may not be compatible, because LPAs may not agree among themselves.
- Plans may not contain policies for new types of proposed development (e.g. new settlements) or new development forms (e.g. factory outlet shops).
- An application for development may be premature in that a plan in preparation may not have caught up with development pressure.
- There may be arguments over interpretation of policies and diagrams in plans.
- Plan inquiries can be long drawn out, so that the status of policies remains uncertain while planning applications continue to be made.
- Land-use plans deal with land-use matters, which give expression to higher-order social and economic objectives, which are ill defined; perhaps this is less so in Scotland with National Planning Policy Guidelines (Bruton & Nicholson 1987: 31–2).
- Large-scale complex proposals may have unforeseen and unintended consequences.

Grant (in Cross & Whitehead 1994: 81 ff.) drew attention to aspects of Section 54A introduced in the Planning and Compensation Act 1991 (Ch. 3). LPAs in determining an application need to have regard to the development plan and to make the decision in accordance with the development plan, unless material considerations indicate otherwise. He drew the very useful distinction between prescriptive plans, conferring legal force on the plan itself (development is then lawful if it conforms to the plan but is illegal if it does not, as in the USA (Ch. 9)) and indicative plans, such as in Britain, where plans in themselves do not give planning permission, but each application to develop is treated on its merits. He also drew attention to a third possibility – development control without plans – which *de facto* has been widespread in Britain since the Second World War. This is to be contrasted with an even earlier situation where it was hoped to implement plans by simply granting permission for development in accordance with the plan and refusing it if it were not. Referring to the 1980s, Grant opined that the principle of a presumption in favour of development, unless it would cause "demonstrable harm to interests of acknowledged importance", led to planning by appeal. In the 1980s the Secretary of State found himself embroiled in national controversy over local schemes, the upshot of which was Section 54A, which gave primacy to the development plan. However, Grant added, so far, in law at least, little has changed. But plan preparation has changed. There is now a tendency to resolve site-specific details and policies at local plan preparation stage, rather than leave matters to the discretionary development control stage. There has been a marked increase in formal objections, especially to specific land-use allocations (Cronin 1993: 16). This has lengthened planning inquiries but perhaps will result in time savings if later planning application appeals can be avoided (Steel et al. 1994: 7). With so much emphasis on plans, one may ask how much influence they have on development control decisions. Statistical analysis of decisions carried out by Davies et al. (1986: 11–15) concluded that "Much of development control has to be conducted without the benefit of formal written policy, whether statutory or non-statutory; it has to rely instead on unwritten policies, local custom and practice, and professional skill, experience and judgement." These findings related to 1982, when the Town and Country Planning Act 1971 §29(1) applied, namely that development plans were only one material consideration, and there were relatively few adopted local plans.

Making planning applications

It is not the purpose of this section to detail how planning applications are made. There are good practical guides available for householders (Willman 1990, Dijksman 1992, Speer & Dade 1995, DoE & WO 1996), businessmen (DoE 1994l) and farmers (DoE et al. 1992). The content of a planning application form, which is customarily used, is given with a commentary in Table 2.1. An application form is normally accompanied by a guide for applicants written by the LPA to assist the applicant to complete the form. The planning officer's view of the process is elaborated in RTPI (1988a).

In outline the applicant informally approaches the LPA to see if planning permission is necessary for the proposal. It may not be: it is best for the applicant to be sure of this in writing, lest doubt and misunderstanding arise. If planning permission is necessary, informal discussions, called preapplication enquiries (below), are usually held between officers and the applicant to match what the applicant wants with what officers think the LPA planning committee will allow. It is not a matter of win/lose but of win/win. The local authority is just as anxious to have good development on the ground as the applicant is. In minor developments, the planning officer has powers delegated to him so that he can make decisions.

Once these informal approaches are completed, a formal planning application is made to the LPA. An outline of the procedures that are followed once a formal application has been made is shown in Figure 3.4.

Preapplication enquiries

Preapplication enquiries by putative applicants to the LPA are recommended by central government (DoE 1992c: Appendix para. 7). They have been researched

31

Table 2.1 Principal headings to be found in planning application forms, with comments.

Heading	Comment
Name of LPA	To establish jurisdiction.
Reference number	Given by LPA to identify application. Entry in planning application register. Receipt of planning application acknowledged.
Date of deposit	The customary eight-week period available for LPA decision starts from this date.
Part I	Part I to be completed for all development.
Address of applicant	For correspondence.
Address of agent	An agent, such as an architect, may act on applicant's behalf: for correspondence.
Site address	So that proposal can be located in terms of development plan policies and site visited by planning officer to check situation on the ground.
Site area	In square metres. Helps LPA understand density, plot ratios and intensification of use.
Brief particulars of proposal, e.g. two-storey house, factory and offices, extension to house	Gives LPA an idea whether proposal will fit policies for site and gives indication of likely problems e.g. traffic generation.
State whether applicant controls adjoining land	Layouts may be improved by using land technically outside boundaries of application site.
State whether proposal involves: new building alteration or extension change of use construction or alteration of pedestrian or vehicular access	Gives LPA idea of scale of development and whether highway authority needs to be involved. Works on highway may be necessary.
Particulars of application:	There are different types as below:
Outline	To establish principles only before details are submitted, although some details may be asked for at this stage.
Full	Contains all necessary details for LPA to make decision.
Reserved matters	Approval of details (reserved matters) following outline approval: siting, design, external appearance, access and landscaping (see Ch. 6).
Renewal of temporary permission	Temporary permissions, say for one year, may be renewed.
Listed Building Consent	If building is "listed" special care is needed by LPA and applicant (see Ch. 7).
Deemed Consent	LPA grants planning permission to itself.
Conservation Area Consent	Special care needed in conservation areas (Ch. 7).
Demolition Consent	Consent may be necessary for demolition (Ch. 4).
Present use, or if vacant, last use	Indicates to LPA if drastic change is proposed or, if site derelict, indicates potential for site improvement.
Does proposal involve felling of trees?	Trees are best kept if possible as they enhance visual amenity, screening, etc. A "tree plan" is often asked for by LPA.
How will surface water and foul water be disposed of?	LPA needs to be assured there will be no flooding or pollution.
Materials to be used: walls roof means of enclosure	LPA wants to know if materials will fit in with nearby development and that fences etc. will be visually acceptable (Ch. 6).

Drawings	Drawings normally accompany application, viz:
	    Location plan – 1:1250
	    Site plan – 1: 500
	    Elevation – 1: 100
	to show existing and proposed development. LPA needs to be satisfied that map matches the situation correctly on site, that proposal is visually acceptable and that it will work. Application site surrounded by red line. There may also be artist's impressions of proposed development.

Part II	Additional information necessary if application is non-housing.
Industrial development – process and type of production	LPA needs to know if there are likely to be problems related to noxious uses (e.g. smell) or hazard (e.g. explosion) (Ch. 7).
Is proposal part of a larger scheme?	Where buildings relate to part of a much larger scheme (e.g. shopping centre), LPA needs to know in advance. It is difficult to refuse subsequent buildings once one is granted, whereas it might have refused a larger scheme.
Is proposal related to an existing use on or near site?	LPA may be concerned about increasing scale of noxious development.
Is proposal related to existing unsatisfactory premises elsewhere?	To allow new development may solve a **non-conforming use** problem elsewhere.

Floorspace in square metres: existing, new, proposed:
  Industrial
  Shop
  Office
  Warehouse
  Other
  Total
	LPA needs to know scale of development to gauge site density, traffic generation, employment potential and so on. These are key planning parameters.

Employment, FT/PT/FTE, numbers Office, industrial, warehouse, retail, others How many new staff, existing staff and staff transferred from other sites?	Upon employment depends the economic prosperity of locality. It affects demand for housing and other facilities. It influences traffic generation and parking requirements.
Parking and loading arrangements	LPA is normally anxious to have adequate parking arrangements for workers, clients and operations so that parking does not take place on adjacent roads. Loading should normally be within the site and not over the pavement (Ch. 6).
Estimated traffic flow from the new development on a normal working day	LPA need to know this to ensure that road network can cope (Ch. 6).
Nature, volume and method of disposal of trade waste and effluent	This can be noxious and/or dangerous. LPA must be assured that proper arrangements are in place (Ch. 7).
Storage and use of hazardous and /or noxious substances (technical list) with quantities	LPA can impose conditions on substances to minimize risks (Ch. 7).
Date Signature of applicant	Necessary as application is a legal document.

The application form is accompanied by a fee and a certificate of ownership which states the ownership of the property and that the owners and tenants know of the application. Explanatory notes accompany application forms to help the applicant. Legal details relating to planning applications are given in the General Development Procedure Order 1995 (DoE 1995l). Different application forms may be used for different types of application (e.g. householders, general and advertisements). (Based on: Dijksman 1992: 27, SODD 1996b.)

by Taussik (1991; 1992: 14–15). She found that nearly all the LPAs she surveyed encouraged them, and major developers encouraged their own staff to undertake them. Although applicants and LPAs had different perspectives, they felt, to a greater or lesser extent, that they improved proposals, made for a more efficient development control service, saved money, time and effort, gave better access to information, fostered good personal relationships between developers and the LPA and were part of the public service. However, they made significant inroads into planning officers' time, the median duration of a pre-application visit being about half an hour. Although preapplication enquiries arguably improved applications, they diverted officers away from the main job of pushing applications through the development control system quickly, especially as some enquiries did not result in applications. A small minority of enquirers found the information given to them was misleading. Neither were all enquirers always happy about amendments to their proposals; over half did not consider their proposals improved. Other concerns were consistency of staff dealing with a proposal and the status of the advice given.

Negotiations

In large and complex cases, more formal negotiations take place at both technical officer level and/or at board director/councillor level. The content of conditions attached to permission, and legal agreements accompanying them, are often the focus of discussion. Studies show that the content and conduct of negotiations vary widely (Wenban-Smith & Beeston 1990, Ennis et al. 1993; Healey et al. 1995: ch. 7). Negotiations can be understood in terms of procedure and substance.

In terms of procedure the sequence is approximately as follows:

1a. The developer carries out design and cost studies to establish what he wants, usually in terms of maximizing profits. He will be conversant with LPA requirements by experience and personal contact. He establishes what he really wants and what the bottom line is. Between these two he is prepared to negotiate conceding what may be of little value to him, e.g. unbuildable land to the LPA as public open space and knowing when he might actually have to withdraw from the project.

1a. Meanwhile, before any meeting of parties, the LPA is generally aware that applications may be made to which they have to respond. They are concerned first to facilitate development in line with development plans, secondly to ameliorate adverse impacts such as visual intrusion and traffic congestion, and thirdly to secure wider community benefits, e.g. road improvements.

1a. Before a planning application is made, discussions of greater or lesser formality usually take place between the applicant and the LPA. The applicant lays out the proposal as he would most like to see it: likewise the LPA. They agree what they agree and identify where there is disagreement. Bargaining then takes place in the format: "If you will do so and so . . . then I will do such and such . . ." and a bargain is struck. (Practice seems to differ as to whether heads of agreement and/or details are thrashed out at this stage.)

1a. A planning application is submitted to the LPA and granted, often in outline only, subject to an agreement. (See Ch. 5.)

1a. Further negotiation takes place, details are settled and agreed in writing for the avoidance of doubt.

1a. The development gets under way and the LPA monitors the situation to ensure agreements are adhered to.

These naïve bare bones conceal the tactics and ploys of negotiation. In times and places of economic prosperity the LPA may be the stronger party; in times of depression it may be the applicant. However, in depressed conditions the applicant may go bankrupt. Negotiations are in private, with the public, and possibly councillors, knowing little of what is being done in their name. The applicant knows that, if he is refused planning permission, appeal will take a long time and it is better to settle and concede to the LPA rather than delay. If the appeals inspectorate could be speeded up, much of the LPA's strength would be lost (Healey et al. 1995: 194). Both parties may have to discuss the proposal with other stakeholders and professionals in order to coordinate the development. The interplay of personalities is vital to the negotiations, as is discussion at the appropriate professional level. Other factors involved are the skills and knowledge of the negotiators, personal contacts and clear, well grounded strategies. Applicants may be in competition, which strengthens the LPA's hand (ibid.).

The substance of negotiations is detailed in Chapter 5, where conditions and planning gain are discussed. Ennis et al. (1993) classified the contents into: negative (e.g. noise control) and positive (e.g. provision of highways by the developer) and the substance of agreements, the most common being highways, sewerage and drainage, landscaping and open space, and parking (ibid.: tables 7, 8). What might be termed social provision, such as childcare, was found to be unusual.

Making development control decisions

Once a planning application has been submitted, it is checked, registered and acknowledged by the LPA. The application is allocated to a planning officer on an area or subject basis (e.g. conservation work). He marshals all the necessary guidance from development plans, Circulars, PPGs, appeals and other guidance with which this book deals. He will consult consultees (see Ch. 3) and carry out a site visit to check the plans, take photographs and so on. When he has sufficient material at his disposal, he writes a report with a recommendation to grant or refuse (RTPI 1988a).

The officer may then make a decision himself using delegated powers or remit it to the planning committee of elected councillors. Where officer delegation powers are in place, there is usually a scheme of delegation. It typically specifies that all applications will be dealt with by officers except:

- those recommended for approval contrary to the provisions of the development plan
- major or controversial applications
- those requested to go to committee by a ward councillor (Reference Services 1992: 35).

The advantages of officer delegation are that it speeds many minor decisions (and many applications are minor household applications) and frees the planning committee to consider what it considers to be important matters.

Planning committees meet regularly, depending on the pressure of business. The frequency may be weekly, fortnightly or monthly. Before a meeting the chief planning officer and chairperson usually go through the agenda, which lists the planning applications for decision and other matters such as local plan preparation. The purpose of this "call over"[1] is to improve the general conduct of the committee, with contentious issues flagged up in advance. The public are usually admitted and may be called to speak. All committee papers are public: typically, they include officers' reports, application decision lists, new central government guidance, and letters and petitions from interested parties. The chairperson calls the items, the planning officer speaks to the applications (or in important cases has a written report), indicating key policies and the results of consultations. He makes a recommendation to grant or refuse. Many applications are approved "on the nod" on the basis of the planning officer's recommendations. More contentious issues may be debated by the committee and the officer's recommendation overturned. Applications may be deferred for further information relevant to the decision to be obtained. In large and complex cases the eight-week period allowed for decision may well be overrun, and deferral needs to be with the agreement of the applicant. In some cases amendments to recommendations are moved. Sometimes a decision is taken by vote. After the committee has met, the decisions are checked, and conditions and reasons refined for legal purposes. Decision notices are then sent to applicants, usually under the chief planning officer's name, and are placed in the statutory planning register. Details of applications and decisions are often put in a computer database for record purposes to enable the LPA to oversee development and employment trends in the district and for recall purposes, should this be necessary.

As will be seen in other chapters, making planning applications is a necessary constraint on business. As Europe becomes more integrated, planning regulations may become more important in business location decisions. Research (GMA Planning 1994) into the experiences of companies operating in five west European countries, including England and Wales showed, inter alia, that:

1. The term for pre-meeting meetings.

- Planning systems and consent procedures were a consideration for two-thirds of companies in their choice of the country in which to invest. They were not a determining factor. Planning ranked 11th out of 20 considerations. The most important considerations were proximity to markets, availability of infrastructure and high-quality land.
- Timescale was important to firms, but their experience in England and Wales was satisfactory.
- The survey of internationally mobile companies did not reveal evidence that the planning system in England and Wales discouraged non-UK companies from investing there (ibid.: 72).

Conclusion

This chapter has drawn attention to the administrative arrangements in place for the consideration of proposals to develop, to the many parties involved and to development plans, which form the basis of development control decisions. It concluded with a description of the process of making applications to develop, with a brief reference to similar processes abroad. Generally, they are no more onerous in England and Wales than elsewhere. Chapter 3 will elaborate on the process by describing the legal procedures in obtaining planning permission and associated matters.

CHAPTER 3

Legal aspects of development control

Introduction

The purpose of this chapter is to outline the legal basis for development control. It should not be looked upon as a statement of law; readers should consult standard reference works such as Grant (continuing), Grant (1995) and Greenwood (1995). The powers for exercising development control come from principal statutes, especially the Town and Country Planning Act 1990, and subordinate legislation, so-called statutory instruments, especially the General Permitted Development Order and the Use Classes Order. The main powers are exercised by district authorities, but in some instances by central government and county councils. The courts and the **ombudsman** may intervene sometimes. Development plans, which are an important framework for development control, also have their basis in law. Readers should be aware of cognate legislation that may impinge on development control. It includes the Wildlife and Countryside Act 1981, which deals with SSSIs and AONBs (Sites of Special Scientific Interest and Areas of Outstanding Natural Beauty), the Rights of Way Act 1990, and the Disabled Persons Act 1970 (regarding access), European directives (e.g. the Environmental Impact Assessment Directive), local government acts, which order and define local government powers, and the Acquisition of Land Act 1981, relating to compulsory purchase. Other legislation relates to pollution, waste, drainage, utilities, highways, building regulations and housing (ILEX 1993b). The law of compensation is of indirect relevance only for development control, is complex and is not normally taken into account when development control decisions are reached (Morgan & Nott 1995: 29; and see Greenwood 1995: xxii). It is not possible to deal with the details of cognate legislation here.

The legal definition of development

Planning permission is required for carrying out any development of land. For legal purposes, development control is fairly strictly defined. In a practical sense it would not be easy to control all development, however trivial (e.g. replacing windows). The LPAs and applicants would be overwhelmed with paperwork. As a principle, all development needs planning permission, but much trivial development is given general planning permission, through the General Permitted Development Order and the Use Classes Order (e.g. replacing windows and minor changes of use such as a grocer's shop to a greengrocer's shop). However, in environmentally sensitive circumstances this general permission may be withdrawn and planning permission may be necessary (e.g. window replacement in some conservation areas). This enables the development control system to disregard that which is not important, concentrate on the matters that are, lessen bureaucratic burdens and speed the process of decision. However, it has the disadvantage that many small uncontrolled cumulative changes can be significant. There may be concern about this but its extent is not clear. Agricultural development is significant and recently has been subject to new procedures. Ripping out hedgerows is of particular concern (Ch. 7). This is an issue separate from development, which has taken place without planning permission when in fact it was needed.

Development means carrying out building, engineering, mining or other operations in, on, over or under land and a material change of use of land or buildings. Demolition and rebuilding are included in this definition (Town and Country Planning Act 1990 §55(1)). In practice it is more complex than this. For example, the following do not constitute development (Town and Country Planning Act 1990 §55(2)): internal alterations to buildings which do not really affect the outside in a major way; road improvements by highway authorities; repairs to utility services; the use of land or buildings within the **curtilage** (i.e. garden, etc. of a dwelling house) for incidental enjoyment (e.g. building a swimming pool) and the use of land for agriculture and forestry, which cover about 90 per cent of the area of UK.

Another category that does not require planning permission is changes of use permitted by the Use Classes Order 1987. However, the following do constitute development: change of use of one dwelling to two or more, extending or raising a waste dump, display of many outside advertisements, and demolition of buildings (Mason 1996: 28). Yet another category of development constitutes development but does not require planning permission: permitted development under Article 3 and Schedule 2 of the General Permitted Development Order 1995, or so-called "permitted development rights" (PDR). Moreover, resumption of a previous use, after a temporary use (§57), and certain advertisements specified in the Advertisement Regulations 1992, do not need planning permission (ibid.: 28). However, "building operations" has difficulties of interpretation: the erection of plant and machinery is not normally a building operation. Mobile structures are not normally development. Mining operations, both underground and on the surface, and engineering operations, including laying out access to highways and possibly demolition, require planning permission (ibid.: ch. 3). Whether planning permission is necessary or not, when there is doubt, it is for the LPA to decide.

Development plans

As mentioned in Chapter 2, development plans are the first consideration when making development control decisions. Their preparation and adoption is subject to legally based processes (DoE 1992b; Morgan & Nott 1995: 170 ff; Mason 1996: 20). The statutory plan-making process enables the LPA to establish policies to safeguard future land uses (e.g. for highways and housing based on survey and analysis of their geographical area). This process allows for landowners, developers and others to make presentations and suggest alternatives. This happens at an early stage (the pre-deposit consultation stage), in the middle of the process at the draft stage and during an inquiry or examination in public, and later when the draft has been modified and before its final adoption. The importance of these inputs and changes to development plans is that development control decisions, when they come to be made, are guided by the policies for particular plots.

The General Permitted Development Order (GPDO)

The Town and Country Planning (General Permitted Development) Order 1995 and the Town and Country Planning (Use Classes) Order 1987 are major pieces of subsidiary legislation within the context of development control. This chapter will deal with their legal implications: Chapter 4 will deal with issues of substance. The General Permitted Development Order (GPDO) 1995 was formerly part of the General Development Order (GDO) (1988) and is referred to as such in this book as appropriate. A comparison of the articles in the GDO, the GPDO and the GDPO is to be found in Circular 9/95 *General Development Order consolidation* (DoE 1995d: Appendix F).

The purpose of the GPDO is to free much minor development from the need for planning permission. Mason (1996: 32) has classified these into:
- minor importance (e.g. painting a house)
- the need for encouragement (e.g. factory extensions)
- lifting bureaucratic burdens (e.g. house extensions)
- environmentally acceptable (e.g. agriculture and forestry) and
- work carried out by a "public body" (e.g. utilities).

The list is given in Schedule 2 of the GPDO and summarized in Figure 3.1 and Table 4.2, and is known as "permitted development rights" (PDR).

However, minor development can be very important in protected and sensitive environments. Permitted development rights may be withdrawn in the following circumstances:

- in conservation areas, national parks and Areas of Outstanding Natural Beauty (so-called Article 1(5) land) (e.g. roof renewal)
- by conditions attached to a planning permission (e.g. minor extensions to a house converted from an interesting old barn)
- where they affect access to a trunk or classified road or create a dangerous distraction
- where development is subject to an Article 4 Direction (see below).

Permitted development rights can be in fact quite complex. For example, Article 3, Schedule 2, Part 7 of the GPDO allows forestry buildings and operations, including the erection of buildings, making paths, obtaining materials for paths and other operations. But development in this class is not permitted if the building is a dwelling, if the building would be over 3m high if within 3km of an aerodrome or if any part of the development is within 25m of a trunk or classified road. Certain conditions may apply; for example, that before the development begins, the developer must apply to the LPA for a determination as to whether prior approval is necessary for the siting, design and external appearance of buildings. Other parts of the GPDO have the following formula: you can have planning permission without the need of a formal application, but certain development is not permitted at all; moreover, if it is, it is subject to conditions (Grant 1995). If there is doubt as to whether permitted development rights apply, the developer can apply to the LPA for a **Certificate of Lawfulness of Proposed Use or Development (CLOPUD)** (Casely-Hayford 1995: 225).

Permitted development rights (PDR) can be withdrawn by so-called "Article 4 Directions" (Article 4 of the GPDO). Withdrawal may be by the Secretary of State for the Environment or by the LPA for any class in Schedule 2 (see Fig. 3.1) or a particular development falling in a class (Part 1 house extensions within a conservation area; Mason 1996: 33). The effect of withdrawal of permitted development rights is to make the developer apply for planning permission when it would not normally be necessary. The upshot is likely to be the grant of planning permission subject to conditions. In the case of a house extension in a conservation area, it may be granted if local materials are used. However, refusal may attract compensation for loss of rights (Grant 1995: 66). An Article 4 Direction cannot be used in retrospect to reverse development that has already taken place (ibid.: 61). Certain types of development are also excluded from the operation of an Article 4 Direction (e.g. mineral exploration; see Circular 9/95, *General Development Order consolidation*: DOE 1995d).

The Circular (ibid.: Appendix D) envisaged that Article 4 Directions should be used sparingly and only in response to specific threat. In conservation areas a special need must be demonstrated, and in the case of Article 4 restrictions on dwellings they should only be used if the dwelling is of particularly high quality.

When a planning application is made in the normal way, the LPA in granting permission may withdraw permitted development rights by imposing conditions. Clearly, the GPDO grants developers freedom and that is the principle behind the GPDO. However, the LPA may have particular concerns, for example preventing the conversion of integral garages into extended living space to inhibit street parking, or preserving the appearance of interesting but obsolete agricultural buildings converted to new uses.

The Use Classes Order (UCO)

The UCO (DoE 1987c) performs a simplifying function similar to the GPDO. It relates to change of use of land and buildings, rather than to new development. It is important that significant changes of use of land and buildings are subject to planning control. Although building work may be minimal in changing, say, a warehouse to a factory, parking and road capacity requirements may increase dramatically.

The GPDO gives general planning permission (i.e. permitted development rights) to uses listed in Schedules at the end of the Order (see Fig. 3.1). Similarly, the Use Classes Order specifies which changes of use are not development and therefore do not need planning permission. A summary of the UCO is given in Figure 3.2. The principle is that planning permission is not needed for minor changes within the specified classes of use, but it is between them. Thus, changing a warehouse (Class B8) to a factory (Class B2) does need planning permission, but changing a grocer's shop to an electrical goods shop does not, because they are both in the same A1 class.

The practical advantages of the UCO are (Mason 1996: 35):
- It gives occupiers commercial security in that they can alter many business uses quickly in response to market demand.
- It cuts bureaucracy.
- By leaving unobjectionable change alone, it is possible to focus on changes that are significant.

The legal niceties of development control revolve around the Town and Country Planning Act 1990 §55(1), which states that: "A material change in the use of any building or other land" is also development. As human activities vary greatly in type and extent, arguments about interpretation abound. They are resolved by the LPA, using its discretion, and by the courts.

A material change is a matter of fact and degree. It may be a matter of fact that a householder is using one room in his house intermittently as an office for business purposes, but the degree may be so insignificant that the character of the domestic use is not changed and the amenity of the neighbours not upset. This kind of use is likely to be relevant, but the degree may not be. Changes must

43

Figure 3.1   General Permitted Development Order (GPDO) (DoE 1995k: Art. 3 Sch. 2; Morgan & Nott 1995: 102 ff; Casely-Hayford 1995: ch. 4).

The provisions of the GPDO are complex. As a principle, all development, however trivial, needs planning permission, but to cut down on excessive regulation the GPDO gives permission for the developments listed below. However, this permission is subject to exceptions, limitations and conditions, which form part of the order itself, to mitigate possible adverse effects. In sensitive areas such as conservation areas, this general permission can be withdrawn by Article 4 Directions of the GPDO. Permitted development rights can also be withdrawn by the use of conditions attached to planning permission (Mason 1996: 32). Some of the conditions and complexities are dealt with in the text.

Planning permission is not necessary for:

Part 1   Development within the curtilage of a dwelling house, for example improvements such as extensions and other developments such as swimming pools incidental to the enjoyment of the dwelling house. However, the extension of houses is limited to 10 per cent of the cubic content for terraced houses and 15 per cent for detached houses, within an overall maximum of 115m^3; otherwise, adjacent property might be adversely affected.

Part 2   Minor operations such as the exterior painting of a building and the erection of walls and fences but not over 2m in height above ground level; otherwise, they might be visually overbearing.

Part 3   Changes of use. This provision has to be read in conjunction with the Use Classes Order (UCO; see Fig. 3.2). The GPDO allows for less environmental damaging changes, for example a hot-food shop to a general shop, but not vice versa.

Part 4   Temporary buildings and uses, including huts, etc. used in connection with the construction of development for which planning permission has been granted. Once development has been completed, temporary uses and buildings must be cleared away. Other land can also be used temporarily for up to 28 days a year without planning permission (e.g. holding a market). Temporary buildings may be made of temporary materials; to leave them *in situ* would be environmentally unacceptable.

Part 5   Caravan sites. Caravan sites may be divided into permanent, tourist and gypsy; they are subject to complex legislation. However, certain caravans are allowed without permission, for example for seasonal agricultural work. There is concern about visual intrusion and infrastructural overload.

Part 6   Agricultural buildings and operations, for example mineral extraction for use on the holding. Certain buildings are allowed without permission, but the LPA must be notified, and it may then require approval lest they cause visual intrusion and other environmental problems (see Ch. 4).

Part 7   Forestry buildings and operations, for example buildings and tracks related to forestry work. As for agriculture, the LPA may have to be notified and approval obtained.

Part 8   Industrial and warehouse development, especially the erection of plant. Extensions are allowed subject to limits (e.g. not more than 25 per cent of the cubic content of the original building) on condition that they do not take parking or turning space.

Part 9   Repairs to private ways as long as they are within the boundary of the street.

Part 10 Repairs to services apart from statutory undertakers and local authorities.

Part 11 Development under local or private acts, for example harbour improvement.

Part 12 Development by local authorities normally of a limited extent on their own property, such as the erection of street furniture (e.g. bus shelters).

Figure 3.1 (contd)

Part 13 Development by local highway authorities, especially improvement and maintenance works.

Part 14 Development by drainage bodies relating to water course maintenance.

Part 15 Development by the National Rivers Authority, e.g. drainage improvement. (The National Rivers Authority was absorbed by the Environment Agency in 1996.)

Part 16 Sewerage works, including maintenance and construction.

Part 17 Development by statutory undertakers, for example the erection of post boxes by the Post Office, although developers are advised to inform the LPA if development is significant, see Circular 15/92, *Publicity for planning applications* (DoE 1992i).

Part 18 Aviation development, for example navigation equipment subject to limitations.

Part 19 Development ancillary to mining operations, for example buildings, although the permission of the minerals planning authority may be necessary (see Ch. 7).

Part 20 Coal mining development, for example development to ensure mine safety. The approval of the mineral planning authority may be necessary.

Part 21 Waste tipping at a mine subject to limitations.

Part 22 Mineral exploration, for example drilling for not more than 28 days, but excluding oil. Any equipment must be cleared and the land restored.

Part 23 Removal of material from mineral working deposits, for example for construction work, subject to conditions.

Part 24 Development by telecommunications code system operations, for example apparatus not exceeding 15 m above ground level. Operators are also licensed.

Part 25 Other telecommunications development, including microwave and satellite antennae, subject to limits.

Part 26 Development by the Historic Buildings and Monuments Commission for England, including restoration but not extension.

Part 27 Use of land by certain members of recreational organizations such as the Scouts, but excluding buildings, for recreational use.

Part 28 Development at amusement parks, for example the erection of booths.

Part 29 Driver information systems, for example in the taxi business.

Part 30 Toll road facilities, for example collection booths.

Part 31 Demolition of buildings subject to exceptions that are listed in the Town and Country Planning (Demolition – description of buildings) Direction 1995, and see Circular 10/95 *Planning controls over demolition* (DoE 1995e).

Part 32 School, college, university and hospital buildings on existing sites subject to limitations, for example by rendering playing fields unusable.

Part 33 Closed circuit television cameras on buildings for security purposes provided, for example, that the building is not a listed building.

relate to land use and not merely to change of occupier or merely to the ownership of goods handled.

Where there is a primary use, the introduction of ancillary use does not normally constitute a change of use. For example, where the occupier of a factory with offices wishes to extend the offices or to put in a works canteen by taking over more existing factory floorspace, this would not normally constitute a change of use needing planning permission; they are ancillary uses, albeit that offices and canteens might be in other classes (B1 and A3).

An important concept relating to change of use is the **planning unit**. In the factory example in the previous paragraph it is a matter of common sense that the factory is one unit for planning purposes. But what if the canteen were converted from a smaller pre-existing factory building in the yard and the canteen were thrown open to the general public? Thus, although the factory and yard might be one planning unit, to change the use of a significant part which had planning consequences (e.g. parking) would probably constitute development. Rather separately, the division of a single dwelling into two or more dwellings constitutes development (Telling & Duxbury 1993: 89, 106 ff), but the division of other types of use does not.

Mixed uses on a site may pose quite different environmental problems. Sometimes the uses alternate over time (e.g. camping and grazing); it appears that the cessation of one use without the intensification of the other does not constitute development. Where an ancillary use becomes the main use, there may be a material change. A new use (not simply an ancillary one) introduced onto a site will normally constitute a material change (Mason 1996: 37).

Intensification of an existing use may also constitute a change of use. For example, a private residential garage used for the part-time repair of cars as a hobby may change to full-time repair as a business. Here the residential character has been changed (Telling & Duxbury 1993: 104).

Difficulties arise when a use is abandoned and resumed. The question is whether planning permission is needed for resumption. Where a new planning permission is granted and implemented, the old use rights are lost. Planning permission runs with the land once implemented; cessation of use does not prevent resumption later on (this is particularly important in mineral working). Whereas a planning permission may be replaced by another planning permission, which is implemented, it is normally only uses that did not originally have planning permission that can be abandoned.

Not all land uses are included in the main use classes. They are called sui generis uses (i.e. each of its own kind). They are of such a character that changes into them cause the LPA specific concern, for example changing a shop into a motor showroom on account of its visual impact (see Fig. 3.3).

A final legal point is the relationship between the UCO and the GPDO. The general principle of the UCO is that planning permission is usually necessary for changes of use between classes. However, the GPDO contains provisions that loosen these constraints (Schedule 2, Part 3). Where a developer wishes to change

---

Figure 3.2 A summary of the Use Classes Order 1987, as amended (DoE 1987b, Grant 1995).

A1 Shops, including retail sales, post offices, ticket and travel agencies, cold food off the premises, hairdressing, funeral directors, display of goods for sale, hiring domestic goods, reception of goods to be cleaned, where the sale is to visiting members of the public.
A2 Financial and professional services, including financial services, professional services (but not medical services) and other services, including betting, appropriate to a shopping area where they are visited by the public.
A3 Food and drink for consumption on the premises or hot food off the premises.

B1 Business, including offices, research and development, and industries which can be carried out without detriment to the amenity of a residential area.
B2 General industry that is not B1.
B3–B7 Special industry absorbed into B2 with effect from 1995.
B8 Storage or distribution.

C1 Hotels and guesthouses.
C2 Residential institutions, including hospitals and residential colleges.
C3 Dwelling houses used by families or by households of not more than six people living together.

D1 Non-residential institutions, including schools, museums and places of worship.
D2 Assembly and leisure, including cinemas, dance halls and swimming baths.

---

from a relatively objectionable use to a less objectionable use in planning terms, then planning permission is not necessary. For example, it is possible to change a noisy and smelly fish and chip shop (Class A3) into a bookshop (A1) without planning permission, but not vice versa. These are referred to informally as ratchet changes or the escalator principle. (See Table 3.1 for further details of changes allowed.)

Figure 3.3 Sui generis uses in the Use Classes Order (as amended) (DoE 1987b: Art 3 (6); Greenwood 1995: 719).

  a Theatre
  b Amusement arcade or funfair
  c Launderette
  d Fuel for motor vehicles
  e Car sales
  f Taxi and car hire
  g Scrapyard, etc.
  h Works registered under the Alkali, etc., Act 1906
  i Hostel

Not all sui generis uses are listed, e.g. garden centres.

Table 3.1 Changes between classes in the UCO which do not require planning permission.

By GPDO Class	From UCO Class	To UCO Class
A	A3 (Food & drink)	A1 (Shops)
A	Sale of motor vehicles	A1 (Shops)
B(a)	B2 (General industrial)	B1 (Business)
B(a)	B8 (Storage & distribution)	B1 (Business)*
B(b)	B2 (General industrial)	B8 (Storage and distribution)*
C	A3 (Food & drink)	A2 (Financial & professional)
D	A2 (Professional & financial with display windows at ground floor)	A1 (Shops)
F (a)	A1 (Shops)	Mixed A1 and single flat other than flat at ground floor level
F (b)	A2 (Financial and professional services)	Mixed A2 ditto
G (a)	Mixed A1 (Shop and flat)	A1 Shops
G (b)	Mixed A2 (Financial services) and flat	A2 (Financial services)
G (c)	Mixed A2 (Financial services)	A1 (Shops)

* Not where change of use relates to more than 235m² of floorspace.
(DOE 1995d: T1)

Planning application procedures

Chapter 2 outlined the practice of making development control decisions; this section deals with the legal requirements and procedures. The procedures are a legal requirement for the grant of a valid planning permission. The legal pathway is in Figure 3.4. It is not possible here to deal with the many detailed aspects of the process (see Salt 1991). However, assuming that planning permission is necessary, there are four main stages: checking the application, consulting the interested parties, making the decision and notifying the decision (Mason 1996: ch. 4; RTPI 1988a).

Once the application has been submitted by the applicant to the LPA, it is checked. It should normally contain four copies of the completed application forms (see Table 2.1 for content), plans at appropriate scales to show location, existing and proposed development and building construction details. Delay is often caused by incomplete information; the LPA may defer a decision and ask for more information. The application is accompanied by a certificate stating that the applicant is the tenant or owner or has informed them. It is possible to make an application for any land; the purpose of the certificate is to prevent possibly controversial proposals being sprung on unsuspecting tenants and owners. The application needs to be publicized by the LPA by newspaper advertisement, site notices or neighbour notification, so that interested parties have the opportunity to comment (DOE 1992i). Additional publicity may be necessary where a proposal is a substantial **departure** from the development plan in force or the proposal might have significant effects on amenity (see Ch. 8). Where rarely a proposed development would have a really significant environmental impact, an

---

Figure 3.4 Planning permission – the decision-making procedure in outline (DoE 1988f; Wright 1991: 18; Thomas, continuing, §5; DoE 1995l).

1. [Preapplication discussion between applicant and LPA.]
2. Application submitted by applicant to LPA.
3. Application checked, registered and acknowledged by LPA.
4. Public consultation period with statutory and non-statutory consultees.
5. Planning officer visits site and starts to compile report on the application for planning committee on the basis of material considerations (Ch. 5).
6. Results of public consultation received by LPA.
7. [Before final decision there may be further discussions between applicant and LPA to make application acceptable.]
8. Planning officer finalizes his report and either makes a decision himself under delegated powers or remits it to LPA planning committee with a recommendation to grant or refuse planning permission.
9. Planning committee decides to refuse or grant planning permission.
10. Applicant notified of decision, which is recorded in planning register.
11. [Where applicant is dissatisfied because of refusal or onerous conditions, he may appeal to Secretary of State.]

[ ] = stages not necessarily in the procedure

---

environmental assessment may be necessary (see Ch. 5). Applications are normally accompanied by fees, which are roughly proportional to the scale of development (see Ch. 8); they are intended to cover part of the costs of the planning service. Finally, a public planning register is held by the LPA; all applications and decisions are recorded in it, so that interested parties are aware of environmental changes likely to affect them.

After these basically clerical stages have been completed, the technical work of appraising the proposal prior to a decision starts. Most applications are dealt with by the planning department of the district council. More unusually, they may go to the county authorities if it is a county matter or to the Secretary of State for the Environment where important matters of principle are involved – so-called "call-in" applications. As land-use decisions may have implications far into the future, it is vital that interested parties are consulted so that important matters are not overlooked. Consultees may be statutory and non-statutory (GDPO: Article 10). Counties are consulted where the proposal would conflict with or prejudice structure plans or be of major importance in their implementation. Other important statutory consultees include other LPAs, when their areas are likely to be affected, the Department of Transport if trunk roads are involved, water authorities when waterworks, sewerage treatment and similar installations are involved, the Ministry of Agriculture when substantial amounts of good-quality agricultural land may be lost, and the Environment Agency if notifiable quantities of hazardous substances may be present. Parish and community councils normally receive applications related to their areas so they can comment. Non-statutory consultees such as residents' associations may also get involved (see Ch. 8). In some cases

49

the effect of a consultation is that the LPA may be overridden in its decision by a "direction". Such a direction may be issued by the Secretary of State for the Environment, using reserve powers for any proposal, if there may be a substantial departure from a development plan and if the proposal involves access to or development near major highways. Consultees normally have a minimum of 14 days to respond (Mason 1996: 52). Delay in responding delays the decision process.

At the decision stage all the information necessary will have been assembled. These are so-called "material considerations", detailed in Chapter 5. These may be reported by planning officers to the LPA planning committee in writing or orally. Material considerations include central government regulations and guidance, development plans, replies to consultations and the physical characteristics of the proposal and the site concerned. The Town and Country Planning Act 1990 §70 requires the LPA to "have regard to the provisions of the development plan, so far as material to the application, and to any other material consideration". In the Jodrell Bank case (*Stringer* vs *Minister of Housing and Local Government* 1971, 1 All ER 65), Mr Justice Cooke said, "all considerations relating to the use and development of land are considerations which may in a proper case be regarded as planning considerations . . ." (Casely-Hayford 1995: 126). Because it is a legal requirement that planning decisions shall take into account material considerations, this is interpreted to mean that the LPA shall not leave out any material considerations and shall not take into account any consideration that is not material (Mason 1996: 57; see Ch. 5.)

The LPA can make the following types of decisions: approve with conditions, refuse, and make no decision, which is termed a deemed refusal. Article 22 of the GDPO requires reasons to be given for refusal and for the imposition of conditions. The LPA must make a decision within eight weeks of the initial receipt of the formal application and fee by them. The period can be extended by agreement with the applicant. The purpose of conditions and reasons for refusals are dealt with in Chapter 5. Failure to make a decision, a deemed refusal, is appealable. This device may be used when an LPA wants to avoid political odium by not making the decision itself, and asks the Secretary of State to decide.

The reader should be aware of two ploys of applicants. First, "double tracking", whereby an applicant submits two almost identical applications for the same site where there may be some doubt as to the outcome. Often, these applications are large scale and complex, to which the LPA cannot readily respond within eight weeks. One application is pursued by the applicant after the eight-week period by negotiation with the LPA; the other, now a deemed refusal, is pursued by appeal to the Secretary of State. The applicant implements the one granted first (if granted at all) and thus saves time. Secondly, the applicant may bombard the LPA with repeated applications once the first has been refused on appeal, in the hope of wearing the LPA down or a change of view with a change in political control. LPAs can refuse to determine an application within two years of a refusal on appeal of a similar application (DOE 1991a: 5, 9; Mason 1996: 56).

Once the LPA has made a decision, it issues a written decision notice to the applicant. It may be accompanied by a planning gain or planning obligation agreement (see Ch. 5). There are further basic points to bear in mind. Several valid permissions can be held for the same plot of land and, as they are all acceptable to the LPA, it is up to the applicant which one he implements, depending on market demand. As planning permission runs with the land, it can be sold on with the benefit of planning permission to another party, who may implement it and profit from it. Applicants are not obliged to implement permission and they may let it lapse. Planning permissions are normally implemented in full; conditions are imposed to ensure this, for example that buildings should not be occupied until landscaping is planted and established. This is to ensure that amenity is secured in spite of the temptation to cut costs. Outline applications (Table 2.1 and Ch. 5) cause difficulties, because more than one set of details may satisfy the outline scheme.

In complex applications, where modifications to original proposals have been made, it is necessary to be quite clear what has been decided. This is done specifically by referring to drawings accompanying the application by number and by stamping. Often, a condition is attached requiring that development is carried out as approved.

In the postwar period, permission was granted in perpetuity, but this prejudiced plan-making. Now full planning permission is granted for five years; outline permission is granted with three years in which to submit details; it expires within two years of the last approval of details. The event that protects a permission from expiry is the start of works such as digging foundations. Sometimes applicants deliberately start development to protect the permission, but do not complete it, because it may not be expedient for them to do so at that time. In these circumstances, the LPA may serve a "completion notice", which requires the development to be completed within a specified time; if not completed, the original consent lapses (Mason 1996: 67).

Planning appeals

If an applicant is dissatisfied with the LPA's decision, say because of a refusal, appeal may be made to the Secretary of State. Appeal cases vary greatly in complexity and procedure. Appeal decisions are usually made by appointed inspectors (reporters in Scotland) and rarely by the Secretary of State himself. A useful guide to the forms used and examples of statements of grounds for appeal is to be found in Lavers & Webster (1990), and guidance for planning officers is given in RTPI (1995a). The Planning Inspectorate has also issued *Planning appeals – a guide* (1992).

Appeals may be held because of refusals, onerous conditions, failure of the LPA to give a decision, and enforcement action. The appeal may take various forms: Secretary of State inquiries, Secretary of State written representations, inspectors' inquiries, inspectors' written representations, and inspectors' informal hearings. Nearly all appeals are decided by inspectors as a result of written representations. Many relate to small-scale housing development. There are between 15000 and 30000 appeals a year in England, of which about a third are allowed (DOE 1992c: para. 14; see Appendix III). An analysis of appellants' perceptions of the planning appeal system is to be found in McNamara et al. (1986).

The purposes of the appeal system are to safeguard the individual against unreasonable LPA decisions and they are a means of ensuring that central government policies are applied consistently in planning matters. However, it does mean taking decisions out of the hands of democratically elected councillors and putting them in the hands of a central government appointee, albeit an expert one. Only the original applicant can appeal, except in enforcement cases. It is not possible for a third party, a neighbour, to appeal against the grant of planning permission because he is aggrieved by it (Mason 1996: 70).

Appeals are a last resort: they can be longwinded and costly. Before deciding to go to appeal, the applicant should negotiate with the LPA. Refusal may be based on a technicality (e.g. landscaping), which can be overcome. It may be possible to alter the original application and to submit it successfully. If an appeal is to be made, it must be within six months of the offending decision.

It is normally for the applicant to decide whether he wants an informal appeal by "written representations" or a more formal public inquiry, although the LPA or the Secretary of State can override the other parties and insist on a public inquiry when the matter is of great difficulty or importance (Telling & Duxbury 1993: 160). Table 3.2 sets out the arguments for and against the principal appeal vehicles; they are basically a matter of cost, speed and thoroughness. "Hearings" are another method of appeal. Written evidence is submitted to the inspector in advance of a meeting of the parties around a table. The inspector takes the lead in clarifying disagreements (Thomas 1994: 69). Procedures for written representations and planning inquiries are outlined in Figure 3.5 and Figure 3.6. (For appeal statistics see Appendix III).

Even after a major overhaul and amendments in 1992 to the public inquiries procedure, the City of London Law Society (1995) felt that improvement was still necessary with savings in time and cost. Pre-inquiry time, they suggested, should be used by forcing the parties to agree factual information and to narrow the issues before the inquiry, with new pre-inquiry procedures backed by time limits and the potential award of costs (ibid.: 3–4).

Enforcement

Development may well take place without planning permission, when in fact it is required; for example, changing a fish shop to a fish and chip shop. Sometimes, planning permission may have been granted for development, but the develop-

Table 3.2 The arguments for and against appeals by public inquiry or written representations (Thomas 1994: 69).

For	*Against*
Public Inquiry	
• Detailed review of evidence	• Expense of experts
• Oral argument may resolve ambiguity	• Delay in organization
• Procedural guarantees	• Delay in decision
• Cross-examination	• Inconvenience of organizing an appeal
• Allows local public to be involved	• Daunting formality because of court-like procedure
Written representations	
• Procedural simplicity, informality	• Superficial review of evidence
• Cheapness	• No oral or cross-examination
• Speed of decision	• Difficulty in resolving ambiguities because of lack of cross-examination

ment has not been carried out in accordance with the permission. Perhaps permission for a house has been granted but it has not fulfilled siting requirements, or a landscaping condition has not been fulfilled; it is not a criminal offence on the part of the perpetrator. Contravention is a high-profile issue as the public becomes increasingly environmentally aware (Arup Economics and Planning 1995a: i). A regulatory system needs ultimate penalties if it is to be meaningful. Guidance on enforcement is given in PPG18 (DoE 1991f). Powers are derived from the Town and Country Planning Act 1990 (Part VII) supplemented by DoE Circulars 21/91 and 17/92 (DoE 1991e, DoE 1992k). Possible contraventions are brought to the notice of the LPA by neighbour complaint or come to the notice of LPA officers in the course of day-to-day work. Sometimes breaches are inadvertent and at other times wilful. Where an apparent breach has occurred the LPA

Figure 3.5 Outline of procedures for appeal by written representations (Mason 1996: 71; DoE 1987a).

1. Once the adverse decision notice has been received from the LPA (or the eight-week decision period has expired), notice of appeal is made within six months to the Secretary of State. Appeal is made on a standard form, accompanied by notices relating to ownership and publicity, as in the case of a planning application.
2. The appeal form requires appellants to indicate whether they will agree to written representations (the appellant, LPA or Secretary of State can insist on a hearing).
3. The appeal form is accompanied by appellants' grounds for appeal, in which they can refute the LPA's position and bring in new evidence. A copy is sent to the LPA.
4. The LPA completes a background information questionnaire for the inspector and includes relevant papers, for example a copy of the relevant LPA committee minutes.
5. Statements and comments are exchanged.
6. Comments and representations by other parties – neighbours, highway authorities, etc. – are circulated. Every party is entitled to comment on the other's submission.
7. The inspector makes a site visit, accompanied or unaccompanied.
8. The inspector makes his decision as if it were on the original planning application.

Figure 3.6 Outline of procedures for appeals by public local inquiry – inspectors' rules (RTPI 1989b; DoE 1992l: annex; ILEX 1993a: ch. 14; Telling & Duxbury 1993: ch. 17; Mason 1996: 73–7).

(The rules that apply to Secretary of State appeals are similar to those for inspectors, but most appeals are dealt with by inspectors) (Telling & Duxbury 1993: 332).

1. The applicant decides to appeal and sends a notice of appeal to the Secretary of State. The Secretary of State gives notice to statutory parties (the LPA, appellant and others) that an inquiry is to be held at a specific date.

2. The inspector's name is notified; he is technically qualified.

3. The LPA, the appellant (and possibly others) prepare written statements (so-called Rule 6 statements) of their cases, which are made available to all, including the public, for perusal and copying, "some weeks" before the inquiry opens. The LPA must send a statement of case to the appellant and others, the appellant likewise.

4. The inspector may convene a pre-inquiry meeting of the main parties to timetable the actual inquiry and make for smooth running.

5a. The inquiry is held. The main parties to appear are the appellant and the LPA. There may be others, such as parish councils and those who may have made applications. The inspector exercises some discretion as to who may appear; he may persuade some parties to present a joint case. If a "direction" has been made, say by a highway authority to refuse the application, then a representative can be required to attend.

5b. Normal procedure is:
- Appellant opens his case and appellant's witnesses are called, followed in each case by cross-examination and re-examination.
- LPA puts its case with witnesses followed in each case by cross-examination and re-examination.
- Cases of other parties with cross-examination and re-examination.
- LPA sums up.
- Appellant sums up.
- Inquiry closes.

(The parties are frequently represented by others who argue their cases for them.)

5c. The inspector may take into account other evidence received before or during the hearing, e.g. letters from neighbours. He has the power to adjourn the inquiry. He can award costs against those whose behaviour is unreasonable, e.g. for late cancellation of the inquiry by one of the parties.

5d. The inspector normally makes a site visit.

6. The inspector notifies his decision to the main parties in writing and with reasons. His decision letter normally contains findings of fact, a statement of key issues raised, conclusions and a decision. The decision may be to refuse or grant permission with conditions. This may be some time after the inquiry has closed.

has to consider whether it is expedient to act. Sometimes the breach is trivial and they decide not to act. But as neighbours look to the LPA to protect their amenity, the LPA may fall foul of charges of maladministration and the ombudsman. The key issue in deciding whether to act should be whether the breach of control would unacceptably affect public amenity or the existing use of land and buildings meriting protection in the public interest.

If the LPA decides to act, it normally approaches the owner or occupier of the land and buildings and points out the problem. It could well be that the matter can be put right by informal negotiation. However, government advice is that negotiations should not be allowed to delay enforcement (DoE 91f: para. 5). Another solution is to request a planning application, which can be granted in retrospect. Conditions can then be imposed to ameliorate harm to amenity and make developments more acceptable to objectors. The government is particularly concerned where small businesses and jobs are involved, especially to allow time to negotiate alternative locations (ibid.: paras 10 and 14). In these cases there is no resort to rather complex legal procedures to abate the problem. Most people are law abiding. There are other pressures also on owners; in conveyancing, a vendor has to convince a buyer that the property has planning permission. If the LPA decides not to act, government advice is that they should explain why to those adversely affected (ibid.: paras 22–3). Normally, building development that has existed for four years, and change of use for ten years without challenge, are immune from further action by the LPA (Mason 1996: 88).

If the LPA does decide to act, it does so through a series of legal devices that say to the owner or occupier what is wrong, how it can be put right and by when. These are best explained in Figure 3.7. They are listed in order of "severity". A planning contravention notice is a shot across the bows of the perpetrator, warning that something is wrong and he is asked to help to put it right. A penalty such as a fine is a fairly extreme sanction. A problem inherent in the enforcement system is that someone in breach of planning law can use legal devices to delay and meanwhile profit.

The most recent procedures are as a result of recommendations of the Carnwath Report on enforcement (Carnwath 1989). Clearly, the system was not working well (ibid.: 21). He reported that a typical LPA may investigate about 500 alleged breaches a year, but only 25 might result in enforcement action (ibid.: 22). But where enforcement notices were issued, a substantial minority were never remedied or were remedied only after unacceptable delay (ibid.: 22). Many of the problem types related to residential caravans, industrial use and retail use in sensitive areas such as green belts, where small-scale developers were struggling with bureaucracy (ibid.: 24).

Carnwath (ibid.: 27) saw the purposes of enforcement as bringing offending activities within planning control, remedying or mitigating undesirable effects and punishing or deterring offenders (ibid.: 27). At that time, enforcement law was seen as so technical and complex as to make enforcement very difficult in practice (ibid.: ch. 5). One of the principal complaints was the failure of the system to deal with breaches of control with sufficient urgency. There was inherent conflict between urgency and fairness. Carnwath (ibid.: ch. 6) considered four major radical changes: making unauthorized development a crime; the formation of a Planning Enforcement Tribunal; the substitution of court remedies, for example injunctions; and empowering aggrieved third parties to institute enforcement proceedings. None of these more extreme measures were subsequently taken up. In the out-turn, Carnwath (ibid.: ch. 7) recommended building on the strengths of the existing system and remedying its weaknesses.

However, McCarthy et al. (1995) found that enforcement was still seen as

55

Figure 3.7 Enforcement devices (Mason 1996: ch. 6; Telling & Duxbury 1993: ch. 10; DoE 1991f, RTPI 1996).

1. Planning Contravention Notice (PCN)
A PCN may be served by the LPA on an owner or occupier where there may have been a breach of control through carrying out development or failing to comply with a condition. It is designed to establish the facts of the situation, not only the names of those with interests in the land, but also whether the land is in fact used as alleged in the PCN and was in the past, when the development began, whether planning permission exists and, if it does not, why the recipient contends it is not needed. The PCN offers opportunities for negotiation by a "time and place" meeting and application for retrospective planning permission. It warns of the consequences of failing to comply. Compliance is fulfilled by giving the required information in writing to the LPA. Failure to comply is a fineable offence. LPAs have power of entry: there are legal remedies for refusal.

2. Breach of Condition Notice (BCN)
Where conditions have been breached, a BCN may be served on a relevant person by the LPA to ensure compliance within a specified period. Non-compliance may result in a fine. It is designed to overcome perceived laxity in fulfilling conditions on the part of developers and has immediate effect (Telling & Duxbury 1993: 203).

3. Certificate of Lawful Existing Use or Development (CLEUD)
As time passes, it may be increasingly difficult to establish what the original use of land was and what changes and developments have taken place. Owners may apply to the LPA to establish conclusively that the development is lawful and immune from enforcement. The LPA may grant or refuse permission. Refusal is appealable.

4. Enforcement Notice
Where a PCN and BCN do not bring the desired results or are not relevant, the LPA may issue an enforcement notice on owners or occupiers. They have discretion: the decisive issue is whether the breach of control would unacceptably affect public amenity. Formal enforcement action would not normally be taken against trivial or technical breaches (e.g. a slight violation of the GPDO on house extensions) or against small businesses (Telling & Duxbury 1993: 204). The notice has various elements, including the nature of the breach to be put right, the remedy, time for compliance and why the LPA thinks it expedient to issue the notice. It is possible for under-enforcement to take place; for instance, the LPA may demand environmental improvements in place of the complete demolition of a building (Mason 1996: 91). Enforcement notices are appealable to the Secretary of State. If there is non-compliance, the LPA may prosecute, enter the land, carry out what is necessary, charge the costs to the offender, or possibly seek an injunction to restrain actual or threatened breaches of planning control.

5. Stop Notice
If an interested person appeals against the issue of an enforcement notice, its effect is suspended. But the objectionable works or uses may continue. It may be some months before an appeal is heard. A stop notice may be served and can be of immediate effect, although normally time is given for the compliance. While the appeal is determined or until the enforcement notice is complied with, the stop notice remains in force. It is a criminal offence not to comply.

weak. The enforcement system was researched again by Arup Economics and Planning (1995) in *Evaluation of planning enforcement provisions*. It was found that in England between 1992 and 1994, the average number of enforcement notices per LPA was 35 (64%), planning contravention notices 26 (over 80%), breach of condition notices 5.4 (85%), stop notices 1.68 (about 67%) and injunctions 0.38 (over 90%), but with wide variations between LPAs (ibid.: 8, 39, 40, appendix A1, tables 4.1, 5.1). The statistics in brackets refer to the proportion successfully pursued in the eyes of the LPAs. Prosecution in court represented a very small proportion of enforcement cases (7% of all enforcement and breach of condition notices served and less than 1% of all planning contravention notices; ibid.: 32). Fines were in the order of £600 per case where there was a conviction (ibid.: 45). However, the perception was that fines were too low and the courts did not take planning matters seriously enough (ibid.: 45–6). Arup's overall conclusion was that the new provisions, introduced as a result of the Carnwath Report, were working well and that significant legislative change was not necessary (ibid.: 49). But they felt that a few persistent offenders continued to play the system to their advantage and that the relationship between the LPAs and the courts was a matter for continuing concern (ibid.: 48–9). As enforcement practice varied considerably between authorities, they recommended that, inter alia, a good practice guide be prepared.

Conclusion

This chapter has dealt with the all-important legal background to the exercise of development control powers. Of all the literature on development control, that on the legal aspects is arguably the most complex and extensive, involving many cases before the courts and on appeal. They have been omitted here (see Alder 1989). The next chapter deals with the simplification and deregulation of the law and regulations in day-to-day practice, in order to facilitate development on the ground. However, the reader may wish to press on to Chapter 5. It deals with the nub of the whole book: the decision whether to grant or refuse permission in response to an application to develop.

CHAPTER 4
Simplifying development control

Introduction

It was argued in Chapter 1 that, as the natural and built environment is complex, it is necessary to have a complex control mechanism if desired states are to be achieved. On the other hand, it can be argued that the operation of the invisible hand of the free market in land and buildings will do the job, and perhaps urban systems are homeostatic anyway. However, it might be a good idea if the invisible hand would show itself from time to time so we know what it's up to.

The potential complexity of the development control system will be evident to the reader. Major efforts have been made to simplify it through the General Development Order/General Permitted Development Order, Use Classes Order, Enterprise Zones and Simplified Planning Zones, which are the subject matter of this chapter. Whereas the legal aspects of the GDO/GPDO and UCO are dealt with in Chapter 3, this chapter will deal with the substantive issues.

Roger Tym & Partners (1995: 1) drew attention to the shifting nature of simplification over time. Roger Tym defined so-called boundaries of control:

- an outer boundary which defines the extreme limits of development control; outside it lie other environmental controls such as public health and building regulations
- an inner boundary within which no exemptions are granted and planning permission is always required
- between the inner and outer boundaries is an area within the definition of development, but development does not need express consent from the LPA.

This is described in Table 4.1 as the permitted development category.

Readers should be aware that it is for the LPA to decide whether planning permission is necessary in any particular case (Town & Country Planning Act 1990: §192). In this way it helps to fix the inner boundary. For example, it is not clear whether it is necessary to obtain planning permission for keeping and breeding dogs on half an acre of waste land with some outbuildings. The keeping and breeding of livestock is an agricultural use for which planning permission is not normally necessary. The LPA has to make a decision on whether planning permission is necessary or not in this particular case (Morgan & Nott 1995: 80).

In some cases special legislation takes away the need for planning permission where it is normally required; most buildings in Enterprise Zones are an example of this (see below). In other cases planning permission is necessary, whereas normally it is not; an example of this is roof renewal in national parks. Minor changes in legislation move the inner boundary around in response to political, economic, social and technical pressures. For example, it was necessary to obtain planning permission to change between certain noxious and dangerous industrial uses. The Use Classes B3 to B7 have now been absorbed into B2 General Industry: such industries are now subject to control by non-planning legislation.

This chapter will now deal in much greater detail with issues that arise from this characterization.

Table 4.1 Categories and boundaries of development control (Roger Tym & Partners 1995: fig. 1 modified).

Categories and boundaries	Comment
The core category	
The core of development control where full controls are in operation.	Within this core, full controls have been considerably relaxed in Enterprise Zones and Simplified Planning Zones (Ch. 4).
The inner boundary	
Inner boundary between the core (above) and the permitted development category (below).	This is the effective boundary of planning control. Whether a particular proposal needs planning permission or not is for the LPA to decide, Town and Country Planning Act 1990 §192 (CLOPUD see glossary).
The permitted development category	
Permitted development category where relaxed controls operate, especially through the General Permitted Development Order (GPDO) and the Use Classes Order (UCO). Planning permission is not normally required in this category.	Planning permission may be required however on so-called Article 1 land (e.g. in national parks and areas of outstanding natural beauty) and where Article 4 Directions withdraw permitted development rights. These are sensitive areas where minor developments, not normally subject to planning control, can have severe impacts.
The outer boundary	
Outer boundary of planning controls between relaxed control (above) and no planning controls at all, because, whatever is involved, it does not constitute development in planning terms. Other environmental controls may operate.	The outer boundary of development control is defined by the legal definition of development.

The General Permitted Development Order (GPDO)

Introduction

The General Permitted Development Order (GPDO) (DoE 1995k) was a consolidation of the General Development Order (GDO) 1988 in the light of intervening
amendments. The overall thrust of the orders was the same: some details were
changed.

Development orders appear to go back to 1919, but in their modern form to
the Town and Country Planning Act 1947. This Act granted powers to ministers
to make orders to relax or tighten development control to encourage or discourage
certain forms of development. The first GDO 1948 was soon amended by the
deregulatory GDO 1950, as some minor operations that required planning permission occupied time and manpower out of all proportion to their importance to
planning. Many GDOs followed, which reflected experience in the operation of
development control. Moves to deregulation more recently have run up against
stiff opposition from the rural and urban conservationist lobby. An interesting
legal difference between the GPDO and the UCO is that the former grants planning
permission for specified development but the latter says planning permission is
not necessary for specified changes of use. This was important under the Town
& Country Planning Act 1947, when development charges were levied on development but changes of use were exempt (see Ch. 8; Grant 1995: 36).

The GPDO is complex and seems to have grown incrementally. Table 4.2 reor-
ders the GPDO in two complementary ways to improve general understanding. It
draws out particularly that some specified land uses have a freer rein and certain
apparently minor developments, such as painting, are granted planning permission. Of course, these developments are dominant in our experience of the environment. Others – utilities, water-related development and technical equipment
– enable vital services to be maintained. Arguably, other groups such as mining
need freedom to boost the economic wellbeing of the community. Ephemeral uses
will not leave permanent problems. But Morgan & Nott (1995: 111) concluded
there was no single explanation for the existence of the 33 parts of the GPDO.
Perhaps because of its wide-ranging complexity, there have been few studies of
the substantive effects of permitted development rights (PDR). The Wootton
Jeffreys & Bernard Thorpe study (1991) of the relationship between one-way
changes of use, facilitated by Part 3 of the GDO, relating to industrial and commercial property, is reported on later in this chapter under comments on the Use
Classes Order. Perhaps the most detailed study of the substantive aspects of PDR
was that related to agriculture and forestry (Land Use Consultants & Countryside
Planning and Management 1995) reported below.

DoE Circular 9/95, *General Development Order consolidation* 1995 (DoE
1995d) is the principal guidance in the mid-1990s. It gives an insight into how
the GDO evolved by incremental change over the years. Closed circuit television
cameras (CCTV) for security purposes, for example, are a relatively new innova-

tion; uncontrolled installations could create a good deal of unsightly clutter. Part 33 extended PDR to include alteration and replacement on shops, houses and other buildings within certain specified limits on size and numbers. Up to 16 cameras were allowed on any one building, but not more than four on any one side, provided they are 10 m apart. Each camera must be sited to minimize the effect on the exterior of the building and be removed once no longer required. However, these PDRs do not apply to listed buildings or scheduled monuments.

Table 4.2 The General Permitted Development Order reordered (Fig. 3.1 above).

Major land uses	1	Residential development within the curtilage of a dwelling house
	6 & 7	Agriculture and forestry buildings and operations
	8	Industrial and warehouse development
	3	Changes of use
Wide-ranging	2	Minor operations
	31	Demolition of buildings
Ephemeral uses	4	Temporary buildings and uses
	5	Caravan sites
	27	Use of land by members of recreational organizations
	28	Development at amusement parks
Utilities, etc.	9	Repairs to private ways
	10	Repairs to services
	13	Development by highway authorities
	17	Development by statutory undertakers
Water related	14	Development by drainage bodies
	15	Development by National Rivers Authority
	16	Development by sewerage undertakers
Technical equipment	18	Aviation development
	24	Development by telecommunication code system operators
	25	Other telecommunications development
	29	Driver information systems
	30	Toll road facilities
	33	Closed circuit television cameras
Special bodies	11	Development under local private acts or orders
	12	Development by local authorities
	26	Development by the Historic Buildings and Monuments Commission for England
	32	Schools, colleges, universities and hospitals
Mining operations	19	Development ancillary to mining operations
	20	Coal mining development
	21	Waste tipping at a mine
	22	Mineral exploration
	23	Removal of material from mineral working deposits

Note also Grant's classification:
(i) Rights conferred on development marginal and incidental to existing uses such as development within the curtilage of existing dwellings.
(ii) Rights conferred on certain types of developer, for example local authorities and airport operators.
(iii) Expansion of rights conferred elsewhere (e.g. Part 3 changes of use).
(Grant 1995: 36).

Commentary on parts of the General Permitted Development Order (GPDO)

The legal aspects of GPDO were briefly described in Chapter 3. Although the GPDO seeks to simplify the development control system by listing over 30 classes of development exempt from planning control, it is paradoxically a very complex document. It itemizes myriad limitations and conditions. The purpose of this section is to comment on some aspects of just a few of the parts listed in Schedule 2 (see Fig. 3.1, Table 4.2), namely agricultural development, a range of urban developments, telecommunications and demolition. Many of the commentaries on PDRs deal with the legal intricacies on which it is not proposed to dwell here. Regrettably there are few commentaries on the substantive aspects.

Agricultural development
Development control in the countryside is dealt with in Chapter 7. Here we are concerned only with agriculture and forestry permitted development rights (PDRs). These are summarized in Figure 7.1, which is perhaps best read at this point. The GDO 1992 (later the GPDO 1995) introduced new controls over agricultural and forestry permitted development rights. The effects of these changes have been reported on by Land Use Consultants & Countryside Planning and Management (1995), whose findings are summarized below. It is an interesting question as to how far the general findings of research on agricultural and forestry PDRs could be translated to other categories of PDRs on which there may be no research, such as residential PDRs. Agricultural and forestry development proposals are somewhat unusual in that, before certain developments are undertaken under PDRs, the developer must apply to the LPA to see if the proposal does have PDRs and whether normally planning permission may in fact be necessary. This is known as a "determination". Details of this are given in Figure 7.1 and the reasons explained in Chapter 7 (see also p. 65).

The relative freedom from planning control enjoyed by agriculture and forestry has been a matter of long-running dispute. In 1991 the Council for the Protection of Rural England (CPRE) (whose prime purpose is the protection of the beauty and character of the English Countryside) published its response to a government consultation paper on the issue (CPRE 1991). The consultation paper suggested a notification procedure, already used in national parks at that time, whereby farmers who proposed to carry out development would need to notify the LPA. This would give the LPA the opportunity to comment on siting and design, but not on the principle of development. CPRE thought this proposal "to be seriously inadequate". Full planning control over farm buildings is necessary if farmers are to win enduring public support (ibid.: 4). From its survey of national parks notification procedure, CPRE was of the view that "prior notification is neither the most effective, in terms of the quality of the decisions, nor the most efficient in terms of time and money, way of controlling farm and forestry buildings" (ibid.: 12). It was concerned about "cow sheds with dormer windows and double glazing and barns for car repair businesses" (ibid.: 14). A survey of about 500 notifications

63

in national parks showed that "only 45 per cent were allowed without modification. 32 per cent were modified or had conditions imposed, 16 per cent actually needed a full planning application, 1 per cent were refused and 6 per cent were still under negotiation or withdrawn" (ibid.: 17). The 1992 changes to PDRs have meant the notification procedure has been extended, the principle of proposed agricultural developments cannot be challenged, and the CPRE failed to persuade the government.

In 1992 the GDO was amended to introduce new controls over agricultural PDRs. These controls took two forms: applied to agricultural holdings over 5ha and forestry land uses and applied to agricultural holdings less than 5ha. In the first category, the developer had to apply in the first instance to the LPA for a "determination" prior to undertaking development to check whether LPA approval was necessary. In the smaller farm category, PDRs were withdrawn for new buildings and major extensions, but minor PDRs were also added (Land Use Consultants & Countryside Planning and Management 1995: 3). Research was carried out to monitor these changes and to assess the effectiveness of the changes in protecting the environment while not imposing excessive burdens on business (ibid.: 4). With regard to smaller holdings, there was concern about economic viability, abuse of PDRs and the problem of farm fragmentation. Further concerns related to carparks, mobile units and temporary structures on farms as they were visually intrusive. The report also reported on the problems of confining agricultural dwellings to agricultural occupancy and the re-use of rural buildings. They are not reported on here as these did not have PDRs. The research was carried out 1992–4 by sampling a range of LPAs, case histories and consultations with various bodies (e.g. CPRE; ibid.: ch. 2). Recent changes in agriculture, especially the decline of the labour force, food surpluses, the growth of commuting and rurally located business, resulted in the planning control priorities in the countryside being shifted from food production to economic diversification. In forestry the aim of a strategic timber reserve has been abandoned so that social and environmental aims have come to the fore (ibid.: 17). These themes are developed in Chapter 7.

Within these general rural changes there have been particular agricultural changes that have engendered pressure for building development, such as replacement buildings for those built in the 1950s and 1960s, new or replacement buildings for new livestock methods, amalgamation of farms leading to increased activities at fewer farmsteads and the creation of more bare landholdings with the need for new farmsteads (ibid.: 25–6). Larger buildings over 465m^2 were subject to normal development control, but a good deal of building will have resulted under PDRs, subject to the "determination" procedure. To put this procedure in its quantitative context, a typical London Green Belt LPA in 1993 would have handled about 1700–1800 planning applications per year, compared with 15–20 agricultural PDRs determinations (ibid.: 63). Of these it was reported that two-thirds were on larger holdings (over 40ha) often owner-occupied, predominantly related to mixed and livestock farms with few for dairy or arable farms.

A significant number were in national parks (ibid.: ch. 4). Typically, the size of buildings was in the 200–300 m^2 range, with few over this limit. Most were on full-time farm units. Of special interest from a development control point of view was that about a half of all PDRs buildings were within farmyards and a further third were on the edge; the relatively small balance were in green fields or on bare land plots (ibid.: table 4.1). This is important in that grouping of buildings is thought to be more visually acceptable than a scattered arrangement in open countryside. It is possible that the research did not pick up determinations that resulted in ultimate refusal of planning permission in the normal way. It was found that, in just over half of cases examined, agricultural developments fitted well in the landscape, because they were adjacent to existing buildings and in muted colours. However, a significant number of cases had adverse effects because of scale and building isolation (ibid.: 59 ff). Nearly 80 per cent of developments were undertaken for sound agricultural reasons; for example, for expansion, replacement, upgrading and the pressure of legislation (e.g. related to waste and slurry). Only a few related to new enterprises and non-agricultural uses (ibid.: Table 4.2). Few determinations related to forestry. However, in this context, contradictory fears were expressed that privatized woodlands may have recreation roads built under PDRs and that, with privatization, public access to woodlands may be curtailed (ibid.: 30).

To qualify as permitted development for agricultural units over 5 ha, the development must have passed four tests: be on agricultural land, be necessary for the purposes of agriculture, not be within 25 m of a metalled road, and not be on parcels of land more than 1 ha forming part of a larger agricultural holding. The determination process (Fig. 7.1) is primarily concerned with the effects of development on the landscape in terms of visual amenity and the desirability of conserving special sites such as listed buildings. Apart from this, permitted development remains permitted development. In the determination, the principle of the development is not an issue (ibid.: 34). It was found that nearly 70 per cent of determinations resulted in approval of proposals unaltered. Very few were refused, had conditions attached or needed full planning permission: in some cases more details were requested and modifications asked for by the LPA (ibid.: fig. 6.3). Most LPAs felt that the determination process worked well for most straightforward applications (ibid.: 46) but there was limited time left for consultations with parish councils. In practice there was considerable confusion about what in fact was in the agricultural permitted development rights category and how the determination process should work in detail. Precise knowledge of the GDO and court rulings was necessary (ibid.: 46). For example, LPAs were not clear whether hardstanding needed planning permission or not. Farmers for their part had limited knowledge of agricultural PDRs, but found the majority of LPAs helpful in handling their queries (ibid.: 52–3). Apart from some procedural matters, an unusual substantive issue related to the lauded re-use of second-hand buildings. Where they were the subject of a determination, it was difficult for the LPA to suggest improvements, by way of conditions (ibid.: 61, 76).

Land Use Consultants found (ibid.: 83) relatively few agricultural PDRs on holdings of less than 5 ha. Such farms are diversifying out of farming or, where farm fragmentation is taking place, resultant holdings are above 5 ha. Much development on small farms lost PDRs in 1992 and is now subject to planning permission (ibid.: ch. 9).

The research also reported on three eyesores: carparks, mobile units and temporary structures on farms. Let us take carparks as an example (ibid.: 98 ff). A grass carpark ancillary to agriculture does not require planning permission, but a carpark ancillary to another use does. The problem is defining when the carpark is no longer ancillary to agriculture. Alternatively, the use of a grass field for up to 14 (or 28 days) unrelated to agriculture, for example for a market, is permitted development. Further, if hardstanding is put down for larger agricultural holdings, no planning permission is required; hardstanding does not come within the determination process. It was found that carparks ancillary to agriculture did not really cause environmental problems. Problems arose where carparking related to non-farm diversification activities such as horticultural units diversifying into shops and then into wholly non-agricultural activities, where hardstanding was used for non-farm activity within a farmstead, and where car boot sales were held under the 14 day rule (with attendant noise and traffic in urban fringe areas or designated landscapes; sometimes they are rotated around a district and are accompanied by temporary structures). The report recommended bringing hardstanding over $465\,\text{m}^2$ (or a limit to be agreed) under the determination process (ibid.: vi).

The report concluded by considering the broad context (ibid.: ch. 21). It noticed particularly that the planning regime and economic pressures resulted in more buildings in the countryside. It was felt that consideration should be given to replacement of buildings on their original sites, the removal of unsightly buildings at the end of their useful lives by the use of conditions, the relocation of surplus buildings where possible, and the re-use of second-hand buildings. Increasing farm diversification will lead in the future to further problems in defining where agricultural PDRs end, for example with the interface with commercial leisure. Because of farm fragmentation, the proliferation of buildings and landscape degradation, the report suggested raising the PDRs limit to at least 10 ha to bring smallholdings of dubious agricultural viability, but in reality "new houses in the country", under full planning control (ibid.: 235).

Urban development

The problem of PDRs in built-up areas is particularly highlighted in conservation areas, as these are singularly sensitive to minor development. They contain both residential and commercial development. Conservation areas contain only about 4 per cent of the nation's buildings and it might be imagined that the partial withdrawal of PDRs within them would safeguard them. But this is clearly not the case (English Historic Towns Forum 1992). In the relative absence of research on the impact of many PDRs, conservation areas are used as a proxy for other areas because of the availability of published information.

Conservation area status does bring environmental benefits in that certain forms of development, which are PDRs elsewhere, are brought under control, such as demolition, felling and lopping of trees, dormer windows, some forms of cladding, some satellite aerials, some hoardings, illuminated advertisements, the size of some extensions, and minor checks on works by utility companies. But English Historic Towns Forum (EHTF) reported in 1992 that "there are in fact more planning controls over the appearance of an inner-city tower block than a house in a conservation area" (ibid.: 6). Listed buildings, often forming the core of conservation areas, do need planning permission for nearly all external alteration. As a result, street façades may have variable levels of planning control. English Historic Towns Forum argued that there was evidence of a slow but steady decline in the appearance of conservation areas, which in part resulted from PDRs not being strict enough. The author argues by extension that this may well be happening in less sensitive environments where the need to improve visual amenity is arguably more important.

EHTF carried out a survey of its 45 member LPAs in 1991 (e.g. towns such as Oxford, Cambridge, York, etc.). It found that the following adverse alterations to non-listed buildings in conservation areas were of concern in rank order: replacement windows, replacement doors, roof materials, removal of garden walls and railings, satellite aerials, destruction of architectural details, and surfacing of front gardens. Since EHTF reported (1992), central government has issued further guidance that enables doors, roofs, windows and frontages to be brought under stricter control (DoE 1994g: 18–19; DoE 1992j) by LPA direction. Painting of buildings, advertisements and porches were excluded from the survey. Significant numbers of LPAs could not keep pace with unauthorized development in conservation areas and many wanted PDRs tightened up (ibid.: 24). It was felt that British people have a strong attachment to "place" and there is a growing interest in the heritage. Tourism and the local economy may depend on it (ibid.: 5).

EHTF argued that what was wanted was restoration and not change. Uncontrolled and unwelcome change sprang from various sources. Owners felt that to modernize a property would increase its value. Often, there was well intentioned but misguided do-it-yourself repairs and alterations to personalize the façades of buildings. Regrettably, some builders and window salesmen acted in ignorance. Not infrequently there is decline, disrepair and decay. But what are the problems in more specific terms? One of the most damaging PDR alterations was the replacement of traditional windows and doors with aluminium or plastic frames. Georgian wooden sash windows have a fine pattern of small panes. To replace these with plastic tilt and turn windows with large panes spoils the fenestration, especially when adjacent buildings and window apertures retain the old style. An illustrated example was given of even glass bricks being used to replace traditional windows (ibid.: 11). EHTF argued that traditional windows could be installed with comparable cost and efficiency (ibid.: 9).

The replacement of Victorian wooden doors with aluminium and glass doors with porch extensions obscures and detracts from façades. Roof materials such as clay tiles may be replaced by concrete tiles creating a patchwork effect in an otherwise more uniform roofscape. Front garden walls and railings less than 1 m high could be removed without consent, greenery is lost and they may be replaced by inappropriate chains and posts to facilitate parking. The appearance of entire brick or stone façades can be changed by painting and rendering. Rendering can cover interesting detail, and black Tudor beams can be painted on. Such changes are particularly infelicitous where semi-detached or terrace properties are involved. In the public domain, natural flagstones can be ripped out and holes badly repaired. Street furniture can be changed, destroying a street's historic character (ibid.: 10).[1]

EHTF put forward these solutions to the problem of deregulation: the education of owners and builders, particularly by issuing detailed guidelines; the tightening of PDRs generally, by including window replacements and other changes known to be particularly troublesome; and the wider use of Article 4 Directions (ibid.: 15–16). As will be apparent, the simplification of development control by the GDO/GPDO leads to complicated limitations and conditions. EHTF argued that fuller control would mean simpler control. In Hove the use of Article 4 Directions encouraged "like for like" restorations that did not need planning permission: this usually pleased the applicants (Sommerville in EHTF 1991: 25–6). It would not lead to increased bureaucracy, because current legislation was complex and time-consuming. Indeed, those LPAs operating Article 4 Directions in conservation areas did not find they were swamped by work (ibid.: 17 and items 11 and 12 on p. 24). This is confirmed by the Roger Tym & Partners findings on Article 4 Directions (see p. 73).

Readers should consider from their own experience whether the degradation brought about by permitted development (or in EHTF words "permitted destruction" (ibid.: 13)) applies outside conservation areas where PDRs are even wider.

Telecommunications
Readers will be aware of the visual havoc that roof-mounted television aerials, pole-mounted telephone and electricity cables, electricity pylons and lines can cause in town and country. As wires, masts and other similar equipment are forms alien to traditional buildings and landscape they are difficult to blend into the existing environment. Burying some of them or fastening them closely to buildings lessens their impact. On the other hand, we all benefit enormously from technical advances in the electrical and electronic industries. They create jobs, make life much easier and reduce the need to travel. Much of the equipment has the privilege

---

1. See also Chater (EHTF 1991: 14 ff) on the erosion of townscape through permitted and minor development. He stressed particularly that part of the definition of development which includes that which "materially affects the external appearance of the building". Does the replacement of Welsh roofing slates by black mineral fibre slates, which have a machine-made appearance, constitute development? The legal tangles of enforcement pose yet other issues (ibid.: 11).

of permitted development rights, but major installations need planning permission. To the author's knowledge, there is no systematic research on this topic in the context of development control. The principal government guidance in the 1990s is contained in PPG8, *Telecommunications* (DoE 1992u) and Circular 9/95, *General Development Order consolidation* (DoE 1995d: appendix E) and a code of best practice (DoE & WO 1996b). It does not deal with electricity transmission.

Telecommunications in the context of development control have come much more to the fore in the 1990s as the communications industry has exploited new techniques and as demand is very buoyant resulting in the proliferation of antennas of various types. Smaller installations and their proliferation are likely to increase the amount of equipment that comes within the PDRs range (Holt, continuing: 29.0). There are thousands of sites, but their number and location appear to be commercially confidential (Thompsett 1995: 14). It is a matter of concern that the telecommunications industry is privileged in being able to carry out development, especially in rural areas and sensitive urban locations, without the requirement for planning permission, whereas others would need it (Anonymous 1996d: 28). The issues are often technical in nature. To help in understanding, it is useful to realize that there are three major areas of planning concern: transmitting facilities, receiving equipment, and development control over other development that might interfere with telecommunications. Sensitive issues arise in designated areas such as national parks and conservation areas and in residential in contrast to commercial areas. Cabling above or below ground, and large and small antennas, all pose problems.

The government is committed to facilitate growth in new and existing systems and to stimulate competition while also being committed to environmental objectives. Competition may also result in the proliferation of installations (Holt, continuing: 28.12). The government asks LPAs to respond positively to applications to develop (DoE 1992u: paras 3, 5). Development control issues spring from the different techniques of transmission. There are three types:

- fixed links, which operate through cable and line-of-sight antennas, which may be on towers up to 60 m
- in height; the radio links involved must be free of obstruction and they require repeater stations
- cellular systems for mobile phone users, with a network of antennas that usually must be placed high up with associated equipment housing
- personal communications networks, which are rather like cellular installations, but with modest equipment housing.

Quite separately, satellite television broadcasting demands outdoor satellite dish receivers, usually mounted in residential areas. Dishes may be up to 90 cm in diameter and their position will be dependent on the position of the transmitting satellite. The construction of new buildings may interfere with transmission and reception. This is a material consideration in development control (ibid.: paras 8–12), as is the insistence on underground cable ducting in new developments at the outset (ibid.: paras 41–3).

69

PPG8 urges LPAs to adopt planning policies such as siting and landscaping requirements designed to minimize the impact of equipment on amenity (ibid.: paras 13–16). In the context of development control the government draws attention to the *de minimis* rule applied to conventional television aerials; that is, they do not constitute development, because they do not, it is argued, materially affect the appearance of buildings.

Planning control of telecommunications equipment is rather like that for farm development: much development has PDRs, but there is a determination procedure whereby the LPA can alter the siting and appearance of equipment to protect amenity but not challenge the principle of the development itself (DOE 1995d: appendix E). The LPA may also intervene with a breach of condition notice, say, if a condition of the PDR is broken, for example by siting apparatus in such a way that it does not minimize its impact on the appearance of a building (DOE 1992u: paras 20–1). PDRs are complex (ibid.: annex 1) but typically for radio masts they must not exceed a height of 15 m above ground level, that is typically higher than many houses and factories. There are further height limits when masts, and so on, are fixed to buildings. Equipment housing must not exceed $90\,m^3$. The determination procedure comes into play when a radio mast or a housing in excess of $2\,m^3$ is proposed. As for satellite dishes on houses, there are size limits, and they must be so sited as to minimize the effect on the external appearance, for example, by fixing them below the roofline. If the LPA thinks a householder has sited a dish badly and could have reasonably positioned it less conspicuously, the householder may be asked to resite it at his own expense (DOE & WO 1992: 9).

Of course, planning permission may be required, especially for large installations. A major problem of siting and design is that installations may be in prominent positions and may not be shielded by landscaping and buildings if they are to work effectively. Mast sharing and minimizing the number of masts will help the applicant's case: higher masts may mean fewer masts. The need to develop national networks and spare capacity are complicating factors. It is apparent from appeal cases that only special landscape designations such as AONB will persuade inspectors to turn down development proposals (Holt, continuing: 28.132 ff).

When all is said and done, we all want to be modern and with it. Perhaps in due course telecommunications equipment will be no more alien than chimneys on houses were in the past.

Demolition and a digression into dereliction
Just as new buildings, alterations and additions may have environmental effects, so also may demolitions.

It is no exaggeration to say, that, apart from hideous architectural fashion in combination with "comprehensive" redevelopment schemes and the inexorable spread of motor vehicles, no single factor has had a more damaging effect on the urban scene since the 1940s than the long agony of frequently wanton destruction followed by years of neglected wasteland. (Fyson 1991: 3)

A contrary contemporary view was that "Many [LPAs] argued for a change in legislation but did not produce systematic evidence of a general and widespread problem" (Milne 1991: 21, quoting Baroness Blatch).

For many years, demolition was held not to be development except for special and specific cases, such as listed buildings, but was the cause of considerable controversy (Holt, continuing: 4.3114). To end confusion, demolition, including partial demolition, is now a building operation and thus normally needs planning permission (Planning and Compensation Act 1991 §13; Morgan & Nott 1995: 78). The principal guidance is DoE (1995e). However, under a direction (the *Town and Country Planning (Demolition – Description of Buildings) Direction 1995*) certain specified designated buildings do not need planning permission for demolition because they are protected by other legislation: listed buildings, buildings in conservation areas and scheduled monuments. Although many other buildings (e.g. factories) are removed from demolition control, dwellings or buildings attached to dwellings are not so removed and are still subject to control. Moreover, small buildings of less than $50\,m^3$, gates, walls and fences are also removed from control, because arguably they are of little consequence. The demolition of domestic gates, walls and fences with concomitant removal of greenery (often to facilitate parking in front gardens) is particularly a matter of concern. These features are in the public eye, next to the highway and often lend architectural unity to the street scene.

Schedule 2, Part 31, of the GPDO deals with the demolition of buildings. The GPDO gives general planning permission for specified classes (called Parts in the Order) of development and the demolition of buildings is one such part. So, generally, demolition has PDRs. But, before demolition can take place, the LPA has to be notified. It may then determine whether approval is required. The purpose of this requirement is to minimize the impact of the demolition on amenity where such impact may be significant (DoE 1995e: 4). If prior approval is required, then the normal eight-week period is allowed for approval or refusal (ibid.: 5). Prior approval may involve restoration of a site. This determination procedure does not apply if demolition is a matter of urgency or planning permission has already been granted for the redevelopment of the land.

Morgan & Nott (1995: 78) described the problem of including demolition as part of the general definition of development and then excluding most acts of demolition as suspect. The introduction of planning controls over demolition has proved to be one of the most technically fraught amendments to the planning system since 1948 (Grant Jul 1995 Monthly Bulletin: 3).

Effectively, factories, offices and shops, and also churches and theatres, have PDRs for demolition and do not come under demolition control. Yet they could be just as important in the street scene, or as buildings in themselves, as dwellings. Total regulation may presumably swamp LPAs. The rules favour freedom

71

for business users but partly protect the immediate environment of voters. Manns (1995: 10) drew attention to the considerable confusion surrounding the subject, including the ambiguity caused by conservation area boundaries running along walls and fences. Demolition is more strictly controlled in conservation areas.

The introduction of controls over demolition partly circumvents some substantive problems. Where buildings are removed, unsightly gap sites may be left which detract from the harmony of the street scene. Sites may be covered in rubble and attract litter. Temporary uses such as carparking may become established, which are unsightly and cause traffic and enforcement problems. When demolition of spacious Victorian houses has taken place in the past without permission, this may well have detracted from the general amenity of the area in which they were situated. It also may involve premature loss of usable floorspace. The developer could then more readily seek planning permission from the LPA for profitable higher-density dwellings, possibly of a substandard nature (Anonymous 1991: 4). To refuse planning permission may mean leaving the land derelict: this was not an acceptable solution in areas of buoyant housing demand. Sometimes in the past, when existing buildings themselves were a bar to obtaining planning permission, developers have tactically demolished buildings to force the LPA's hand. In some cases developers demolished property to bring undue pressure on neighbours to sell perfectly sound housing. Dobry (1974: 5) was concerned with the loss of amenity and the general deterioration of neighbourhoods. He felt it was wrong to cause a wasteland over which the LPA had no effective control. Houses may sometimes be demolished to open up land behind existing frontages for further development (DoE 1990e). Gap sites, particularly if left a long time, blight the amenity of surrounding property and have a depressing effect on confidence (Cowan 1983: 71 ff).

Demolition and the appearance of derelict and vacant sites is a necessary part of the development process. As far as the author is aware at the time of writing, there were no recent research studies *per se* on the impact of demolition as PDRs. However, Arup's study of derelict land prevention and the planning system threw some oblique light on this problem (Arup Economics and Planning 1995b). The report was not concerned with PDRs, or with mineral working, where conditions are widely used to ensure restoration. Derelict land includes buildings that needed treatment before re-use (ibid.: 5). The focus of government concern is to bring such land back into productive use and to avoid the need to use greenfield sites. The reasons for dereliction and vacancy were identified as (ibid.: 6, 13): redevelopment costs exceeding development value, land held to await future rises in value, land held for future expansion, financial failure of the site owner leading to abandonment, tax burdens, piecemeal acquisition prior to comprehensive development, and temporary buildings and structures. Much dereliction is attributable to industrial change, with further change anticipated (ibid.: 7). A significant amount of such land is contaminated. Future dereliction problems can be anticipated from the chemicals industry and telecommunications, for example where the nature of the development is such that it cannot readily be put to alternative uses. Sites in urban areas may be readily recycled, but those such as military establishments in rural areas are more problematic. Arup drew attention to the fact that currently it is not an explicit purpose of the planning system to prevent dereliction. Future use is not normally a material consideration when planning permission is given (ibid.: 8). Currently, the planning system is reactive rather than proactive; demolition control is still in its early days in this context.

Existing limited powers can be used, for example to preserve listed buildings, to clear sites when buildings are dangerous and for the LPA to require an owner-occupier to remedy a situation where amenity is threatened (ibid.: vii). Among other measures Arup Economics and Planning suggested (ibid.: 15–19) were rehabilitation conditions modelled on those already attached to mineral workings (on the "polluter pays principle") not normally used on permanent development, the difficulty of forecasting after-use notwithstanding. This was suggested especially where developments were known to be of limited life-span and specialized, such as structures unlikely to be re-usable, and where developments were in sensitive areas where permission would not normally be granted except for that particular use (ibid.: 17). The review of planning conditions in the light of changing circumstances is another possibility, of which examples were given.

It was also argued that conditions requiring proper maintenance of buildings should be explored (ibid.: 18). Continuing to report on planning powers rather narrowly defined, Arup drew attention to the Town and Country Planning Act 1990 (§215 provisions), which allowed LPAs to enter land, carry out remedial action to improve amenity and recover costs from the owner (ibid.: 22). Current provisions were regarded as protracted, cumbersome and ultimately "toothless", partly because it was difficult to demonstrate that amenity was adversely affected and partly because it was difficult to recover costs from, possibly unknown, owners. However, Sennitt reported where it was used to good effect to clear a fire-devastated site (1993: 17). Much of course depends on clearance costs and the market value of the land involved. In this context, performance bonds, compulsory purchase orders and tax relief on rehabilitation expenditure and on holding derelict land were financial measures also explored (Arup Economics and Planning 1995b).

If it is possible to summarize this complex set of issues and solutions, one can say that we are now in a climate of the need for sustainability and that the planning system needs to become proactive rather than reactive. Rehabilitation planning conditions were thought to have the most effective and practical potential (ibid.: x).

Article 4 Directions of the General Permitted Development Order

This section summarizes the Roger Tym & Partners report on the day-to-day working of Article 4 Directions (Roger Tym & Partners 1995; see also Larkham & Chapman 1996). Although all development may need planning permission, the GPDO (previously the GDO) grants an automatic planning permission – permitted development – for a wide variety of relatively uncontentious developments. However, in sensitive circumstances such as conservation areas and the open countryside even trivial development may need to be controlled if the environment is not to be spoilt. This claw-back of control is facilitated by Article 4 of the GDO/GPDO. A Direction may be issued under this article which brings specified development for specified geographical areas back under control until cancelled. Typically, Directions relate to architectural details of buildings.

The Roger Tym & Partners research was conducted using questionnaires in a sample of LPAs, face-to-face interviews with relevant parties, and case studies in England and Wales. It was estimated that about 2000 Directions were in force in England and Wales; a typical LPA will have between one and five Directions in force. The impetus for Article 4 Directions, it was found, came frequently from the public, parish councils or conservation groups who perceived a threat to the environment. LPAs then reacted. The most common type of geographical areas subject to directions were residential conservation areas, agricultural areas and other residential areas. The most common purposes were protection against threat to conservation areas, protection of the countryside and the prevention of temporary uses. With conservation areas the principal reason for restricting permitted development rights related to the alteration of dwellings to preserve area character. In agricultural areas, they were much more concerned with controlling particular activities such as Sunday trading and car racing. Other cases involved control of otherwise legitimate changes of use of retail buildings. Where the building character of an area was threatened, consultations with the public were often carried out; in contrast, where particular activities were involved, they were made quickly without consultation, so the activity did not get established. Surprisingly, once an Article 4 Direction was in place it did not result in a substantial increase in the number of planning applications. Most applications made in this context were granted. Where permitted development rights are withdrawn by an Article 4 Direction, compensation may be payable. Very few cases were found where compensation had been paid. It was suggested that the possibility of paying compensation made LPAs very cautious in the use of Directions. Most LPAs had no formal monitoring in place to gauge the effect of Directions. Very few Directions have ever been cancelled; LPAs saw them as being necessary in perpetuity.

Although there are four routes by which Article 4 Directions may be initiated and approved, in practice nearly all use one route. Normally the LPA (usually district or borough) prepares the Direction; it comes into effect immediately, but lapses if not approved by the Secretary of State within six months (Roger Tym & Partners 1995: fig. 3). The LPA is under no obligation to notify owners of its intention to make a Direction. The reason for this is that consultation may trigger pre-control implementation of the very development the LPA is seeking to control. Once a Direction is made, owners are notified. Directions cannot be made to control a development which has already been carried out. Compensation may be payable to owners for the withdrawal of permitted development rights, as it is for the **revocation** of normal planning permission already granted.

Guidance on Directions is given in Circular 22/88 (withdrawn) and in PPG15 and PPG8 relating to historic environments and telecommunications. To give the flavour of the reasoned justification necessary for Directions in conservation areas, LPAs should ensure that the Direction helps to protect features that are key elements, the LPA provides a clear assessment of the area's architectural character and historic interest, and establishes the importance of this interest, and the LPA must demonstrate local support (DOE 1994g: para. 4.23).

Although the Roger Tym & Partners study was about Article 4 Directions, it drew attention to the fact that permitted development rights can also be withdrawn by planning conditions on the grant of planning permission, but of course this can normally apply only to new developments. This is administratively simpler than Directions and does not attract possible claims for compensation. It is a commonly exercised power in spite of guidance in Circular 11/95 (and 1/85 withdrawn) on planning conditions, which suggested the freedom granted by permitted development rights should not be limited in this way. Readers should be aware that certain categories of permitted development rights are also withdrawn in national parks and areas of outstanding natural beauty – so-called Article 1(5) land and Article 1(6) land of the GDO/GPDO.

The Roger Tym & Partners overall findings were that current policy guidance was not clear enough and placed an unreasonable onus on the LPA when confirmation of Directions was sought. Directions were seen as generally effective in conservation areas but of limited effectiveness where control of activities was sought. The most significant deterrent to the use of Directions was the threat of compensation payable on the refusal of planning permission following an Article 4 Direction. Roger Tym & Partners recommended that policy guidance should be clarified, best practice should be promoted and inter alia that compensation provisions should be removed.

The Use Classes Order (UCO)

Changes of use generally

The legal background to, and the purposes of, the Use Classes Order were outlined in Chapter 3 (Figs 3.2, 3.3, Table 3.1). The purpose of the UCO is to simplify the need for planning permission related to changes of use. Figure 3.2 lists the use classes. Changes of use within classes do not require planning permission; changes between them do. The purpose of this section is to explore the matters of planning substance involved with changes of use.

Human use of land and buildings is extremely varied. Two of the purposes of planning and development control are to separate activities or uses geographically which are not thought to be compatible with each other by zoning, especially factories from housing; and, if changes in the use of existing buildings are involved, to prevent them, or, if they are allowed, to mitigate the effects. Figure 4.1 tabulates the main activities with which planners are concerned and separately the range of planning characteristics which may or may not accompany them, plus other matters arising. The figure is a rough and ready approach to the subject of change of use; the classification is somewhat arbitrary. Traditionally, planners have been concerned with activities in adapted spaces – "folk, work, play". As these three have become geographically separated to varying degrees, these land uses have generated traffic, hence the fourfold classification of activities to include transport. Whether consciously or not the classes in the UCO 1987 reflect "folk, work, play" but omit principally agriculture, forestry, mineral extraction and transport uses, very important as they are. The UCO 1972 omitted dwellings.

The utility of Figure 4.1 as a checklist is best illustrated by an example. An LPA has received a planning application for the conversion of a warehouse (Class B8) to a general industrial factory (Class B2). The warehouse is characterized by very few workers per hundred square metres of floorspace, has limited carparking and moderate commercial vehicle flows. The factory use is expected to have far more workers and moderate commercial vehicle flows and will have dusty processes which neighbouring factory occupiers will not like. Waste materials may need to be stored in the open. The checklist highlights what needs to be considered in changes of use applications. What should the LPA do? Refuse because of likely parking difficulties, or grant subject to conditions and agreements? Issues such as these underlie the following sections.

Changes of use constitute a significant proportion of planning applications

---

Figure 4.1 A checklist of the main land-use activities and planning characteristics

Land-use activities
- Work – Jobs: factories, offices, shops, warehouses, schools, hospitals, mineral extraction, agriculture and forestry . . . and advertisements
- Folk – Homes and living: dwellings, residential institutions, residential colleges, hostels and hotels
- Play – Leisure: places of worship, museums, cinemas, theatres, dance halls, swimming baths, playing fields and stadia
- Transport: walk, road, rail, water, air . . . routes, terminals and parking

Planning characteristics
- Amenity: noise, soot, dust, grit, dirt and litter, vibration, smell, fumes, privacy, vehicle movement
- Danger: fire, explosion, poison, vermin, other injury
- Visual appearance: glare, colour, architectural style, advertisements, landscaping, ugliness
- Other: employment, parking, traffic generation

Other matters arising
- Moral issues: gambling, alcohol, sex uses, political issues, unwelcome neighbours
- Intensification: increasing plot ratios, double-shift working, building subdivision

---

made or decided. In 1993–4 of 428 300 applications made in England 39 100 related to change of use (DoE 1995b: table 7.3). As far as I am aware, there has been no study of change-of-use phenomena in the round. Much of the literature is concerned with the problems of operating the UCO, the effects of the UCO on the property market and reports of cases on appeal and in the courts. An obvious question to ask is: "What uses are changing to what uses?". My study of changes in what are now the London Boroughs of Bexley and Bromley and Dartford District for the 1950s in terms of the UCO 1948 showed that applications were frequently from residential to shop and office use and to some extent to hotel-, "home-" and school-type uses (but not vice versa), shop-to-shop type uses and industry-to-industry uses. If the number of change-of-use applications is related to the total number of properties in the study area, it is quite small. Where applications were refused, they were frequently on grounds of residential amenity. None of this is surprising: residential premises greatly outnumber commercial properties, and house changes are likely to upset neighbours' amenity. Moreover, the physical nature of the buildings would inhibit other types of change (Thomas 1972: ch. 5).

A useful way of explaining change-of-use issues is to look on the major revisions in the UCO 1987 as a watershed. From the first Use Classes Order in 1948 until the 1987 revision, the UCO had undergone only minor revisions, which were consolidated in the 1972 version. Three events precipitated the change. First, a new government, elected in 1979, sought to remove what it saw as restrictions on business enterprise. Secondly, the commercial property market was changing as the distinction between factories and offices (classes II and III of the UCO 1972), became blurred with the advent of high-tech industry. Increased affluence brought a rapid growth of hot-food outlets and financial services outlets in traditional shopping streets. Thirdly, the Care in the Community programme precipitated the demand for hostel-type accommodation in residential areas.

The Property Advisory Group Report

The Property Advisory Group (PAG), set up within the Department of the Environment, was charged with reviewing the UCO 1972 in 1985. Forerunners were the White Paper, *Lifting the burden* (1985), and Circular 14/85 (withdrawn), which urged LPAs to "respond positively and promptly to proposals for development . . . unless that development would cause demonstrable harm to interests of acknowledged importance" and to help small firms by avoiding "unnecessarily onerous and complex controls" (Home 1989: 15). The PAG was charged with a wide-ranging review:

- to reduce the number of classes compatible with environmental protection
- to permit, without prior permission, a mixture of uses within one building
- to incorporate the escalator principle whereby noxious uses could change to less noxious uses without the need for permission.

As Home pointedly said, they had six months to report, had no local authority planner in their midst (being largely property professionals) and apparently did not consult widely with others. This was at a time when the DoE had a considerable funded research programme. Critics of their report claimed it favoured developers and owners and gave scant attention to users, tenants, neighbours and the public as a whole (Home 1989: 17).

The rationale of PAG's ultimate recommendations was based on changing industrial and commercial building use, both geographically and by sector, and with the emergence of business parks, new retail formats and the motorway network. The PAG considered the possibility of geographical variations in the definition of use classes, but took the view that local measures should build on, rather than detract from the UCO. If an LPA wanted greater freedom, it could set up Simplified Planning Zones.

Among contentious recommendations were a new "small business at home" class and a new shop class to embrace certain types of office and the sale of hot food. They also suggested open land-use classes for retail sales and industry. A small business-at-home class with up to five workers met vociferous opposition. It was feared that amenity would be spoiled, non-residents would come in and parking restrictions would be difficult to enforce. It would result in a proliferation of business in residential areas. The proposal, for what can be described as an omnibus shop class, raised the spectre of dead frontages. That is to say, if market forces were uncurbed, service uses that sought ground-floor locations with good pedestrian flows could readily enter and disrupt the continuity of retail frontages selling goods. Here the concern was not with environmental consequences but with relationships with other uses.

In the out-turn these two contentious proposals were dropped. A further contentious proposal, a business class, was ultimately incorporated into the UCO 1987. The UCO 1972 clearly separated Class III Light Industry from Class II Offices, as they were believed to have different planning characteristics (see Fig. 4.1), especially parking requirements and employment characteristics. The B1 Use Class combines these and includes research and development. Normally, proposed subsidiary legislation does not cause such a stir on the floor of the House of Commons. However, in this case, the MP covering the Saville Row tailoring area of the Westminster North constituency raised the matter in an adjournment debate. Not only were 3000 workers involved in a trade with £43 million a year turnover, but people visited Westminster, stayed in hotels, consulted distinguished lawyers and Harley Street doctors, and saw a variety of professionals, including their bespoke tailors. The fear was that the tailors' workshops would be converted into offices at much higher rents and the bespoke tailoring would disappear. The government argued that planning should not be concerned with property values. Besides, leases limiting property to manufacturing uses fell due in a phased way, so there was little need to worry. The tailors lost their battle, and offices and light industry were ultimately combined (ibid.: ch. 2).

The modernized and clarified UCO 1987 had 16 classes compared with 18 in the 1972 version. As the new UCO was published, modifications were made to the GDO, which incorporated the escalator principle that ministers had sought. This facilitated certain one-way changes (e.g. hot-food shop A3 to A1) without planning permission (see Table 3.1). Many of the difficulties of the PAG proposals were foreseen in the consultation period after the publication of their report. Some of these will now be reported on in the light of experience at first in the sequence in which they appear in the UCO itself. Research has shown (Wootton Jeffreys & Bernard Thorpe 1991: vi) that the implications have been much greater for the business sector than the High Street and residential sector. The scale of activity and change has been greater in the business sector; the other sectors have merely been clarified. Readers should be aware that trade cycle effects may significantly affect results: longer-term studies may modify findings.

Retail tenant mix in the High Street

There are two main planning issues related to the UCO and retail outlets: tenant mix and hot food, which will be dealt with separately.

The attractiveness of the High Street to the user is in part dependent on tenant mix. It also depends on size, bus routes, parking and general physical attractiveness. The tenant mix not only involves retail outlets but also leisure facilities, which users patronize on multipurpose journeys, including journeys to work in town centres. This mixture of uses contributes to character and vitality, which are important to maintain if traditional High Streets are to compete with retail warehouse parks and other new retail formats in new locations. Central government policy has stressed this for some time (DoE 1985f withdrawn, DoE 1996c). With growing household affluence, the demand for (a) financial services and food and drink consumption away from home and (b) durable goods (e.g. clothes and electrical goods) has been buoyant in the long term. This has led to a changing retail mix in the High Street and new shopping formats in non-traditional locations. This changing mix has given rise to planning problems.

Much of the concern about the changing retail mix in the High Street arose before the reissue of the UCO in 1987, which essentially tidied up the UCO 1972 into A1, A2, A3 and a group of sui generis uses. As such, LPAs cannot control retail mix in the traditional High Street in the same way as owners can in planned shopping malls. Indeed, their success is partly predicated on tenant mix. However, the LPA can address issues which they see as problems. Character and vitality can concern mix and appearance. There is, or better was, a traditional wisdom that financial services and other outlets selling services constituted "dead frontage", as did those with few callers, disliked by other retailers. Such outlets, it was argued, were unattractive to customers because of uninteresting window display and detracted from pedestrian flows. Research (URPI 1981) in the early 1980s showed that banks and building societies were highly attractive to pedestrian flows and were frequently visited. But this was not so of estate agents, or of jewellers with displays thought attractive. How often do you buy a house or a jewel?

The dead frontage argument may now be a dead duck. An associated argument is whether local plan policies should seek to earmark specific shopping streets for service uses to avoid dead frontages or whether to favour dispersion. Shoppers preferred dispersion (URPI 1981). DCPN 11 (withdrawn) suggested planning policies that divided shopping streets into primary, with traditional shops, and secondary, with a mix of service and traditional outlets (DoE 1985f: paras 10–14). Many change of use appeals revolve around these arguments and the balance of shop uses in particular centres.

Wootton Jeffreys & Bernard Thorpe (1991: 14) reported that since the 1987 revision of the UCO and the loosening of control the workload of LPAs had not slackened significantly although this is likely to be a reflection of activity in the market. Case studies showed that A2 Financial Services continued to cause concern to LPAs because some professional offices could be markedly less lively than banks and building societies. Indeed, the new UCO may have precipitated some LPAs to draw up policies, where they had had none, to incorporate in local plans. The type of policies involved are exemplified in High Wycombe, where there was a presumption of no new A2 uses next to an existing A2 use. They found too that, although there is an implicit assumption that the UCO should not be limited by the imposition of restrictive use conditions, in practice such conditions were imposed; for example, allowing a restaurant but restricting its conversion to fast food or takeaway without express planning permission. As for the operation of the escalator or ratchet effect, whereby no permission was needed for one-way changes from A3 to A2, the GDO did not seem to stimulate a change in that direction. However, Bell (1992a: 14–16, citing Simmie) reported that in the Thames Valley between 200 and 300 pubs (A3) had closed and were subject to change to office (A2) applications since 1987. It is not clear why these were subject to applications, as this is not normally necessary; perhaps other operations were also involved such as façade changes. Public houses may also be converted to restaurants or wine bars without planning permission. Pubs are thought to lend character to an area. DCPN 11 was widely used for policy guidance until its withdrawal. The Bell survey of London Boroughs (1992b: 45) did not seem to encounter this problem.

If High Street tenant mix is important to compete with new locations, what might be done if development control is ineffective? Aggressive town centre management through fortuitous purchase and lease may be one answer. Or should all land be municipalized and the mix be controlled through leasing?

Hotels and hostels

The new residential classes C1, C2 and C3 (Fig. 3.2) are a reordering of five previous orders. The economic and social background pressures are varied. In large tourist cities it is profitable to change hostels to hotels. In seaside resorts, where there has been a decline in all but short-stay visitors, it is expedient to turn hotels into residential flats or residential institutions. The Care in the Community programme has led to the closure of large residential institutions and the opening of small group homes. The growth of higher education has led to a demand for student hostels. Each of these changes can involve changes in planning characteristics (Fig. 4.1).

Hostels are used particularly in central London for service workers such as nurses and for students who otherwise would find accommodation difficult to secure. Residents are likely to be long stay, have no cars and have meals provided at work. Bell postulated (1992b: 21) that a change from hostel to hotel within the C1 Class, once allowable without planning permission, would result in more traffic, with an estimated 30 per cent of visitors coming by car, 20 per cent by coach and the rest by taxi, as well as commercial deliveries early and late in the day. A case was quoted in Kensington and Chelsea where a nurses' hostel was to be changed to a hotel within the C1 Class but needed planning permission for an extra storey. On appeal, as it was deemed contrary to the borough's hotel restraint policy, the inspector said he was in no doubt that the introduction of a hotel in this primarily residential area would have some detrimental effects on its residential character. The appeal was dismissed. The Use Classes Order was later amended to remove hostels from any use class (Greenwood 1995: 720).

Wootton Jeffreys & Bernard Thorpe (1991: 46–51) reported that LPAs and operators were satisfied with the inclusion of small-group houses with up to six residents in Class C3, so that they looked and operated like ordinary dwellings. Problems really sprang from the possibility of "unwelcome neighbours" coming into a residential area where planning permission is being sought for changes of use within Class C as a whole. Wootton Jeffreys & Bernard Thorpe drew attention to bail and probation hostels, hostels for drug rehabilitation and ex-offenders, and possibly homes for those with mental and physical disabilities. These uses are potentially sensitive and emotive, against which neighbours' opposition can build up. Where group homes were dispersed in residential areas, amenity was not adversely affected to a significant degree. Indeed, in the case study areas no formal complaints had been formally recorded. Overall the revision of the residential class was one of clarification in a relatively quiet market.

However, it is not so nice beside the seaside. British seaside resorts have been in decline. In Ilfracombe (Devon), for example, between 1976 and 1991 40 per cent of hotel beds were lost (Fair 1994a: 11). Both hostels and hotels were for some time in the same C1 Class. This facilitated the conversion of tourist hotels to social security claimant hostels. The arguments are nicely summed up by quoting Heritage Minister Ian Sproat in a debate on tourism in the House of Commons:

> What was once a small hotel becomes a hostel. It is filled not with guests who stay by the night or week but by people, usually DSS claimants, who stay for months on end. It is essential that we find proper accommodation for DSS claimants or unemployed people but it is idiotic to place a hostel next to a good hotel that is bringing in good tourist money and jobs to an area. (Anonymous 1993: 4)

People who retire to somewhere like Scarborough hope to spend their retirement in peace and quiet. They suddenly find however that their house is next door to some noisy drug-infested hostel. (ibid.)

The threat to tourist amenity persuaded the government to take hostels out of the C1 Class so it is now necessary to seek planning permission for hostel use (Anonymous 1994a: 3). However, the dilemma remains. If hoteliers are to make a living, do the LPAs refuse permission and allow the hotels to become vacant? If hotels do take in some claimants sometimes, how does the LPA demonstrate this and that there is harm to amenity? (Fair 1994a: 11).

Hot food

Class A3 uses – food and drink for consumption on the premises or hot food for consumption off the premises – can be the source of amenity problems, specially smell, fumes, litter, vehicle movements and out-of-hours operations. This is especially so when the outlets operate close to residential property in suburban locations. It is therefore right that planning permission is necessary for change into this class. Besides these core problems, Thomas & Thomas (1990: 12) have identified other associated issues such as external alterations, loss of a retail outlet, proximity to other incompatible uses, cumulative effect of similar developments in the area, effects on the vitality of the shopping street, access for the disabled and the impact of hot-food outlets on the character of the area. More serious control problems occur when permitted changes take place within the A3 Class. The loss of characterful pubs has been mentioned above. This was partly precipitated by the report of the Monopolies and Mergers Commission 1989, which resulted in brewers being required to sell off tied houses (Wootton Jeffreys & Bernard Thorpe 1991: 14).

It is hot-food takeaways and fast-food restaurants that cause most difficulty. There are two types (Wootton Jeffreys & Bernard Thorpe 1991: 16–17). First, there are well managed high-profile national chains that seek prime pitches in town centres, in locations often occupied by A1 Class shops. Loss of residential amenity is not normally a problem, although change of tenant mix may be. Secondly, small independent operators, such as fish and chip shops, sometimes occupy premises in secondary suburban locations where restaurants have failed. Some problems are within the control of the operator, particularly smell, fumes, storage of trade waste and the control of vermin. Where planning permission is necessary and is granted, planning conditions can be imposed to control nuisance (e.g. the installation of fume extractors). It is usually necessary for such outlets to open late in the evening to be commercially viable. The Thomas & Thomas survey of Leeds and Cardiff (1990: 13) found that, by numbers of conditions, hours restriction and fume extraction were the most commonly imposed, but they also found conditions related to litter bin provision, sound proofing, personal permissions and temporary permissions. In a third of the cases examined, conditions limited the use to hot-food takeaway.

Other problems relate to customers entering and leaving, over whom the proprietor has no effective control: litter, the noise of voices, radios and car doors and illegal short-term parking on busy radial roads in spite of traffic management schemes. Bell reported (1992b: 27) that takeaways generated more callers with concomitant traffic and parking requirements than restaurants. Admittedly, other legislation may control these nuisances. It has been found that such legislation is reactive; that is, it seeks to control the nuisance once it has occurred and it is less effective than planning conditions, which are imposed with foresight. LPAs often seek to avoid takeaway businesses by using conditions to control uses within the A3 Class where possible (Wootton Jeffreys & Bernard Thorpe 1991: 17). In view of these difficulties, it has been suggested that takeaways should form a separate use class (Bell 1992b: 13).

Cold-food sandwich bars are not contentious. They are in A1 Class. Thomas & Thomas went so far as to conclude from the case studies that, because of the use of restrictive conditions, it was doubtful whether the government had actually achieved the flexibility within the A3 Class that it had envisaged.

The business class (B1 uses)

In practice, the blurring of industrial processes between offices (Class II) and light industry (Class III) of the UCO 1972 led to their being reorganized into B1a offices (but not A2 offices), B1b research and development and B1c industry in the UCO 1987. Such activities are defined as passing the residential test, that is, they "can be carried out in any residential area without detriment to the amenity of the area by reason of noise, vibration, smell, fumes, smoke, soot, ash, dust or grit". Presumably, associated traffic falls within this definition, but visual impact presumably not (Wootton Jeffreys & Bernard Thorpe 1991: 33). The concept of "any residential area" is general and not specific to the actual surroundings. However, it is not the activity which is important but its impact on amenity. Thus, it would be possible by installing effective smoke and grit arresters to change a building from B2 to B1 Class (Grant 1995: 20).

Property market pressures in the late 1980s led to an increasing demand for offices and the construction of business parks. An obvious likely effect was to change into offices premises hitherto in the light industry class, as higher rents could be obtained. In the upshot there was an oversupply of premises, at least partly brought on by the loosening of planning control engendered by the flexibility of the new B1 Class (Wootton Jeffreys & Bernard Thorpe 1991: 29). The changes did not seem to have really significant effects on the workload of LPAs, although it threw development plan policies based on Classes II and III into some confusion (Wootton Jeffreys & Bernard Thorpe 1991: 31–2). The overall finding of the Wootton Jeffreys & Bernard Thorpe report was that, putting traffic aside, there was no evidence that amenity was adversely affected. Normally, changes and rebuilding were from industry to office within the class, rather than vice versa, so that amenity was enhanced (ibid.: 34).

Traffic is a different matter. Wootton Jeffreys & Bernard Thorpe reported that white-collar workers worked at higher floorspace densities, with resultant parking and traffic flow problems. Bell (1992b: 27) reported that, in Hillingdon, studies had shown that offices drew workers from a much wider hinterland than manufacturing industry, leading to higher overall average trip lengths. To circumvent the parking problem, LPAs have insisted on office parking standards for new B1 buildings and for B8 and B2 buildings because of the ratchet provision, although they might be used initially for industrial or storage purposes (ibid.: 36, 16–17). Of course this does not alleviate the problem of changes of use of existing buildings, which may not need planning permission. To circumvent this difficulty Article 4 Directions of the GDO/GPDO have been suggested (ibid.: 20–1) which would require planning permission for B8 and B2 to B1 changes. It is not known if any have been approved. The traffic generation characteristics and parking requirements of different uses are given in Tables 6.2 and 6.8.

A quite different issue is that of strategic employment planning, not for particular sites but for whole districts. An aim of employment planning policy is to reserve land and specific areas for office or manufacturing use to provide a diversity of employment opportunities appropriate to the skills of residents of a district. This is particularly important where some sectors are in decline and fresh job opportunities need to be created. The effect of combining light industry and offices, and possibly the B8 and B2 to B1 ratchet changes, is a decisive shift to office accommodation as it commands higher rents. Wootton Jeffreys & Bernard Thorpe (1991: 36 ff) found the retention of industrial land difficult in their case studies of Crawley and High Wycombe, where demand was high and available land limited. The situation seemed to be exacerbated by the decline of indigenous manufacturing employment and by the fact that incoming firms tended to take on white-collar workers. In Newport (Gwent) the LPA made sites available for diversification employment, but limited the permission to B1a and B1b. Attempts to market the land had met with limited success and the developer sought to alter the condition to allow B1, B2 and B8. A spate of appeals reported by Wootton Jeffreys & Bernard Thorpe (1991: 38) in London went against the LPAs seeking to limit B1 uses by condition, as being contrary to the spirit of the new UCO in encouraging enterprise. On the other hand, they also reported a High Court case in Camden and a structure plan approval in Cambridgeshire where the UCO order was overridden in favour of strategic manufacturing objectives. Bell reported (1992b: 19) that Westminster had designated a Special Industrial Area to protect workshops in the West End. It included bespoke tailors, jewellers, recording studios, publicity and advertising, considered essential to the character, function and vitality of the area. It is not clear whether this has been effective, although Wootton Jeffreys & Bernard Thorpe argued they were in long-term decline (Wootton Jeffreys & Bernard Thorpe 1991: 42).

A knock-on effect of Business Class changes has been on housing allocations in development plans. Housing land allocations are often based on employment trends, which changes in the UCO could well upset. Research by West Sussex CC in relation to Crawley showed that average work floorspace ratios for manufacturing were one job per 33 m² and for offices one job per 19 m² (Wootton Jeffreys & Bernard Thorpe 1991: 41). These differences are substantial and in the context of development control could lead to efforts to restrict the effects of the UCO by conditions and to changes in land allocation policies in development plans.

In the context of development control, both the Wootton Jeffreys & Bernard Thorpe and Bell studies were published in 1991 and 1992, only a short time after the new UCO came into effect in 1987. This was a property boom time, which subsequently died away. The effects of the flexibility of B1 and the B8 to B1 ratchet were introduced at a time when manufacturing employment had been in long-term decline. It is difficult therefore to see how important the UCO order changes really were. Ironically, the changes encouraged increased traffic when it is realized more and more that we should be curbing it. A further irony is that much new office building took place in the late 1980s at the very time that UCO controls were relaxed, leading to oversupply.

Changes to the UC(S)O took place in Scotland somewhat later in 1989 with the introduction of Class 4, which is very similar to B1 in England and Wales, and have been the subject of study by Hartop (1993) and Brand et al. (1994). Hartop's study of its effects in Edinburgh (1993: 30) concluded that much new floorspace was proposed that is likely to be used for offices rather than industry. There had also been a noticeable increase in proposals for inner suburban sites adjacent to the city centre, where hitherto structure plan policies would have discouraged them. It was also opined that existing industrial policies could no longer prevent industrial land from going over to office use, although it was thought unlikely that existing industrial uses had been displaced by offices on any significant scale. As the City was a major landowner, it could use feu² agreements, akin to covenants in England and Wales, to control land use. It was also felt, as found in England and Wales, that the Business Class changes weakened important strategic planning policies, for example where office development would increase traffic flows and parking problems. Finally, she concluded flexibility in the use of business space had not been achieved. Brand et al. (1994) carried out a larger-scale study of Scotland as a whole. They reported that the most telling findings were that prevailing economic changes were a much greater influence on market activity (which was depressed in the study period) than were changes in legislation and, in terms of fostering enterprise and employment, that the provisions of the UCO were but one, and possibly a minor, contribution. They also reported tension between government objectives relating to deregulation and emerging policies on sustainability (ibid.: iii). Also, LPAs had lost a measure of control over Class 4 uses (B1 in England and Wales), but had sought to regain it through

---

2. A term in Scottish land law for a perpetual lease at a fixed rent.

conditions, agreements and amendments to development plans (ibid.: 50), and the business class had net beneficial effects on the environment albeit that there was concern about traffic and parking. As for the retail Classes 1, 2 and 3 (A Classes in England and Wales), it was found that the vitality of shopping centres may be adversely affected by permitted changes from Class 3 (A3) to Class 2 (A2) by an increase in office uses, and hot-food takeaways raised significant amenity issues (ibid.: v, vi).

The London Boroughs Association's report on the UCO (Bell 1992a) had revealed that 31 out of the 33 London boroughs were experiencing problems with the new classes. They made representations to a junior Minister of the Environment. He recognized the problems, but described them as "localized" (Bell 1992b: 15). In contrast, new business classes in rural areas were mooted in 1996 (Baber 1996b: 4).

Classes B3–B7 special industrial use classes

Classes B3–B7 – so-called special industrial use classes – have been abolished. They included "alkali works", processing metals and minerals, and processing non-metalliferous minerals, processing "chemicals" (e.g. distilling) and processing organic materials (e.g. skins and animal feed). They contained noxious industries (e.g. involving smell) and dangerous industries (e.g. those that might involve explosions or fire). Their abolition throws historic light on the simplification of the development control system.

As stated above, the purposes of the UCO are to control changes of use where otherwise they may be unacceptable in planning terms, but to keep the classes wide enough to give flexibility to operators. With specific regard to classes B3 to B7, the Waller report (Roy Waller & Associates 1989) showed that changes of use between classes B3, 4, 5, 6 and 7 were very rare, that improvements in industrial processing and control had rendered the distinction between B3–7 and B2 General Industry indistinct and that special industrial uses were carried on as ancillary uses in B2 premises. Commercial trends have meant that the number of firms in these classes has declined since 1948 when the classes were first defined. They found that, among industries themselves, B3–7 uses were not uniquely bad neighbours. Indeed, industrialists were more concerned about bad neighbours next to them than about the burden of planning permission, should they apply.

The government saw two shortcomings in defining special industry for development control purposes. First, the impact of a particular process varied widely from site to site, depending on the technology and buildings used. Secondly, in order to fulfil its purpose the schedule of processes would need to be updated in line with technical change. In 1989 (DoE 1989c) the DoE suggested some solutions to the problem:

- a modification of the B2 general industry class, but with some special sui generis uses (compare sui generis shops in the A Class), all of which would require planning permission

- combining classes B2 to B7, leaving "problems" to environmental and pollution control
- removal of all classes B2 to B7 to give flexibility where in any event planning permission would be necessary for physical development
- status quo.

In the event, the Special Industrial Use Classes were merged with the B2 Class in 1995 (Grant, continuing, 3B–971).

Intensification of use

We now turn to changes of use issues not closely related to the UCO but conveniently discussed here. **Intensification of use** has legal and substantive aspects. From a legal point of view, it comes about in two ways. First, a use may be ancillary to another use, but the ancillary use becomes dominant. For example, a householder may use outbuildings for intermittent business-type uses such as offices or car repair. However, if these uses really increase and become material, then a change of use may have taken place for which planning permission may be necessary (Redman 1989: 60). Secondly, uses that already have planning permission may intensify, in which case planning permission is not likely to be necessary. Examples of this are outside storage in an industrial estate where only a small part of a plot is occupied by buildings (but see Redman 1989: 22), the building of mezzanine floors within factory shells for storage and offices, multiple-shift working and longer opening hours in offices, shops and factories, the rearrangement of equipment and workers in a given floorspace, which increases the numbers of workers, and changes of occupier entailing changes in productive processes. A third perhaps rather different category is the subdivision of units. It is clear that the subdivision of a dwelling to make more dwellings needs planning permission. However, the subdivision of shops, offices and factories does not (Home 1989: viii, 8–10, quoting the Housing and Planning Act 1986). **Town cramming** is a controllable aspect of intensification.

Intensification of use may lead to changes in planning characteristics (Fig. 4.1). For example, there may be increased burdens on infrastructure such as schools. Home (1989: 26–7 citing RTPI) drew particular attention to the problem of subdividing old large factories on cramped sites: subdivision may result in higher parking demand than could be accommodated, resulting in parking on residential streets.

Enterprise Zones and Simplified Planning Zones

Introduction

Development control is procedurally and substantively complex. The GPDO and the UCO are used to reduce procedural complexity on a countrywide basis. Two other initiatives, Enterprise Zones (EZ) and Simplified Planning Zones (SPZ), have been used to simplify development control procedure on a small geographical area basis. Both use the same formula, that planning permission will not normally be necessary for development as long as proposals fall within the rules of the zone scheme. The rules of the scheme usually exclude noxious development and residential development. Enterprise Zones have an array of financial and other incentives; Simplified Planning Zones do not have such incentives. Both are property-based rather than people-based initiatives. Both types of zone were set up on the assumption that planning controls were burdens on enterprise which are best removed as far as possible. They follow US and European models of development control. Arguably, they were set up to test overseas experience in the UK, with a view to much wider adoption. The effect of wide adoption would be to take a significant amount of development control power out of the hands of locally elected councillors. The importance of the zones lies not so much in their extent, which is small, but in possibly presaging major changes in the development control system as it has existed for 50 years.

Enterprise Zones

Enterprise Zones were first mooted in the late 1970s and were formally legislated for in 1980. They were set up in two rounds; in 1981 (9 zones, e.g. Corby) and in 1983–4 (13 zones, e.g. Invergordon), with an initial ten-year life. When this period ended, the experiment was subject to an evaluation on which this account largely draws (PA Cambridge Economic Consultants 1995). This study divided the zones by location into: inner-city urban (e.g. Dudley), accessible to major population centres (e.g. Tayside), and remote areas (e.g. Milford Haven) – reflecting fundamentally different property markets. The largest EZ reported on was in Tyneside at 454 ha and the smallest in Glanford at 50 ha (ibid.: iii). The study covered most but not all the designated zones. The main objectives of the zones were to generate additional economic activity in and around the zones and to improve the environment and stimulate the local property market.

Enterprise Zones were predicated on local property market failure, particularly related to the existence of dereliction and decay, which individual entrepreneurs found difficult to overcome because of the high risks involved, institutional factors (e.g. planning controls) and the considerable scale of the sites involved (ibid.: 2–4).

To overcome market failure, developers were given a series of incentives in the zones (ibid.: 6 ff):

88

- exemption from property rates
- enhanced capital allowances for industrial and commercial buildings for corporation tax purposes
- exemption from Development Land Tax (abolished 1985)
- exemption from industrial training board levies (also abolished)
- a simplified planning regime
- speedier decisions by local authorities on planning matters
- improved customs facilities
- a reduction in statistical requirements.

With multiple goals and policy levers it is not easy to isolate individual components for the purposes of evaluation. Leaving aside planning and development control matters for the moment, it was found inter alia over the ten-year period that:

- There was a considerable build-up of floorspace and employment, although this was described as lack-lustre in the remote zones (ibid.: ch. 2).
- If EZs had not been designated, over a third of firms weighted by employment in the EZs would have gone elsewhere in the locality, a quarter in the region and a sixth elsewhere in the UK. Only 1.6 per cent would not have started up (ibid.: table 2.1).
- Excluding grants under other policies which firms would have received anyway, rate relief and capital allowances were the main public expenditures; infrastructural and land acquisition costs were a small part of the total (ibid.: tables 3.2–3.5).
- EZ measures were instrumental to a considerable degree in overcoming market failures (ibid.: ch. 4).
- EZ incentives provoked significant firm start-ups and growth (ibid.: ch. 5).
- Employees were largely recruited locally. Although local unemployment rates continued to be above the UK average, they tended over time to fall more generally into line with UK rates (ibid.: ch. 7).
- Retail development was significant only in some EZs. It was about 10 per cent of developed floorspace. EZ managers sought to exclude retailing to reduce local area displacement of retailers (ibid.: ch. 8).

Let us turn now in more detail to the simplified planning regime (ibid.: ch. 6). Normally developers must apply for planning permission to develop. In the context of the EZ initiative, this was seen as costly (payment of fees and negotiating with planners), leading to delay (holding firms back from having proper premises), uncertain (LPAs have discretion) and preventing development (owing to refusal of planning permission). Equally, an unplanned free for all in the property market would introduce considerable uncertainty and risk for developers. Each zone was subject to a "scheme" which used the following formula: planning permission is not normally necessary for development, subject to specific exclusions (usually hazardous and noxious development and sometimes retailing) and to conditions (e.g. parking and access standards). This is the formula used in the General Permitted Development Order (see above). Firms were still subject to other controls, for example building regulations, health and safety at work and

89

pollution control. There were fears that the relaxed planning regime might have spill-over effects outside the zone (e.g. visual intrusion and traffic generation) and that environmental standards inside the zone would be poor. The report by PA Cambridge Economic Consultants (ibid.) made no apparent mention of the relationship between EZ policies and local and structure plans. It was reported merely that "development may in some cases have had negative effects on surrounding areas through increased traffic pressures, reduction in the visual quality of the landscape, or for other reasons" (ibid.: 138). In further detailed case studies, a variety of impacts was found. For example, in Corby there was little visual impact as the sites were screened by planting. However, in Dudley retail development brought traffic congestion and negative impacts on nearby shopping.

It was found that "just under a quarter of companies have made some significant investment in land or buildings requiring approval from the Enterprise Zone management" (ibid.: 135). Unfortunately, the expression EZ management does not clarify entirely whether these are landowners and/or LPAs. An implication is that, the existence of an EZ scheme notwithstanding, a quarter of companies still required planning permission to overcome the restrictions and conditions of the EZ schemes. Of these companies, 60 per cent were encouraged to invest by the relaxation, nearly half reported they would have found it more difficult to obtain planning permission outside an EZ, a quarter said it might have delayed investment and a quarter discouraged investment (ibid.: 135–6). Apparently no mention was made of firms that developed land and buildings without the need for planning permission because of the existence of the EZ schemes. After the ten-year life of the EZs, normal planning controls will have been introduced. When the same firms were asked what they thought of the reimposition of controls, nearly 80 per cent said it was of no consequence, about 4 per cent welcomed it, but the balance did not, fearing increased bureaucracy associated with getting planning permission (ibid.: table 6.1). The report's executive summary of the planning findings was as follows: "The relaxation of statutory planning has been felt to be beneficial to those companies who undertook investment in buildings in zones mainly because it helped [to reduce] uncertainty associated with planning delay. Around a third of companies who invested in buildings on zones felt that this would have been discouraged or delayed had normal planning regulations been in place" (ibid.: ix para. 30).

Fears that lack of planning control would lead to low-quality buildings and environments, and to inappropriate uses, were unfounded. There were two reasons for this. First, there was a general desire for good-quality buildings and environments; poor quality could not readily be marketed. Secondly, local authorities and/or zone managers owned the land and influenced what was built; indeed, much of the land was in public ownership at designation (ibid.: 140). Of companies surveyed in the zones, very few thought that the relaxed planning regime had had adverse effects and very few welcomed the reintroduction of normal planning controls. A further factor affecting quality was that building control regulations were still in place (ibid.: 137).

Within the zones there were considerable environmental improvements, especially the re-use of derelict land which had dominated them (ibid.: fig. 6.2). Overall, the resultant appearance of development had been good in comparison with comparable similar developments elsewhere in the case study areas (ibid.: 143). Although rate relief and suitable premises were considerably more important than other factors influencing the decisions of new firms to set up in the EZs, an attractive physical environment was the next most important (ibid.: fig. 6.3).

The report also addressed the question as to what would happen after de-designation and the re-establishment of normal planning controls? Survey showed that "8 per cent of companies felt that the reintroduction of controls would affect the decision to invest in land or buildings in the future". Although this percentage is relatively small overall, this should be seen in the context of the proportion of companies likely to wish to carry out development (ibid.: 224 paraphrased). Regrettably, it is not clear from the report (ibid.) whether this small proportion of firms would be encouraged or discouraged, although clearly some may be discouraged. Designation and development has resulted in considerable environmental improvements, but what would happen at de-designation? About two-thirds of firms surveyed felt that there would be little change in environmental quality and a few thought there would be improvement. But a significant third thought there would be a deterioration as land was split up and sold off, and soft landscaping may not have been maintained (ibid.: 224–5).

"In terms of being able to focus on the removal of hard core market failure in these relatively defined areas and bring about property led economic regeneration in these areas, the Enterprise Zone policy has been successful" (ibid.: 227). The report did not address the burdens placed on LPAs in the preparation of EZ schemes, dealing with developers' queries, and the need to reassure developers in writing that development carried out without the need for planning permission was in conformity with EZ schemes. This was necessary to ensure that the planning status of development was not in doubt once the EZ regimes ended.

Simplified Planning Zones

As a generality, Simplified Planning Zones (SPZ) follow the Enterprise Zone (EZ) model for stimulating development. Their establishment was postulated on the premise that obtaining planning permission was a burden to enterprise, best circumvented by using the US model of development control (Ch. 9). In a nutshell, planning permission is automatic and need not be applied for as long as proposed development keeps to the rules laid down in the SPZ scheme. They may be promulgated by LPAs or private landowners. The difference between EZs and SPZs is that the only advantage an SPZ enjoys is the simplified planning regime. It does not enjoy the other benefits listed in the EZ section above. Planning-free zones were mooted as early as 1977; SPZs were legislated for in 1986–7 and PPG5 SPZs was issued in November 1988 (DoE 1991h: 70). By 1996, six SPZs were in existence (Allmendinger 1996).

PPG5 *Simplified Planning Zones* (DoE 1988d) sets out government views on the following:

- An SPZ, once adopted, grants planning permission for types of development specified in the SPZ scheme: there is no need for developers to submit planning applications or to pay a fee.
- The SPZ will allow the planning system to work more efficiently and effectively.
- The initiative lies with local government and landowners (and not central government as for EZs).
- They are seen as most appropriate in areas in need of regeneration, but excluding such areas as national parks and hazardous installations.
- It is envisaged that SPZs would be used in conjunction with financial assistance and grants.
- The procedure for establishment would involve a draft scheme, public participation in a public local inquiry, an inspector's report, modifications, further objections, notice of adoption, scheme adopted and the possibility of High Court challenge.
- SPZs are likely to vary in size and character, as are the planning permissions thereby granted.
- Two types are envisaged:
  - specific schemes where itemized development is allowed
  - general schemes where all types are allowed subject to exceptions.
- Possible uses include land allocated in a development plan as an SPZ, old industrial areas, old and new residential areas and the conversion of development briefs to SPZs.
- It is envisaged that certain types of development would be excluded (e.g. aerodromes, funfairs and scrapyards).
- It is likely that schemes would include planning conditions (e.g. carparking standards).
- Subzones are envisaged (e.g. for landscaping adjacent to residential areas).
- Other permissions may still be required (e.g. building regulations).

Two recent studies have reported some very modest progress (DoE 1991h, Allmendinger 1994, 1996). Six schemes have been adopted in Britain (e.g. in Corby and Slough) and six are in various draft stages, for example Delyn (Allmendinger 1996: 15). The DoE study found inter alia that officers often initiated them and many were in Labour LPAs, which took a pragmatic view of economic regeneration and promotion. Some authorities opposed them on philosophical grounds, but it was commonly held that planning permission was just one of many factors firms considered, and SPZs were no solution. Schemes took a long time to get through and it was difficult to meet market demand quickly. There was caution by LPAs in restraint and conservation areas. Certificates of compliance with the scheme and enforcement procedures were still found to be required. The study found practical problems such as landownership, infrastructure provision, environmental uncertainty inherent in SPZs and staff time taken.

As for the content of schemes themselves, it was found that B1, B2 and B8 uses (industry, offices and warehouses) were commonly allowed in. Cleethorpes SPZ was unusual in excluding these, but included shops, hotels, dwelling houses and leisure facilities (C1, C3 and D2). They commonly included conditions restricting uses (e.g. hazardous substances) or enforcing standards (e.g. for estate roads and parking). Sometimes further submissions were required from developers (e.g. landscape schemes) and subzoning within the SPZ to safeguard amenity (e.g. landscaping along boundaries). One gets the impression that a simple idea – no need for planning permission – was made more and more complex in schemes when the ramifications of the simplicity were realized. The amount of actual development in SPZs has varied. The current situation is not clear and it is probably too early to gauge success. Apparently one major beneficial effect has been the promotional coverage that the promulgation of schemes has engendered. That so few schemes have been mooted or have got off the ground is perhaps an indication of their limited value.

Allmendinger (1994) sought to examine SPZs as an aspect of Thatcherite deregulation. He concluded from a study of five SPZs actually in operation that local authorities substituted their own objectives for the zones and used them for a variety of reasons at variance with what the government intended, giving considerable scope for autonomous local policies and politics (ibid.: 1, 49 ff). More particularly, in Birmingham it was used to fend off an urban development corporation, in Cleethorpes as a local development plan, and in Slough to avoid highway contributions. There were problems relating SPZs to adjacent uses such that conditions and subzoning arrangements were more than in the normal discretionary planning regime. As deregulation meant a vacuum in central government policy, local government substituted its own objectives, which went beyond the regulation in the erstwhile regime. Indeed, far from the normal planning system acting as a supply-side constraint on the market, it appeared to provide a framework of certainty by regulating adjacent uses. The SPZ adoption process is rather like that for a normal development plan, but "why bother going through the rigmarole of adopting a zone when you can grant planning permission for a company in eight weeks" (Allmendinger 1996: 15).

Three alternatives to SPZs have been suggested (DoE 1991h: appendix 2). Development and planning briefs are in widespread use. They do not confer planning permission but act as guidance as to what LPAs might allow in response to applications. It has been suggested that they could be used as the basis of outline planning permission, with the officers using delegated powers to deal with details. Another variant involves the LPA granting permission on land it does not own. Currently, LPAs cannot submit a planning application and grant planning permission on land they do not own unless they intend to carry out development themselves. The advantages of being able to do so in the context of a local plan are that it would be more positive than the normal system and give developers certainty. Yet another concept is the Local General Development Order, which would widen the range of development permitted in the General Permitted Development

93

Order at local level. It may be viewed as an Article 4 Direction in reverse. All these suggestions would give LPAs more power and discretion.

Conclusion

One may conclude by saying that, paradoxically, attempts to simplify the UK development control system have led to complexity. The American system started simply with zoning, but the need to deal with myriad problems has led to complex regulations (see Ch. 9).

CHAPTER 5

Granting and refusing planning permission

Introduction

Arguably, the most important class of decisions in the day-to-day operation of the town and country planning system is that related to the granting and refusing of planning permission. Development plans, important as they are, can normally be implemented only through the development control mechanism. Planning initiatives, such as town centre redevelopment, also pass the scrutiny of the same mechanism. Of course, as explained in Chapters 2 and 3, there must be legal powers and administrative arrangements in place. The decision point – to grant or refuse in response to a planning application – is the nub of the matter and the hub around which this book revolves.

The chapter begins by explaining those matters that are taken into account when a decision is made. These are called "material considerations" and they are very wide-ranging. The chapter then considers environmental impact assessment, which is important for only a very few but highly significant applications. Most planning applications are granted with conditions attached, taking account of material considerations. Conditions, imposed to safeguard and improve the environment, are described in some detail. A few planning applications are granted subject to other agreements, popularly termed "planning gain"; these are considered. A minority of planning applications are refused; three sections deal with the reasons for refusal, the effects on applicants and determinant factors in appeals. Finally, research on outline, as distinct from full, planning applications is reported.

Material considerations

When a planning application is made, it is not decided by a formula or by reference to a fixed set of rules. LPAs use their discretion; each application is unique.

Those matters that are taken into account are called "material considerations". Material considerations have been defined by the courts; they are not normally laid down by statute. For a full legal critique of material considerations, see McAuslan (1980: ch. 6). Holt (continuing: Section 4) has ordered material considerations into nine main groups; his work is summarized below. One can also systematize the kind of matters that a reasonable person would take into account in making a development control decision and use it as a checklist. Davies et al. (1986) have done this: their scheme is reproduced as Table 5.1. Casely-Hayford (1995: chs 4–7) divided material considerations into: the need for consent, for example changes of use; area designations, for example national parks; site-specific considerations, for example roads; and planning conditions and obligations.

Before describing Holt's work more fully, it is useful to report his fundamental precepts:

- LPAs must observe the rules of natural justice. They must be seen to act fairly, reasonably and without bias. They must consider all relevant material considerations.
- There is a legitimate public expectation that decisions will be made with regard to all plans, policies, etc.
- A further fundamental requirement is that the material considerations must be relevant to the development and to the use of land – albeit indirectly and obliquely – and related to the public interest. The boundaries of the planning system are blurred and "quite often transgressed by local authorities and inspectorate alike" (Holt continuing).
- The consequences of approval for harm or good ought to be foreseen and a balance struck. But who can be certain? One can only act reasonably.
- The consequences of refusal should be taken into account. What are the practical consequences of leaving existing buildings and uses on a site?
- Court cases have confirmed that the planning history of a site, including previous applications, is relevant.
- The threat of the award of costs against the LPA, should they take a particular course of action, is a material consideration.
- LPAs may impose conditions. Failure to do so, where they might impose them instead of refusing an application, may lead to penalties for the LPA.
- Ministerial policies in Circulars, PPGs, etc. are material considerations and as a planning long-stop so are "interests of acknowledged importance": preservation of the heritage, improvement of environmental quality, protection of the green belt and conservation of good-quality agricultural land.

The following nine groups of material considerations can only give the flavour of what is involved.

Group 1: economic and financial factors

The cost details of proposed developments are not submitted with planning applications, but economic and financial considerations are relevant to planning decisions. National economic considerations are material, such as economic growth, the provision of jobs, the safeguarding of key installations such as international airports and the need to promote exports. Energy conservation and sustainable development are of crucial importance, for example encouraging development that reduces vehicle journeys and emissions.

Profitability and financial viability are not usually taken into account in proposals; it is up to the developer to decide. However, where there is a linkage to planning matters, they may be permissible, for example where a firm wishes to sell land with planning permission in order to finance manufacturing operations and save jobs. Appeals have been allowed where the track record of the developer is good. Commercial competition is not normally a planning matter, but it is where substantial shopping proposals might affect the viability of nearby centres. However, new commercial developments can change the character of an area and this may be used as a ground for refusal. LPAs can prevent an incompatible development that may upset the economic success of the enterprise next door and prevent a development that might prejudice the expansion of an adjacent firm. Sometimes objectors to a proposal on a specific site may correctly argue that there are better alternative sites for the proposal from the point of view of public advantage. One of the purposes of planning is to facilitate the comprehensive redevelopment of old areas; applications may be refused if the redevelopment may be prejudiced. However, the problem arises of knowing whether the comprehensive redevelopment will ever take place.

Group 2: social and cultural matters

Conservative government policy has been that the operation of the market should decide what development is built; social engineering is not one of the purposes of planning. Government guidance is against LPAs imposing specific types of housing mix in new developments, say, to have an "adequate balance of families". However, in larger housing developments the government is anxious to produce a reasonable mix to include "affordable housing", that is, low-cost housing. The maintenance of the housing stock, by preventing changes to other uses, is a material consideration. Normally tenure, private or public, rented or owned, is not a planning matter however desirable it might be in some areas to foster low-rental housing. Arguments rage as to whether substantial extensions to small villages will swamp existing communities, infrastructure considerations apart; it is particularly significant in Wales, where the Welsh language is a material consideration (WO 1996: para. 49; Thomas 1993: 20–1). Conditions aimed at limiting the growth of second homes in North Wales and the Lake District have not been very successful. Development control problems related to race, morality and criminality are dealt with in Chapters 6 and 8.

Table 5.1 Checklist of planning considerations.

1st tier	2nd tier	3rd tier
101 Amenity (including appearance)	201 Site characteristics	301 Topography 302 Landscape features: vegetation, water, etc. 303 Impact on historic etc. buildings 304 Archaeological site
	202 Design (visual quality)	305 Issues of architectural style 306 Intrinsic architectural merit: scale, mass, etc. 307 Relationship with surroundings 308 Treatment of external spaces 309 Density/plot ratio
	203 Physical impact/ quality	310 Daylight 311 Sunlight 312 Protection from noise 313 Visual privacy 314 Orientation 315 Outlook 316 Noxious/hazardous uses
	204 Operation/ amenity (effect on amenity)	317 Hours of operation 318 Effects of construction 319 Litter 320 Obstruction (i.e. "comings and goings")
	205 Relationship to surroundings (i.e. off site)	321 Impact on historic etc. buildings 322 Impact on protected land – amenity 323 Non-conforming use – removal
102 Arrangement	206 On-site layout	324 Roads – layout 325 Roads – capacity 326 Parking – layout 327 Parking – capacity 328 Pedestrian movements: gradients, etc. 329 Creation of new pedestrian routes 330 Cyclists 331 Disabled persons 332 Refuse collection 333 Children's play space – layout 334 Children's play space – space provision 335 Residential internal accom. – layout 336 Residential internal accom. – position/facilities 337 Residential private open space – layout 338 Residential private open space – provision 339 Residential amenity/open space – layout 340 Residential amenity/open space – provision 341 Non-residential ancillary accom. – layout 342 Non-residential ancillary accom. – provision 343 Backland development 344 Security: e.g. defensible spaces

Table 5.1 (contd)   Checklist of planning considerations.

	207 Off-site relationships	345 Compatible/related uses & activities – proximity 346 Compatible/related uses & activities – capacity 347 Proximity to incompatible uses and activities 348 Highway network – proximity 349 Highway network – capacity 350 Public transport – proximity/access 351 Public transport – capacity 352 Utilities – proximity 353 Utilities – capacity
103 Efficiency	208 Resources on site	354 Subsurface conditions 355 Condition of buildings 356 Conversion potential of buildings 357 Vacant land/buildings 358 Loss of natural resources: agricultural land, etc.
	209 Off site	359 Blight – physical
104 Coordination	210 Phasing: on site	360 Linkages in mixed-use schemes 361 Interim measures
	211 Phasing: off site	362 Other linked proposals: physical 363 Other linked proposals: socio/economic 364 Phasing – by quality 365 Phasing – by areas
	212 Operation/time	366 Temporary uses
105 Quantity and distribution	213 Quantity	367 Loss of existing use 368 Addition to or increase in use 369 Residential mix/non-residential unit 370 Ancillary uses 371 Special categories (residential) 372 Special categories (non-residential) 373 Expansion of existing premises 374 Employment generation 375 Impact on existing uses – off site
	214 Distribution location	376 By subareas 377 By groups
106 Other considerations	No 2nd tier	378 Planning gain 379 Agencies 380 Prejudicial to another (preferred) scheme 381 Competition 382 Applicant's needs (including personal occupancy) 383 Site assembly 384 Financial viability 385 Impact on existing occupier – on site 386 Impact on existing occupier – off site 387 Precedent

Source: Davies et al. (1986: fig. 3).

Group 3: design and amenity matters

Design is one of the most contentious of all material considerations. In the 1980s, central government sought to inhibit control over design. Holt (continuing) put forward the following reasons why this should be so; there is disagreement about what constitutes "good design" (Ch. 6) and the building industry believes design is better left to the market to decide. The architectural establishment has lobbied against planning controls that stifle "good design". Current government policy is found in PPG1 Annex (DOE 1992c). Elevational design is material, and materials are material, but LPAs get short shrift on appeal except in areas of acknowledged sensitivity. However, control of massing and scale are more likely to be acceptable, especially when proposed new building is likely to be alien or intrusive in the context in which it finds itself. Particularly difficult are proposals at the boundary of two different contexts. In former times pre-set densities, say for housing, were in development plans; latterly they have been abandoned. However, "town cramming" is to be avoided (ibid.: paras 5, 20). Plot ratio control has been used in commercial development, but matters of traffic generation and parking are likely now to be more important in industrial areas.

Layout – the spatial arrangement of buildings in relation to themselves and to neighbours – is material. Overshadowing and overlooking are the main problems in housing layouts. Landscaping is material and should be considered in relation to crime, the provision of public open space and road layout. Garden size is usually considered in relation to other matters such as privacy, but according to PPG3 (DOE 92d: para. 6) is a matter for the market to decide. Building lines, once sacrosanct, are still material, although rarely, where infill development is envisaged. The right to a private view is not a planning matter but the preservation of public views is. Conversely, that development may be seen by few people is an argument in its favour. Overdominance may be a ground for refusal. The BRE (1990) has produced guidance that safeguards daylight and sunlight standards for new and existing development. Noise is material: it may emanate from proposed development, or new development may be affected by an existing noise source (DOE 1994h). Glare, smell and fumes are material and effects may be mitigated by conditions. Lights fixed to buildings do not normally need planning permission (J. Weston, pers. comm.).

Group 4: existing site uses and features

Holt (continuing) usefully classified existing features into three classes. A proposal may: remove something undesirable (e.g. an eyesore); remove something which it is desirable to retain in planning terms (e.g. trees, or the use of County Hall as the seat of London government (Alder 1989: 28)); and sterilize a resource (e.g. minerals). These three groups are all material. Examples of the undesirable are: derelict buildings, contaminated ground, overgrown and untidy sites, abandoned mineral workings, defence installations, builders' obsolete yards, unsightly extensions in conservation areas, old mine workings, dangerous accesses and nonconforming uses. Examples of features that are desirable and may be threatened by a proposal to remove them are: trees, which have a special section in a planning application form (Table 2.1), hedges, wildlife, see PPG9 (DoE 1994j), including site designations (e.g. SSSIs), attractive buildings that do or do not have statutory protection, playing fields (DoE 1991b), housing stock, old schools and churches for community use, A1 retail uses, manufacturing jobs (weighed against the removal of unsightly buildings), tourist hotels, theatres and cinemas, pubs, medical and professional uses (particularly in "quarters" in Westminster), high-grade agricultural land (DoE 1992a: para. 2.5), and allotments *per se* and as urban open space. Examples of sterilization of resources are overbuilding of coal and aggregate deposits (DoE 1988a: para. 5d) and of archaeological remains known, suspected and unsuspected, above and below ground (DoE 1990c).

Group 5: requirements of other authorities and undertakers

"Planning legislation should not normally be used to secure objectives achievable under other legislation" (DoE 1992c: paras 24, 25). However, planning does impinge on other areas of control, especially those related to infrastructure, which are a material consideration. As transport is one of the four main land-use activities (Fig. 4.1) with which planning is concerned, all aspects – road, rail, air and water – are highly relevant to development control. Highway authorities (counties and/or districts) are always consulted on access to any highway over which they have jurisdiction. The Department of Transport is always consulted over new access, increased traffic volumes to trunk roads and development within 67 m of the centre of a proposed new road. It has power to direct refusal (DoE 1994c). The following are material considerations: safeguarding the routes of new roads, and rail and road widening; the burden that proposed development would throw on the road network; detailed highway standards, for example width and visibility (Ch. 6), often derived from local highway authority guides; bin-carrying distances in pedestrianized layouts; parking standards; water supply, drainage, water pollution and sewerage; flood risk; some public health matters; arguably, internal standards of housing, hazardous materials storage, access for disabled people (DoE 1985g), crime prevention, school provision and "public safety zones" near airports. An associated problem is what Holt termed "hypothetical illegalities". When certain uses are proposed, such as clubs, pubs, hostels, amusement arcades and hot-food takeaways, it is argued that disturbance, vandalism, threatening behaviour, theft, litter and traffic offences may result. Such grounds, possibly based on fear, prejudice or ignorance, do find their way into reasons for refusal under political pressure from constituents. One aspect is lack of evidence that such threats exist and the other that such problems are subject to control by other legislation.

Group 6: external environmental factors

Some factors that emanate from outside a planning application site are material. Either the external influences are so great that a proposal should be refused or they should be mitigated by the imposition of conditions. The main material

101

considerations are: noise (mainly from road, rail, air and factories), smell (e.g. from farming), smoke, dust, fumes, contaminated and unstable land below the proposed use, liability to flooding and impedance of water flow and storage, the presence of buffer zones around airports and hazardous sites, and proximity to pipelines and power lines. A quite different set of material considerations is involved when proposals are within the setting of listed buildings, ancient monuments or conservation areas; this is unusually embodied in statute (Planning (Listed Buildings and Conservation Areas) Act 1990: §66). The area over which a setting can stretch can be considerable if safeguarded distant views are involved. In conservation areas, settings are more closely confined geographically. Proximity of proposals, but not necessarily immediate proximity, to SSSIs is material, as disturbance by light and movement may affect wildlife. Buffer zones between villages may also be material (J. Weston, pers. comm.).

Group 7: public opinion
It is the statutory duty of LPAs "to take into account" representations received from the public about proposed development. However, local opposition is not a ground for refusal, unless it is founded on good evidence (DoE 1992c: para. 42). Even though public opinion may be ill founded, fears may be real enough to be material, for example an explosives store near a residential area or the psychological harm that may ensue from funeral and slaughterhouse uses near residential areas.

Group 8: creation of precedent
Holt differentiated two aspects of this difficult and abstract material consideration. First, cases where applications for similar development in similar locations would be difficult to resist in all fairness. Secondly, situations where applications and sites were sufficiently unique as to render the risk of parallel situations small. Precedent cases are often in rural areas. However, "the fact that a single house on a particular site would be unobtrusive is not by itself a good argument; it could be repeated too often" (DoE 1992a: para. 2.18). Once one development is allowed, there may be others, so that the cumulative effect is significant. Holt quoted a case where an LPA was concerned about creating a precedent by allowing a developer to build houses on the edge of a village. They were willing to grant permission as long as he agreed not to attempt to develop adjacent land in his ownership, to prevent a precedent being set. He declined to agree. Precedent rarely stands on its own as a reason for refusal (J. Weston, pers. comm.).

Group 9: personal circumstances of the applicant
Planning permission normally runs with the land. The personal problems of applicants are not normally given much weight, as their problems are transient. Personal hardship is material in exceptional circumstances. Holt gave some of the following examples: where a house in the open countryside is burnt down but there is no right to rebuild, the hardship to the occupants may override planning considerations.

Further sections in this chapter will consider how material considerations are used in coming to a decision to grant or refuse planning permission. Before that, however, it is necessary and logical to discuss environmental impact assessment.

Environmental impact assessment

Arguably, all development control is about environmental impact assessment (EIA). Even quite minor proposals need to be assessed by the developer and the LPA to see if they are likely to have adverse effects and whether these can be overcome. In the context of this section, however, concern is with large or significant projects, such as an oil refinery or industrial estates, especially in sensitive locations. Environmental impact assessment (EIA) is a process, part of which is a statement (ES) that may accompany a planning application. The LPA takes the statement into account when coming to a decision to grant or refuse planning permission. The main central government guidance is contained in Circular 15/88, *Environmental assessment* (DoE 1988b), as amended, introduced as a result of a European Union directive (85/337). Circular 13/95 (DoE 1995h), dealing with EIA and unauthorized development, and Circular 3/95 (DoE 1995c), dealing with permitted development rights, describe how these categories of development are drawn into the ambit of EIA, where they would have significant impacts on the environment. Further government advice is given in *Preparation of environmental statements for planning projects that require environmental assessment* (DoE 1995j) and *Evaluation of environmental information for planning projects* (DoE 1994p). Professional guidance is given in PAN 13, *Environmental assessment* (RTPI 1995c).

The background reason for EIAs is growing concern with the quality of the environment and the impact of large installations on it. The basic philosophy is that prevention of damage is better than cure and that problems should be foreseen as early as possible in the planning process. Many of the basic concepts have come from the USA, where EIAs have been necessary since about 1969, following the introduction of the National Environmental Policy Act.

The following account is drawn from Glasson et al. (1994). EIA is only necessary for a few of the massive annual throughput of planning applications, but it is very important when it is required. Glasson (ibid.: 2) estimated about 300 a year in the UK out of about half a million planning applications in the early 1990s, but this was thought to be the tip of the iceberg and there may be a growth in EIA activity. The cost of producing statements has been estimated at between 0.000025 per cent and 5 per cent of the value of a project (ibid.: 21). Statements are produced at the expense of the applicant. Whether it is necessary for a statement to be produced to accompany an application is described in Circular 15/88 (DoE 1988b: para. 12 ff) and it is for the LPA to decide if it is required. So-called Schedule 1 projects require environmental assessment in every case: for example, they include power stations, chemical installations, motorways, ports and waste disposal installations. So-called Schedule 2 projects need assessment if they are likely to have significant effects on the environment by virtue of their size, nature and location (ibid.: para. 17; see DoE 1995h: annexes 1–3). These include agricultural development, such as very large pig and poultry rearing installations; extractive industry such as open-cast mining; new manufacturing plants and industrial estates requiring sites larger than about 20ha, for example if there are large numbers of dwellings nearby; urban (re)development projects, especially if they are very large or in sensitive locations, for example near conservation areas; local roads, especially if in proximity to specially designated areas, for example an SSSI; airports; other infrastructural projects and waste disposal, for example landfill (DoE 1988b: appendix A; Glasson et al. 1994: appendix 1). Another perspective on the need for environmental statements under Schedule 2 (DoE 1988b: para. 18 ff) is to consider whether the major project is of more than local importance, the project is in a sensitive or vulnerable location or is unusually complex, with potentially adverse environmental effects. Circular 15/88 stresses the likelihood of significant environmental effects and not the amount of opposition or controversy that the proposal will arouse. It also stresses that it is not possible to lay down clear criteria and threshold sizes as to when a statement may be necessary.

The procedures for an EIA differ from the methods of EIA. The former deal with what might be termed the planning procedures, including preapplication consultations; the latter refer to the method and content of preparing the EIA and the statement itself. Circular 15/88 (ibid.: para 7 ff; Glasson 1994: fig. 3.4) suggests that the developer approaches the LPA with some details of the proposal to see if an EIA and statement are necessary. The LPA may request further information: it may also consult others (e.g. English Nature) for advice. The LPA should decide within three weeks if an EIA is necessary. If it is necessary, the LPA issues a direction to that effect and makes the information public. The developer may appeal to the Secretary of State if he disagrees with the decision of the LPA. If it is decided an EIA is necessary, the developer prepares it and submits it with the planning application. The LPA then has 16 weeks to make a decision to grant or refuse permission and meanwhile carry out the customary consultations with the public, and so on. Refusal is appealable. A decision by the LPA not to require an EIA does not imply that planning permission will be granted (DoE 1988b: para. 38). This is an outline of a more detailed procedure. About 70 per cent of EIAs prepared so far relate to those under planning regulations; other EIAs were prepared under other regulations, for example related to highways (Glasson 1994: fig. 8.3). Methods depend on circumstances (ibid.: ch. 4). The first stage in the process is deciding whether an EIA is needed. This is the screening process and it depends on Schedules 1 and 2 and the concept of significant impact mentioned above. The next is scoping, that is, deciding which impacts of the proposal and which issues to consider. This involves the LPA, the developer, consultees and the public, it and can include social, economic and physical aspects. Reference is made to development plans and other planning guidance. At this stage, alternative proposals (e.g. alternative locations or scale of development to limit environmental damage) should be considered but are frequently not (ibid.: 77). As installations may be large and complex, many internal factors bear on alternatives; for example "no action", scale, processes and equipment, layouts and operating conditions, and external factors such as the planning policy context, transport, labour and housing markets, potential hazards, wastes and the flow of expenditure into the community. The next stage is EIA report preparation, including establishing the environmental baseline for the site and its environment so that any potential impacts can be matched against it to see what they and their extent may be. Again many factors are taken into account: human population, flora and fauna, soil, water, air, heritage features, landscape and topography, recreation and so on. This involves much data collection from imperfect sources. The impact identification stage brings together the characteristics of the proposed project and the baseline data. When this is done it should identify, inter alia, compliance with regulations, ensure full coverage and short-, long-term, large- and small-scale impacts, and include qualitative and quantitative results. The use of checklists, matrices and maps seeks to ensure that nothing is left out. Direct impacts may be easy to identify; indirect impacts may be more difficult. The relative weighting of many factors is also problematic, especially when some are unquantifiable and it means comparing things that are unalike. Glasson saw (ibid.: ch. 5) impact prediction, evaluation and mitigation as the heart of EIA. Predictive techniques need to be applied to the variables identified in the baseline study and, if possible, quantified, for example likely population changes and air quality changes. Most important to establish are the magnitudes of changes and their significance, and whether they are beneficial or adverse. And so many predicted variables are fraught with uncertainty. Once likely impacts have been predicted, they need to be evaluated as to their importance and how the impacts vary between alternative variants of the proposal. Judgement has to be exercised in the evaluation ranging from the rational analytical mode to the intuitive. Evaluation may range from those in money terms (e.g. cost–benefit analysis) to those that are not (e.g. goals achievement). Once the impacts have been evaluated for magnitude and significance, thought can be given to mitigation, that is avoiding, reducing or remedying adverse effects. These can be divided into site planning, technical measures (e.g. pollution control) and aesthetic and ecological measures (e.g. landscaping). These in turn need to be evaluated for their likely effectiveness. Planning gain may be involved. If the proposal goes ahead, mitigating measures need to be implemented and monitored, which may take many years.

Eventually when the environmental statement (ES) is completed it is submitted to the LPA with the planning application. It must contain a non-technical summary. The LPA considers it along with all other material considerations and the results of consultations and at this stage may negotiate further mitigating measures with the applicant (RTPI 1995c). These are likely to result in planning conditions or §106 agreements if the application is granted. As with other planning applications there may be appeals against refusal, public inquiries and call-in by the Secretary of State. In practice, EIA is an iterative process, rather than the strict stage-by-stage approach described.

Among comments and observations made on EIA and EIS by Glasson (ibid.: ch. 8) surveying UK practice to 1993 were the following. Most LPAs, whether districts or counties, had received some. About two-thirds related to town and country planning regulations, others to utilities, for example electricity. About 40 per cent were produced for the public sector and 60 per cent for the private sector. Most were produced by consultancies that probably had limited experience of producing them. Some of the limitations of EIA are that, for example, they are not required for defence projects and public participation is not mandatory. Regulations allow developers to carry out their own EIAs and focus is narrowly confined to project level. As LPAs are given discretion as to the need for Schedule 2 projects, there was inconsistency in applying the European Union Directive 85/337 between authorities for very similar projects. The scope of industrial EIAs varied considerably; although mandatory elements were carried out, non-mandatory ones, for example consideration of alternatives, were not always done. Public consultation was often limited, and the review of the EIS, once received, was often ad hoc and without the help of outside experts. The quality of EISs was very variable, but it appeared that they did improve the quality of the decisions, in that they modified proposals.

Granting planning permission with conditions

Planning permission may be granted by an LPA with or without conditions, except that there will always be time-limit conditions (see below). Reasons for granting planning permission are not given to the applicant, but reasons for imposing conditions must be given. For example, permission may be granted for housing development on condition that the developer and subsequent occupiers plant and maintain trees so that amenity may be enhanced. Inspectors may also impose conditions when they grant planning permission on appeal against refusal by an LPA. The purpose of conditions is to enhance the quality of development and enable development to go ahead that otherwise would be unacceptable. Circular 11/95, *The use of conditions in planning permissions* (DOE 1995g), is the principal central government guidance. It does not appear to list the purposes of conditions although it deals with many aspects of conditions.

The Roger Tym & Partners (1989b: 19) survey of applicants found that they thought that the conditions were sound, but had reservations. However, many of the conditions imposed were to the benefit of the applicant anyway (e.g. good-quality landscaping). Sometimes conditions were imposed by councillors contrary to officers' advice and seemed irrelevant. Draft conditions negotiated with one officer might be changed by another. From the LPA officer's perspective, the advantages were improved environmental control, speed, flexibility and a demonstration to the public of concern for the environment. Another view was that conditions tested the ability of the applicant to implement a viable scheme when an application lacked detail (ibid.: 20).

A good deal of explanatory guidance is given with model conditions in Circular 11/95 (DoE 1995g). A summary of it is given here with some explanations added. As with many Circulars and PPGs, it takes on the following format: "on the one hand, this but on the other hand that". For example, the use of conditions on the grant of planning permission will enhance public confidence, but the use of conditions in an unreasonable way will damage such confidence (ibid.: para. 4). Similarly, the Town & Country Planning Act 1990 §70(1a) enables LPAs to impose "such conditions as they think fit", but the power is not as wide as it appears (ibid.: annex, para. 2). Conditions should not be confused with planning obligations (§106 agreements), sometimes called planning gain, which are not normally imposed but freely entered into by the parties (ibid.: annex, paras 12–13; see below).

Powers are all important. However, conditions can be imposed only to regulate the use of land and not for other purposes often covered by other legislation. They can also be used to regulate the use of land in the control of an applicant but outside the site that is the subject of the application (ibid.: annex, para. 3). Developers who find conditions onerous can apply to have them altered, for example if a restrictive condition made the development subsequently difficult to market. Where unauthorized development has taken place, the situation can be regularized by the applicant making a retrospective application. At this point, conditions can be imposed by the LPA.

As mentioned elsewhere, major policy guidance – particularly PPGs and Circulars from central government and development plan and other policies at local level – often determine the context of conditions. The Circular itself gives model conditions that LPAs can use. LPAs often have standardized lists of carefully worded conditions they can apply to save time in drafting. But, under the pressure of work, there is the danger that they may not suit a particular application site well and therefore have to be modified.

All conditions imposed on the grant of planning permission must be accompanied by reasons, although the model conditions given at the end of the Circular do not contain reasons. If reasons are clear and concise, the developer can see more clearly what is required of him. On the other hand, if a condition is onerous and the condition is appealed against, the reasoning may be refuted on appeal. One of the main purposes of preapplication discussions between applicant and the LPA is to make proposals more acceptable by conditions which can be negotiated before the formal stages are reached. This saves time and possible refusal of an application (ibid.: annex, para. 10).

Normally conditions should conform to six important tests (ibid.: annex, para. 14 ff):

- *Need*   A condition should not be imposed if there is no clear need. If the application would have been refused, then the condition is necessary for granting permission. Another way of looking at need is to say: if this condition were breached would the LPA enforce it – if not, then it may be unnecessary. Conditions should tackle problems head on. The absence of a specific condition does not preclude enforcement action being taken if the completed development does not conform with the plans as submitted, for instance where materials have been used different from those in the plans, although not specified by conditions.

- *Relevance to planning* Conditions which have no relevance to planning are *ultra vires* (i.e. beyond the powers of the LPA). A condition requiring open space in a housing development is proper; but to insist that it is dedicated to the public would not be. Where other legislation or regulations cover the issues involved, the planning conditions should not be used (e.g. advertisement or pollution control). The Circular specifically says that conditions cannot be imposed just because the LPA is not the relevant authority or because another licensing control is time-limited or to avoid paying compensation. This is to avoid confusion and duplication. But on the other hand, says the Circular, a condition may be necessary where other available controls cannot secure land-use objectives. (Ch. 7 discusses the relationship between planning and pollution controls.)

- *Relevance to the development to be permitted* A valid condition must relate to the development permitted. For example, it would be wrong, in a permission to build a new factory, to require that an adjacent site in the applicant's ownership be tidied up. But on the other hand, a condition requiring demolition of existing buildings on the application site may be permissible if the result of the new development would constitute overdevelopment of the site.

- *Enforceability* A condition should not be made unless it can be enforced. Detection of the fulfilment of a condition may be very difficult. For example, a condition limiting the number of residents in a block of flats, in order to control traffic generation, would be difficult to enforce because it would be difficult to count them. On the other hand, a condition limiting the opening times of an amusement arcade, to control amenity problems, is easy to monitor. Philips (1995: 2) drew attention to the difficulties of enforcement by an LPA when an inspector granted planning permission for the flying of light aircraft , subject to 16 conditions, including reference to aircraft use, weight and flying altitudes.

- *Precision* Conditions must not be so vague that the applicant does not know what is required (e.g. "to keep the buildings in a tidy state"); even adding "to the satisfaction of the LPA" does not help. However, where occupancy conditions for a building, for example, are laid down, the criteria to be satisfied can be specified in a development plan (e.g. for affordable housing). Conditions can also be clarified by providing a plan of what is required.

- *Reasonableness* Conditions must not be so tight as to vitiate the development and make it impossible to operate. For example, it may be desirable to restrict the working hours of a factory near a residential area because of noise or the movement of traffic. However, if it made the business impossible to run, this would be unreasonable. Or again, if a condition were imposed on a new factory such that it could only be disposed of to another local firm – to discourage in-migration in an area of housing shortage – then it may be difficult for the applicant to get a mortgage. Once completed, the building may be very difficult to dispose of and be poor security. Sometimes a developer is dependent on the actions of others. For example, a development may depend on sewerage yet to be provided. In this case it would be reasonable for a condition to say that the development should not be occupied until the sewerage had been provided. Even if the applicant consents to an unreasonable condition, this does not make it reasonable, because the conditions run with the land and will affect future occupiers.

What is noticeable about the tone of the Circular is that it seeks to box the LPA in, so that they cannot really impose "such conditions as they think fit". This is partly the result of court cases, but may be partly the desire of central government to shackle local democratic bodies in favour of property interests.

There are various types of planning application. An important type is "outline". Conditions may be imposed on outline applications. They normally relate to key matters dealt with at the outline stage (e.g. access from the road net to the site). Matters not dealt with at outline stage are called reserved matters (e.g. siting). Where a matter is to be decided at the outline stage, any conditions related to it are imposed at that point. Conditions that relate to matters reserved for later consideration are imposed later. Even if all matters are reserved, the LPA can impose conditions at the outline stage if wishes it to secure its position. Whether outline or not, a condition can be imposed, requiring more details to be submitted and approved before development can start.

The Circular continues with many items that are more subject specific, accompanied by model conditions, the flavour of which is given in Figure 5.1.

Conditions are an important way of improving the environment. But what is the effect of conditions and do they work? The Roger Tym & Partners study (1989b) of conditions imposed, answered some of these questions. As a generality, although most permissions had conditions, not many conditions were imposed and they were not very onerous. They were relatively uncontroversial and well received. Concomitant legal agreements were few.

Roger Tym & Partners identified about 200 different conditions used by LPAs, which were grouped into 17 types (ibid.: 6, Appendix 5). A selection of these is to be found in Figure 5.2. Highway, materials, "avoidance of doubt" and car-parking types of conditions between them accounted for just over half of all conditions imposed, roughly in equal measure. The "avoidance of doubt" condition is used by LPAs to clarify applications. For example, an application for a house is likely to contain a garage. A condition may be imposed stating that "the garage shall be used only for purposes incidental to the dwelling" and not, by implication,

Figure 5.1 Conditions which may be imposed on the grant of planning permission with commentary (DoE 1995g).

Design and landscape (see Ch. 6 below)
The appearance of a proposal and its relationship to its surroundings are material considerations. Conditions can be imposed to control these. Because of the somewhat transient nature of soft landscaping and the need to put in landscaping once the building work is nearly complete, conditions need to be framed to ensure the approval of the scheme and possibly ensure that the buildings are not occupied until landscaping works are actually carried out. Conditions can ensure that landscaping is maintained in future.

Trees (see Ch. 6)
Trees enhance any development. Preserving existing ones can be enforced by condition, for example fencing to preserve them during construction or limiting lopping. Planting and maintaining new ones can be secured by conditions which ensure that LPAs approve planting schemes in advance and maintenance and necessary replacement are continued for a specified period, say two years.

Time limits
New development must start within three or five years depending on the type of application imposed by condition. However, a condition can relate to the phasing of building development over a specified number of years, after which a fresh application has to be made so that the LPA can reconsider it in the light of changing circumstances. It is possible to review it before it expires.

Completion of development
Half-finished development may be an eyesore but the imposition of a condition at the outset requiring completion would be difficult to enforce in the case of bankruptcy or market changes. However, to prevent developers wriggling out of reasonable obligations it is possible to impose a condition requiring that certain elements of a development be completed before the whole is developed or occupied.

Highway conditions
PPG13 (DoE Mar 1994) recognizes that land use generates traffic. Conditions can specify the number of parking places to be provided at a development. They may be intended to be generous to prevent parking on adjacent roads or restricted to lighten flows on the adjacent road network. Conditions can also be imposed to ensure that vehicles turn within the development and do not back into main roads, in the interests of safety, and that carparks are used as such and not for storage, for example. Access conditions can ensure that, say, only a side or service road is used to a development rather than a main road and that the site access is laid out in a certain way. Safety is particularly important.

Contaminated sites
Contamination can pose threats to people and buildings now and in the future. Conditions can be imposed to ensure hazards are overcome by remedial measures. Where it is uncertain that hazards exist, permission can be granted on condition that investigations and assessment are carried out and that remedial measures are incorporated into the development.

Environmental assessment
Where environmental assessment is necessary for a development, the assessment itself may suggest conditions designed to mitigate environmental problems.

Noise
Noise can be overcome by separation of uses, suppression and insulation. Conditions can limit noisy activities to be within buildings or site boundaries, or not above a specified noise level outside the buildings, e.g. 50 dBa and are limited to specific working hours and days. See MPG11 and PPG24 (DoE 1993d, DoE 1994h).

Archaeological sites
Conditions for archaeological sites are designed to protect what is found and give reasonable access to archaeologists to watch, investigate and record before and while development is under way. However, Circular 11/95 (ibid.: Model 54) warns that conditions should not require work to be held up while investigation takes place, although developers may allow this. See PPG15 and 16 (DoE 1994g, DoE 1990c).

Paying for planning permission
It is not permissible for an authority to demand money or other resources, e.g. land for public use as a condition of planning permission. But it can certainly ask for works to be done within the site, e.g. the provision of an access road, to overcome planning objections. See Circular 16/91 on Planning Obligations (DoE 1991c).

Conditions modifying applications
When an application is submitted to an LPA it may be unacceptable as it stands. It may be sent back to the applicant for minor modification, or be so altered as to constitute a new application, or conditions may be imposed to make it acceptable.

Conditions regulating development in the long term
Conditions may be onerous and restrictive in the long term for subsequent owners and occupiers. As a generality there is a presumption against restrictions. One of the purposes of the GPDO and the UCO is to deregulate and lighten the burden on LPAs and landowners alike (Ch. 4). It is possible to impose conditions which restrict permitted development rights if necessary. For example, normally it is possible to change a furniture shop to a food shop within Use Class A1 of the UCO without permission. However, if this happened at large-scale premises it could considerably increase undesirable traffic generation. It would be possible in this case to impose a condition restricting the sale of goods (see ibid.: Appendix 1 Model 49).

Occupancy
The occupancy of a building is not normally subject to planning control but it can be in the following cases:
(a) Personal compassionate conditions. For example, building a workshop in the garden of a house for a named disabled worker may be permitted but would have to cease if the worker stopped work.
(b) Employment restraint conditions. Where, as in Central Oxfordshire, the LPA wishes to restrain employment growth, it is permissible to limit occupancy to local firms (e.g. from within the county).
(c) Domestic occupancy conditions. In specific circumstances (e.g. affordable housing and agricultural dwellings) it is possible to limit the type of occupier. As there is a presumption against building houses in the open countryside, conditions may be imposed on essential agricultural workers' houses limiting the occupancy to agricultural workers.
(d) Size of units. Normally large buildings in one use can be split into smaller units in the same use without planning permission and without altering their planning characteristics. However, in the case of shopping the subdivision of a retail warehouse park into small units may threaten the viability of nearby town centres.

Temporary permission
It is possible to grant permission on a temporary basis with a time limit. The two main cases are: the applicant's intention is that the use will be temporary, or the LPA considers a trial period is necessary, in the face of currently inadequate information, to see what the effects will be. It would not be justified because the building materials are temporary. Where temporary permission is given, a condition should be added to ensure the removal of works and structures and reinstatement. Otherwise, dereliction may result.

Disabled people
Conditions may be imposed to ensure adequate access for disabled people.

Seasonal use
Where caravans and chalets are of unsuitable design and construction for continuous occupation in the winter, conditions may require their removal or vacation at specified times.

Nature conservation
Nature conservation is a material consideration in granting planning permission. Where development may damage sites, conditions requiring fencing or time restrictions on operations may be imposed. See PPG9 (DoE 1994j).

for commercial purposes. This type of condition does not restrict the applicant more than he or she is already restricted; this is not mentioned in Circular 11/95. As a generality, the larger the development the more conditions were imposed (ibid.: 7). Among non-household applications the average number of conditions were three (ibid.: v) and among householder applications just over one (ibid.: 9). Applications for the modification or deletion of conditions were very rare (ibid.: 8–9). Fewer than 1 per cent of applications involved legal agreements. Other findings showed that, for the most part, applicants found conditions "precise" and "reasonable" (ibid.: 12–13). For 27 per cent of applicants surveyed, costs of development were increased by conditions and for a further 13 per cent the conditions reduced gross financial benefits. In the majority of cases where conditions did incur extra cost, it was less than 10 per cent of the cost of the development (ibid.: 15). In about 70 per cent of cases, the conditions confirmed what the developer would do anyway. The vast majority of applicants intended to comply with conditions; of those who did not, some altered proposals and others appealed – few disregarded them.

There was some evidence (ibid.: 32) that, where development pressures were weak, LPAs were reluctant to impose conditions, but where they were strong more conditions were imposed. Another view advanced was that conditions clarified applications and made enforcement easier.

As for suggested improvements, no major alternatives surfaced in the Roger Tym & Partners enquiry (ibid.: 30–1). All parties interviewed thought that large proposals were best concentrated on rather than the small, which seems to be what happened in practice.

Having imposed conditions, it is up to the LPA to enforce these (ibid.: 27). From the applicant's point of view the great majority of conditions could be easily complied with and they had few problems with LPAs. From the LPA's perspective, enforcement processes varied widely by authority. Some authorities checked up on compliance, but most relied on neighbours' complaints to bring non-compliance to their notice. Both applicants and officers had a low opinion of the thoroughness of enforcement of conditions. An ombudsman case over the failure to enforce conditions (Friend 1996: 7) highlighted the invidious position in which LPAs found themselves. The resource implications of checking all conditions was alleged to be huge. Circular 11/95 only makes a brief mention (annex, para. 26) and its predecessor Circular 1/85 not at all.

Brooke (1996: 83) found in a study of conditions related to nature conservation that relatively few permissions had nature-protective conditions; planning agreements were more common. There was also considerable concern over the apparent lack of monitoring and enforcement of conditions (ibid.: 67–71).

Figure 5.2 Classification of planning conditions by type with some examples (source: Roger Tym & Partners 1989b: Appendix 5, in which over 200 conditions are listed).

1. Details to be submitted and approved by the LPA before works commence
   • Details (&/or samples) of materials to be submitted and approved.
   • Details of refuse storage to be submitted and approved.

2. Carparking, loading and unloading
   • Carparking to be for residents only.
   • Carparking to be provided in accordance with the Council's standards.

3. Trees and landscaping
   • Existing trees/hedges (shown on plan) to be retained.
   • Trees/landscaping to be planted in accordance with plan.

4. Noise
   • No power tools/machinery without consent.
   • Power driven plant restricted to specified times.

5. Materials
   • Materials to match existing facing materials.

6. Highways
   • Specified access points to be closed.
   • No occupation till turning space provided within the site.

7. Archaeological sites
   • No commencement of development till specified area fenced off.

8. Use
   • Restricted to specified Use Class(es).
   • Restricted to use incidental to the enjoyment of the building.

9. Sales
   • Use restriction to sales of specified goods.

10. Construction
    • Hours of construction restricted.
    • Wheel cleaning equipment to be installed within the site.

11. General amenity
    • No process to be carried on which by reason of noise, smell, vibration, fumes, soot, smoke, ash, dust or grit would be detrimental to residential area.
    • Open storage forbidden.

12. Caravan sites
    • No caravan to stay on the site within specified period.

13. Detailed site considerations
    • Specified windows to be obscure – glazed and/or non-opening.
    • No external alterations to be carried out without consent.

14. Occupancy
    • Restricted to specified numbers of persons and/or, e.g., to elderly people, children in day nursery, etc.

15. Outline permissions
    • Siting restrictions specified. Density/plot ratio specified.

16. Miscellaneous
    • Development to be completed within specified time.
    • Specified buildings to be demolished prior to occupation.
    • To be implemented in complete accordance with plans submitted.
    • Permission hereby granted is an alternative to x (sic) permission. If one is implemented the other shall not be implemented.

17. Foul and surface water
    • Arrangements to be made for surface water to be intercepted (through traps) and disposed of (to avoid discharge onto highway).

Planning gain, planning obligations or planning agreements

Most simple planning applications are granted with imposed conditions such as "the materials shall be agreed with the LPA before development starts". In a more complex development the LPA and the applicant may agree in addition that the developer will pay for works which will:

- facilitate the development, which cannot go ahead without them, e.g. road junction improvements for an industrial estate
- benefit the community, for example public open space in a housing scheme or agree to restrict the use of the development, e.g. confine agricultural workers' housing to agricultural workers.

These restrictions on and expenditures by the developer are popularly called "planning gain". Planning conditions are appealable, but planning gain agreements are entered into willingly by the negotiating parties and are not appealable, although they may be modified (see Circular 28/92: DOE 1992r). The enabling provisions are in the Town and Country Planning Act §106, modified as §106 A & B by the Planning and Compensation Act 1991.

Planning gain has become more important in the 1980s and 1990s for two reasons. First, in the past, local authorities provided associated development such as highway improvements and public open space. Recently they have been very constrained financially. Planning agreements are a way of providing necessary improvements. Secondly, the grant of planning permission by an LPA greatly improves the market value of a development. This so-called betterment does not accrue to the LPA that granted planning permission locally. It is also known that completed development can be very profitable on disposal. Planning gain is a way of returning some of this surplus value to the local community to fulfil planning policy objectives and to mitigate adverse effects. This is part of a long-running argument about the relationship between development control and compensation, betterment, worsement and recoupment (see Ch. 8).

Annex B to DOE Circular 16/91 (DOE 1991c) outlined the principles on which agreements may be drawn up between a developer and an LPA. It starts by stating that the term "planning gain" has no statutory significance. The Circular referred to "planning obligations". The Circular turned its face against "planning gain", as the "price of planning permission" where developers make offers to an LPA unrelated to the development proposal. Planning obligations are material considerations, for example in appeals. Where it is reasonable to impose conditions on the grant of planning permission, they should not be duplicated in a planning obligation agreement, as this would probably frustrate a developer's right of appeal.

As with conditions, planning obligations should be sought only where necessary for the grant of planning permission, where they are relevant to planning and where they are relevant to the development to be permitted.

The Circular continues with tests of reasonableness in seeking planning obligations:

- They are needed for the development to go ahead (e.g. adequate access).
- In the case of financial contributions they should provide facilities in the near future.
- They are related to the development and its use and it should not be permitted without it (e.g. open space).
- They are designed to ensure, in mixed development, a balance of uses (e.g. affordable housing in a larger residential development).
- They offset the loss of a resource (e.g. by the provision of a nature reserve).

Planning obligations may relate to land which is not the subject of a planning application but where there is a reasonable connection between the two sites under consideration. The developer's contribution should relate in scale and kind to the development. Subsequent recurrent expenditure should be met by the body in whom the asset is to be vested.

The Circular introduces a new form of planning gain: the unilateral undertaking. Where a developer considers negotiation with the LPA over planning gain to be protracted or unreasonable, the developer can offer unilaterally to do works, and so on, in order to overcome planning objections to a proposal. It is envisaged that these would be used particularly in appeals.

To overcome concern that planning obligation negotiations take place behind closed doors, the Circular urges LPAs to list the relevant papers in planning committee minutes and to register agreements in the local land charges register. Finally, the Circular warns LPAs that, if they act unreasonably, and matters go to appeal, costs may be awarded against them.

Studies by Grimley J. R. Eve (1992) and Healey et al. (1995) showed that the content can be classified into two groups. First, negative obligations that regulated and restricted owners' rights, which included the extinguishment of previous planning permissions, limitation on working hours and occupancy restrictions. These negative agreements were numerically the most commonly found (Grimley J. R. Eve 1992: 21). Secondly, positive obligations which involved the developer providing benefit: numerically highway provision, sewerage and drainage, landscaping and open space, parking and community facilities were the most common. Various forms were used, for example conveyance of land, carrying out works and financial payments. Sometimes a bond was demanded up front to ensure compliance. Of all development sites studied by Grimley J. R. Eve (ibid.: 20, 24), residential sites were the most numerous; average site size, which included minerals, was about 5 ha, and where financial payments were made they were "essentially insignificant when compared to the costs and values of the development permitted."

Research has shown that local authorities use planning agreements sparingly – fewer than 1 per cent of planning applications involve them – and largely in terms of the Circular 16/91 Guidelines (Macdonald 1991, Grimley J. R. Eve 1992, Elson & Payne 1993). However, Grimley J. R. Eve (1992: vii, 21) found that planning conditions were included in agreements and there was delay: both were contrary to Circular guidance.

It would appear at first sight that planning gain is a burden on the developer, but it has its advantages (Healey et al. 1995: 118–19, 152–3, quoting various sources). Planning gain:

- removes an obstacle to planning permission being granted
- ensures infrastructure is provided
- provides a more robust control of development than conditions
- avoids appeals and delays and reduces their likelihood
- facilitates a trade-off between advantages and disadvantages of a project so that it can proceed.
- produces a public relations benefit
- enhances the development itself
- provides support in the case of an appeal
- provides a contractual basis for providing benefits
- helps to coordinate other stakeholders.

Most of these benefits also accrued to LPAs and in addition:

- were seen as more enforceable than conditions
- enabled an LPA to coordinate action among stakeholders
- secured long-term management of a development
- indicated commitment from the developer.

The practice of using planning gain has given rise to concern. Where developers offer substantial community benefits or cash, seemingly related to a proposal to develop in only a general way, this may be condemned as cheque book planning or paying for planning permission. The LPA may be tempted to allow poor development in exchange for inducement. Secondly, negotiations over planning gain are usually behind closed doors, with the public and councillors knowing little for reasons of commercial confidentiality. A new draft Circular suggested that LPAs would need a strong case to keep the public and the press out of negotiations (reported Anonymous 1996b: 1). Little if any consultation takes place with other relevant stakeholders. They are not included in the planning register (Burton et al. 1991: para. 11). Thirdly, developers may sometimes be in competition for a limited number of sites and they will then effectively bid for permission. This seems to have been the case in Plymouth, where three superstore operators were applying for nearby sites (Healey et al. 1995: fig. 4.2). The impact of the "extras" may be overlooked. An LPA may be particularly anxious to bring about a road improvement, but in its eagerness does not consider side effects. Environmental assessment may be necessary. Large-scale easy-to-develop sites in healthy local economies may readily offer the opportunity for planning gain. Conversely, complex, difficult, small sites in weak local economies, particularly where redevelopment is needed in the inner city, offer much less opportunity for planning gain, perhaps where it is most needed (ibid.: 67). There is uncertainty as to how much and in what form the LPA can effectively demand contributions. Highway improvements may be acceptable, social provision such as creches are more uncertain. A way of clarification is for planning gain requirements to be included in development plans. These will then be negotiated and debated in plan inquiries.

The introduction of **unilateral undertakings** by the 1991 Act means that developers can ignore an LPA, by-pass negotiations and present their proposals to an inspector on appeal. The purpose of unilateral undertakings was to circumvent the LPAs, who might demand excessive planning gain at negotiations (Burton et al. 1991: para. 14 ff).

It should be noted that a developer's financial calculations, such as the cost of land, construction costs and expected profit, cannot be demanded by the LPA when a planning application is made. The extent to which the LPA can negotiate planning gain, or conditions for that matter, depends on the knowledge, skill and experience of the negotiators involved.

More recently legislation has opened up the possibility of developers being able to modify agreements after five years (ibid.: paras 20–21) in the light of changing circumstances. Where LPAs do not act, or refuse modifications, an appeal may be made to the Secretary of State for the Environment (DoE 1992r: para. B1).

The incidence of planning gain has distributional effects. Planning is supposed to regulate the use of land "in the public interest", but actual practice means that different localities or sectional interests will benefit or disbenefit differentially (Burton et al. 1991: para. 33 ff).

Elson & Payne (1993) reported a range of planning-gain case studies related to sport and recreation. One example (ibid.: 22) was of a prestigious office campus at Hedge End, northeast of Southampton near the M27. The site was specifically mentioned in the local plan, where a list of sports and other requirements were set down. The planning obligation allowed inter alia for a football pitch, a bowling green, or two football pitches on a 2ha (approx.) site, a pavilion, a car-park, a footpath linking nearby housing to the facilities, and the transfer to the local borough council at no cost. All these facilities were within the application site. Other cases show the land subject to agreement geographically distant from the application site (ibid.: 33–4). Further cases show cash sums being paid for specific purposes such as improvements to sports facilities.

Refusing planning permission

Reasons for refusing planning permission

When a planning application is refused by an LPA, the applicant must be given the reasons for refusal (DoE 1992b: para. 16). This will enable the applicant possibly to submit a revised application successfully by overcoming objections or to appeal to the Secretary of State for the Environment and successfully refute the reasoning.

Most planning applications are granted (about 80%); relatively few applications are refused and of these only some go to appeal and only some are successful (about one third). LPAs have considerable help in drafting conditions on the grant of planning permission through Circular 11/95 (DoE 1995g). Scrase (1988) commented that there was very little central government guidance or case law on drafting reasons for refusal. Refusal is not listed in the subject index in the DoE's *Index of planning guidance* (DoE 1995f). Holt (continuing: para. 5.232) gives very modest attention to the subject. He comments that reasons for refusal are often bland, as off-the-peg lists are used by LPAs to speed the development control process. He also felt that sometimes an LPA would intimidate an applicant into not appealing by "throwing the book" at him.

Both Rawlinson (1989) and Roger Tym & Partners (1989a) empirically generated tables of reasons for refusal found in their studies, although the headings are very cryptic and hardly explanatory (Tables 5.2, 5.3). The Rawlinson study was of six LPAs involved in the Time for Design initiative in the late 1980s; the study represented a reasonable cross section of LPA development control work. The Roger Tym & Partners study was narrowly focused on the effects of refusals on 518 small firms. Land-use policy considerations, such as green belts, loss of residential land and shopping policy, figure strongly in both studies. Unfortunately, they are reported in such a way that it is not possible to unpack the constituent policies; presumably they are derived from development plans, but may be from central government guidance. "Size" (bulk and scale), which figured prominently in the more general study (perhaps understandably) because small firms may occupy small buildings, does not appear in the small firms study. Parking and access are important in both studies. Precedent as a reason for refusal appears in the general study but not in the sharply focused one. A ground for refusal not mentioned, but which is in PPG1 (DoE 1992c: paras 32–4), is "prematurity". Where an application is made and is of such significance that it may prejudice policies in a development plan in the course of preparation, then the LPA may refuse it. Rejection would not normally be justified where the effect of development would be marginal. However, notwithstanding problems of definition and coverage, the two studies between them will give the reader a general overview of reasons for refusal.

Scrase (1988), in an admittedly dated commentary, drew attention to the following miscellaneous considerations. When an inspector refuses an application on appeal, he gives a balanced argument. When an LPA refuses an application, the reasons are rather short, sharp and bald. It is not really possible for the applicant to appreciate the arguments behind the decision. They may be vague, poorly worded and contentious. Advice in PPG1 (DoE 1992c: para. 16) is that: "In every case where a proposal for development is not acceptable, the LPA must state clearly and precisely the full reasons for refusing planning permission." A vital test for an LPA as to the validity and clarity of the reasons for refusal is whether they will stand up on appeal. If an applicant does appeal, the LPA and the applicant will be involved in trouble and costs – something to be avoided if possible. LPAs and appellants alike are at risk in appeals of having costs awarded against them if they act unreasonably (DoE 1993c: appendix). For example, an applicant may appeal against refusal, even though the proposal "flies in the face" of national policies, or an LPA may fail to provide evidence to substantiate reasons for refusal. The LPA will also be mindful of its track record on appeals: the proportion of refusals going to appeal and the proportion of appeals it wins and loses.

Since 1947, the normal presumption has been that an applicant should receive planning permission unless the LPA has sound reason for refusal (Scrase 1988: 20). Circular 14/85, *Development and employment* (DoE 1985b: para. 3, withdrawn) stated that "There is therefore always a presumption in favour of allowing applications for development, having regard to all material considerations unless the development would cause demonstrable harm to interests of acknowledged importance." PPG1, *General policy and principles* (DoE 1992c: para. 5) states that ". . . applications for development should be allowed, having regard to the development plan and all material considerations, unless the proposed development would cause demonstrable harm to interests of acknowledged importance." A brief history, and wording of, this important principle since 1949 is given in Lee et al. (1988: 10). To say that a proposal is contrary to the development plan is inadequate. The LPA needs to produce evidence of harm. On the other hand, "An applicant who proposes a development which is clearly in conflict with the development plan would need to produce convincing reasons to demonstrate why the plan should not prevail" (DoE 1992c: para. 25). "Interests of acknowledged importance" and "harm" have to be demonstrated. "Harm", thought Scrase (1988: 20), was clear. "Interests of acknowledged importance" included the protection of residential amenities, policies protecting the viability of town centres, the protection of good farmland and rural character, SSSIs, nature conservation and conservation areas. Circular 14/85 (para. 4, withdrawn) stressed that reasons for refusal needed to be "precise, specific and relevant to the application." Compare this with Circular 11/95, *The use of conditions in planning permission* (DoE 1995g: 8, 9, 14), which states that conditions should not be vague and obscure but should be clear, reasonable and relevant to the development permitted. If an LPA is mindful of refusing an application, it may be made acceptable by the imposition of conditions (see DoE 1992c: para. 46–7).

If an applicant is refused planning permission, he may want to refute the reasons given by the LPA on appeal. Scrase (1988: 22) suggested two lines of attack: "ad hoc" and "policy". By "ad hoc" he meant that the reason could be refuted by common sense. For example, refusal of an industrial application on the grounds of harm to residential amenity could be countered by confining uses to light industry only. He suggested (quoting McNamara 1986) that an attack on policy grounds could be mounted in the following ways: legality, internal logic, application and terminology of the policies. Under legality, arguments may be mounted which highlight the fact that a policy may be used but does not appear in a statutorily approved document (ibid.: part 1.7). Questioning the internal logic of development plans may point to policies that are basically ill founded in fact and/or a particular policy may not apply in the application case under consideration. A further line of attack on reasons for refusal under the policy umbrella is to question the meaning and the interpretation of policy statements in development plans and exploit ambiguity. Readers not familiar with the details of the way these arguments are mounted should refer to McNamara (ibid.) and Keeble (1985: ch. 7).

Table 5.2 Reasons for refusal with an indication of their relative importance (number of mentions) in a study of development control in six LPAs. (Rawlinson 1989: 19)

Reason	1984	1987
Land-use policy	58	68
Access	46	38
Parking	27	34
Density	11	8
Landscape	14	15
Size	88	84
Intensity	28	27
Layout	40	44
Appearance	55	56
Overlooking	45	56
Noise	33	26
Amenity of area	34	25
Precedent	16	31
Presentation	13	10
Number of cases	258	251
Number of reasons	508	522

The effects of refusing planning permission

The reasons for refusing planning applications have just been dealt with. About 20 per cent of applications are refused. But what effect does refusal have on the applicant?

Light has been thrown on this in a study by Roger Tym & Partners (1989a) with respect to 518 small firms that had been refused planning permission for the period 1984–5 in 32 districts. Small firms are job and wealth creators; it is important that regulations do not unnecessarily hold up business. The majority of planning applications are granted, so that it must not be thought that the development control system holds up job creation in a major way. Indeed, LPAs surveyed stressed strongly that, far from refusing applications for small businesses, a good deal of help and encouragement was given (ibid.: 4). Roger Tym & Partners found that industrial and commercial refusal rates varied by region and by type of use involved (ibid.: Appendix 3). The following statistics, so-called "minor" categories and change of use, give the flavour of the situation. Refusal rates for the Northern Region are given, with the South East Region in brackets: offices 4 per cent (15%), manufacturing 5 per cent (12%), retail 9 per cent (12%), other (e.g. fencing) 8 per cent (12%) and changes of use 18 per cent (25%). Of these refusals, further discussion with LPAs took place in 19 per cent of cases, 19 per cent submitted revised applications, 33 per cent went to appeal and no further

Table 5.3 Reasons for refusal with an indication of their relative importance (% of total) in a study of small firms (Roger Tym & Partners 1989a: appendix iv and table 4).

Amenity	01	Visual amenity	(4%)
(56%)	02	Residential amenity	(35%)
	03	Pollutants	(3%)
	04	Unsocial hours	
	05	Pedestrian and vehicular activity	(10%)
	06	Privacy	
	07	Loss of light	
	08	Loss of outlook	
	09	Amenity areas	(3%)
Design	10	Design of buildings	(3%)
(11%)	11	Relationship with surroundings	(3%)
	12	Site layout	
	13	Existing buildings on-site	
	14	Density/plot ratio	(3%)
	15	Internal space provision	
	16	Site characteristics	
Infrastructure	17	Access to road network	(17%)
(43%)	18	Road/footpath pattern on site	
	19	Off-street (on-site) parking	(11%)
	20	Offsite parking (incl. on street)	(13%)
	21	Public transport	
	22	Utilities	
	23	Social infrastructure	
Strategic	24	Physical resources	
(11%)	25	Social/ecological resources	
	26	Agricultural resources	
	27	Loss of landscape/townscape	
	28	Containment	
	29	Strategic location inc. green belt	(9%)
	30	Phasing	
	31	Land availability	
	32	Social balance	
Social &	33	Public opinion	
economic	34	Moral/religious/ethnic/cultural	
considerations	35	Security and public order	
(34%)	36	Employment	
	37	Financial viability	
	38	Appellant's circumstances	
	39	Local needs	
	40	Prejudicial to another preferred scheme	(6%)
	41	Use of resources	
	42	Temporary uses	
	43	Competition/impact on existing offsite occupiers	
	44	Impact on existing occupiers off site	
	45	Property values	
	46	Other, largely policy grounds	(27%)

The total percentage of reasons for refusal is in excess of 100 per cent as applications are refused for more than one reason.

action was taken in 38 per cent of cases. Of those who resubmitted revised applications, 60 per cent were granted and of those who appealed 53 per cent won their cases (ibid.: 15–16). In refusals of initial applications , about a third were refused because of residential amenity, about a quarter on "policy grounds", a fifth on access and highway grounds and about a tenth because of parking (ibid.: table 4). Over two-thirds of applications made were for change of use: the main reason for applications was to expand businesses.

But what of the impact of refusals on business? About 40 per cent of firms said the effect was significant, but equally another 40 per cent said there was no effect or it was marginal. The most common direct impacts were being unable to achieve anticipated turnover and losing orders and being prevented from reorganizing activities (ibid.: 16–17), but 60 per cent of firms said employment levels were unchanged. Over 40 per cent carried on business as before the refusal, 18 per cent moved, but only 6 per cent closed down (ibid.: fig. 16).

Roger Tym & Partners (ibid.: 22) felt that the main implications for the planning system were to improve dialogue between applicants and the LPA and to improve the chances of success on application and on appeal.

An analysis of planning appeals against refusal

When a planning application is refused, the applicant may appeal to the Secretary of State. Many appeals relate to minor development and householders' applications. The reasons for refusals by LPAs are listed and commented on above. However, it is reasonable to ask what is the outcome of appeals and what are the key determining factors. Appeal outcomes are a direct reflection of central government policy, which one may contrast with the LPA policy, which is in turn revealed when it makes the initial decision to grant or refuse planning permission. Of course, initial LPA decisions are constrained by central government guidance in Circulars and PPGs.

One of the most detailed analyses of determinant factors in appeals has been carried out by Lee Donaldson Associates into retail appeals (Lee Donaldson Associates 1989, Lee et al. 1987, 1988). Planning for retailing was highly contentious in the 1980s and remains so in the 1990s. PPG6, *Town centres and retail developments* (or documents with similar titles), has been issued three times – in 1988, 1993 and 1996 (DoE 1996c) and its predecessor, *Development control policy Note 13*, twice – 1972 and 1977 (Lee et al. 1988: 12). This is not the place to describe the arguments in detail, but they include trading impact of off-centre developments, traffic generation (Thomas 1990) and wider issues, such as the very strong grip that a handful of food retailers have on national food distribution. Normally the government of the 1980s and early 1990s was in favour of the free market in property, unhindered by planning, but they took fright over the effect of major out-of-town-centre shops on town centre viability and vitality. Very large sums of money and town centre land of the highest value are involved. A significant number of vacant shops "in town", rather like post-industrial land dereliction, does not create a good impression. Pension funds have considerable investments there (Guy 1994). The arguments are forever moving on.

An important central government policy extant in the 1990s but not in the 1980s is the so-called sequential test to encourage town centre development. Shop property developers should consider town centre sites first for their proposals, then, if this is not possible, edge-of-centre, and out-of-centre sites as a last resort. To bolster town centres, LPAs are urged to provide parking for shoppers but not commuters, and to insist on high-quality design (Baber 1996a: 1).

At the risk of being dated, I shall summarize Lee's *Superstore appeals review* (Lee et al. 1988), which reported an analysis of 221 superstore appeals over a ten-year period in England and Wales. Superstores and hypermarkets normally sell food and are $2500 m^2$ ($25000 ft^2$) and over in floor area; they are different from regional out-of-town shopping centres, which are over $50000 m^2$ (over $500000 ft^2$) and from retail warehouses, which are normally over $1000 m^2$ ($10000 ft^2$) in floor area and sell only bulky durable goods. Readers should be aware of the locational terms: town centre, off-centre (i.e. adjacent to the town centre), suburban, edge-of-town (i.e. edge of the built-up area) and out-of-town (i.e. in the countryside). For the period (1970–85) that Lee reported, only about one-eighth of superstores had been established as a result of appeal (ibid.: 2). From 1970 to 1988, 221 superstore appeals were reported, of which 83 were accepted – a 38 per cent success rate for retailers (ibid.: 73) – by which time about 400 were operating. By the mid-1990s, about 800 were operating and it is likely that the planning regime has become more difficult for superstore developers. Appeals, Lee pointed out, highlight crucial problems and their outcome reverberates through the development plan and control system (ibid.: 2).

Traditionally, the town and country planning system in the UK has sought to protect the countryside, contain urban growth and create self-contained balanced communities with a range of shopping. The advent of superstores from the late 1960s led to demands by retailers for 2–4 ha uncluttered greenfield sites, which, if developed, may adversely affect existing shopping. Determinant issues in appeals centre on this incipient conflict. With the benefit of a quarter of a century of superstore planning experience, we know matters are more subtle than this. Unobjectionable sites have been developed and the trading impact has been diffuse.

Lee found (ibid.: 1–15) that issues were in three broad categories: land use, shopping and traffic. Within the land-use category there were two subcategories: environmental matters and land supply. The major environmental concern at that time was incursion into the green belt or open countryside. This forced the applicants to look for urban sites. The land supply issue arose when a superstore application was made, say, on land zoned for industry or housing. The question was then whether there was an adequate supply locally of that particular type of land and whether it would be reasonable to allow its use for retailing. Shopping problems were divided into adverse trading impact on existing town centres and the significance of allowing the proposal while shopping policies were being prepared (the prematurity argument for refusal). Now that there is considerable experience of superstore trading impact, it is clear that it is diffuse and subtle rather than gross. A more interesting issue is whether to allow several superstores relatively close together, where they would have an adverse effect on each other, especially if one of the stores was an anchor store[1] within the confines of an existing centre, and whether a number of superstores would have an adverse cumulative impact. The second shopping argument involved preferred shopping policies under preparation by an LPA. Where an LPA favoured, say, a superstore as an anchor to an existing centre, a competing application may well undermine that particular LPA policy. Traffic problems were the third area of appeal contention. The principal issues were whether the road network could take the additional traffic flows, and the safety and adequacy of site access. Parking was not normally an issue, as retailers would have been keen to attract car-borne shoppers. Moreover, as experience of superstores and traffic was gained, these issues were resolved in preapplication negotiations.

Lee made the point that, although these appeal issues appear negative, LPAs are keen through their development plan policies to improve the quality and quantity of shopping in their areas. The planning system has not necessarily proved a major inhibition to superstore development, but has affected form and location. Shops provide local employment and may result in road improvements and the use of disused and derelict sites.

Reserved matters in practice

About one in ten planning applications is made in outline (see Ch. 3; Davies et al. 1989). Full planning applications contain all the details necessary to make a full decision. Outline applications have details missing, called reserved matters – siting, design, external appearance, access, landscaping – which may be decided later, once the outline has been granted.

In 1985–6, there were about 31 000 applications in outline in England and about 10 000 for approval of reserved matters. Approximately 45 per cent of outline applications were refused, but fewer than 5 per cent of reserved matters applications were refused. Surprisingly, Davies found no evidence that outline applications and reserved matters were decided more quickly than full applications.

Much of Davies's report is concerned with the practicalities of procedure. He drew attention to the fact that, once permission is granted in outline, reserved matters become subsidiary. It is vital therefore to have some detail, even at the outline stage, as the application itself may be very brief. For example, consider an outline application for housing on an awkwardly shaped plot without knowing the layout. It is important at this stage to know which plans are part of the

---

1. A key retailer with considerable drawing power for customers.

application and which are merely illustrative, so that it may be clear subsequently to what permission has actually been given. Once outline permission has been given, reserved matters – siting, design, external appearance, access and landscape – can be dealt with later. In practice, it is a matter of discussion between the LPA and the applicant which of the reserved matters are dealt with at the outline stage, say access, and which at the later stage. Applications for reserved matters may be dealt with separately or together. Powers of decision are sometimes delegated to officers.

Two things may be said about the time between approval of the outline and the submission of permission for reserved matters. First, the outline permission may be "sold on" by the first applicant to another who applies for subsequent approval of reserved matters. Secondly, the intentions of the second applicant may be different from those of the first. Furthermore, market conditions may change and the policy stance of the LPA may alter. Misunderstandings can arise.

Davies also drew attention to the difference between the five standard reserved matters from the GDO/GPDO and "reserved conditions". LPAs may impose conditions on full, outline and reserved matters applications. A reserved condition is imposed by the LPA and may call for further details to be approved on further specified matters (e.g. noise control and drainage). Eight of the 38 model conditions listed in Circular 1/85 (now withdrawn and replaced by four in Circular 11/95) were of this type. Such conditions can be used to clarify the content of applications.

Davies drew attention to a spectrum of application types used by the parties, depending on what they were trying to achieve:

- A "pure" outline application consisting of a red line on a plan to identify the site and no reserved matters decided at the outline stage. This would be useful to a landowner to establish the market value of a site for future sale.
- A "hybrid" outline with some reserved matters decided at the later stage, typically external appearance and landscape. This would be very useful to the LPA where it was particularly concerned to fix access at the outline stage.
- A "quasi-full" application where the application is "full" but there are one or two details to be decided later (e.g. materials). This may be used in a conservation area when the LPA needs to know virtually all the material considerations before making a decision.

In practice there is great variety and complexity in the use of the outline and reserved matters system. The public is now much more aware of the importance of detail through public participation, sites are complex and there is a blurring of the difference between principle and detail. Rarely, reserved matters may be refused, which may result in a new full planning application. Other agreements such as planning obligations may be involved. As the GDO/GPDO does not define each of the reserved matters clearly, there is scope for argument over the meaning of reserved matters in individual applications. For example, access may have been fixed at outline; design may be a reserved matter but access is a design matter. What, therefore one may ask, has been decided at the outline stage? The usual

125

expedient adopted to cater for ambiguities is to use reserved conditions that seek to clarify the position.

The Davies et al. study (1989: ch. 5) concluded that discussions between the parties were beneficial, LPAs could and did influence details (e.g. to ensure privacy), and apparently there was little dispute between LPAs and applicants over design, external appearance and landscaping. Applicants were rarely able to quantify and cost any delay arising from planners' attempts to get details right. Other significant causes of delay were incomplete applications, problems of site assembly and supplies of materials. Conditions were frequently used to constrain and guide reserved matters. There were no general rules as to when applications across the spectrum from outline to quasi-full should be used. There was no evidence that the "famous five" needed to be added to, but they do need clarifying. Particular gaps in the five are:

- "Site layout", including density and phasing.
- There is ambiguity over access – access to the site and access within it, which may follow later.
- Siting, design and external appearance are treated as a group in practice. If they were separated, the expression "footprint" could be used for siting. Both design and external appearance relate to the use of materials; but in practice, materials are decided late in the approval process and depend on their availability. Perhaps materials should be considered separately.
- Although landscaping is a reserved matter, it may be one of principle regarding the relationship with surrounding development.

The overall conclusion from the study was that the outline and reserved matters procedure is a very useful instrument in a limited but significant number of cases. It is a matter of leaving well alone, or more reserved matters and definitions could be added in an amended GDO/GPDO. The arguments were pretty evenly balanced.

Conclusion

This chapter has considered the wide variety of considerations taken into account when a decision is made to grant or refuse planning permission. It has also discussed the imposition of conditions imposed on the grant of planning permission and the reasons for refusing planning permission, both of which help to maintain and to improve the environment. Interestingly, central government provides guidance on the imposition of conditions, but little on giving reasons for refusal. Planning gain and environmental impact analysis were late arrivals in the post-war history of development control and are significant in only a very small proportion of proposals to develop. The next chapter will consider matters of substance rather than matters of procedure, namely building and engineering operations in development control.

CHAPTER 6

Major issues in development control

Introduction

The purpose of this chapter is to discuss a core area of issues in development control which are the substance of most planning applications. So called "reserved matters": siting, design, external appearance, access and landscape, are a convenient, if somewhat arbitrary, way of structuring a complex subject area. They are building and engineering operations. The reader will be aware that there are different types of planning application (see Ch. 2). The two most important numerically are "full" and "outline" applications. An outline application is submitted to an LPA to establish the principles of a proposal before much, possibly abortive, effort is expended in solving detailed problems. The application is granted in outline and reserved matters are decided upon subsequently. Reserved matters may be settled at either stage, depending on the result of informal discussions between the LPA and the applicant (Davies et al. 1989). Reserved matters do not apply to change-of-use applications as they are subject only to full applications. The list of reserved matters is derived from the GDO, going back to at least 1950.

Others could be added, such as "quantity" (e.g. housing density), "boundary treatment" and "layout". Definitions are not clear and they vary from authority to authority (ibid. 1989: 3, 23, 24–6, 36). Neither are they discrete: design and external appearance overlap. Davies's practical definitions are a useful starting point:

- *Siting* The two-dimensional location of buildings within the site, that is the size and placing of their footprints, perhaps also showing or implying access to the buildings themselves.
- *Design* The two-dimensional arrangement of buildings and uses, their three-dimensional form in themselves and in relation to their surroundings, that is their massing, height and number of storeys; and in broad terms their external appearance.
- *External appearance* External elevations and the colour and type of facing

127

materials to be used for external walls and roofs, often treated separately.
- *Means of access* The location and detailed, two-dimensional design of vehicular and pedestrian access to the application site from the surroundings, but also circulation and access to individual buildings within the site.
- *Landscaping* According to the GPDO, the treatment of land for the purposes of amenity, including screen walls, planting, earthworks, laying out of gardens.

The last sections of this chapter will seek to synthesize these apparently separate matters and report briefly on related research.

Siting

Siting and location

Siting describes how buildings sit within a plot and relate to their immediate surroundings. Readers will readily appreciate the siting differences between a traditional shop, in a traditional shopping street, which sits immediately next to the pavement so that pedestrians can look in, and a hypermarket on a ring road with virtually no windows, surrounded by carparking and landscaping. Siting is different from location. The location of a building describes its position in a region and/or a town, or perhaps in a deep rural setting. For example, department stores normally *locate* in the centres of larger towns; they are normally *sited* next to the pavement in prime shopping streets and may be sited close to a bus station, a multistorey carpark and other traditional shops. Location is also a material consideration in development control, as described in this chapter ("Access" on p. 147 ff).

Siting constraints

The siting of buildings within plots has much to do with their type and function – residential uses, shops, factories, offices and leisure uses – each with their special needs, such as gardens for houses and buffer zones along factory estate boundaries. At a very basic level, siting of individual buildings within plots will depend on the pre-existing plot characteristics. Apart possibly from housing and open space, most uses avoid steep slopes. The bearing capacity of the soil may have been compromised by infill, undermining, underlying geology or water-logging. It is customary to retain certain features, especially trees, hedges and buildings of value and interest, to give the development a feeling of maturity. Water features may be retained and their potential exploited. As drainage is best by gravity rather than pumping, topography helps to determine the position of pipe runs. As services tend to be laid along roads, for easy maintenance, road layouts to an extent are predetermined by the need for drainage. Drainage and flood control must be discussed at the pre-planning and outline stages of planning applications on a "prevention is better than cure" basis. But in spite of the use of conditions and agreements for new developments, drainage problems have still resulted (DoE 1992s; Institution of Civil Engineers 1993: ch. 10). In turn, the siting of buildings is influenced by the road layout, but the siting of buildings for other reasons, such as design ("Design" on p. 134 ff), helps to determine road layouts. A good deal of new building is adjacent to pre-existing distributor roads (Table 6.1), so that a key factor in internal site layout is the position of the access between the road network and the plot itself, including the need for visibility splays ("Access" on p. 147 ff). It is possible also that there may be other pre-existing constraints, such as way leaves for power and sewerage and rights of way (DoE 1993a).

The immediate environs of the plot may have favourable–compatible and unfavourable–incompatible factors which influence the siting or footprint of the development. Favourable factors may include the possibility of distant views or views of amenity spaces, or development of a similar kind with which it is compatible or complementary, such as housing next to housing or to open space. On the other hand, noise, poor outlook or hazard may influence siting. It is possible by careful siting of buildings within a plot to maximize one set of influences and minimize the others.

Building densities and unit sizes

It is useful under siting to consider the closely related issues of plot ratio, density and footprint. The plot ratio of a development is the floor area of buildings on a plot expressed as a percentage of the area of the plot. Plot ratio is a measure of density, but density may also be expressed in other ways, for example houses per hectare, or bed spaces per hectare in residential developments or workers per hectare in commercial developments. Footprint is also a density measure: it is the ground-floor area of buildings as a percentage of plot area. Readers will readily relate to semi-detached houses at 30 houses per hectare, which is very common in Britain, and run-of-the-mill industrial estates with a plot ratio of 50 per cent, which contrasts with a well landscaped business park at say a plot ratio of 20–25 per cent. An office block completely covering a site in a city centre could easily have a plot ratio of 300 per cent or more (see Fig. 6.2). Clearly, the density philosophy that might be applied to a site – low-rise high-plot-ratio housing or higher-rise low-footprint offices in a park – will affect the siting of buildings. Density is a determinant of massing or bulk of buildings dealt with under design ("Design" on p. 134 ff). Overdevelopment of a site may be a reason for refusing a planning application.

The size mix of buildings within a development may help to determine the position of an individual building within the development as a whole. Size mix in housing development is measured by numbers of habitable rooms or bed spaces per house with a mixture of house sizes. Small four-roomed houses in terraces sit differently from ten-roomed detached houses within their respective plots, as detached houses will be surrounded by garden. A development of small houses will have siting arrangements different from one dominated by larger ones. With regard to shopping development, the market demands many small "unit shops" (up to 300–400 m² in floor area) with relatively few very large units (anything over say 1000 m² in area). Small shops are sited in malls against the heel of the pavement, as with traditional shops. Large shops in new planned developments may be either at the ends of malls, and sited away from each other if there are more than one, to even out pedestrian flow through the mall (so-called magnet stores), or free-standing superstores, hypermarkets or retail warehouses placed within extensive parking.

Offices, factories and warehouses come in a range of sizes from very small office suites and workshops of say 50 m² to tens of thousands of square metres; the emphasis, by size of unit, is at the lower end of the scale. As with shops, the market demands small units speculatively built with future occupiers unknown, and large units built for specific clients. Small firms can expand by adventitiously taking over adjacent small units; this is not possible with larger firms. Small factories usually range up to about 500 m² in floor area. They are often arranged in terraces, sometimes back to back and sometimes with yards at the back. Siting within a development is often dependent on the need for adequate road access and parking. The clients occupying larger purpose-built offices and factories may wish to be sited next to a district distributor road, but perhaps without access to it, or in a prominent site within a development to convey a high-profile prestigious image to the public. Smaller office suites, especially in town centres, are sited above shops, in which case they need pedestrian access entirely separate from the shops or in subsidiary town centre positions somewhat away from the main shopping streets: they may be sited against the pavement or back from it, depending on the urban design characteristics of the context.

Building and improvement lines

Building lines and improvement lines were devices used earlier in the twentieth century to determine the siting of buildings within their plots. Building lines were specified in new developments so many feet back from the centre lines of roads to ensure airiness and light, in contrast to the squalor and airlessness of earlier unregulated development. Once specified, buildings had to be sited behind them. The result is a level of regimentation that is now rejected. However, the siting of infill development may still be required to conform. Improvement lines were laid down so many feet from the centre line of heavily trafficked but already developed road frontages, with a view to ultimate road widening. The reconstruction of obsolete buildings was required to be behind the improvement lines. The result has been idiosyncratic broken frontages, which are visually and functionally unsatisfactory.

Residential and commercial development

At this point it will be useful to consider the special siting characteristics of residential and commercial development separately. Human dimensions and the needs of family life drive the internal layout of houses and their relationship with their surroundings. Internal arrangements are not normally a planning matter. Sunlight and daylight, privacy, views out and surveillance, parking, garden size and landscape are closely related planning matters. These factors influence the siting of housing.

Daylight and sunlight
Good daylight within buildings is much appreciated by residents, workers and customers, whatever the building. Sunlight is also appreciated, especially as solar gain can reduce energy requirements. Buildings can obstruct both daylight and sunlight by overshadowing. Correct siting is vital for both. The design of the interior environment is important as well, especially the size and position of windows, the depth and shape of rooms and the colours of internal surfaces (Littlefair 1991: 1). The depth of rooms affects building bulk, a design consideration.

The quantity and quality of daylight inside a room will be impaired if obstructing buildings are large in relation to their distance away. Imagine that you are standing close to a ground-floor window of your property and looking out. A neighbour is proposing either a building opposite or perhaps an extension to his property immediately to your left or right. If you raise your gaze 25° above the horizontal and if the ridgeline of the proposed building breaks through and above this 25° line, then it is likely that your daylight will be significantly impaired (ibid. 1991: fig. 2; Speer & Dade 1995: 123). Trees should normally be ignored unless they form dense continuous belts; it is best to site them away from windows.

Where extensions to existing buildings are proposed adjacent to existing windows, the 45° rule is used as guidance to avoid the extension making adjacent rooms gloomy. Imagine again that you are standing close to a ground-floor window looking out. Your neighbour proposes an extension to his property immediately to the left or right. Turn your gaze horizontally 45° to the left or right as appropriate towards the proposed extension. If the proposed extension breaks into and beyond the 45° line, then your daylight will be significantly impaired (Littlefair 1991: fig. 8; Dijksman 1992: 38).

Sunlight is a wonderful boost to the spirits: most people like it as long as they can move or have shade if it proves too much. This is important in domestic and non-domestic buildings. Maximizing sunlight in site layout involves a consideration of orientation and overshadowing. South-facing windows receive most sunlight, north-facing ones only in the morning and evening in the summer in the UK. A dwelling with no main window wall within 90° of due south is likely to be perceived as insufficiently sunlit. The overshadowing of one building by another can be reduced if the site is south-facing, taller buildings are on the north of the site, low-density housing is on the south and terraced dwellings are on the north. Overshadowing can also be reduced if terraced housing is on east–west roads and semi- and detached on north–south roads. Low-pitched roofs also reduce overshadowing. Thus, a building will appear reasonably well sunlit if at least one main window wall faces within 90° of due south and this window wall receives at least a quarter of annual probable sunlight hours, including a due proportion in winter (Littlefair 1991: 11). Buildings that satisfy these criteria may have their sunlight prejudiced if new buildings are sited near them. It is therefore important to check for this in the development control process.

Good site planning ensures good daylight and sunlight for gardens and open spaces throughout the year. This is valuable to provide attractive views, to make sitting out and playing more pleasant, to encourage plant growth, for warming and drying the ground and for drying clothes (ibid.: 12). Where focal points such as fountains are used, it is important that they are well lit. Shade does have its uses, especially for carparking in summer. Opaque fences and evergreen hedges over 1.5 m high can cast significant shadow. As a rule of thumb, no more than a quarter of an outside amenity area should be prevented by buildings from having any sun at all on 21 March. If it is, the loss of sunlight is noticeable (ibid.: 14).

With greater sustainability in mind, passive solar gain can be improved in all buildings by trying to ensure that collecting façades face within 30° of due south and overshadowing is minimized. Barton et al. (1995: 25) reported that building services consume approximately 40 per cent of UK delivered energy, so that energy can be saved by improved siting and other measures. To achieve this in residential layouts requires careful layout, ideally with roads running east–west and with living rooms facing south. In non-domestic buildings, stores, toilets and computer rooms are best sited on the north side of buildings. It is also useful to set buildings well back from the southern boundary of a development in anticipation of future development farther south, which may cast shadows (Littlefair 1991: ch. 4).

Littlefair usefully drew together a series of daylight-related issues in site layout (ibid.: ch. 5). He stated that the need for a view from a building rarely conflicted with the need for daylight. Where privacy in homes and gardens is concerned, the rule of thumb that facing windows should be typically at least 18 m and up to 35 m apart ensures that the building faces get adequate daylight. Where domestic windows are large for solar-gain reasons, gardens may have to be lengthened or roads and paths situated to avoid overlooking. There may be conflict between sunlight, daylight and security objectives; for example, shading of carparks may inhibit surveillance. Fortunately, the need to open up pedestrian and vehicular access to buildings favours sunlight and daylight provision. He particularly drew attention to the potential conflict between the psychological need for enclosure between buildings and the need for light. Even at higher residential densities, where two linear terraces enclose a street space, with a space-to-height ratio of 2.5:1, it will still feel enclosed but not obstruct too much light. The worst conflict occurs in courtyards, which can be gloomy. Littlefair stressed that the above guidelines are not mandatory. Their use will depend on the difficulties of individual sites.

Climatic considerations

Opening up layouts for light draws attention to other climatic considerations. Littlefair warned not to allow large flank-walls to face the wind, or have openings under buildings near the ground, or have funnel-like gaps between buildings.

Further advice (BRE 1990: part III, 7) suggested avoiding multistorey buildings and flat roofs. Gable ends should be hipped instead of upright and, where wind-speeds increase near corners of buildings, planting can mitigate the effects. Buildings should be arranged in irregular patterns but of regular height: irregularity of height produces downdrafts. Distances between buildings should be small; ideally between 1.5 and 2.5 times their height, but without gaps between buildings of less than 3 m, otherwise wind funnels may be created. It is suggested that the maximum length of a block should be 25 m and that steps and staggers in façades will reduce windspeed. As for planting, this should be designed with buildings to improve microclimate, especially to maintain the "roughness" of the development. Planting conifers on the north and deciduous trees on the south of a site can provide shelter but allow for winter sun.

Building Research Establishment Digest 350 (BRE 1990) drew attention to more intractable problems, particularly related to the geography of the UK: accumulated temperature differences, solar irradiation and driving rain, which vary markedly between north and south (ibid. 1990: part I, 2). At local level the best sites are in the "thermal belt", part way up south-facing slopes, avoiding frost pockets and windy ridges (ibid.: part II, 2). The spacing of terraces is significantly different between north- and south-facing slopes (ibid.: part II, 2) if overshadowing is to be avoided. For example, in March at noon, at latitude 50° north, with terraces 7 m high running east to west, each on 10° gradient slopes, the terraces on the southern slopes would need to be only 12.8 m apart to ensure that one terrace did not overshadow another, but 21.2 m apart on northern slopes (ibid.: part III, 2).

Privacy, outlook and landscaping

Internal privacy can be safeguarded by ensuring an adequate distance between facing windows (usually up to 35 m), by setting housing back from pavements and angling the alignment of one house to another so it is not possible for the interior of rooms to be inter-visible. These privacy matters are to an extent safeguarded by having a parking space at least 6 m long in front of the dwelling and at least a 100 m^2 garden at the rear. Fencing and planting at least 2 m high further safeguard privacy (Essex County Council 1975: 31). Where the siting of house extensions may lead to loss of neighbour privacy, this may be mitigated by the use of windowless walls, high sill windows and opaque glass; these can be subject to planning conditions. The desire to exploit pleasant views of distant landscapes out of buildings, amenity spaces or merely of the access roads, with their comings and goings, affects the siting of buildings. Views out over access roads, parking and other buildings improve site security.

The presumption in favour of retaining old trees and hedges in new layouts, as features to add to the pleasure and maturity of a site, will help determine the sites of individual buildings. Once proposed buildings have their sites fixed, the siting of new landscape features will soften the development and provide privacy and a sense of enclosure and rurality.

Phasing and expansion space

On substantial business parks and industrial estates, the siting of buildings is strongly influenced by the road layout and by phasing. Road layouts are dealt with below ("Access" on p. 147 ff). Sites are developed over a decade or more and properties released onto the market as demand arises. To avoid having capital tied up in works before demand, phasing can take place in two ways: successive expansion of the road layout to open up fresh plots, and allowing expansion space within plots, which may be only partly developed initially. Ranging from smaller to larger developments, the road net may be just a simple spine, with one access to a distributor road and a turning area, and each property having direct access to the spine. This spine may be extended as the need arises. In some cases a spine may run as a loop between two distributor roads. Only slightly more complex is a spine and spur arrangement, where both spines and spurs may be extended and spurs added to open up fresh plots. On larger developments, modified grid layouts are used; the grid can be completed piecemeal as required. In each of these cases, the first buildings to be built should be sited near the main access point: scattered buildings with vacant plots create a half-completed unmarketable atmosphere. As for expansion space for buildings sited within plots, there are two schools of thought. First, private developers may take the view that it is best to develop the plot fully initially to maximize rental income for a given outlay on infrastructure. Secondly, a local authority view may be to allow for expansion space to keep firms in the area and to diversify employment. It has not been proved possible to forecast how firms will expand their property requirements. However, space can be left in layouts to extend terraced buildings and detached buildings in plots can be so sited as to be extended in virtually any direction.

A further feature of larger industrial and business parks is balancing ponds. As roofs, carparks and roads can have very rapid rainwater runoff, it is necessary to site ponds where topographically suitable to avoid flooding. They form admirable landscape features and they double as emergency water supplies for fire fighting (English Estates et al. 1986). If you want a successful development, just add water.

Design

Sense of place – genius loci

Davies (Davies et al. 1989) defined design as "the two-dimensional arrangement of buildings and uses, their three-dimensional form in themselves and in relation to their surroundings, that is, their massing, height and number of storeys and in broad terms their external appearance". Bridger (1987) has described many of the key terms and elements in the context of development control (Figs 6.1, 6.2).

The design of a development springs from the needs of owners, users and occupiers. There should be a sense of arrival: "when you get there, there is a there there". There is also getting there: the journey through spaces, from one to another, should equally be a joy.

In the context of development control, owners and others need access and other services, a feeling of community and visual delight. The internal arrangement of rooms in buildings in development also needs to satisfy them, but this is not normally a matter for development control. The over-arching objective of the designer and the development controller is the creation of a sense of place – *genius loci*. In part, a sense of place is created on the one hand by the arrangement of buildings in three dimensions to create spaces between them (consider a modern enclosed shopping mall or an eighteenth-century residential square), and on the other hand by a single building standing alone in space (consider a hypermarket with its car-parking and an eighteenth-century country house in its parkland).

Maslow (quoted by Preece 1991: 107) suggested that there is a hierarchy of human needs which is reflected in building development. First, we have physiological needs such as food and warmth. Secondly, we have a need for physical security, expressed in our feelings of territoriality, and the need for surveillance (see below). Thirdly, we have social needs such as friendship expressed in the built environment in job and leisure provision. Fourthly, we seek esteem; in the built environment this is expressed in the personalization of our houses and the construction of flagship buildings for firms. Finally, we seek what is called self-actualization, which is an internally self-sufficient experience. Aesthetic pleasure, the enjoyment of quality and the provision of leisure facilities express this in the built environment. It is argued that we satisfy the physiological needs first, and so on up the hierarchy. We are willing to sacrifice higher-order needs to satisfy lower-order ones, for example by putting up ugly fencing to ensure security. The siting of buildings to bring about these purposes has been dealt with above: external appearance, access and landscaping will be dealt with below.

All development proposals start with the site constraints and site potential dealt with above (see pp. 128–30). Constraints include internal factors such as hydrography, topography, geology, existing landscape features and buildings worthy of retention. Off site there may be poor views and sources of noise, dust, smell and so on. The skill of the urban designer lies in satisfying the needs of the user by turning problems into opportunities. Consider the difficulty and delights of steeply sloping sites for housing.

Space between buildings

Spaces engender specific but contradictory feelings within the user (GLC 1983: 23 ff). Large spaces inspire both exhilaration and exposure (e.g. being in a very large civic square). Small spaces inspire privacy and claustrophobia (e.g. being at the bottom of a light well in a tall building). Spaces of whatever kind relate to human scale: spaces therefore should be scaled appropriate to their use. Compare an intimate residential cul-de-sac with a square in front of a city hall. Buildings take on a group value. This is particularly highlighted in the need to obtain consent for the demolition of a building of little merit in itself in a conservation area (Ch. 7). Outdoor spaces are rather like rooms and corridors in buildings. Each has floors (floorscape), walls (buildings and planting), ceilings (forest tree canopies), doors (access ways) and windows (views out). Each is characterized by scale and proportion, height to width to floor area, related to human scale. They also have surface treatment which, as far as buildings are concerned, is dealt with below ("External appearance" on p. 141) under external appearance, as a reserved matter. Here we should leave the room and corridor analogy. By moving buildings, planting and access in terms of siting (previous section) and altering their mass (height to width to depth) it is possible to alter the degree of enclosure of the space between them and alter their dynamic character. A traditional residential street with semi-detached houses has a limited degree of enclosure, but a residential terraced square with only one access point has a high degree of enclosure. Where the enclosure is entirely one of buildings, the character is hard, but where the enclosure is partly or largely provided by planting, character is softened and may become arcadian. We also describe spaces as static and dynamic. Buildings arranged in squares, circles or cul-de-sacs have a feeling of rest and completeness. Buildings arranged along a boulevard create a dynamic space, which implies movement and change (McCluskey 1992: ch. 3).

The height of the enclosing buildings and planting in relation to the plan shape of a development creates a sense of scale and proportion in three dimensions. It has been found from observation that, where the height of buildings exceeds the distance between them, in a linear space, the feeling of enclosure starts to be rather uncomfortable. Where the distance between buildings is more than 2.5 times their height, there is a low feeling of enclosure (GLC 1983: 33). Sometimes we like enclosure, for example a narrow quaint shopping street on medieval building lines because it affords protection from the weather. At other times we value openness, especially where it gives extensive views of the sea or countryside. Enclosure is not an end in itself.

As we move from space to space, we are aware of the variety of spaces possible, the connections between them and the experience of serial vision. This is felt strongly in old town centres, where spaces of different shapes and sizes, such as markets and churchyards, open onto each other through a succession of irregular streets. Here we are aware of communities and neighbourhoods, such as the town centre, the interwar suburb and the village, each with its own character.

The character of spaces has already been described: enclosure, proportion, floorscape, formality, hardness and softness. Between spaces are thresholds and portals. Sometimes there is a change of road surface, a narrowing of the road or an archway. Gates separate the public street from the private garden. A related concept is a "sense of arrival": a house door or a cathedral door. This is particularly important in shopping development, so that customers are attracted. Traditional shop fronts, with fascias, hanging signs, stall risers, windows and shop doors evolved to attract customers. In newer developments, such as planned malls in town centre back-land,[1] attractive portals are constructed on principal streets. Free-standing superstores and retail warehouses can attract by their bulk, colour and bold signage: features such as clock towers indicate entrance doors.

As we move through spaces we experience a succession of constantly changing views as we approach our destination; this is serial vision. It heightens interest and involvement in the environment. It evokes mystery, suspense and anticipation. Long straight terraces on either side of a straight road create a vista when all is revealed at a glance. Where buildings are arranged more irregularly on short straight stretches of road or in a curve, views are closed, and there is a sense of suspense, anticipation and sometimes surprise as we move through the spaces. This design phenomenon is exploited in all types of development.

Formality, informality and character

McCluskey (1992), the DOE and Department of Transport in Design Bulletin 32 (1992), the GLC (1983), Phillips (1993a,b) and Beddington (1991) described many designs of greater or lesser formality which may be described as the character of the development. Whether designs are formal or informal relates to our innate desire for order on the one hand and our dislike of regimentation on the other. Formality is derived first from the geometric shapes in the plan, such as circles, squares, crescents and oblongs with many variants, which form the pattern of the roads. The roads themselves form another tree-like order in a hierarchy from primary distributors to pedestrianized streets, dealt with below ("Access" on p. 147; Table 6.4). Secondly, formality is derived from the geometric order with which the buildings are sited in relation to the roads and finally from the order and regularity of the building façades. Many designs mix the formal with the informal, for example a business park with a grand tree-lined boulevard flanked by a mix of buildings in different styles.

To state the obvious, buildings not only have the function of defining spaces, but have functions in themselves; for example, shops sell goods. The spaces about the buildings have the function of providing the setting in which buildings and groups of buildings can be appreciated. The spaces also have functions in the same way that shops do, particularly pedestrian and vehicular movement and parking

---

1. Land behind traditional built-up frontages.

("Access" on p. 147). Some open-space functions are important but relatively rare, for example, market trading, pomp, ceremony and celebration.

More important are territoriality and social interaction, including play and leisure. The urge to claim territory is a basic animal trait. Legal ownership is one expression of this; familiarity, use and overlooking are others. "Neighbourhood" and "village" attachment engender weaker feelings of territoriality. Territorial associations of residents or retailers are organizational expressions that embrace buildings and space. The recently created town centre management schemes are in the same category. Buildings and spaces are designed to foster this instinct. The private ownership and control of space promotes self-esteem and care for spaces and buildings. Public ownership and control promote corporate care. Environmental problems such as unchecked vandalism and lack of care arise where there is lack of spatial clarity as to who "owns" what and when the level of commitment to territory is low. In practice, development control has very little influence on the quality of the environment once it has been developed, other than through the enforcement of continuing planning conditions. Relatively trivial but important matters such as painting and the erection of fences are permitted development. Or the problem is in other hands, such as dealing with litter and graffiti. It is important therefore at the development control stage to get the design right. Front gardens of houses, or the forecourts of shops and factories, are clearly private. Public open space is clearly public and is maintained by public authorities. But some spaces are semi-public, such as open space in residential areas and factory estates (see Fig. 6.2 Bridger "SLOAP"). Clear definition of territory depends on how well the entrance, whether vehicular or pedestrian, is defined (GLC 1983: 55). Steps, gates, doors, portals, bollards, arches, clear change in floorscape, signage, narrowing roads and paths, changes in gardens and landscape, and semipublic arrival spaces help to define entrances or thresholds. Territoriality is also defined by enclosure. Private and semi-private spaces, such as residential and factory cul-de-sacs with the possibility of surveillance by occupiers, are enclosed by buildings, planting and "means of enclosure". Walls, hedges, close-board fencing, railings, chainlink and wire fencing are all "means of enclosure". They define territory and may provide privacy and security. But depending on height and opacity they may obstruct sightlines at junctions, be overbearing because of their height, hide miscreants and be ugly if made of materials inappropriate to the setting. The erection of means of enclosure is often permitted development under the GPDO, Schedule 2, Part 2, Minor Development (DoE 1995k).

Roofscape is a topic lying between design and external appearance. In the context of development control roofscape or skyline is important in two ways: highbuildings policy and infill. High buildings may be a blessing or a curse. In certain sensitive towns – Oxford, Edinburgh and London for example – skylines are a particular attraction. In Oxford the delicate pattern of spires and domes, in Edinburgh the Old Town dominated by the castle, and in the City of London the prominent position of St Paul's Cathedral viewed from the surrounding hills, demand that proposed high buildings be subject to restrictive control (DoE 1991d). This necessarily influences the siting and design of proposals in and near sensitive areas. On the other hand, high buildings can be used to advantage in town centres to mark their presence, where otherwise it would not be visible from a distance, for example the Brunel Centre in Swindon. Where infill is proposed, it is accepted practice to use similar materials, for example red tiles, with similar roof forms, for example gables to the street at a similar height from the ground, say two or three storeys.

Development control and crime

Reported crime and the fear of crime has greatly increased in the last decades of the twentieth century (Central Statistical Office 1996b: table 9.3). Some are against the person, many are against property. Crime prevention is a material consideration in development control. Circular 5/94, *Planning out crime* (DOE 1994b), is the principal guidance, which stresses that development control solutions to the problems of crime are essentially local (ibid.: 1). The Circular argues that the causes of crime are complex, but desolate surroundings foster hostility, and attractive environments may discourage anti-social behaviour. Although crime prevention involves landscaping and access considerations, it is conveniently dealt with here.

The Circular makes some over-arching points (ibid.: 2–3). Security and crime considerations are best dealt with early on in the design stages of an application. LPAs are advised to consult with local police **architectural liaison officers** where there is an opportunity to reduce crime. If these opportunities are not taken, then the possibility of incorporating appropriate design features may be lost. Two themes run through all aspects of coping with crime: prevention and detection.

As for siting and location, the following are advised: mixed uses, such as residential and commercial, or mixed house types, to ensure that the property is surveyed throughout the day. The LOTS initiative ("living over the shop") facilitates this in shopping areas where the upper storeys of shops have become disused. The provision of diversionary sport, recreation and leisure facilities for young people is to be encouraged through development plans. The Circular draws attention to "trouble spots", but is coy about specifying what and where they are (ibid.: 4). On the other hand, it does advocate area-wide strategic approaches, for example ensuring that security measures respect the character of conservation areas and that housing developments are mixed, small in scale and diverse with local amenities, rather than monolithic and lacking in amenities. It is argued that one of the main reasons why people shun town centre locations at night (ibid.: 3) is fear about safety, and one of the main reasons for that fear is the fact that very few people are about. The Circular argues that LPAs should encourage a wide mix of uses to foster lively and welcoming environments and to discourage fortress-like security structures. Increased opportunities for mixed uses will increase the opportunity to see what is going on (passive surveillance). Readers should be aware of the promotion of the "24 hour" or "night economy" in this context and of town centre management schemes that seek to integrate all town centre concerns, including security and development control.

As for design, the key concept is defensible space. Access ways and buildings should be so laid out that occupants of surrounding buildings overlook them, so that criminals feel under constant surveillance and the "ownership" of property is clear. Vehicle parking, play space and waste storage should be as close as possible to the buildings to which they relate, not only to minimize fetching and carrying distances but to facilitate surveillance. The external appearance of a development is affected by security considerations. The Circular draws attention to security shutters (ibid.: 6) and closed circuit television equipment (CCTV) (ibid.: 9). External security shutters on shops, offices and houses present a forbidding fortress-like appearance and in the case of shops present dead frontage disliked by customers and traders alike; they detract from environmental quality. As they materially alter the external appearance of buildings, planning permission may be necessary for their installation. Less intrusive, more open grille shutters inside buildings may circumvent this problem. Also, with regard to shops it is suggested that reinforced but appropriately clad stall-risers and laminated glass may be a protection against theft (ibid.: 10). CCTV helps deter and detect crime. Although equipment may materially alter the external appearance of buildings, it normally has permitted development rights (see Ch. 4) and needs no planning permission.

Applying the need for surveillance to access matters, the following are recommended (ibid.: 5). Well intentioned segregation for pedestrians and cyclists should not lead to over-isolation, especially at night. Unrestricted rear access to premises is best avoided. Alleyways and subways should be direct, wide, clear of hiding places and well lit. Carparking areas can be especially crime-prone. Potential problems can be avoided by good lighting, by CCTV and staff surveillance, and by limiting the number of access points.

Landscaping – embracing planting, street furniture and means of enclosure – is frequently permitted development, although much depends on the circumstances (Ch. 4). The Circular (ibid.: 5, 7, 11) advises landscape schemes that avoid creating hidden areas, where crime is easier to commit, and the use of thorny plant species as a deterrent to intruders. Kerbside bollards and railings near shops may deter some types of crime. Installing security lighting needs to strike a balance between security and light pollution of neighbouring properties. Surprisingly, the Circular makes virtually no mention of means of enclosure, their design or siting in the context of enhancing the security of development. Finally, special care needs to be taken where listed buildings and conservation areas are involved.

However, design is only one aspect of crime prevention. Social and economic policies related to the family, education, housing and economic polarization may be much more important (Osborn & Shaftoe 1995: 31).

External appearance

Aesthetics and development control

Town planning as a regulatory activity is judged very much by what the public see built. Development is public art. External appearance is a major material consideration in development control decisions and is a reserved matter specifically highlighted in the GDPO. Operations that "materially affect the external appearance of the building" are one of those tests that distinguish those works to a building that constitute development from those that do not (Millichap 1996: 20). When planning permission is granted, imposed conditions frequently relate to matters of appearance, particularly the use of building materials such as stone or brick. Some of our key planning tools, such as conservation areas, listing of buildings, areas of outstanding natural beauty, national parks and green belts, are a dominant theme. They have wide public support.

Delafons (1994: 85, 86) made the telling point that standard planning law books do not contain index entries on design and aesthetics. Apparently there are no classic legal judgements in British law relating to this aspect of planning. Perhaps problems are settled at LPA level before they get to the courts. Yet the DoE has issued design guidance for many years. Aesthetic control is closely associated with the word amenity, the quality of pleasantness. When neighbours and consultees are alerted to the possibility of new development, they are likely to be concerned more with amenity than with refined aesthetic considerations. Although buildings are public art, it is doubtful whether we look on them as works of art other than in unusual circumstances such as places of worship, great houses or art galleries. Design, aesthetics and amenity are ambiguous, elusive but connected concepts. Aesthetics is concerned with beauty: both man-made buildings and the works of nature can be beautiful. But are these aesthetic qualities objective or subjective? Are developments beautiful or ugly independently of the minds of those who make development control decisions? Development control is a rational process, but are aesthetic judgements more to do with emotional and spiritual appeal? What is good taste and bad taste? Are architectural styles merely a matter of fad or fashion? Are there basic objective rules that we can apply to aesthetic judgements or are aesthetic judgements subjective? And what do we mean by quality in the environment? Part of the difficulty with aesthetic control springs from the differences of perception and interests of the general public and planners or others with design training (Hubbard 1994: 271–87). When building materials and plants are skilfully arranged, they become something more than say just houses and trees. They give aesthetic pleasure.

In the practical context of development control we are dealing with difficult subject areas in which problems may never be resolved to the satisfaction of the parties. Is the purpose of development control merely to prevent harm to an area or is it to preserve and/or enhance? Will external appearance be enhanced by bureaucratic rules and regulations imposed by the state or by letting patrons, architects and craftsmen have free rein?

141

Much of the charm of older development lies in local materials used by local people in well defined localities. Modern development has been built by national companies transporting material over some distances. Local occupiers are then left to make anywhere into somewhere (Hillman 1990: 21). Hillman's book, which summarizes many of these arguments, noticeably has no site plans, elevations or photographs.

It is not possible to teach design in a book of this nature. But the reader can be alerted to the elements of design under discussion in the context of development control.

Terms and concerns

At a basic level it is useful to be conversant with the main concerns and terms used. Bridger (1987: 68 ff) usefully divided terms into forms in buildings, buildings and space, and other matters, such as subjective reaction to design. The terms used to describe building forms are listed in Figure 6.1, and buildings in space in Figure 6.2, which are more appropriate to the section on design as a major component of development control. Regrettably, it is not possible to give a full explanation of the figures. It is possible however to see how the concepts might be practically applied in the solution of aesthetic problems involved in roof extensions in houses. Both Dijksman (1992: 52 ff) and Bridger (1987: 56) deal with this aesthetic problem.

Dijksman suggested that a roof extension of whatever kind will alter the existing roofline to some extent. The knack is to minimize visual impact. Extensions facing away from the street are likely to have less impact than those facing it. Smaller, dormer windows have less impact than large box-like ones. Extensions should not be above the existing ridgeline, nor should they normally extend immediately vertically upwards above the main front wall of the building, altering the pattern of eaves in the street. Where a dormer is inserted in a roof, as a guideline it should represent less then half the distance between the eaves and the ridgeline. The slope of the roof of the dormer should reflect the slopes of the adjacent roof. Where a flat-roof dormer window is used to gain interior floorspace, it is best facing the rear, at least 1 m from the eaves and 30 cm from the adjacent property. The use of dark or matching colours also reduces impact.

Bridger (1987: 92) has provided some useful practical observations for those involved in aesthetic decisions in development control. As there is no statutory requirement for plans to be drawn up by a trained designer, they can be quite poor. Many minor applications are submitted by those without formal training. Councillors not used to dealing with plans may not fully understand them. Two-dimensional plans can falsify three-dimensional effects: house roof extensions may appear more recessive when built. Artists' aerial perspectives may help, but they are quite unlike the normal view from the street: few normally have a bird's-eye view except birds. Punter (1985: 147) in his study of Reading showed that proposals shown in artists' sketches could considerably mislead those charged with making decisions. Computer-based visualization may be a solution to the problem of seeing how proposals might appear when built (Hall 1995: 16–17). The colour and texture of building materials are difficult to represent accurately and, in drawings, give an impression of homogeneity that in fact may not exist. Sample materials may be submitted with applications. Scaled-down models of proposed development are rather like toys, so one needs to beware of being misled.

Aesthetic guidance

Formal aesthetic (design) guidance is given in two main sources, Circular 22/80, *Development control – policy and practice* (paras 18 to 21, now cancelled; DoE 1980) and in PPG1, *General policy and principles* (DoE 1992c: annex). Supplementary professional guidance is given in an accord between the RIBA and the RTPI (Hutchinson & Fidler 1991: 5). These documents highlight the incipient conflict of views between central government, which is trying to give an overall steer to development, lay councillors who make key decisions, architects who advise developers, and planners who advise councillors. Many applications are submitted without professional advice.

Figure 6.3 shows the advice. The 1992 DoE advice largely follows the RTPI/RIBA accord of 1991. The 1980 Circular suggested that "aesthetics is an extremely subjective matter": the 1992 advice is that "aesthetic judgements are to some extent subjective". However, common elements relate to scale, context, character and the importance of professional advice. Furthermore, it was advised that LPAs should not normally be concerned with the details of building design; **design guides** and development plans were available as guidance for applicants and warnings were given to LPAs about imposing their tastes. The 1980 guidance did not specifically encourage high standards of design: it asked the LPA to reject poor designs. Later guidance stresses high quality. Earlier guidance had a market emphasis – developers should not be asked to adopt designs unpopular with customers – and the implied threat that LPAs would be brought into line at appeal and have costs awarded against them. Both publications mention the importance of aesthetic control in special areas such as national parks; presumably other areas, arguably in need of higher environmental standards than at present, do not warrant special treatment. The need for the RIBA/RTPI accord and for professional advisers lies in the clashes of the professional views of individual planners and architects, in informal consultations prior to the submission of formal planning applications. Professional architects undergo a five-year academic course with a design stress, undergraduate planners four years with a more modest design content. Clashes come when they disagree. The guidance suggests not unreasonably that architects' views should hold sway particularly on details. It should be borne in mind that many applications are submitted by those without design training.

A study by Building Design Partnership (1990: 41) found that, taken overall,

Figure 6.1 Forms in buildings and landscaping (Bridger 1987: 70 ff; Bell 1993, augmented).

Point
A point marks a position in space. Point features may be assertions of power or ownership, for example a distant spire.

Lines
Forms start with lines. Lines in buildings are modified by direction. Vertical lines embody more "force" than horizontal lines because they have to overcome the perception of gravity. Curved lines have intrinsic liveliness. Lines can be part of the texture of materials, such as courses of brickwork. Vertical lines stress height: horizontal lines emphasize width.

Planes
Lines in two dimensions create planes. Fronts of buildings are façades. Façadism stresses frontage appearance. The proportion of a building is partly the relationship of horizontal to vertical surfaces. A squat building is one of low height in relation to its width. Planes include water surfaces, lines of trees and the Earth itself.

Forms
Forms are typically cubes, shafts, cylinders, rectangular blocks, pyramids, spheres, etc. Each has its own quality; for example, pyramids incorporate direction while cubes appear as static. Forms may be solid as with buildings or open as with the spaces between buildings.

Mass
Mass conveys a sense of volume. Square buildings appear larger than rectangular buildings of the same volume. Spheres and cylinders do not combine easily with other forms but cylinders can be a focus and add strength to a corner.

Time
Time brings about perceptual changes in values, fashion and design in buildings and brings seasonal changes in landscape.

Light
Light displays the surface modelling of buildings. Modelling varies with cultural and regional differences. Light is an important element in itself: it emphasizes roofscape and streetscape character.

Colour
Colour is a subdivision of light and an attribute of building materials and planting. It creates patterns, variety, contrast and harmony and has emotional and cultural connotations. Painting is usually permitted development.

Materials
Building materials embody colour, texture and pattern. Texture is small-scale surface modelling (e.g. smooth glass and rough stone). Patterns such as brickwork lend cohesion to development.

Proportion
Proportion is a matter of the relationship of the component parts of a building to the building or building frontages to the street as a whole. It applies also to landscape elements. Classical proportions are pleasing because they embody order. Proportion is closely related to scale. Fenestration is the pattern and proportion of windows and the proportion of glass to wall.

Human scale
Building scale is related to human form. Consider – human:cottage:cathedral. People are endeared by the small scale but awed by the large.

Scale
Buildings are related to each other and to the landscape. A power station in a plain is different in scale from the same one in the hills.

Genius loci
Genius loci, the spirit of the place, refers to the unique quality that one place has over another, with which we often identify as individuals.

Figure 6.2 Buildings in space (Bridger 1987: 78 ff, augmented).

Part I Glossary

Space between buildings Buildings depend for their impact on their relationships to the surrounding space. Consider a residential square or a shopping street. Floorscape, paving or grass, affects the quality of the space. Gaps between buildings and infill affect feelings of spaciousness. Building density and plot ratio are cognate concepts. Increasing floorspace in proportion to site area, that is plot ratio, increases density and may result in loss of space about buildings.

SLOAP Space left over after planning. Spaces left as a by-product of building without thought to landscaping, etc.

Roofscape The pattern that roofs form on the skyline. It may be large scale, e.g. Edinburgh Old Town, or small scale in a suburban street. Roofscape gives character to a place and involves gables, chimneys, spires, dormer windows, etc. and materials such as slate and clay tiles.

Townscape Townscape and streetscape are to town as landscape is to countryside. It may be picturesque as in many traditional villages or grand as in classical Bath and Edinburgh.

Floorscape Surface treatment of external spaces. It may be hard or soft and may be patterned and coloured with a variety of textures. Grass and other plants are the main elements of soft landscape.

Serial vision Cumulative and sequential visual experience as one travels through the space between buildings often with a sense of anticipation.

Privacy Personal desire not to be overlooked, especially in residential environments. It contrasts with personal desire to have an outlook or view.

Territoriality Individual instinct to experience "ownership" or control over territory close by. When designers neglect this instinct, territory may be neglected. It is important to have clear boundaries to avoid disputes. Territoriality is related to surveillance.

Continuity Historical and cultural continuity considers what we know about our environment, as much as what we see, e.g. the role of famous people there. More simply we like most what we are familiar with.

Legibility The presence of factors which enable us to know physically and mentally where we are and what we are looking at. The use of a disused church as a warehouse sends out a mixed message in this context.

Amenity The quality of pleasantness. It includes the presence of trees, a spacious view, as well as the absence of noise, ugliness, etc.

View Instinctively we enjoy outlook or view, especially if it is pleasant. Development control activity may preserve views but it is often difficult to prevent loss of view.

Trees Best preserved as an amenity. Age, disease and danger may make trees difficult to keep.

Part II Development context

Ribbon development Buildings fronting main roads in regular fashion. Thought to be bad practice because of many dangerous accesses, excessive length of piped, etc. services.

Linear development Buildings fronting streets in irregular patterns particularly in old villages. Bends in roads give sense of containment. Such development is thought worthy of protection.

Infill development Normally acceptable development in vacant plots on otherwise built up frontages.

Rounding off Completion of settlement, e.g. building on land within an envelope defining it and separating it from open country.

Backland development Building land behind existing frontages. It is undesirable if it adversely affects privacy and servicing.

Accessibility Access to buildings can involve visually dominant roads, visibility splays and pavements. Joint use surfaces and narrower road widths can circumvent this dominance.

Listed buildings Buildings especially listed for their intrinsic qualities. Alterations and settings need to be strictly controlled visually. Buildings may be listed for their group value.

Conservation areas Areas of architectural and historic interest in which detailed design changes are subject to closer scrutiny than usual.

Vernacular buildings Buildings using local materials in traditional styles usually without assistance from trained designers. Neovernacular building takes old styles and reworks them in new ways, possibly using new forms of construction.

Figure 6.3 RTPI/RIBA Common policy on design and PPG1 Annex – design considerations – reformulated to bring out main points (Hutchinson & Fidler 1991: 5; DoE 1992c: annex).

1. For those making decisions on planning applications, material considerations are:
   - the appearance of the proposed development and its relationship to its surroundings.
   This applies to:
   - those who determine applications and those who determine appeals.
2. Good design should be the aim of all involved in the development process but it is primarily the responsibility of designers and their clients. (However)
   - applicants and LPAS
   should recognize the benefits of skilled advisers [and advice of architects] and should recognize the benefits of encouraging high design standards.
3. LPAs should reject obviously poor designs [which are out of scale or character with their surroundings].
   - Aesthetic judgements are to some extent subjective and (therefore)
   - LPAs should not impose their taste on applicants simply because they believe it to be superior. (Nor should)
   - LPAs interfere with [PPG1 seek to control] the detailed design of buildings [unless the sensitive character of the setting justifies it], *especially where applicants can demonstrate that the building was designed by an architect for the particular site.* (Moreover) [A2] in considering a development proposal LPAs should recognize the design skills and advice of architects and
   - be closely guided by their own professionally qualified advisers
   - [although the final decision remains that of the LPA itself].
4. Applicants for planning permission should always demonstrate that they have considered the wider setting of buildings.
   - New developments should respect but not necessarily mimic the character of their surroundings.
   - Particular weight should be given to the impact of development on existing buildings and the landscape in environmentally sensitive areas such as national parks, AONBs and conservation areas [where the scale of new development and the use of appropriate building materials will often be particularly important].
5. The appearance and treatment of the spaces between and around buildings is also of great importance.
   - Where these form part of the application site, the landscape design – whether hard or soft – will often be of comparable importance to the design of buildings and
   - should likewise be the subject of consideration, attention and expert advice.
   - [The aim should be for any development to result in a benefit in environmental and landscape terms.]
6. Development plans and guidance for particular areas and sites should provide applicants with clear indications of the LPA's design expectations.
   - Guidance should avoid excessive prescription and detail and
   - concentrate on broad matters of scale, density, height, massing, layout, landscape and access.
   - It should focus on encouraging good design, rather than stifling experiment, originality or initiative.
   - Indeed, the design qualities of an exceptional scheme and its special contribution to the townscape may justify departing from LPA design guidance.
7. LPAs should encourage applicants to consult them before formulating development proposals.
   - LPAs' consideration of proposals will be assisted if applicants provide appropriate illustrative material to show their proposals in context.
   - It may be helpful for the applicant to submit a short written statement setting out the design principles involved.

Key ( ) parentheses, added by author
     [ ] square brackets, material added to RTPI/RIBA Common Policy in PPG1 Annex
     italic RTPI/RIBA material not in PPG1 Annex

a very large proportion of planning applications were submitted by those with limited design experience. Registered architects were found in a majority of LPAs surveyed in 1985, only to be involved in major applications. In surveying LPA staff in England and Wales, it was found that about half the staff in development control sections were professionally qualified (presumably the others were clerical and technical support staff); of these 80 per cent were planners but only 4 per cent were architects (ibid.). What is surprising is that there was no suggestion in their study that applications should be drawn up only by those with specified design qualifications, such as registered architects or planners, as a way of improving design in the environment.

None of the guidance gives practical examples nor refers to any text where such guidance can be found. Punter described DOE views as "agnostic" (Punter 1990b: 14).

In this context, Raine (1995: 2) drew attention to the role of inspectors at appeal. As a professional advocate he was involved in cases where competent designers argued cogent cases why they were right and their opposite numbers wrong. In his view, the inspector needed to ascertain the design constraints of the site and to ensure that design was in accordance with established principles. But what then if both schemes passed these tests? Would the inspector substitute his own artistic preferences?

Access

Land use generates traffic. Access to sites is a key issue in development control. As far as road access is concerned, the main issues are strategic considerations, access to the site and within the site, and parking. Access may be vehicular or pedestrian. The special aspects of development involving direct water, air or rail access will not be dealt with: concern will be concentrated on road access. PPG13, *Transport* (DOE 1994c), is the main central government guidance. It is expanded on in *PPG13, A guide to better practice* (DOE & Department of Transport 1995).

Strategic considerations

Although development control usually deals with relatively small-scale individual site matters, the cumulative effect of many decisions affects traffic movement patterns. Decisions therefore should be made within a wide strategic framework. Many of the problems spring from the extremely rapid growth in road use in the last quarter of the twentieth century. The number of vehicle kilometres driven in Great Britain increased from 303 billion per year in 1984 to 422 billion per year in 1994, that is, 39 per cent (Central Statistical Office 1996a: 221). The number of dwellings in the UK increased from 21.6 million in 1981 to 24.3 million in 1994, an increase of 12 per cent (Central Statistical Office 1996b: 176).

147

The need to manage demand springs from the need to have an efficient economy while fostering sustainable development and the protection of the habitat, but at the same time reducing congestion and delay and noxious vehicle emissions. New and dispersed patterns of development and economic growth stimulate the demand for transport, and new transport infrastructure provides the opportunity for new development. Infrastructural development in itself can have an adverse effect on the landscape and townscape. Land-use policies in development plans are therefore aimed at promoting acceptable alternatives to the private car by promoting walking, cycling and public transport, and by reducing the need to make journeys by concentrating development in established centres. Limiting parking provision on and off the street will discourage car use.

PPG13 sets out advice on location strategies. For housing, it suggests the maximum amount of housing should be allocated to towns of market town size and above, so that all service amenities would be near at hand, with an emphasis on redeveloping **brownfield** sites. If this is not possible, then housing is best located near rail and other public transport. Small new settlements are to be avoided. At local level, maintaining and increasing housing densities are suggested. Juxtaposition of mixed uses is advocated. As for employment, concentration in urban areas is to be encouraged to reduce private car dependence. Freight transport should be encouraged to use rail and water: warehousing should be located close to these and with access to the trunk road network. Retailing should be concentrated in existing centres to maintain its vitality; the sporadic siting of comparison goods shops along radials is to be avoided. Leisure facilities constitute the fastest area of traffic growth and, like shops, should be concentrated in existing centres served by public transport.

Facilities for further and higher education and similar establishments should be located where they are well served by public transport, but lower-level facilities need to be in residential areas where they can be reached on foot or by bicycle. As a generality, a wide range of facilities should be made available in neighbourhoods.

PPG13 opines that location strategies in development plans must be accompanied by transport strategies, especially increasing modal choice, other than the car, thus increasing the attractiveness of urban facilities as against peripheral ones. As the availability of carparking is a major determinant of travel mode, parking standards should be set at minimum levels: carparking charges (and the enforcement of restrictions) can be used to reduce commuting. LPAs should consider "commuted payments" from developers for the promotion of walking, cycling and public transport, rather than the provision of parking. As very many journeys are short and/or on foot, every effort should be made to provide cycling and pedestrian facilities, especially by vehicular separation. Advice is given on the encouragement of public transport and park-and-ride schemes.

Road building needs planning permission (DoE 1994c: para. 5.14, 5.26). Road building should aim to support location policies, improve the environment and reduce accidents. In granting planning permission, LPAs should ensure that proposed routes and disused transport routes are not unnecessarily severed by new development. New and improved roads enhance the development potential of sites; site development will throw fresh traffic onto the road network. New roads may also lead to the relocation of traffic and reduce it.

Advice is given (ibid.: paras 5–15, annex B) on new roads *qua* development, particularly the need to avoid specially designated areas such as SSSIs, landscape preservation and enhancement through screening, the need to avoid good quality agricultural land and farm severance, the disruption of drainage and sterilization of mineral deposits. Further considerations are "need", alternative routes, the disposal of spoil and the re-use of suitable waste for road building. Planning applications for roads may be accompanied by formal environmental assessments. Consultations are necessary with local highway authorities when new accesses are opened up into existing roads, and with the Department of Transport if a trunk road is involved or development is within 67 m of the centre of a trunk road. Safety and extra traffic generation are the main concerns. A 5 per cent increase in traffic flow on a trunk road as a result of a development proposal is regarded as material in the context of development control.

The road hierarchy and access to the road net

The last section dealt with very broad strategic considerations, but what of access to and from individual sites that have been the subject of planning applications? Without access to the road net, development would be of limited value.

PPG13 (DoE 1994c: para. 5.6) lays down some general principles:

- The purpose of long-distance routes should not be undermined by short trips.
- New development must be "traffic safe".
- Development proposals must take into account their demands on the road network.

Plans and development control should aim to inhibit the use of long-distance routes by short-distance traffic by strictly limiting direct access from sites to trunk roads. The type of access provided should reflect the type of road and traffic involved. PPG13 (annex D) lays down safe visibility splay design standards, which ensure that when drivers emerge from minor roads onto major roads their vision is unobstructed by fences and the like on corner plots. Heavy vehicle generators such as industrial and warehouse estates should be so located on local distributors as to inhibit movement through town centres, residential neighbourhoods and minor rural roads. Traffic management schemes can deny heavy vehicles access to roads unsuitable for them.

Developers' contributions may be used to provide infrastructure to overcome planning objections to a particular development: they are normally provided first before site development starts. Mention may be made at this point of so-called "Grampian conditions". Normally a condition cannot be imposed on the grant of planning permission related to land outside the applicant's control. However, it is possible for the LPA to grant planning permission on condition that development

149

may not start until some obstacle such as highway access has been overcome. Such conditions are necessary to facilitate safe access to the development, for example, by the construction of a roundabout, without which the development would have been refused.

Fundamental to traffic planning is the concept of the road hierarchy. Roads are generally designed for the purposes for which they are required, for example long-distance traffic on motorways and pedestrianized streets for shoppers. Roads not only carry traffic but also are the site of piped services and form part of the space about buildings which acts as a setting for the buildings themselves. Conflicts arise as a result of roads being multifunctional, for example the problem of personal injury, visual intrusion of vehicles in sensitive environments, and noise and atmospheric pollution everywhere. Designing roads is a balancing act between traffic capacity, the environment, speed, safety and user comfort for the road in question (IHT 1987: 31).

Roads are arranged in a hierarchy of size and capacity by primary function from the pedestrian ways to motorways. The hierarchy is shown in Table 6.1. The benefits of the hierarchy are that roads can be designed to suit their prime function:

- Activities related to frontages can be given adequate space (e.g. pedestrianized shopping streets).
- Traffic on long-distance roads can be speeded up by excluding local turning movements (e.g. by minimizing the number of junctions and access points).
- Road capacity can be increased.
- Accidents can be reduced (e.g. by excluding pedestrians from primary routes).
- Environmental amenity can be improved by routing traffic around "environmental areas" such as housing, town centres and industrial estates which may not have routes through them.
- The rate of return on new investment designed to improve the traffic flow, save accidents and reduce intrusion can be increased by concentrating traffic onto a few selected corridors (ibid. 1987: 32).

The advantage of the hierarchy from a development control point of view is that the need for access from a plot to the network can be judged in terms of it. To give two extreme examples: a new house is likely to be served by an access road, rather than a district distributor road and an international airport may have direct access to the motorway network. For historical reasons, matters are not clear cut. Should one allow housing infill along a heavily trafficked district distributor road already lined with houses with direct access? The hierarchy is usually more clearly defined in large urban areas than in small settlements.

Table 6.1 The hierarchical classification of urban roads based on function (IHT 1987: tables 5.1 and 5.2, simplified).

	Pedestrian streets	Access roads	Local distributors	District distributors	Primary distributors
Main activities	Walking Meeting Trading	Walking Vehicle access to plots Slow traffic	Vehicles near ends of journeys	Medium-distance traffic Public transport Local through traffic	Fast long-distance traffic No frontage access
Pedestrian movement	Free Main activity	Crossing at random		Controlled crossings	Minimum safety emphasis Segregation
Stationary vehicles	Service and emergency only	Some	Considerable	Some	None
Heavy goods traffic	Servicing only	Servicing only	Minimum through trips	Minimum through trips	Suitable for all HGV trips
Vehicular access to property	Very limited	Main activity	Some	Little	Nil, apart from sites of national importance
Local traffic movements	Nil	Nil	Main activity	Some	Very little
Through-traffic	Nil	Nil	Nil	Main role	Main role
Speed	Less than 5 mph	Less than 20 mph	30 mph limit	30/40 mph limit	More than 40 mph
Parking	Ban except for loading	Limited	Limited	Severely limited	Total ban

Traffic generation and land uses

The amount of traffic a development proposal is likely to generate is a material consideration in development control. Relating potential traffic generation to road capacity is a matter of calculation and ultimately judgement. Probably the most detailed studies of traffic generation by different types of land use, now dated, were carried out by the Greater London Council (GLC 1985) (see Fig. 6.4 and Table 6.2) The difficulties of estimating traffic generation from development can be appreciated by considering the following:

- Many permitted development changes such as light industry to offices within the B1 Class result in different traffic outcomes.
- Road traffic has increased greatly since the mid-1980s, although the amount of new development in relation to the stock has been modest.

Table 6.2 Traffic generation by a selection of different land uses in different locations in London and elsewhere.

Type of retail outlet	Number of goods trips generated
Food retailer (excl. supermarkets)	4.0 trips per day per 100m² GFA
Department store	0.36 trips per day per 100m² GFA
Clothes/shoes	1 trip per day per shop

(Most arrivals and departures between 0900 and 1300 hours)

Percentage modal split of shopper group trips to superstores/hypermarkets

Location/type	Car	Bus	Walk	Other
Out-of-town	80–90	8–4	10–5	2–1
Suburban	80	5	14	1
District centre	50–60	13–10	35–28	2
Town centre	40–50	25–20	25–20	6–5

(Peak time for arrivals and departures on Friday 1700–2000+ hours)

Industrial premises, work trips per person per day per 100m² GFA* by employment density class

Employment class	Range
Very high, e.g. electronics	5.5–7.8
High, e.g. pharmaceuticals	4.1–4.4
Medium, e.g. vehicles	3.4–3.7
Low, e.g. textiles	2.6–3.1
Very low, e.g. bricks	1.4–2.3

(Arrivals peak 0700 to 0900 hours and departures peak 1600 to 1800 hours)

Total person trips per day, offices per 100m² GFA, numbers and modal split with free on-street parking in minor roads, outer London locations

Numbers of person trips per day 100m² GFA
13.8

Modal split for offices with free on-street parking in minor roads
Car driver/passenger	38.5%
Bus	13.0%
Tube/rail	8.0%
Walk	39.1%
Other	balance

*GFA = gross floor area
(GLC 1985: tables 2.1, 2.3, 2.4, 3.1, 5.4; based on earlier studies but still quoted in PPG13, *A guide to better practice* (DoE & Department of Transport 1995: 89))

- The amount of traffic on roads will depend on the availability of alternatives for travellers, for example road to rail, public to private, cycle to private car.
- Traffic generation of specific land uses depends on their location: car-borne shopping in the suburbs is greater than in city centres as a proportion of shopping trips.
- The construction of roads themselves induces traffic which might otherwise not have flowed.
- Car ownership rates depend largely on personal incomes, which have been rising.

Figure 6.4   Examples of trip generation by different land uses (IHT 1994: Appendix based on TRICS data and JMP Consultants 1992). GFA = gross floor area.

Food superstore 2000–8000 m²
Highest daily trip rate Saturdays: 120–160 trips (summed in and out) per 100 m² GFA
Peak trip rate: 11% of daily rate
Mode: 95% by car
Average trip length: usually under 10 minutes

Offices
Daily trip rates: weekday 10–15 trips (summed in and out) per 100 m² GFA
Peak trip rates: 33% of daily traffic arrives 0800–0900 hours
Mode: unless very restricted site probably greater than 85% by car
Average trip length: about 25 minutes

Industry
Daily trip rate: 5–15 trips (summed in and out) per 100 m² GFA
Peak trip rate: 0830–0930 hours with possibly 60% arriving within half an hour
Mode: highly variable
Average trip length: about 20 minutes for highly skilled operatives

Residential, all housing types
Daily trip rate: 7 to 9 trips per household (summed in and out)
Peak trip rate: 0800–0900 and 1700–1800 each with 14% of daily flow

Road network capacity

Quite separate from the traffic generation characteristics of land uses is the capacity that road networks have to cope with flows. Road capacity can be considered under three headings: physical, economic and environmental. The physical capacity of a road is the number of vehicles it can carry in a day or an hour. It is not a fixed unique quantity but may well depend on the weather or on drivers' familiarity with the route, for example in holiday areas. The capacity of a road is, in practice, usually determined by the vehicle throughput of the junctions along it (IHT 1987: 39). Capacity is dependent on:

- the physical characteristics of the road, for example width and alignment
- the composition of the traffic, especially vehicles' performance capabilities
- operating conditions, for example the number of parked cars
- speed, in that, as speeds rise, the distance between vehicles increases for safety reasons and capacity declines.

For design purposes it is normal to determine the required design speed in order to provide a certain "quality of service". "The economic capacity of a road is the traffic flow at which the investment cost of providing new road capacity is just equal to the present value of the net benefits to traffic that the investment would achieve" (ibid.: 39). Put crudely, do you go for a cheap improvement now, knowing that congestion will occur sooner rather than later, or do you pay more now and postpone congestion? However, it is not now considered acceptable that continued traffic growth should necessarily be catered for. The two solutions give different economic capacities. Finally, the environmental capacity of a road is its ability to absorb moving and parked vehicles without sacrificing safety, without excessive noise and without excessive visual intrusion. Typically an access road or local distributor will have an environmental capacity of 300–600 vehicles per hour, which is substantially below its physical capacity (ibid.: 40). Environmental conditions are improved by speed and other vehicle restrictions. An indication of design flows for roads is given in Table 6.3.

Table 6.3 Some examples of design flows for two-way urban roads. Peak hourly flow vehicles per hour (IHT 1987: table 36.1).

Road type	Two-lane, both directions of flow, width 7.3m	Four-lane, one direction of flow, width 13.5m

All-purpose road with:
  no frontage crossings
  no standing vehicles
  negligible cross traffic
	2000	2800

All-purpose road with:
  frontage development
  side roads, bus stops, etc.
  waiting restrictions
	1700	1900

Traffic impact assessment

The two main variables – traffic generation by land use and road capacity – can be drawn together in practice by the use of traffic models, which help to establish the traffic consequences of new development. These models are beyond the scope of this book. Financial, social and environmental constraints have now made society rethink the whole basis of private car use and public transport as indicated above.

However, LPAs are still faced with the problem of relating road capacity to major proposals such as superstores, major housing estates, offices, factory estates and leisure facilities. The possibilities of major developments are usually signalled in development plans, so that land use can be related to the road network at an early stage. When a major application is made, the LPA and the developer need to investigate the highway and traffic implications. The data are derived inter alia from traffic censuses, studies of existing developments and the details given in the application itself (see Table 2.1). A summary of requirements is given in Table 6.4. It is recommended (IHT 1994: 5, 6) that a traffic impact assessment be carried out if one or other of the following thresholds is crossed:

- traffic to and from the development is expected to exceed 10 per cent of the two-way flow on the adjoining highway
- traffic to and from the development exceeds 5 per cent of the two-way traffic

Table 6.4 Highway and traffic investigations necessary for major new developments (derived from: IHT 1987: tables 29.1 and 29.2; 1994).

Investigations	Comment
Traffic volumes by mode and time period	Problems of peaking especially for journey to work and journey to shop. Use of public transport, private car, cycling and walking.
Adequacy of the road network	Impact on different parts of the network. Consideration of site access and consequential changes, e.g. cycle tracks, bus stops and roadworks. Development plans for the area.
Site access	The relationship of the internal circulation of site to the wider road network. Deals with road widths, geometry, safety, visibility and possible pedestrian/vehicular segregation. Turning movements. Needs of the disabled.
Internal site layout	Safety, operating efficiency, aesthetic considerations. Prevention of tailback onto the network. Need to separate cars, HGV and pedestrians. Parking for workers, residents, clients and operational use. Signage.
Estimate number of workers, residents, clients, customers, etc.	Related to number of rooms, floorspace, etc. Relationship of people to spaces is very variable for a single type of use.
Identify catchment areas in relationship to the transport net	Where will residents work? Where will customers and workers come from? Competing opportunities. Future traffic growth.
Estimate mode of travel to and from the development – car, bus, etc.	Related to journey time, cost and availability of modes.
Estimate number of trips by time, by mode	Problems of peaking – morning, evening, weekend, etc.

flow on the adjoining highway, where traffic congestion exists or will exist within the assessment period or in other sensitive locations. A sensitive location may be a large quarry in a country area. Other thresholds are given, for example more than 200 houses, $5000\,m^2$ of Class B1 and B2 uses, $1000\,m^2$ of Class A uses, 100 trips in and out in the peak hour and 100 on-site parking places.

With so many variables involved it is ultimately a matter of judgement whether to allow a major development. Planning conditions and agreements often relate to roadworks or traffic management to mitigate effects.

Road layouts

Roads and circulation are the two-dimensional aspects of layout to which design, as a reserved matter, provides the third dimension. Topography is not to be ignored. Siting, as a reserved matter, is the two-dimensional placing of buildings on a site and it implies access to them. Access, siting and design are inseparable.

155

Road layouts (and associated matters) focus attention on the need to make siting and design work in a functional sense distinct from an aesthetic sense. Road layouts are determined in part by the land uses they serve – housing, shops and industrial estates – and in part by the technical characteristics of the vehicles needing access to them. New roads themselves need planning permission if they are built other than as an integral part of a development; they are usually local, district or primary distributors (see Table 6.1). New developments may be modest in scale and use existing local distributor roads; or in larger-scale developments local distributor roads need to be built which then feed into district distributors. Arguably, we have been far too concerned with building road layouts to cope with vehicle mobility and not enough with roads as places that people can enjoy (Hirst 1996b: 4).

In the case of new residential layouts, the great majority of new housing developments in urban areas are relatively small infill and redevelopment sites which already have existing roads on one boundary. Layout is then a matter of getting safe access(es) onto existing roads and siting houses adjacent to the access road in what may be a very constrained site. Siting issues such as daylight and privacy were dealt with in the siting section above. On large less-constrained sites designers have more freedom (IHT 1987: ch. 31). Road layouts play a very important part in creating surroundings that are safe, convenient, nuisance-free, visually attractive and economical to maintain and construct. The most basic road layout expression of these requirements is that there should be adequate visibility splays at junctions, junctions should be T-shape and show priorities clearly (rather than X-shape earlier rectangular grid layouts), as in loop and cul-de-sac layouts to prevent through-traffic should be used, there should be parking within the curtilage of dwellings, and roads and paths should be of adequate width. In many residential contexts, roads that satisfy traffic requirements can be visually intrusive. An important determinant of road widths and the way parking is arranged is the density of development, which is usually expressed in dwellings per hectare (Table 6.5).

Table 6.5 Housing density and its effect on parking layouts (IHT 1987: fig. 31.3).

Dwellings per acre/hectare	Housing type	Parking	Comment
Over 25/60	Flats	Grouped	High density
Up to 25/60	Narrow frontage terraces	Integral and grouped	
Up to 20/50	Medium frontage terraces	Curtilage and grouped	
Up to 16/40	Semi-detached narrow frontages	Curtilage	Middle income
Up to 12/30	Detached narrow frontages	Curtilage	
Up to 8/20	Detached, medium and wide frontages	Curtilage	High income, low density

In new residential developments there are always roads that give access to individual properties. These may include shared surface access roads where vehicles and pedestrians are not separated because traffic flows are so low. This improves visual appearance. Design speeds are less than 20 mph/32 kph. Access roads may have pavements in which services are located. In shared access ways, these may be located in residential frontages.

Normally highway authorities lay down highway standards to which developers build. When development is complete, its roads are adopted and maintained by the public at large.

More detailed guidance on residential areas is to be found in Design Bulletin 32 (DoE & Department of Transport 1992). Carriageway widths are dependent on the number of houses served, taking cars parked on the carriageway into account. Footways, where provided, are normally 2 m wide. Speed control can be facilitated by limiting the length of straight stretches of road or by building in traffic-calming devices. It is advisable to allow a space 6 m × 3.2 m for parking within the curtilage of dwellings. It is vital to have clear sightlines at junctions. The faster the priority road the longer the horizontal visibility splay (vertical clearance should be 1.05 m above the ground; see Table 6.6 for some of the variables involved). In addition, there should be consideration of large emergency vehicles (maximum distance from dwellings 45 m), bin-carrying distances (maximum 25 m), cycle routes, proximity to bus routes (maximum five minutes walk). Vehicle

Table 6.6 Some road layout variables in housing development (IHT 1987, DoE & Department of Transport 1992).

Carriageway widths and numbers of houses served			
	Around	Around	Up to around
Dwellings served	50–500	25–50	25
Carriageway width (m)	5.5	4.8	4.1
Minimum centre line radius (m)	30	20	10

Design speeds for residential access		
	Design speed well below	Unrestrained road lengths not greater than
Shared surfaces	20 mph	40 m
Minor access roads	20 mph	60 m
Major access roads	30 mph	80–120 m

Footway widths	
Less than 50 houses	possibly shared surface
More than 50 houses	2 metres

"Eye heights" to be safeguarded in landscaping, etc.	
Commercial vehicle driver	2 m above ground
Child	0.6 m above ground
Car driver	1.05 m above ground

Parking spaces within curtilage of dwellings, preferred dimensions	
Length	6 m
Width	3.2 m

drivers should be aware that they are entering a residential area where vehicle speeds are low and pedestrians and cyclists take precedence over the free flow of vehicles. Access should be well lit and protected from inclement weather (DoE & Department of Transport 1992: 17–18).

The layout of roads in the form of squares, crescents, grand boulevards and cosy cul-de-sacs to create urban design effects is dealt with above ("Design" on p. 134 ff).

New industrial estates are best accessed from distributor roads so that heavy vehicles do not pass through residential or shopping areas. Factories are normally oblong in plan and do not share the more exacting requirements of housing. Modified grid layouts from simple spine and spur arrangements, to loops, to fuller grids, are adequate. Visibility splays are of the same order of magnitude as for housing. Cul-de-sacs up to 250 m long are acceptable as long as adequate turning areas are available for large vehicles, but with circular or banjo form to avoid the necessity of reversing. On very large estates, access to distributor roads may be from a service road. Road dimensions are determined by the size of large vehicles, whose maximum is 2.5 m wide and normally 15.5 m long. Traffic volumes on industrial estates are usually low, so that in small developments footways (1.8 m) may not be necessary although services need to be accommodated. The radii of bends on roads and turning areas have to be large enough to accommodate large swept areas when vehicles manoeuvre (see Table 6.7). Parking for cars and operational vehicles should be as close to buildings as possible to facilitate surveillance and to minimize carrying distances. Parking bays for large vehicles are 3.5 m × 18.5 m. Vehicles frequently need to enter buildings (headroom 4.75 m). Factory and estate operators seek to keep the number of access points to estates and to buildings to an absolute minimum, to improve surveillance. Emergency exits from buildings and from larger estates are normally closed. This has an influence on road layout.

Table 6.7   Minimum design standards for industrial estate roads (IHT 1987: table 32.1, ch. 32; English Estates et al. 1986: ch. 9).

Design speed	Minimum carriageway width	Mininimum centre-line radius	Minimum junction spacing	
			Adjacent	Opposite
40 km/hour	7.3 m	60 m*	90 m	40 m

*English Estates et al. (1986: 122) suggested desirable minimum 300 m and absolute minimum 90 m.

New science and business parks, which include a mixture of traditional factories and offices in new clean formats, follow linear, grid and loop-road layouts associated with traditional industrial estates; but, of course, design and siting standards are much higher than they have been in the past (Trafalgar House 1987, Philips 1993a,b).

The road layouts for new shopping developments vary greatly from small suburban shopping centres and superstores, to city centre redevelopment sites, to major out-of-town shopping complexes, of which there are a few in Britain. Retail warehouse parks and factory outlet shopping centres are new shopping formats. All are best located on distributor roads, so that traffic is not drawn through residential areas. Road layout designs normally seek to separate pedestrians from customers' cars, and both from large service vehicles and service access, in the interests of safety and security.

Within these shopping formats the degree of segregation of pedestrians, cars and service vehicles varies (Beddington 1991: chs 4 and 5). Within large planned shopping centres, pedestrians are usually separated into malls. These are normally simple (e.g. Y or X in plan) and without cul-de-sacs, so that shoppers can find their way easily and provide maximum flow past all shops. Frontages are normally irregular, and malls open out into courts forming major foci in centres to avoid monotony. Straight-through malls are to be avoided, as shoppers do not linger. As a rule of thumb, malls should not be more than 200–250 m long between points of interest. Malls may be two storeys and aligned with major pedestrian traffic generators outside the site and "magnet" stores inside the site. Mall width varies between 6 m (minor malls) to 13–15 m (major malls, including planting and seating), which is narrow enough for shoppers to linger without obstructing flow and be able to cross from side to side to shop. Getting all goods in and bulky customers' goods out is best achieved by ground-level service courts and ways to which the public do not have access. Vehicles may be large, arrive irregularly and park. Through-ways and loops at least 3 m wide and parking are needed; gradients should not exceed 1 in 10 if underground or overhead routes have to be used. In small suburban shopping centres, operational traffic is quite low in volume, and rear access is probably not necessary. Indeed, small retailers would prefer to trolley to one front entrance for security reasons. Parking provision, whatever the scale of shopping, is best placed as close to shopping as possible to minimize walking and carrying distances.

Cycling, walking and rights of way

All journeys begin and end by walking. Cycling is a very efficient, healthy and environmentally friendly way of making journeys. Because of the effort involved, it has been found empirically that, where distances exceed about a mile (1.6 km) only a small proportion of people will walk, and, where distances exceed about five miles (8 km), few will cycle regularly (DOE & Department of Transport 1995: 6). About 81 per cent of all journeys under one mile are by foot and journeys under one mile account for 30 per cent of all journeys by all means of travel. About half of all journeys are under five miles (8 km). Cycling is an ideal mode for journeys up to five miles, but fewer than 3 per cent of journeys are made this way, whereas car journeys account for 45 per cent. Only 2 per cent of all journeys are made by cycle, but in Oxford and Cambridge 20–25 per cent are made this

159

way. Clearly, there is scope for improved cycle use (ibid.: 98 ff, 102 ff).

Within the context of development control, it is a matter of integrating appropriate cycling and walking routes and secure cycle parking within old and new developments. Locational policies for new development (whether residential, commercial or recreational) should promote local self-sufficiency. To minimize effort, desire lines (the shortest straight-line distance between origin and destination) should be followed as closely as possible. As a rule of thumb, cyclists will not accept diversions of greater than 10 per cent of journey length (Barton et al. 1995: 127). Normally, for safety, cycle and pedestrian routes should be separated from other vehicular routes but not necessarily cyclists from pedestrians. However, routes should be aesthetically attractive, well surfaced, not generally in lonely isolation from other routes and activities, and well lit and have user-friendly road crossings. To be effective, walking and cycling policies need to be combined with other measures such as parking control (DoE & Department of Transport 1995).

The effect of a development on a public right of way is a material consideration in development control. Advice is given in Circular 2/93, *Public rights of way* (DoE 1993a: annex D: 41 ff). Rights of way developed for local access needs and are still important as such. However, many rights of way are used principally for recreational purposes by a large and increasing number of people (ibid.: 2). There are two areas of concern: the need for adequate consideration of the rights of way before the decision on the planning application is taken, and the need for the right of way to be kept open until other statutory procedures authorizing closure or diversion have been completed (ibid.: 41). Where it is agreed that rights of way need to be altered, these are best routed through landscaped areas or open spaces away from traffic and not along estate roads. The grant of planning permission does not give developers the right to obstruct a public right of way. Nor should it be assumed that the grant of planning permission will eventually lead to its closure or diversion. For the avoidance of delay it is advised that negotiations for planning permission and for alteration to rights of way are undertaken in parallel.

Parking

Every development results in the demand for a parking or loading space. Parking needs to be provided for cycles, cars and much larger vehicles. Shops, leisure and transport interchanges can have very large demands concentrated in a relatively small space and time. Demand is influenced by location and the possibility of parking at the destination. Consider shopping in a town centre or in a suburban superstore. The availability of alternative transport modes affects parking demand, as does the cost of parking to the user. Parking policy varies with time and place (IHT 1987: ch. 30). One school of thought says that we should deliberately limit parking to reduce vehicle use and traffic congestion. Another school says that, wherever possible, parking should be provided for those who wish to park, as this would improve the marketability of the development (DOE & Department of Transport 1995: ch. 6).

Parking needs in housing areas can be divided into residential and visitors and elsewhere for workers, clients, customers and operational use. Some parking has a rapid turnover (e.g. in shopping areas) but elsewhere residential and commuter parking can be long term. Where firms own and operate their own commercial vehicles, their parking demands may change dramatically if they decide to dispose of their vehicles and use an outside contractor.

Parking provision to some extent depends on land costs, construction costs and maintenance costs. These vary dramatically with location, being particularly high in multistorey development in town centres. Hilton (1981: 66 reporting Munro) quoted the following range of costs of parking provision depending on parking standards applied to a 4000 m^2 (40000 ft^2) gross floor area store (excluding land costs): at the least onerous standard 6.6 per cent of total building costs, at the retailer's assessment of need 20.6 per cent, and when the most onerous parking standard applied 32.5 per cent. Some LPAs grant planning permission for town centre development and accept payment in place of the applicant's obligation to provide parking. These commuted payments are used by the LPA to provide parking elsewhere, for example on the periphery of a town centre. The main determinants of the payment are land and construction costs (Nathaniel Lichfield & Partners 1990).

From the design point of view, parking needs to be close to the ultimate destination, to minimize walking and carrying and to improve surveillance. Allowance must be made for disabled people, by having ramps for example. The geometry of the entry and exit points should be such that there is no tailback of waiting vehicles. Where there are many workers or shoppers likely to leave a large carpark in a short period of time, checks should be made that the junctions and the distributor roads can handle the flow without undue delay.

Parking requirements and carpark design guidance for different types of development are given in Tables 6.8 and 6.9. In this case, parking spaces are related to the built form; it is possible to relate parking spaces to people, e.g. customers, clients and workers. But of course the number of people can change over the lifetime of a building (see Ch. 4, where Class B ratchet changes are discussed).

Thus, although the literature and development plans speak of "parking standards", there is no single parking standard as such. Standards vary with time and place and may be negotiated between developers and an LPA, depending on the exigencies of the site, including the proximity of nearby public parking. It has been suggested that, where a traffic generator feeds into an overloaded network, parking should be subject to a maximum standard; where the network is underused, minimum standards should be set to ensure that on-street parking does not take place (Hilton 1981: 42). Arguably, this principle is the dominant theme in transport planning and development control in the 1990s. Ultimately, it is a matter of balancing three variables: accessibility, environmental quality and the cost of

161

provision (ibid.: 44, quoting Buchanan). What the future holds is difficult to predict. The availability and cost of public transport and the advent of road pricing will clearly have an effect on parking standards. Hilton (ibid.: 116, reporting Woods) suggested that outside city centres LPAs would continue to press for development proposals to be self-sufficient in parking.

Table 6.8   Some typical carparking levels required by type of development (IHT 1987: table 30.1).

Type of development	Resident	Visitor/ employee
Typical family dwellings	One space per dwelling usually excluding garages	One visitor's space for every two dwellings outside the curtilage
Offices – non-central locations	n.a.	One space for every 25–50 m² of floorspace
Shopping – non-central locations	n.a.	One space for every 10–50 m² of gross floor area (Financial viability of shopping may be dependent on high levels of provision)
Industry	n.a.	One space for every 25–50 m² of gross floor area

Suggested parking levels for new business development, London:
   Central London: 1 space per 1500–1600 m² floor area
   Inner London: 1 space per 1200–1400 m² floor area
   Outer London: 1 space per 1000–1300 m² floor area
(DOE & Department of Transport 1995: 96)

Table 6.9   Some typical parking space dimensions for different types of vehicle (IHT 1987: table 30.3).

	Car	Coach	HGV articulated
Vehicle dimensions (m)	Up to 5.0 × 2.0	Up to 12.0 × 2.5	Up to 15.5 × 2.5
Allocated parking area (m)	4.8 × 2.3	14.0 × 3.5	18.5 × 3.5
Overall space per parked vehicle (m²) including access and manoeuvring space	20/25	100/150	150/200

Landscaping

Introduction

Unlike siting, design, external appearance and access, landscaping is defined in the GDPO. Paraphrased, it means the treatment of land for the purposes of enhancing or protecting the amenities of a site and the area in which it is situated, and it includes screening by fences, walls or other means, the planting of trees, hedges or grass, forming banks, terraces or earthworks, the laying out of gardens and the provision of other amenity features. Presumably other amenity features include other aspects of floorscape – hard floorscape – for example setts and gravel, water features and street furniture, and public and private open spaces.

Landscape, as distinct from landscaping, is also very important in development control work. Scenery, landscape and the countryside carry strong emotional associations (Preece 1990: xv). Special designations have been devised in the context of development control to protect areas of landscape value, especially national parks, areas of outstanding natural beauty and green belts. These cover very substantial areas of countryside. Landscape has positive pictorial connotations: landscaping may convey the idea of shallow cosmetic treatment of development. Landscaping is often the subject of conditions imposed on the grant of planning permission, mentioned in Chapter 5 (see Ross 1990: 24–5).

In the context of development control it is useful to describe landscaping in terms of site characteristics such as topography, the living environment of plants and animals, and floorscape such as street furniture. Another useful division is between what exists, such as hedgerows, and what we might add, such as trees to complement buildings. Yet another perspective is to discuss the purposes of landscape in the context of development.

The shape of the Earth

The basis of landscape design is the shape of the Earth's surface. At the largest scale the pattern of rivers, hills, valleys and plains makes up the much loved and protected British landscape. The lakes, the sea and the coast are especially prized. This scale is so vast that the features are beyond anything but puny alteration by man during the course of development. Where major development proposals are involved, such as airports, motorways, mineral workings, reservoirs and major town expansions, current practice is to blend the new development into the existing landscape as far as possible and to work with nature. An opposite philosophy could be adopted in which man imposes his will upon nature. "Major engineering works are nearly always treated as far as possible in the English landscape tradition, that is, although the structures themselves are obviously artifacts, they are given a naturalistic setting in terms of ground shaping, and of planting" (Preece 1991: 193). With new roads, straight stretches are avoided, curves are not circular but transitional in form, and cuttings may be made to resemble valleys by using S-shape rather than Z-shape slopes, which accord with natural processes (ibid.: 196). In this context, skylines are sensitive; for example, where a settlement is visually contained by hills, development over the crest spoils the effect of enclosure.

Much development takes place on relatively flat sites, so that the need to shape the land surface significantly may not arise, although, as Pinder & Pinder (1990: 235) quipped, "The proportion of the Earth's surface which is entirely flat is very small but the proportion of drawing boards which are flat is very high." It is all too easy to design as if a site were flat and later to have to confront the fact that it is not. Changes of level are best designed for at the outset.

163

Earthen banks may be used along roads, carparks and adjacent to mineral workings to reduce noise and visual intrusion. They also provide shelter on leisure sites and to private gardens. Where terracing is necessary, cut should equal fill to minimize cost; allowance has to be made for settlement. Slope stability depends on the type of rock involved, but for many soils a slope of 1:2 is adequate; care needs to be taken not to undermine the stability of neighbouring property. Adjusted contours are best natural and flowing in shape unless formal terracing is intended. Where proposed road gradients in a layout may be excessive, cuttings and embankments are necessary. Preece suggested (ibid.: 205) in housing layouts that ramps for pedestrians should not be steeper than one in ten, grass slopes for mowing no steeper than one in four, and football pitches should have a slope of between one in thirty to one in eighty to ensure drainage. Roads with a design speed of 30 mph should not be steeper than one in ten and cycle tracks about one in twenty. Residential development at high and medium densities should not be developed on slopes much steeper than one in ten, and industrial and commercial not more than about one in twenty-five (Barton et al. 1995: 149).

Any cutting and filling is likely to upset existing drainage patterns and the health of existing trees. The problem with all cut and fill is that the cut material may not be suitable for structural fill, and imported materials may be toxic and liable to collapse and decomposition. Most material bulks up during excavation. The handling of topsoil is a separate issue when it is stripped and stored; it does not always take kindly to long storage and mixing with subsoil (Preece 1991: ch. 9).

Sun, wind and water

Energy from the Sun drives all climatic phenomena. Its position in relation to site and building development is crucial. Daylight and sunlight and their relationship to the occupants of buildings were dealt with above (see pp. 131–2). Plants need sunlight. Preece made the telling point that gardens in Britain on the north side of houses (say) will be in shadow; at the height of summer the shadow will be half the height of the building, but about ten times longer in winter, which is longer than many gardens (ibid.: 211).

What happens to solar energy depends on the nature of the surface it strikes. Dry sandy soils warm up and cool down more than moist clay soils. Grass surfaces will be cooler than tarmac. Topography has a significant effect on local climate, especially whether slopes face north or south and whether frost pockets form or not under still-air conditions. Exposure to sunlight and wind are generally the two most important factors in microclimate. To some extent airflow can be modified by buildings, walls and hedges reducing its speed and altering its direction. The chill factor and its destructive force on plants is thus reduced.

Drainage is best under gravity. Surface water and foul water are normally kept separately, so that sewage works are not overloaded in times of flood. Normally, surface water goes into soakaways and surface streams so that it is available for plant use; much rainfall is retained for plant use in the soil. Many surface water features are filled in and culverted in urban areas for child safety and are only unusually turned into attractive water features in public parks and business parks.

Circular 30/92 gives guidance on development and flood risk (DoE 1992s). The Environment Agency (previously the National Rivers Authority) has general responsibility for flood defence. This is important as sea level and climatic changes augur more flooding both by fresh and sea water. The Environment Agency is the consultee in development plan preparation and for proposals for development. Flood protection works may need planning permission. In the context of applications for development the main concerns are to:

- prevent development which might subsequently be flooded, risking life and property
- prevent development in the floodplain that would hinder flood control, for example leading to loss of flood storage capacity
- prevent interference with flood defences
- prevent development that might restrict flows
- consider the impact of new development on water runoff
- consider the diversion or culverting of water courses.

Mineral workings cause special flood control and water storage problems, as does the flooding of contaminated land. Caravan sites may be subject to extra risks. Where alleviation works are necessary, these may be secured by planning conditions and agreements.

Planting

There is a specific section on a planning application form which enquires about trees (Table 2.1). Does the proposal involve lopping, topping and felling? Is a tree plan included with the application? Does a tree preservation order cover part of the site? Preece opined (1991: 223) that "in their contribution to visual effects and shelter, trees represent in most situations the best value for money of any of the components of landscape design. A young tree need cost no more than a pot plant or half a dozen flower bed plants." Once planted, many trees last a human lifetime. Shrubs and grass are smaller in scale and easier to alter than forest trees. The reader will appreciate that with the many plant species and their varied habitat requirements, it is not really possible to comment in more than a general way about planting.

Site conditions can be divided (not very clearly) into intrinsic site conditions and those conditions occasioned by the development itself. Much amenity planting, in contrast to commercial planting, does not need detailed site and soil analysis (Preece 1991: 234–6) other than to distinguish the main types of soil (clay, sand, chalk, loam and waterlogged soils, with their varying degrees of acidity). Trial holes on the site and the examination of successful trees nearby will provide most of the information needed. Beech, for example, will flourish on chalk where other trees might find it difficult. Plant species also need to be matched to withstand

165

wind (sycamore) and frost (European larch), exposure and more unusual hazards such as salt (evergreen oak) and industrial pollution (London plane). In addition to their visual relationship to buildings, trees need to be planted to avoid underground services, the foundations of buildings, and paths and roads, where they may cause dangerous frost or wet leaves to lie. Apart from, say, frost hardiness, all trees have individual characteristics, particularly size (height and diameter of spread) – which makes them suitable for, say, ground cover, hedging or specimen trees – and colour – spring and autumn colour, deciduous or evergreen – which lends variety to the landscape. Preece said that knowledge of a few dozen species only is required; the eighteenth-century landscape gardener Capability Brown used only a handful.

As intimated at the beginning of this section on landscape, the LPAs are very concerned to retain existing trees in a proposed development, as are developers, because it increases sale value. The problem is ensuring that the right trees are kept and then conserved, but at the same time that they do not cause a nuisance. The tree plan that may accompany a planning application should show position, species, spread and likely age and condition. Ultimately, the LPA may have in mind granting permission on condition that specified trees are retained and new ones planted. **Tree preservation orders** and conservation area status mean that owners need permission to lop, top or fell trees, irrespective of the need for planning permission for other development. Whether existing trees should be felled or retained in the interests of amenity is a matter of judgement. If they are dangerous to buildings or persons, diseased, at the end of their lives or in poor aesthetic shape, then there may well be a case for felling or trimming. Where trees can readily be seen in places frequented by the public, are good specimen trees or may be rare, then they should be preserved. When design for construction work is started, the developer should differentiate between trees that must be kept if planning permission is to be secured, those that must be kept if possible and those that can be sacrificed. Fitting in buildings, roads and services may regrettably involve felling good trees. Once construction work starts, large trees can be readily damaged by quite small changes, for example stripping and dumping topsoil, drainage changes, trenching, compaction caused by vehicles, dumping building materials near them, and bark and root damage; this can be countered by imposing fencing conditions. As for the proximity of old trees near proposed buildings or new trees near buildings, much depends on the type of tree and the type of soil if buildings are not to be seriously damaged. Clay soils expand and contract with moisture, others not so much so. For example, poplars and willows on clay are probably the most dangerous and should not be placed closer to buildings than their eventual height. Other trees on non-shrinkable soils should be placed no closer than one third of their eventual height (Preece 1991: 256; O'Callaghan 1996: 12–13).

Tree preservation orders

At this point it is useful to consider tree preservation orders (TPOs), which are a particular contribution of the development control system to the conservation of the landscape. TPOs have given special protection to specified individual trees, groups of trees and woodlands since 1947. Trees in conservation areas have been subject to similar control since 1975. The principal effect of TPOs is that trees etc. cannot be lopped, topped or felled without the consent of the LPA. Wilful damage or destruction is an offence. TPOs are normally made by LPAs. The principal guidance is given in Circular 36/78, *Trees and forestry* (DoE 1978), *Tree Preservation Orders: a guide to good practice* (DoE 1994i), from which this account is taken, and the 1969 Regulations as amended and which are reprinted in the *Tree Preservation Orders* (ibid.: Annex 2; DoE 1969). *Tree Preservation Orders* has a legal rather than an arboricultural perspective.

For legal purposes "the High Court has held that a 'tree' is anything which ordinarily one would call a tree" (ibid.: 3). TPOs can protect woodlands but not hedges or shrubs (ibid.). TPOs may be made by LPAs where it is expedient in the interests of amenity. Guidance on criteria are given. Trees:

- make a significant impact on the environment and its enjoyment by the general public
- should normally be visible from a public place
- may give present or future benefit
- may be protected for their intrinsic beauty or to hide an eyesore
- may have scarcity value
- may have group value
- may involve other matters, for example, wildlife habitats
- threatened by destruction may be the subject of TPOs (ibid.: 5).

The effects of development proposals on trees, either felling or planting, are a material consideration when planning applications are considered (ibid.: ch. 5). Development plans may have policies dealing with them. Pre-application discussions may involve which trees might be felled and retained and what potential there may be for planting. Planning applications accompanied by a tree plan should identify trees:

- which must be retained at all costs
- whose retention is very desirable
- whose retention is desirable
- not worthy of protection.

Apart from these amenity considerations the *Tree Preservation Orders* (ibid.) drew attention to danger and so on dealt with above, to the use of planning conditions (e.g. the protection of trees during construction) and to the use of planning obligations involving trees.

It is possible to lop and fell trees without the consent of the LPA, for example if they are an immediate danger or a legal nuisance or if planning permission has been granted for development (ibid.: ch. 6). Applications for consent to the LPA are normally made on a simple form specifying the applicant's name, the location, a TPO reference number or reference to conservation area status, a schedule of trees with the type of work and reasons, plus a tree plan (ibid.: annex 5). Arrangements are in place, rather as for a planning application, for limited publicity, site visits, the decision usually to grant or refuse, consent conditions and appeals to the Secretary of State (ibid.: ch. 7). Conditions typically require replacement planting on or near the site of felled trees or work to be carried out to British Standard 3998:1989, *Tree work*. However, where consent for tree work not subject to TPOs has been applied for in a conservation area, the LPA can either make a TPO or not make a TPO and inform the applicant that the proposed work can go ahead. The LPA cannot refuse consent, nor can it grant subject to conditions, but it may give arboricultural advice (ibid.: ch. 9). There are penalties for wilful destruction of protected trees and also enforcement powers to facilitate tree replacement (ibid.: chs 10 and 11).

Hard landscaping and floorscape

So far, all the natural elements of landscape and landscaping have been dealt with: topography, climate and planting. That which is neither building nor landscaping in the obvious sense constitutes another important part of what we see in development: floorscape. Floorscape provides that part of outdoor "rooms" for which building façades and large trees provide the walls and possibly the ceiling. For the purposes of description, it includes road surfaces, grass and shrubs, means of enclosure and street furniture.

The functional need for access has been dealt with above. Road and path dimensions and layout are in part determined by their positions in the road hierarchy (Table 6.1) and the type of traffic they are expected to take. For example, footpaths need to be about 2m wide if pedestrians with prams are to pass without stepping off them. There is also the natural desire, for walkers particularly, to take the shortest route between two points and "cut across the grass rather than keep to the path". In this context, roads and paths are constructed to prevent damage to and destruction of planting. In the context of landscaping, surface treatments have more than mere function: they have symbolic value. Surface treatments may be smooth, such as in shopping malls, to entice the shopper and to look clean and businesslike. They may be very rough and cobbled to slow vehicular traffic in towns or perhaps inhibit pedestrians looking through dwelling-house windows in a street predominantly consisting of shops. Cobbles and setts recall an earlier age and are suited to use in conservation areas. Paths and roads, especially in rural settings, meander, rather than take more direct routes, and in so doing become inviting and very possibly mysterious. Preece noted the eighteenth-century maxim that "the foot should not tread where the eye has gone before" (1991). The role of serial vision is dealt with in the paragraphs on design above.

Surface treatments are characterized by colour, texture and scale. They need to be chosen and designed with the same care as building façades (McCluskey 1992: 218). They are secondary to the vertical elements in a townscape and therefore should not be obtrusive (ibid.: 247). Colours should be restrained, such as black, grey, red or brown, often derived from the colour of the surfacing material itself. They should be harmonious, calm and restful. Road markings are in brighter colours. The surface treatment of distributor roads is likely to be smooth and large scale, appropriate to the speed of vehicles and the scale of the engineering works themselves. On shared surfaces, say in residential cul-de-sacs and industrial estates, the use of blocks, bricks and setts is more appropriate to the human scale of the development. The judicious use of bricks and setts in various patterns and colours differentiates where vehicles should run, where they should park and where pedestrians should take precedence. Changes in surface treatment signal to drivers and walkers that they may be entering a different ownership realm and indicate the direction they should follow or that they should exercise caution. Bollards and other street furniture complement the messages sent by the surfacing. Surfaces, besides having a strong sense of direction, may also have a sense of repose, such as in a square or cul-de-sac (Pinder & Pinder 1990: 2; McCluskey 1992: ch. 9).

Surfaces should take the weight of traffic, drain readily and usually be frost proof. To be sure that this is so the structure may be divided into surface, edge and gutter. Each element may be of a different material, colour and texture. The treatment of these elements conveys formality or informality of character. Consider the prominent kerbs of a distributor road and the apparently edgeless gutterless gravel path in the countryside (Pinder & Pinder 1990: 4; Preece 1991: ch. 8). A minor, but usually significant, element in floorscape is the treatment of grass and other low ground-plant cover. They can be established relatively quickly in comparison with trees, which provide vertical elements. Preece took the view that in informal layouts a pleasing effect can be obtained by grass being an inch or two above adjoining paths, as hard surfaces and buildings appear to be resting on a yielding pillow of grass. In open layouts such treatment has a unifying effect on development (Preece 1991: 200–201).

Means of enclosure

Fences, walls, barriers, railings, gates and hedges provide means of enclosure. Although they can be visually dominant in a development, they may be permitted development as permission is not normally necessary unless they are over 2 m high. Enclosure may variously inhibit trespass, provide security, provide visual enclosure, delineate property ownership, provide shelter from wind and rain, provide privacy, sometimes retain the ground, retain noise and be works of art in themselves. They should be vandal proof and easy to maintain. They also have a mysterious quality that provokes the questions: What is on the other side? Why am I excluded? They have varying degrees of opacity, from solid walls to open fences and rails, which repel or invite further curiosity. Where local materials and styles are used, they give a sense of place. However, cheap mass-produced components result in much poor and uninspiring enclosure (Pinder & Pinder 1990: ch. 2). Enclosure, as already described in the section on design, is an important concept in landscape design, with similar rules.

Other minor but important elements in landscape include lighting, seating, signage (see pp. 202–207), bus shelters, substations and works of art.

The purposes of landscape and landscaping

So far, the main elements of the preservation of the landscape and landscaping have been discussed, but we have only implied what the purposes of the activity might be. The British tradition is to work in harmony with nature to modify climate, especially microclimate, control runoff and erosion, and to provide for wildlife. These factors are of particular importance in the context of sustainability. Secondly, where possible, aspects of the landscape should be productive, whether in terms of commercial crops, stock and woodland in the countryside, or gardening for leisure in domestic gardens. Thirdly, landscape and landscaping provide for outside activities in "outside rooms", especially back gardens, public parks, playing fields and countryside recreation. Fourthly, landscape provides the setting for buildings, often softening their appearance, whereas forest trees and hedges complement buildings by becoming architectural features in themselves. Fifthly, it engenders a sense of privacy, security and territoriality, especially in housing development. Sixthly, landscape features can hide the ugly, such as mineral working, help to restore damaged and derelict land, and cope with SLOAP (space left over after planning). Finally, and importantly, landscape and landscaping should bring repose and delight to the soul: it is an end in itself.

However, landscaping is not without its problems, especially maintenance costs, the interruption of sightlines and views, damage to buildings and services, hiding places for miscreants, and overshadowing. There is a constant need to be aware of the effects of new development on the wider landscape and the need to enforce landscape conditions attached to planning permissions.

Some research findings on design

In 1984–5 six LPAs launched a pilot three-year initiative inter alia to improve the quality of design in the environment and the operation of the planning process; it was called "Time for Design". The results of the exercise were researched by the Building Design Partnership (1990). The monitoring exercise did not attempt to devise any objective measure of design quality or of whether the "Time for

Design" initiative itself had resulted in improved design. The situation was and is very complex, and there were far too many variables (ibid.: 5). The DoE was particularly concerned about the speed and efficiency of the operation of the planning process. The monitoring exercise sought to determine the extent to which design issues featured in development control decisions. This was done by analyzing planning applications and appeals, and by an analysis of design guidance used by LPAs in England and Wales. The policy background at the time, based on Circular 22/80, was that central government advised LPAs not to interfere with design matters unless there were exceptional circumstances (ibid.: 5). The word "design" was not defined in the monitoring report, but it is clear from the contents that design meant far more than design as defined for the purposes of reserved matters, and in fact it embraced all reserved matters.

Five ways were used to improve design in the six LPA areas: design award schemes, the use of design guides, seminars and lectures, environmental education, and design and tender (ibid.: ch. 3). It was found inter alia that LPAs were preaching to the converted, but they were continuing with the award schemes. Design guides were widely used, but with various degrees of support from the LPAs. Typically they involved shop fronts and home improvements such as house extensions, many of which had permitted development rights in any event and detailed design guidance for conservation areas (ibid.: 39). Design guides were thought to be the most successful part of the initiative (ibid.: 9). Seminars were particularly aimed at "plansmiths", that is, non-architect applicants such as builders. Environmental education in schools was thought to have long-term benefit. In the design and tender process, the LPAs acted as exemplars by producing **design briefs** for sites they owned. A two-stage tendering process ensured that design criteria rather than financial criteria dominated. The overall view was that the "Time for Design" initiative had a positive but unquantifiable effect on improving the quality of design.

Statistical analysis in the relevant period showed that the proportion of applications dealt with in the eight-week period fell (ibid.: ch. 4). This was because of increasing numbers of applications and staff shortages. There were no significant changes in approval rates and no evidence that higher design standards had resulted in higher refusal rates. The number of appeals rose in the period in the six LPAs, but only in eleven cases out of 944 appeals was intrinsic design an issue, and nine of these were dismissed (ibid.: 35). Very often appeals involved multiple issues (ibid.: 36). However, in a survey in England and Wales in 1985 to which 153 LPAs responded, a third of authorities said that "design" was a major issue in less than 10 per cent of "major" applications and a third said it was a major issue in over 50 per cent of "major" applications. "Design" was rarely an issue in change-of-use applications (ibid.: 40–41). It was found that pre-application discussions in conjunction with design guides produced a consistent approach to design within planning departments. An analysis of approvals in the six LPAs showed that 30 to 40 per cent of applications were approved without conditions. Of the conditions imposed, most were concerned with materials, landscape, access, parking, positioning of windows and restrictions related to the classes of use. It was argued that refusals weeded out poor designs. The most frequent reason for refusal was that a proposed development was "too large", followed by reasons of policy, appearance and overlooking. However, there was no evidence to show that design-related reasons for refusal increased in significance as a result of the design initiative (ibid.: 14). The report concluded (ibid.: 15) that, as a guide to other LPAs, a declaration of high standards, the production of design guidance and the use of professionally trained urban design staff within planning departments were important ways to improve design standards.

Synthesis of major issues

In conclusion this section seeks to synthesize matters described separately above. Reserved matters – siting, design, external appearance, access and landscaping – are a part, a major part, of the control of development. They are the concern of the emerging urban design profession and of many commentators.

For the purposes of exposition, the five reserved matters have been treated separately with cross references between them. No mention has been made of the design process whereby a designer or design team starts with the client's brief and the characteristics of the site, and systematically works through to a design solution that will obtain planning permission for major development. At this point I shall try to synthesize the strands by drawing on the work of Bentley et al. (1985), who took quite a different line from the reserved matters approach, and Punter (1990b), who has boldly drawn together the philosophies of ten writers, including Bentley et al.

The starting point of Bentley's philosophy is that "the built environment should provide its users with an essentially democratic setting, enriching their opportunities by maximizing the degree of choice available to them. We call such places responsive." (Bentley et al. 1985: 9). It should be said at this stage that the approach is geared to sites of street block size in towns rather than smaller sites and the countryside. He identified seven qualities of so-called "responsive environments", some of which find echoes in the reserved matters described, although others do not. They can be compared with the qualities sought by other writers in Table 6.10.

The seven qualities of a responsive environment sought after in the design process are as follows:

- *Permeability* (ibid.: ch. 1)   This quality affects where people can and cannot go. Cul-de-sac layouts mentioned in the access section above detract from this quality; through-streets foster it.
- *Variety* (ibid.: ch. 2)   Variety means a variety of building types and land uses at street, block and district level, the purpose of which is increased choice for users, especially those with low mobility, in a relatively small

area. Planners have been nervous about mixed uses until recently because of the threat of poor amenity.

- *Legibility* (ibid.: ch. 3)   Legibility is the quality that makes a place grasp-able in the mind of the user. It has two facets – physical form and activity patterns – and corresponds to *genius loci* mentioned earlier. Key physical elements from Lynch (1960), are "nodes", "edges", "paths" and "land-marks". Legibility in modern cities has been reduced in comparison with traditional ones.
- *Robustness* (ibid.: ch. 4)   To use buildings and environments for different uses as demands change gives them robustness. The way that old buildings have had various uses over the years illustrates this quality. Changes of use are subject to development control.
- *Visual appropriateness* (ibid.: ch. 5)   This quality combines variety, leg-ibility and robustness to communicate to the user the choices available, and echoes external appearance and landscape as reserved matters.
- *Richness* (ibid.: ch. 6)   Much of our experience of the environment is through our eyes. Richness seeks to cater for other senses as well: the feel-ings of motion, smell, hearing and touch (e.g. the texture of the floorscape). Visual richness is particularly important.
- *Personalization* (ibid.: ch. 7)   In spite of public consultation, most people work and live in places designed by others. Designers should cater for the need to personalize buildings, improve facilities and/or alter their image. Much personalization, such as minor building extensions and painting, has permitted development rights.

Punter (1990b: 10–14) drew the work of several commentators together and distilled and tabulated key principles. His distillation is reproduced as Table 6.10.

Regrettably, there is inadequate space in this book to explain individual phi-losophies. They are best read in the original; most of the bibliographical items Punter used are included in the bibliography for this book. He started with the Prince of Wales's list (Table 6.10: col. 5) and bent the work of other commen-tators to it. He opined that the Prince drew his ideas primarily from neoclassical architects and designers, whereas the other commentators drew on the American experience of Lynch and Jacobs. It is a simplification, but there are two themes buried in Table 6.10: first façade control and secondly people issues, such as safety and social justice. Suffice it to say that they interact. Punter warned par-ticularly against the checklist or formula approach to design and design control, because it stifles initiative and creativity, although it might promise a quick route to planning permission.

Punter's table (Table 6.10) is merely a structuring device for marshalling basic ideas. He made the point that commentators seemed to base their ideas in town centre contexts. He was not convinced that they could be used in areas where townscape was subordinate to landscape. Moreover, any set of urban design principles must be relevant to relevant users' experience, such as cleanliness, which may be more important than architectural delight. Ecologically sustainable

Table 6.10 The ten commandments/principles of the Prince of Wales and other checklists for urban design.

Kevin Lynch 1982	Jane Jacobs 1961	Bentley et al. 1986	Tibbalds 1988	HRH The Prince of Wales 1989	Holyoak 1985	Urban Design Group 1987	Wates 1988	Buchanan 1988
1. Vitality (include biological and ecological)	Appropriate activity before visual order	"Responsive" environments	Places before buildings	The place		Responsive forms	Urban environment in broadest sense	Place making public realm outdoor rooms
2. (See Sense)		Visual appropriateness	Respect history	Harmony and context	(i) Retain the best (ii) Respect street line			Dialogue with context and history: re-contain street
3. (See Fit)	Mixed use Mixed age Mixed rent Concentration	Variety	Encourage mixed uses		More than one use	Mixed uses		
4. (See Vitality)	The street	Human scale	Scale enclosure	In scale with context				
5. Access	Permeability (short blocks)	Permeability	Encourage pedestrian permeability			Public access		Public space and movement systems
6. Control	Social mix and consultation	Personalization	Social mix and consultation	Community	"Acceptable" personalization	Consultation	Individual responsibility, professional enablers, local action and control, integrating experience, optimizing resources, envt education	

				Hierarchy	Visual accessibil-ity reflects uses		(i) Respect conventions (ii) Articulate meanings (iii) Connect inside and out
7. Sense (clarity with which it can be per-ceived)		Legibility	Legibility				
8. Fit (adaptability)	Robust spaces	Robustness and adaptability					
9. (See Efficiency)	Gradual not cata-clysmic money		Small-scale change				
10.	Activity richness	Richness	Visual delight	Materials and decoration	"Visible" construction integral ornament	Stimulating	Natural, rich materials good weathering decoration
Two meta criteria: efficiency (relative cost) justice (social equity)	Automobile attri-tion surveillance (safety)			Signs and lights		Protection, security, comfort, shelter	

Source: Punter (1990b: 12).

development, he felt, must be integrated more fully into the analysis, not only in the sense of sustainability but in the enjoyment of landscape and of diverse flora and fauna. Finally, he emphasized that improved urban design and control was only one way of enhancing the public realm. Other initiatives are vital, particularly related to moving vehicles, such as emissions and speed control.

What, he asked, do these principles mean for improving the British development control system? He rejected binding design rules used in European plans and on privileged private estates. He advocated instead using what we have. First, the local plans system can incorporate design principles that can be tested in the approval process; they incorporate local concerns and have the support of a cross-section of public opinion. Secondly, supplementary guidance can be tailored to local circumstances, warning of the mindless plagiarisms that followed in the wake of the Essex Design Guide (Essex County Council 1975; Punter 1990b: 13). Disseminating best practice through the Department of the Environment, the RTPI and other bodies is a way to make development control more positive in the face of developers and funders, and less reactive to individual proposals. Indeed, developers recognize that good urban design enhances and maintains property values. Research and analysis may show that there is a good deal of consensus on what constitutes good design. Punter's final concern was with the largely negative advice given by three paragraphs in Circular 22/80, now replaced by the annex of PPG1 (DoE 1992c), which he described as agnostic.

Continued concern with the issues raised in this chapter were expressed in the Department of the Environment's discussion document, *Quality in town and country* (DoE 1994f), which is touched on in Chapter 9.

CHAPTER 7
Other topics, other perspectives

Introduction

This book has already dealt with many important topics in development control, for example the legal background and physical layout, which are important in all circumstances. This chapter brings together matters that do not fall readily into a logical pattern but are of such importance that I feel they deserve explicit treatment. They frequently figure in practice and in the literature. They are arranged from the relatively nice to the relatively naughty in terms of the difficulty of the planning issues that they raise: conservation, development control in rural areas, advertisements, minerals and hazardous development. The remaining chapters of the book – 8 and 9 – deal with development control controversies and with the future.

Conservation

Introduction

Conservation in the context of development control is concerned with reconciling development, which may be destructive, with our built and natural heritage, which is worth keeping. Much of this book has dealt with new development looking forwards. It is now worth turning to what we need to keep from the past. At its core, conservation means preserving what we have as it is, while actively using and enhancing the resource itself. Conservation does not mean pickling in aspic with no prospect or cognizance of the possibility of change. Indeed, change may be harnessed to bring about conservation. The growth of tourist income particularly can be used to safeguard and enhance what we have inherited. Our heritage for this purpose can be divided into the natural environment and the built environment.

Conservation of nature

Our natural environment provides everything we need to exist. It is foolhardy to destroy it wantonly through development. In terms of Maslow's hierarchy of human needs, the need for food and shelter derived from living and non-living resources is basic. The topmost need for self-actualization finds its expression in our spiritual awareness and the intrinsic joy that nature brings.

As we are entirely dependent on the natural environment for our basic needs, it behoves us to conserve it, so that it will sustain us. Wildlife acts as a genetic resource for all the domestic plants and animals we use, is a sensitive indicator of our environment that we should be unwise to ignore, and in itself is of intrinsic worth – the joys of nature. The natural environment can be conserved through policies in development plans and through the development control system. Current government guidance is contained in PPG9, *Nature conservation* (DOE 1994j).

The resource we seek to conserve consists of living plants and animals in their respective habitats on the one hand, and geological and geomorphological phenomena on the other. Plants, animals and habitats of special concern in this context are listed in annexes to PPG9. Although PPG9 draws attention to the safeguarding of natural phenomena everywhere, Sites of Special Scientific Interest (SSSIs) are set aside specifically in the context of development control to further conservation policies. There are nearly 4000 covering 840000 hectares in England (Comptroller & Auditor General 1994: 2, 7, 11). Ultimately, perhaps 8 per cent of the land area of Great Britain will be notified. SSSIs vary in status. Some are of international importance, for example Ramsar sites (wet lands), and others are of national importance, for example National Nature Reserves. Many other sites have SSSI status and below them in importance are Local Nature Reserves (without SSSI status), non-statutory nature reserves and finally sites of importance for nature conservation (DOE 1994j: 5). LPAs are under an obligation to have regard to nature conservation in development plans where these designations may be found. Outside these designated areas are rural, urban and coastal areas where nature conservation is not to be ignored. Because natural phenomena do not respect man-made boundaries, development plans provide a strategic framework in which development control decisions can be taken. Part of development plan policy is to encourage landscape features that provide havens for wildlife, such as ponds, heaths, woods, and linear features, such as rivers and hedgerows, which encourage wildlife dispersal. These have become ever more important as wildlife habitats have declined through agricultural development and afforestation (Comptroller & Auditor General 1994: 6).

SSSI notification in England is carried out by English Nature. It is a complex and lengthy process involving site survey, prioritizing sites, "potential" status, consultation with owners and occupiers who may object, resolving objections, including the use of management agreements, and final notification to LPAs and owners and occupiers (ibid.: 10). Since 1981 many sites have been reassessed (ibid.: 11). The selection criteria for biological sites involve naturalness, diversity, typicality, size and rarity, and, for geological sites, representativeness, exceptionality and international importance (ibid. 1994: appendix 4).

The main statute is the Wildlife and Countryside Act 1981, which is underpinned by the network of SSSIs. English Nature (with the Countryside Council in Wales and Scottish Natural Heritage) are the agencies advising local and central government. Inter alia, it maintains nature reserves, notifies and protects SSSIs, although they are often in private ownership and in active use (e.g. estuaries), and carries out research (DoE 1994j: 5). This is an expression of central government's commitment to the Habitats Directive under European law (DoE et al. 1995).

Nature conservation is a material consideration in development control. Where development near or in SSSIs is proposed, there is a statutory requirement to consult English Nature (DoE 1994j: 7–8). The consultation area may be up to 2 km from the SSSI. Where there is likely to be an adverse impact on the SSSI, permission may be granted subject to planning conditions and agreements to mitigate effects.

Permitted development rights in an SSSI, for example recreational uses such as clay pigeon shooting, are withdrawn. Such activities are subject to a planning application, which can then be considered on its merits and possibly granted subject to conditions to limit damage. Environmental impact assessment may well be necessary where development in or near SSSIs is proposed (see Circular 15/88) (ibid.: 8–9). Mineral extraction is singled out in PPG9 (ibid.: 9) as being both a blessing, in that it may create new habitats or expose new geological features, and a curse, in that extraction and drainage changes may lead to destruction. Minerals applications need very careful scrutiny and consultations with English Nature. Many species of plants and animals, and their habitats, are subject to protection. In granting or refusing planning permission, LPAs must generally be mindful of this special designation (ibid.: 10).

Holt (continuing: 4.255) has reported some of the substantive issues involving SSSIs, for example an obtrusive bird-shooting and -watching shed in a Ramsar site, hospital redevelopment posing a threat to improved grassland in a National Park, gravel working threatening mires, and moorings for 40 boats along an estuarine SSSI, as creating a precedent. He also drew attention to local nature conservation designations that do not have SSSI status. In one appeal case, housing was proposed for such a site, which it was intended would act as a buffer to an SSSI. The inspector noted that the LPA offered no ecological evidence, whereas the applicant did. It showed that only the hedgerows would be affected and these were for the most part to be retained. The inspector concluded that the development would not cause demonstrable harm to conservation interests.

An insight into the effectiveness of SSSIs in England was provided by the Comptroller and Auditor General (1994). Sites are monitored by English Nature normally on a three-year rotation basis (ibid.: 13). Changes for the better and for the worse can take place in various ways: natural change, unauthorized development, authorized development, pressure of use (e.g. recreation and management changes). Losses may be total or partial, sometimes with compensatory gain. Many changes are beyond the control of English Nature and the LPAs. Changes may be induced by influences both inside and outside the SSSIs. The fact that notification does not always protect a site does not mean that designation is of little value. "There is no way of knowing how many proposals to develop on or near SSSIs have never been progressed because of notification, but it is likely to have had a significant deterrent effect" (ibid.: 15). In the period 1987–93, one site was totally lost, 57 were partially lost and about 800 suffered recoverable damage (ibid.: 15), which may well have been offset by enhancement elsewhere. Recent surveys of the causes of loss and damage found that roughly a quarter each could be attributed to agriculture (e.g. overgrazing), poor management and miscellaneous causes (e.g. burning). Those attributable to the grant of planning permission were only about 4 or 5 per cent of all causes. Damage by statutory undertakers, including road building, accounted for substantially more than this (ibid.: 7). No breakdown was given of planning problems but it was noted that English Nature's efforts had led to a strengthening of development plan policies and a fall from 18 per cent (1989–90) to 4 per cent (1992–3) of cases suffering damage from activities operating with planning permission (ibid.: 26).

However, the Royal Society for the Protection of Birds (RSPB 1992) was scathing about the UK government's performance in designating Special Protection Areas (SPAs). These all have SSSI designation as being internationally important to bird life (ibid.: 2). Further research on the imposition of planning conditions by the RSPB on applications involving nature conservation found an unsatisfactory state of affairs. In an examination of 560 relevant cases, 1990 to 1995, it was found that only in 12 per cent of the cases were conditions used to protect or mitigate adverse effects of development (Brooke 1996: 4–8). The RSPB itemized many threats, with case studies such as the "Greater Thames" showing threats from port expansion, marinas and recreation.

The soil is a major natural resource. The conservation of agricultural land has long been a prime objective of the planning system, as once developed it cannot readily be returned to food production. However, domestic gardens may be significant food producers. Currently, development control policy concentrates on protecting the best Grade 1, 2 and 3a land. There is encouragement to develop brownfield (previously developed) rather than greenfield sites as a contribution to sustainable development. This is a complex issue. There are arguments about the grading of land, the role of good farm management, set-aside policy and the trade-off between the quality and density of urban development and the need to keep land in agricultural production (see Worthington 1996: 20 ff). If the rate of transfer of agricultural land to urban use in England from 1945 to 1990 continued for another century, the country would lose about one sixth of its cultivated and pasture land (Anonymous 1996c: 5, quoting Royal Commission on Environmental Pollution 1996).

Conserving the built environment

"A town without old buildings is like a man without a memory" (source unknown). Throughout Europe and elsewhere, efforts have been made for much of the twentieth century to keep old buildings and remains and prevent them from being destroyed or from decaying (Jones & Larkham 1993: 26–8). We do this because:

- old buildings may have individual intrinsic worth as works of art
- they may have strong historical associations, for example the birthplaces of the famous
- they may have unusual or epoch-making technical innovations
- they may be excellent or rare examples of particular architectural styles
- individual buildings may not have much merit in themselves but collectively form interesting and attractive street scenes – so called "group value"
- buildings and archaeological remains may be very old and that in itself makes them part of our historical records
- older buildings, indeed all buildings, are a capital resource in themselves and are worth keeping in spite of the short-term gains that may be made from destroying them – a sustainability argument
- they are part of our national and local cultural identity
- their presence adds quality to our lives by enhancing familiar scenes and giving character and continuity to localities.

Rather separately, many older buildings are of considerable economic and commercial importance, being in the centres of old towns and serving as retail outlets, residential property, museums and so on. Our old buildings and archaeological remains are a major part of the tourist economy.

In the context of development control it is useful to divide the subject matter into conservation areas, listed buildings and archaeological remains. Whenever planning applications are made for development affecting these subject areas, more stringent controls may apply than is normally the case. The main policy guidance is contained in PPG15, *Planning and the historic environment* (DoE 1994g) and PPG16, *Archaeology and planning* (DoE 1990c). The Planning (Listed Buildings and Conservation Areas) Act 1990 is the principal statute covering this aspect of planning.

Conservation areas

The 1990 Act (ibid.) requires development plans to include policies to conserve the natural and built environment (DoE 1994g: 3). Conservation areas are an expression of this; there are over 8000 in the UK and they appear in local and unitary plans. Conservation designation is very significant in making decisions on planning applications. Designation, which first started in 1967, is in the hands of the LPAs. They have a duty to designate "areas of special architectural or historic interest the character or appearance of which it is desirable to preserve or enhance" (ibid.: 15). Whereas "listing" is designed to protect individual buildings, conservation area designation is the main instrument to conserve neighbourhoods and areas. Designation introduces general control over demolition and provides the basis of policies designed to preserve and enhance character and appearance that define an area's special interest (ibid.: 15). The policies help determine the character of infill development, changes of use and extensions and alterations to buildings. Consent is necessary for demolition in a conservation area. Normally, outline planning applications are not entertained by LPAs in conservation areas, as details are of considerable importance (Thomas, continuing: ch. 8).

The criteria for the designation of conservation areas, which does much to determine the character of continuing development, are not absolute (Jones & Larkham 1993: 32). Each case is considered on its own merits (ibid.: 45) and as a result there is considerable variation in the quality of conservation areas. One set of criteria quoted (ibid.: 45) was "one where the pattern of streets and enclosed urban spaces, the scale of the buildings, their silhouette, the massing of groups of buildings, make a coherent visual unity that has not been spoilt by insensitive development or redevelopment." Other criteria include landscape and open space, which help to protect the setting of buildings. Conservation areas can thus be highly urbanized ones but also be in rural villages. A survey suggested that fewer than 50 per cent of LPAs consulted residents and pressure groups before designation, the fear being that trees would be felled and buildings altered, thus defeating the purpose of designation before it had taken place (ibid.: 47). Conversely, pressure for designation may come from local residents anxious to resist change and preserve their amenity. Thus, conservation areas may become gentrified: local shops may become antique shops and the nature of the residents may change (ibid.: 63). However, consultation is advocated in PPG15 (DoE 1994g: 15–16). Special characteristics frequently found in conservation areas include well grown trees, key public buildings such as churches, houses of note and groups of terraced houses, early planned development, early industrial and transport sites (e.g. canal locks) and historic gardens (Jones & Larkham 1993: 63–6).

Occupying buildings in a conservation area can be a mixed blessing. On the one hand, amenity is better protected, there is kudos from occupying the buildings, and property values may increase. On the other hand, occupiers and owners are more restricted in developing their property. Permitted development rights (PDR) over demolition and minor development are restricted (Ch. 4), advertisements may be tightly controlled and trees are protected as if subject to a tree preservation order (TPO) (see Ch. 6). More particularly there are tighter controls on cladding, dormer windows, satellite dishes and permitted extensions to houses and factories. LPAs may also use Article 4 Directions withdrawing PDR from changes to doors, windows, roofs and frontages. PPG15 advocates using these sparingly, which may mean we are back to the problems identified by the English Historic Towns Forum (EHTF), mentioned in Chapter 4 (DoE 1994g: 18–19).

Permission to demolish buildings is required in most cases in conservation areas. The procedure is essentially the same as for listed building consent (ibid.: 19). The general presumption is that buildings should be retained which make a positive contribution to the character or appearance of an area. Proposed replacement development can be taken into account in the demolition decision. Routine maintenance and replacement of windows, and so on, are held not to be demolition. (The problems of demolition are dealt with in Ch. 4.) Changes of use of buildings may be a way of conserving them, especially when uses become obsolete or economic pressures indicate more profitable uses. Central government views are that no special change of use regulations should apply in conservation areas (ibid.: 5–6).

Regrettably, minor alterations, subject to but without the benefit of planning permission, may take place. This is particularly so where newcomers move in and plead ignorance of conservation area designation or the controls involved. This can be circumvented to an extent by leafleting households regularly with design guidance and with guidance on the need for planning permission (Jones & Larkham 1993: 50).

As for planning policies in conservation areas, PPG15 is somewhat thin. In the section on designation (ibid.: 15 ff) it refers to the layout of property boundaries, the mix of uses, characteristic materials, scaling and detailing of contemporary buildings, the quality of advertisements, shop fronts, street furniture, the treatment of hard and soft surfaces, vistas along streets and between buildings, and the extent to which traffic intrudes and limits the pedestrian use of space between buildings. Conservation area designation should be seen as recognizing the importance of these factors. Others mentioned in addition were archaeological factors, the character and hierarchy of spaces, the quality of the buildings in the area, and trees and other green features. It also stresses the need to mesh conservation area policies with others, for example bringing vacant residential property over shops back into use by carefully considering planning applications that seek to eliminate separate access to shops and living accommodation (ibid.: 17). Policies must not prevent all forms of development, but must ensure prosperity by avoiding unnecessary control over businesses and households. New buildings need not imitate the old but must be designed to respect their context. As a policy, PPG15 urges LPAs to use design briefs detailing scale, height, massing, the pattern of frontages, fenestration and so on. Standards should be applied sensitively (e.g. parking).

PPG15 (ibid.: 18) also draws attention to a key legal case in which it was decided that "whilst the character and appearance of conservation areas should always be given full weight in planning decisions, the objective of preservation can be achieved by development which makes a positive contribution to an area's character or appearance, or by development which leaves the character and appearance *unharmed*" [author's emphasis].

Many conservation areas contain businesses that wish to display advertisements. Central government's view (ibid.: 20–21) is that outdoor advertising is essential: it attracts business, which in turn will maintain the conservation area. LPAs are urged to adopt policies that will indicate to developers what types of display will be acceptable. Certain categories of "deemed consent" advertisements, which have significant visual impact, may need specific consent from the

LPA (see below). In any event, LPAs are asked to use their powers sensitively – advertisements must "preserve and enhance" the area. Fascia boards on shops belonging to national chains are best scaled down and Holt (continuing: §30) reported examples of appeals failing because of floodlighting, signage clutter inappropriate to a building, and internally lit fascias. Hand-painted hanging signs and signboards found favour.

Trees are valued features in conservation areas and have protection rather like that given by Tree Preservation Orders (TPOs) (Ch. 6). Developers proposing to lop, top or fell trees must give LPAs six weeks' notice of their intentions, which gives them the opportunity to make TPOs. New planting may be necessary to retain the character of a conservation area. The imposition of conditions requiring new and replacement planting provides the developer with the opportunity to do this (DoE 1994g: 21).

New roads are best sited away from conservation areas, partly because of amenity considerations and partly because they may induce unwelcome development pressure in the conservation area itself. Within conservation areas, traffic management schemes can reduce traffic intrusion. Traditional floorscape and street furniture need to be retained, although uneven surfaces are not favoured by cyclists. Road signs and markings have a significant impact on streets. But this can be mitigated by, for example, attaching signs to buildings instead of to poles (ibid.: 22 ff).

With these points in mind, it is interesting to speculate on what we are conserving in conservation areas. Conservation area policy and implementation has only been phased in over the last third of the twentieth century. Apparently there are geographical differences between northern England and the South East in the number of conservation areas designated per LPA, and many conservation areas lack proper management funding and a sense of purpose. An important part of the debate over buildings in conservation areas is whether to restore them to their original design (the pragmatists' approach) to bring the economic benefits of tourists or to live with the alterations that are part of the building's history (the purists' approach) (Fair 1994c: 10). With constant authorized and unauthorized changes to buildings, in 50 years' time photographic records will probably show substantial changes in conservation areas.

Listed building control: ecclesiastical buildings
The Secretary of State for National Heritage has "listed" about half a million buildings in England as being of special architectural or historic interest, that is about 4 or 5 per cent of the stock of buildings. It is a criminal offence to demolish, alter or extend such buildings, internally or externally, without the consent of the LPA (DoE 1994g: 7). (It is not normally a criminal offence to do this to other buildings; ibid.: 15.) Wales and Scotland have similar arrangements (Cormier 1995: 1). There is a fine line between repair, which does not need consent, and development, which does; it is a matter of fact and degree, which the LPA can decide (painting, which affects the character of the building, would need permission).

Ecclesiastical buildings are fully subject to planning control, but those used for ecclesiastical purposes, and which are listed or are in conservation areas, are exempt. This exemption is predicated on churches exercising their own internal controls (Department of National Heritage & Cadw 1994). Where buildings are no longer used for ecclesiastical purposes, PPG15 urges that alternative uses be found, rather than demolition, as very often such buildings occupy convenient locations and are important features in townscape and landscape (DoE 1994g: 34 ff).

The "listing" referred to above divides listed buildings into the following categories in England: Grade I (2%), Grade II* (4%) and Grade II (94%) in order of importance and as a percentage of the stock of listed buildings (DoE 94g: 25 ff). Listing takes place by systematic survey and by suggestions from LPAs and others; "spot listing" protects buildings under immediate threat. The criteria for listing, not all of which apply in all cases, help in the understanding of the development control issues involved and reflect the reserved matters dealt with in Chapter 6. They include the following: architectural and aesthetic merits, historic interest and association, group value (e.g. model villages), age, type (e.g. housing and industry), national importance and local interest. LPAs can draw up their own lists, integrate them into plan policies and protect buildings through development control. De-listing, and certificates of immunity from listing, may help owners by giving them greater certainty in terms of what they may do with their buildings.

Generally, the best way of securing the upkeep of historic buildings is to keep them in active use. This may well involve changes of use and additions and alterations to the fabric. To secure a balance between change, conservation and viable use may mean less profitable or unprofitable outcomes, in which case charities such as the National Trust may become responsible for upkeep.

Whereas planning permission may be sought to develop most buildings, listed building consent is sought for listed building development (ibid.: annex B). However, if proposals are such that one would need planning permission for an unlisted building, then planning permission is necessary as well (Cormier 1995: 15). Listed building consent is rather like a normal planning application, but there is much greater attention to detail. Conditions, on the grant of consent, may typically ask for the preservation of particular features or the use of original materials. Where demolition of a listed building is to be allowed to make way for new development, a condition may be imposed to ensure that it should not be demolished until contracts have been let and planning permission for the new development obtained. This is intended to overcome the problem of gap sites. Readers should be aware of "Listed Building Enforcement Notices" to enforce compliance with the law (ibid.: 9). There is an appeals procedure (ibid.: ch. 4).

Procedures ensure that English Heritage and/or similar bodies are consulted about applications for consent: their comments are taken into account. LPAs may refuse consent or, if they are mindful of granting consent, the Secretary of State may call in the application. English Heritage may direct the LPA to refuse (DoE 1994g: annex B). PPG15 Annex C (ibid.) gives guidance on the detailed substantive matters to be considered when alterations to listed buildings are under consideration. There are too many to be listed here. But it is instructive to ponder on them, as alterations to buildings without any protective status, such as "semis in the suburbs", also need to be sensitively treated during alteration if the quality of the environment is to be preserved. Normally, of course, relatively minor alterations are permitted development; cumulatively insensitive alterations lead to environmental degradation. Considerations are grouped into major divisions: external elevations, roofs, external doors, windows, shop fronts, interiors, floors and new services. As for external elevations, alterations to walls have the most damaging effects. Every effort needs to be made to retain original materials (e.g. stonework). Painting and cleaning usually need listed building consent. Details such as ironwork need to be carefully repaired. Roofs are a dominant feature of many buildings: the shape and type of cladding need to be retained. External doors and door detail must be retained; modern off-the-peg doors should not be used. Windows should be repaired or replaced, like for like; new windows should respect existing fenestration. Old shop fronts should be retained and steel security grilles avoided. Unlike most other buildings, internal alterations, including flooring, are also subject to planning control. New services such as security cameras and wiring need to be unobtrusively integrated into the fabric.

Protection for listed buildings notwithstanding, 51 consents for demolition were granted in 1995–6 in England, but 2056 buildings were added to the list in 1995. The total number of sites recorded by the Department of the National Heritage was 448835 (Anonymous 1996f: 5, reporting English Heritage and the English Tourist Board).

Archaeology and planning

Archaeological remains in the UK stretch back millennia. They are often found in town centres during commercial renewal, but can be found virtually anywhere where building or mineral working is likely to take place. They are a small but discrete facet of development control. PPG16 (DoE 1990c) is the main central government guidance. It stresses that remains are a finite non-renewable resource, often fragile and vulnerable to damage. They contain irreplaceable information about our past, give us our sense of national identity and are valuable for their own sake and for their role in education, leisure and tourism. They have to be managed so that they are not needlessly destroyed. There is therefore a presumption in favour of physical preservation. Preservation *in situ* is possible, especially if remains are suspected and confirmed, by careful siting of landscaped areas or preserving them securely under new buildings. Excavation and preservation for the record is a second-best option. These approaches can be implemented through development plans and development control.

Not all remains are of equal importance; policies for nationally important sites are usually detailed in development plans. The desirability of preserving an ancient monument and its setting is a material consideration in development control (DoE 1990c: para. B18). Where remains are important it is possible to withdraw permitted development rights with an Article 4 Direction (Ch. 4).

If remains are known or suspected, it is best for the developer to negotiate with the LPA and the area archaeological officer as soon as possible in the development process. Designs can then take cognizance of remains. Prior investigation can be both field and desk study; such studies accompany planning applications. Where LPAs suspect remains, they normally consult experts. Developers should not expect planning permission in exchange for financing archaeological work. LPAs should seek agreement with developers for watching briefs, preserving, recording and publication, or by the imposition of conditions, usually in the form that no development shall take place until archaeological work has been carried out in accordance with a scheme submitted by the applicant and approved by the LPA. Ultimately, the LPA has to strike a balance between the intrinsic need to preserve the remains and the need for the development; it may refuse planning permission. In this context, readers should be aware of the schedule of ancient monuments and areas of archaeological importance, such as the centre of Chester, where special development control rules apply under the Ancient Monuments and Archaeological Areas Act 1979.

So much for government guidance. But what has the outcome been? Roger Tym's review of PPG16 (Roger Tym & Partners & Pagoda Associates 1995) found that many LPAs, in their preparation of development plans, allocated new land for development without a prior evaluation for archaeological considerations. But county and district archaeological officers (CAOs/DAOs) were reluctant to provide archaeological constraint maps, partly because planning applications outside constraint areas may not get referred to them, although practice had shown that this was not a significant problem. Normally LPAs pass planning applications lists to CAOs as a matter of routine for checking against Sites and Monuments Records (below). Article 4 Directions were apparently not used to protect archaeological sites, although Roger Tym recommended they should be. Each county or district keeps informal Sites and Monuments Records. Quality and access are very variable: they should be made statutory and more accessible to help LPAs and developers. Large developers appear to be sympathetic to the need for preapplication research but smaller ones rarely get involved; perhaps they do not wish to if they are not certain of getting planning permission. Because many archaeological officers operate at county level and the LPA is operating at district level, it is sometimes difficult to resolve archaeological problems. A further problem is with smaller utility companies that insist on their permitted development rights to carry on their operations, possibly to the detriment of archaeological remains. Ideally, predetermination evaluations (of planning applications) should be carried out, but this may be inhibited by the desire of LPAs to make a decision inside the eight-week period set by the Department of the Environment. As for evaluation costs, these are modest and should be looked on as just another site investigation cost.

The overall scale of archaeological concerns in the context of the development control process is very small (Table 7.1).

Surprisingly, there is no routine way in which CAOs know if developers have

Table 7.1 Categories of planning applications related to archaeological matters in 44 counties in 1993. Some categories overlap. (Roger Tym & Partners & Pagoda Associates 1995: 16).

Total planning applications	413882	100.00
Applications with potential archaeological significance	22512	5.4
Applications requiring archaeological recommendation	8148	2.0
Applications requiring archaeological recommendation	8148	100.00
Approved with archaeological conditions	5730	70.42
Recommended for redesign	486	6.0
Those involving watching brief	3493	42.9
Those involving full recording	1284	15.8
Refusal on archaeological grounds	164	2.02
"Archaeological appeals"	12	0.15
"Archaeological withdrawals"	48	0.6

started work so that they can be monitored. LPAs do not routinely provide copies of relevant decision notices to CAOs, and counties vary greatly in their views as to what proportion of recommendations should be and are monitored. In 1993 only 40 per cent of sites recommended for monitoring by CAOs/DAOs were actually monitored. Roger Tym recommended that monitoring of all kinds – excavations, archiving records, etc. – should be tightened up.

In 1993, 3493 applications involved a "watching brief": only in 43 cases (1 per cent) did remains come to light after planning permission was granted. Conditions normally secure the funding of excavations – 1111 cases in 1993. Excavation is one thing but the recording, archiving and storage of finds are different and may be the responsibility of different bodies. For a further report with case studies, see Brenan (1994).

In general, Roger Tym & Partners reported that archaeologists considered PPG16 to be working well (1995: 24).

Development control in rural areas

Introduction

Although the UK is highly urbanized, 77 per cent of the land area is used for agriculture and a further 10.5 per cent for forestry (Land Use Consultants & Countryside Planning and Management 1995: 15–17). About 80 per cent of the population live in towns and cities (DoE 1992a: para. 1.3). As a result, town planning is spoken of as synonymous with town and country planning. This section stresses country planning, which raises issues rather different from town planning and offers a different perspective on development control. The reader will appreciate that development control is a wide-ranging activity. To condense country planning to a section of a chapter is to do the subject an injustice. To add insult, tourism, sport and recreation are included here as often being rurally based. Minerals, almost invariably rurally based, are allocated to a separate section. The main central government guidance policy is contained in PPG7, *The countryside and the rural economy* (DOE 1992a), PPG2, *Green belts* (DOE 1995a), PPG9, *Nature conservation* (DOE 1994j), PPG17, *Sport and recreation* (DOE 1991b), PPG20, *Coastal planning* (DOE 1992m), and PPG21, *Tourism* (DOE 1992q). The Countryside Commission, which has statutory responsibility for the countryside, felt that the town and country planning system had been successful in conserving the beauty of much of our countryside. But the system faces major new challenges, particularly that of sustainable development (Countryside Commission 1996: 2).

The countryside and green belts

PPG7 (DOE 1992a) is the main planning guidance dealing with plans and development control in the early 1990s. Population and employment have been increasing in the more accessible parts of the countryside, but population and traditional employment in the more remote areas has declined. The Common Agricultural Policy has resulted in food surpluses. Farmers, landowners and occupiers therefore have to look to new economic opportunities. In small towns and villages, the quality of the environment has attracted new employment, but there are rural areas where economic problems remain. The government wishes to diversify the rural economy but at the same time protect the environment. This can be done by strictly controlling development in the open countryside and encouraging it sensitively in settlements (ibid.: §1).

Economic and technical changes have greatly increased pressure on traditional landscapes and wildlife habitats. There has been a longstanding priority planning policy to restrict the transfer of agricultural land to non-agricultural use, but the government has shifted its priority to rural diversification to provide employment opportunities. In making development control decisions, the government advises LPAs to take into account special designations (e.g. national parks); the need to encourage rural enterprise; the protection of the landscape, wildlife and historic features; the quality of agricultural land (especially Grades 1, 2 and 3a, which are the best land); and the need to protect non-renewable resources.

The use of land for agriculture and forestry is not development for the purposes of development control (Town & Country Planning Act 1990: §55, §336); some development is "permitted development" (see Fig. 3.1). PPG7 (DOE 1992a: annex B) describes agricultural development control in detail and there is a popular version, *A farmer's guide to the planning system*, summarized in Fig. 7.1).

Some agricultural development is subject to development control, depending whether the holding is larger or smaller than 5 ha and/or in a national park. Farmers wishing to carry out permitted development may need to inform the LPA so that they can determine whether planning permission is required (Fig. 7.1). Agricultural dwellings are excluded from permitted development (ibid.: appendix,

Figure 7.1 Development control and the farmer – an outline.

Introduction
As mentioned in the text (Ch. 3) the General Permitted Development Order Part 6 allows significant agricultural development without the need for planning permission: these are so-called permitted development rights. However, some types of development may need planning permission. In order to clarify whether planning permission is necessary or not for agricultural development, a special procedure has been set up for farmers, called a "determination". The farmer notifies the LPA of proposals. It then has 28 days to reply. The LPA may approve the proposals. Planning permission may or may not then be necessary. These procedures and substantive advice have been set out in popular form by the DoE et al. (1992) in *A farmer's guide to the planning system* on which this figure draws. Of necessity it deals with many aspects that are the subject of this book. The issues have been researched by Land Use Consultants (1995) and are reported in Chapter 4. The GPDO Part 6 is subject to many detailed conditions and exceptions too detailed for inclusion here. It is also subject to frequent changes.

Permitted development rights (DoE et al. 1992: 8, 28–31; Land Use Consultants & Countryside Planning and Management 1995: 33, 79; Casely-Hayford 1995: 68 ff).
Planning permission is not necessary for:
- Temporary uses of land, but not buildings, for not more than 28 days a year (14 days for some uses)
- Agricultural buildings below a certain size (465 m² or 12 m high) except farm dwellings and livestock units and slurry storage near housing. Proposals must be more than 25 m from a trunk or classified road. Erecting a new building, forming a private way, excavating or depositing waste may involve a "determination" from the LPA whether or not planning permission is necessary. (This is the special provision for farmers mentioned in the introduction and dealt with below.)
- Extensions up to 10 per cent of the cubic content of a building; in certain cases (e.g. in national parks), "determinations" may be necessary.
- Working minerals for use on the holding.
- Caravan sites in certain circumstances.
- Forestry building, etc. (but not forestry dwellings), subject to similar restrictions as agricultural buildings (Part 7 of the GPDO); may be subject to "determination" procedure.
- Erection of walls, gates, etc., as means of enclosure provided that they are not above 1 m from a highway and 2 m elsewhere and the setting of a listed building is not affected.
- Recreational use of land by specified organizations like the Scouts and the Caravan Club (Part 27 of the GPDO).
- Certain operations related to fish farming.

These permitted development rights apply to holdings larger than 5 ha. Below this size further restrictions apply.

The "determination" procedure (DoE et al. 1992.: 30–1)
As agricultural buildings and uses can be visually intrusive and noxious, the "determination" procedure was introduced so that an LPA could decide whether a proposal should be brought under control or not. For the determination procedure to operate, the proposed development must have permitted development rights. Details are given in PPG7 (DoE 1992a: Annex C). Under this procedure a farmer notifies his LPA of proposals, on a form rather like a simplified planning application form. It then has 28 days to decide whether prior approval is necessary for:
- the siting, design and external appearance of agricultural or forestry buildings
- the siting and means of construction of a private way
- the siting of excavations or waste deposits with an area exceeding 0.5 ha
- the siting and appearance of fish tanks.

The LPA may decide that prior approval is necessary; it may ask for further details. It then (Ch. 3) may make a decision to grant or refuse within eight weeks. Other consents may also be necessary related to listed buildings, conservation areas, tree preservation orders and advertisement consent. There is a right of appeal. In some cases planning permission may be necessary (Land Use Consultants & Countryside Planning and Management 1995: 39–40, 166).

Special rural policies
As great swathes of countryside are subject to special development control restrictions, the attention of farmers is drawn to national parks and areas of outstanding natural beauty (where appearance is very important), sites of special scientific interest (where consultation is necessary with special bodies such as English Nature) and the green belts (where agriculture, forestry and leisure uses are allowed but not others, other than the re-use of redundant rural buildings) (ibid.: 5).

Some of the farmer's questions answered
Does one need planning permission for:
- the conversion of farm buildings to non-farming uses – yes
- holiday accommodation – usually yes, but may not if the residential nature of a farmhouse is not changed
- stables for horses – generally, yes, but not for farm workhorses
- caravan sites – generally, yes, subject to exceptions
- farm shops – sometimes, especially if goods are bought to be sold
- food processing – depends on the scale involved
- "pick your own" – sometimes, but depends on amount of traffic and safety at junctions.

An example of good practice: a livestock unit (ibid.: 38)
As the acceptable siting of large new buildings in the countryside is difficult, advice is given. Farmers are urged to give the following information to their LPAs when making planning applications: the use of building (e.g. number and type of livestock), proximity to other buildings, ventilation, arrangements for storage and disposal of slurry (tanks, etc., within 400 m of certain buildings need planning permission), and type and colour of external materials, plus plans and photographs.
    Proposal plans showed softening with native, deciduous trees and sensitive siting next to existing buildings. As for colour, it was advised that green was an obvious choice but as it was difficult to achieve a natural shade, browns or dark blues were preferred (DoE et al. 1992).

annexes B and C). The main concerns are visual intrusion, traffic hazards, malodorous and pollutant slurry from livestock units, and farm shops on busy roads. A key test is whether the proposal will have a significant impact (ibid.: §3). The whole tone of PPG7 on this matter is one of "don't hinder the business of farming unreasonably". All developments should be assimilated into the landscape. For example, new buildings should not normally be in isolated locations, but grouped with others and related to them in scale and colour. Buildings should be set into slopes or near woodlands; new planting can soften the impact of buildings. As a generality, all development should conform to the principles set out in Chapter 6 on reserved matters (ibid.: annex C).

The re-use and adaptation of redundant buildings in the countryside poses different problems (ibid.: para. 2.15 and annex D). One abuse mentioned by PPG7 is the construction of new buildings, using permitted development rights with a view to early conversion to uses that would not normally be allowed, especially to residential use. Another issue is extensive change to historic farm buildings.

191

Conditions can be used to withdraw permitted development rights and improve the appearance of old buildings in these cases. Re-use of old buildings is a way of preserving them and avoiding the need to build new buildings in new locations. Generally, there is a presumption in favour, as the alternative may be dereliction.

Unless strictly controlled, new building in the countryside would spoil the very qualities householders may have sought. Widespread car ownership would make this so easy. There is particular concern about this issue in Northern Ireland. New housebuilding in villages is acceptable as it helps to sustain rural services. But "New housebuilding and other new development in the open countryside, away from established settlements, should be strictly controlled. The fact that a single house on a particular site would be unobtrusive is not in itself a good argument; it could be repeated too often" (ibid.: para. 2.18). A particular justification for housing in rural areas is building for those on modest incomes who cannot compete with commuters, the wealthy retired, second-home owners and entrepreneurs who bring new jobs to the countryside (see DoE 1992d). Arrangements should be made for affordable housing (DoE 1992a: para. 2.19).

PPG7 ends by drawing attention to development control in specific areas: national parks, areas of outstanding natural beauty (AONB), green belts and the urban fringe (see DoE 1995a), sites of special scientific interest (see DoE 1994j), historic and archaeological sites (see DoE 1994g, 1990c), and other designations, including locally devised Areas of Great Landscape Value and Environmentally Sensitive Areas, which can be protected and enhanced by specific agricultural practices (ibid.: §3). It particularly draws attention to the (partial) withdrawal of permitted development rights (PDR) in national parks, AONBs and conservation areas by the reduction of particular permitted limits (e.g. there are lower volumes for permitted house extensions) and by the complete withdrawal of PDR (e.g. roof extensions to dwellings, the application of stone cladding to the outside of houses and the installation of satellite dishes facing roads or on buildings over 15m high (ibid.: para. 3.1). In national parks, national parks authorities are responsible for development control in their areas. Their purpose is to conserve natural beauty and promote enjoyment, but where there is conflict in the context of development control, recreation should take second place, having due regard to the social and economic welfare of local people (ibid.: para. 3.2). The development control difference between national parks and AONBs is that the latter do not cater specifically for recreation and the LPAs' control development. Between them they cover nearly a quarter of England and Wales. There is particular sensitivity to major industrial and mineral developments. The development control regime in green belts (ibid.: 3.12), SSSIs (ibid.: para. 3.14), archaeological sites and conservation areas (ibid.: para. 3.15) is dealt with elsewhere in Chapter 7.

Green belts are subject to possibly the longest-standing central government development control advice, in that parts of Ministry of Housing and Local Government Circular 42/55 were not cancelled until PPG2 was issued (DoE 1995a). Green belts have five purposes:

- checking urban sprawl

- preventing towns merging
- safeguarding the countryside from encroachment
- preserving the setting of historic towns
- assisting urban regeneration by recycling derelict and other urban land.

Within green belts some types of development are allowed (ibid.: §1):

- to provide access for townsfolk
- to provide outdoor recreation
- to improve damaged land
- to conserve nature
- to facilitate agricultural and forestry uses.

Green belts are seen as permanent and are included in development plans as such. Central government advises that, once set, detailed boundary changes should be seen as exceptional, and warns that changes should not be made merely because the land has become derelict (ibid.: para. 2.6). In the context of development control it seems to face two directions at once: boundaries "should be carefully drawn so as not to include land which it is unnecessary to keep permanently open", but "If boundaries are drawn excessively tightly around existing built-up areas it may not be possible to maintain the degree of permanence that green belts should have" (ibid.: para. 2.8). Possibly the most striking development control policy related to green belts is the presumption against development. "Inappropriate development is, by definition, harmful to the green belt. It is for the applicant to show why permission should be granted" (ibid.: para. 3.2). Elsewhere there is a presumption in favour of development (DOE 1992c: para. 5): it is for the LPA to demonstrate good planning reasons for refusal. However, some development is allowed:

- for agriculture and forestry
- for outdoor recreation
- limited extension of existing dwellings
- limited village infill
- on certain major sites (e.g. hospitals)
- the re-use of buildings
- mineral working.

Overall concern is the desire to preserve the openness of the green belt, which may be preserved by conditions and planning obligations.

Elson et al. (1995a, 1995b; see also 1996: 8–9), in their studies of rural diversification in England and Wales, reported on some aspects of PPG7 and PPG4. They considered particularly the inclusion of central government guidance in making development control decisions. Their studies included national parks, AONBs and green belts, and considered rural areas thought to be "remote" and those thought to be "accessible". The study was concerned primarily with economic diversification and commercial development, and not with housing. Their overall conclusion with regard to development control and appeal statistics was that the LPAs studied were not being restrictive on economic diversification proposals (Elson et al. 1995b: 45) and that they had gone a long way to integrate

PPG7 policies into development plans (ibid.: 90). However, LPAs had a rather low understanding of local labour markets and there was little monitoring of the process of economic diversification and the re-use of buildings (ibid.: 91). In terms of re-use and intensification of uses, pressure was high in "accessible" areas, but in "remote" areas there was a low level of implementation of permission for employment re-use and no evidence of a great shortage of premises (ibid.: 92). Relaxation of policies and development control were therefore unlikely to create new jobs. The study did not include studies of unemployment, personal incomes or other economic indicators. The relationship between planning policy, development control and the wider aims of rural diversification remained unclear. The two studies quoted contained development control case studies of LPA areas, individual planning applications and examples of good practice; a taste of these is offered in Figure 7.2.

Elson et al. (1993) reported on the effectiveness of green belts in 1993. Whereas Elson et al. (1995b) reported on the operation of PPG7 promulgated in 1992 *ex post facto*, the green belt study reported before PPG2 was promulgated in 1995 and influenced its content. For example, earlier guidance suggested that institutions surrounded by extensive grounds could be allowed in the green belt. It was found that this category was difficult to define in practice (Elson et al. 1993: v) and it did not appear in the more recent guidance PPG2 (DoE 1995a). The 1993 report therefore considered the effectiveness of earlier green belt guidance. Nonetheless, it is instructive because of the light it threw inter alia on

---

Figure 7.2   Development control and rural diversification.

An example of a rural local planning authority, Leominster District, Hereford and Worcester, a "remote" district, 1991 to 1993
Leominster had about 150 non-residential planning applications a year (approval rate 90–94% per annum) out of a total of about 860 (approval rate 84–88% per annum). In the non-residential group, agricultural, industrial and tourist applications were the most numerous and, of these, new buildings were by far the most common, followed by re-use; extensions and others were few. Applications were somewhat more numerous in rural settlements than on farms or in the open countryside. Business-related residential applications were significant. Approved applications in 1993 included general agricultural buildings such as cattle sheds, school extensions, garden centre developments, industrial buildings split half and half into new and change-of-use, offices, retailing (including shop front changes), recreation (including golf courses), tourism (including conversions to holiday lets), transport and storage (Elson et al. 1995b: 114 ff, paraphrased).

Examples of rationalizing formerly inappropriate uses on large sites in the countryside
Four examples of rural industrial uses were given, some of which involved farm buildings and others defence property. One example was the permitted conversion of 50000ft^2 of storage, plus other buildings previously used for defence purposes to light industrial units. The buildings were in "open countryside" as defined in the local plan (Hambleden District, North Yorkshire) and would not normally be permitted. It was argued that the buildings were not new; they were well located on the highway network, caused minimal damage to neighbouring communities, 60 jobs were to be created, and the buildings received grant aid. The overall lessons of the four cases cited, inter alia, were that the use of low-cost buildings near rural settlements was very important to those starting up in business (Elson et al. 1995a: 30 ff, paraphrased).

development control practice throughout the English and Scottish countryside.

As with the 1995 study of rural diversification, the authors had two main areas of concern: the effect of central government guidance on development plan-making and on development control. As plans are an important consideration in development control (Ch. 2), it is useful to report briefly on some aspects of plan-making before dealing in more detail with development control. It was found inter alia that green belt policy was successful in checking urban sprawl and preventing the merging of towns in the study period in the eight years to 1993. Less than 0.3 per cent of green belt land had been affected by alteration of boundaries (Elson et al. 1993: i, 9, 10). However, the effects of green belt restraint policies on the cores of historic cities were unclear (ibid.: 18). On the other hand, green belt restrictions had assisted urban regeneration where LPAs had a portfolio of sites awaiting development, although again the effect is not all that clear-cut (ibid.: 25). A particularly contentious issue was the permanence of green belt boundaries (ibid.: ch. 9). Green belts are seen as long term, to be altered only in exceptional circumstances. They have had very strong support from the general public (ibid.: 136–7, quoting Consumers' Association 1989). Exceptional circumstances were not clearly defined; discretion lay with the Secretary of State, who may alter policies in plans (ibid.: 85). It was found that exceptional circumstances often related to high-amenity employment sites (ibid.: 94).

For the purposes of development control in the green belt, three or four different types of land need to be differentiated. There is the green belt proper. This is open country in which there is a presumption against development. Some types of development are appropriate in the green belt, for example agricultural buildings, outdoor sport, mineral working, roads, utilities, the re-use of redundant buildings, housing for local rural needs and, under earlier guidance, institutions standing in extensive grounds. Also in the green belt are small settlements that carry green belt notation; they are called "washed-over" and they include hamlets and ribbon development. In these either there may be no development allowed at all or, in a specified list of settlements, infill may be permitted. Elson et al. (ibid.: 254) found in fact that infill was allowed in both. Furthermore, there are "inset villages". These are enclaves within the green belt but do not have green belt notation. They include low-density development or land that might be an eyesore in need of enhancement or where there is spare capacity in the infrastructure. Within them, limited expansion is permitted (ibid.: 29). Insets are likely to contain valuable employment sites that would be inappropriate in the green belt proper.

Elson et al. (ibid.: 36–40) found in four districts studied with green belts that two-thirds of all planning applications for land in the green belt proper were for houses and most of these were for extensions and alterations to existing dwellings. About 10 per cent were for educational and community use. Others, such as retail, leisure and agriculture, were a very small proportion of the total. Approval rates in the green belt proper were consistently 10 to 15 percentage points lower than in relevant open countryside, urban land and inset land. However, by the time of the study there was little difference in approval rates between green belt

195

and open countryside sites, except for the treatment of employment sites and redundant buildings. As in other studies of this type, it is not possible to gauge applications not proceeded with, because they are weeded out as hopeless cases with no chance of success in the green belt. Actual applications are not only small in scale but also very small in number. In the Chester green belt, for example, covering 14000ha, only 15 applications for leisure were approved in 4 years.

The report went into considerable detail on the development control arguments surrounding particular types of development in the green belt: affordable housing, agricultural dwellings, the re-use of redundant buildings, institutions in extensive grounds, redundant hospitals, existing employment uses, outdoor sport and recreation, golf, tourism, park-and-ride, motorway service areas, utilities and unauthorized uses such as tipping. Let us take existing employment uses to illustrate some of the arguments as local authorities seek to protect them. Such uses include offices in country houses, isolated industrial estates and oil depots, some of which may have been established before 1948 (ibid.: 51). However, they are inappropriate uses in the green belt. The earlier version of PPG2 (DoE 1988h: para. 14) advised that plans "should make no reference to the possibility of allowing other development in exceptional circumstances". It was found in practice that most LPAs allowed for redevelopment and expansion for fear that firms might move elsewhere.

A study of the outcome of appeals against refusal of planning permission and enforcement appeals in the green belt showed that fewer than a quarter were upheld (Elson et al. 1993: appendix H). Of appeals made about a half related to dwellings and of these a majority related to extensions, of which only a third were upheld. Of applications for new dwellings that went to appeal, fewer than 10 per cent succeeded. Proposals upheld on appeal most often related to the re-use of redundant buildings for commercial and office uses, and land for **gypsies**. LPAs normally permit limited extensions to dwellings in the green belt and have policies in development plans for this purpose. For example, extensions up to 50 per cent of the original floor area may be allowed. In appeal cases, infill was sometimes allowed in washed-over villages where they would not have harmed green belt objectives. Where agricultural dwellings for agricultural occupancy were refused and went to appeal, the success rate was low at 19 per cent. Tests were applied, for example that the holding would be financially viable enough to sustain one agricultural worker and that there was an agricultural need. LPAs were very aware that applications for agricultural dwellings were a way of circumventing the virtual prohibition on building dwellings in the open countryside. Conditions were imposed on those allowed, to restrict them to agricultural use.

As mentioned earlier, green belts have multiple purposes. Three objectives – checking unrestricted urban sprawl, preventing towns merging, and protecting the countryside from encroachment – do seem to have been fulfilled. The effects of green belt policies on historic towns, urban regeneration and urban intensification were not so clear-cut (ibid.: i–iii). But these aims and findings ignored the activities that need to go on in the green belt itself and which are also subject to development control. In particular, these are agriculture, which is subject to continuing economic and technical change, and ever-growing leisure pursuits, which have been included in the green belt discussion so far. Development control arguments about agricultural dwellings, the effects of fragmentation of holdings, bare land farms (devoid of the usual farm buildings) and the re-use of rural buildings were reported by Land Use Consultants & Countryside Planning and Management (1995). The management of the countryside, which is so important to its attraction, is not subject to planning control. Elson et al. (1993: ch. 4) suggested inter alia that neglected sites could be enhanced by allowing enabling development to finance projects and community forests to include recreation. As development is allowed in the green belt, planning conditions and planning obligations could be attached to them to enhance the landscape. Such developments include mineral working, waste disposal, golf courses and the redevelopment of hospital and industrial sites.

Recreation and tourism

Readers will recall that in Chapter 1 attention was drawn to the four main activities in adapted spaces with which town planning is concerned: workspaces (e.g. shops, factories and offices), living spaces (especially houses), and leisure spaces (e.g. cinemas and camp sites) and transport spaces, especially roads and parking, which facilitate movement between the other three categories of activity ("work, folk, play"). Arguably, the planning characteristics of job spaces, residential spaces and transport spaces, each taken in turn, exhibit a certain homogeneity each within itself. Chapter 6 on major considerations in development control, such as design and, especially, access, was illustrated using examples drawn from these three activities. It is argued that leisure activities exhibit great variety and are worthy of separate consideration here. On the other hand, PPG21, *Tourism* (DoE 1992q: paras 2.2, 2.3), opines that "The kinds of facility and development needed for (these) various types of tourism and the problems that they can generate, are not necessarily different, in terms of land-use planning, from similar types of development serving other types of demand . . . For (all) those reasons 'tourism' cannot be regarded as a single or distinct category of land use".

Tourism is defined as "the temporary short-term movement of people to destinations outside the places where they normally live and work and the activities during their stay at these destinations" (ibid.: para. 2.1). This might be for business or domestic purposes and for holidays and recreation. Recreation is usually thought to be within and near the home, but of course tourists share sport and recreational facilities with locals. The coast provides rather special tourist and recreational facilities. The demand for leisure over the past century has shown an upward trend, but more recently trends in visitor numbers to the countryside have not been clear cut. Participation in indoor and outdoor sports is increasing (DoE 1991b: para. 5). Less quantifiable activities have grown in recent years; for example, holiday villages and current concern for health and fitness create a

197

demand for active leisure opportunities. Common to many countryside leisure activities is its impact on sensitive environments (House of Commons Environment Committee 1995: xxi ff). Principal central government guidance is given in PPG17, *Sport and recreation* (DoE 1991b), PPG20, *Coastal planning* (DoE 1992m), and PPG21, *Tourism* (DoE 1992q). They will be commented on in turn. Further guidance occurs in other PPGs, for example, PPG2, *Green belts* (DoE 1995a), and PPG7, *The countryside and the rural economy* (DoE 1992a).

PPG17 (DoE 1991b: para. 2), *Sport and recreation*, is concerned primarily with outdoor leisure either of an organized kind (e.g. in stadia), or of an informal kind, such as walking in the countryside. It is not concerned with indoor urban recreation such as theatres. The perspective is one of plan preparation rather than of development control. The development control implications are oblique and at a high level of generalization. The government argues that sport and recreation are important components of civilized life, promoting health and national pride, and it seeks to promote them in their widest sense (ibid.: para. 2). It is part of an LPA's development control responsibilities to ensure that deficiencies are made up and to resist the development of open space where it conflicts with the wider public interest. Open space is not only an amenity but a contribution to the conservation of the natural and built environment (ibid.: 4). Typically development plans have (ibid. paras 8–15):

- policies for major facilities of local, regional or national importance (e.g. motor sports)
- policies for landscape, open space and wildlife
- policies for the urban fringe and green belts
- a statement of the implications for sport and recreation of new development
- policies for rights of way
- policies for playing fields.

PPG17 also draws attention to the concept of standards, for example an outdoor playing space standard of 2.43ha per 1000 population and to the hierarchy of spaces, from regional parks to small local open spaces, each catering for different needs (ibid.: tables A and B). It stops short of recommending standards of provision. It also advocates the provision of facilities through §106 agreements attached to planning permission for housing, commercial development and mineral working (ibid.: para. 20). (See Elson & Payne 1993, who researched case studies of §106 agreements briefly reported in Ch. 5.)

PPG17 continues by drawing attention to a series of planning issues (ibid.: para. 25 ff). In urban environments, LPAs are urged to safeguard open spaces from encroachment and especially cater for children and the elderly. Where floodlighting might be used, planning conditions can be attached to time-limit their operation. On the urban fringe, LPAs are asked to give sympathetic consideration to change of use from agriculture to recreational pursuits. In the green belt "outdoor sport" is an appropriate use where in special circumstances ancillary buildings may be built and where the re-use of redundant sites might improve environmental quality. In the countryside more generally, tourist facilities may help local residents who otherwise would not have access to them, for example country parks. The distinction is drawn between national parks, where conservation and recreation are of equal importance, and AONBs, where natural beauty is paramount, but where nonetheless there are recreational pressures. The aim must be to balance and reconcile competing interests, for example by management measures (implicitly planning conditions) to limit time, space and season. Rather separately, playing fields should be kept for recreational and amenity value. However, in some cases they may be used for development, where by developing a small part of a site the whole facility can be enhanced, where alternative provision can be made, and where there is more than adequate provision locally.

PPG17 makes suggestions related to particular sports (ibid.: para. 45 ff). As a result of the Hillsborough disaster, many soccer stadia are being reconstructed or relocated. Many old grounds are boxed in by residential development where access and parking are poor. Strategic relocation may solve planning problems at an old site and, where derelict land can be used, solve other problems at a new site. Besides the customary development control issues such as traffic generation, attention can also be paid to safety and public order. The opportunity can be taken to incorporate multi-use non-football leisure facilities for the whole community. Noisy sports, such as motor sports, can be contained by banks or steered to suitable sites such as degraded land or land near noisy activities such as main roads. Where sports such as war games can take place under permitted development rights, Article 4 Directions (Ch. 4) may be used to control them when they are a threat to amenity. To satisfy the buoyant demand for boat moorings, PPG17 argues that they can be created in redundant mineral workings, disused docks and elsewhere without undue damage to the natural environment. Where golf courses are suggested in the open countryside, concomitant hotels and associated developments should be considered on their own merits.

PPG20, *Coastal planning* (DOE 1992m), not only deals with leisure but also with sea defence, industrial plant, ports and wastewater treatment. The coast is a very important resource because certain economic and social activities, such as ports and leisure, need a coastal location and it contains special landscapes and habitats. As ever, it is the task of the LPAs to reconcile development with conservation.

About 30 per cent of the coastline of England and Wales has been developed, much of it before the Town and Country Planning Act 1947. In 1972, the "Heritage Coast" designation was introduced, covering another third of the open coastline, which is protected by the planning system, including other designations such as AONBs. Inter alia, the purposes of the Heritage Coast designation are to protect habitats and natural beauty, facilitate leisure activities and take account of the social and economic needs of coastal communities (ibid.: para. 1.7). LPAs define coastal areas above low water mark by reference to the nature of the topography and the extent of coast-related activity. Activity below low water mark (e.g. gravel extraction), is subject to other controls. Onshore activities, for example industry, may have an effect offshore (e.g. on shellfish stocks; ibid.: §1).

199

Coastal development can be particularly visually intrusive, so that curbing it may well bring development pressures on less protected parts. Central government urges LPAs to adopt development plan policies that steer developments, which do not need a coastal location either away from the coast or to an already developed coastline. In fact few developments need a coastal location (ibid.: para. 2.10). New development should not generally be allowed in areas needing expensive engineering works, for example flood control. Planning permission is necessary for new sea defence works; marinas and holiday villages may well need environmental impact assessment. PPG20 draws attention to the need to provide carparks and other development and to the need to regenerate rundown seaside resorts (ibid.: §2).

Tourism and recreation are uses that may need coastal locations. Pressures are building up which bring people to the coast for its beauty and for water-based recreation. If there is irreconcilable conflict, the conservation and enhancement of natural beauty must take precedence (ibid.: para. 3.3). The demand for boat moorings in particular has been growing, which brings pressure for carparking, access and onshore facilities; these are best steered to old docks. LPAs should discourage the loss of disused boatyards to other uses which do not require coastal locations. Central government also declares that public access to the coast should be a basic principle that should be secured through the development control process, possibly by using §106 agreements (ibid.: para. 3.9; Elson & Payne 1993).

PPG21, *Tourism* (DoE 1992q), is wider in its leisure scope than PPG17 and PPG20, and devotes a good deal of attention to development control issues (ibid.: §5 and annexes A, B and C, devoted to hotels, caravans and seasonal occupancy planning conditions).

Tourism is a growing and major part of the national economy, generating a wide range of jobs and earning foreign exchange. It is based on growing incomes, leisure and mobility. It involves a wide variety of development, including shops, hotels, conference centres, tourist attractions such as historic sites, the coast, sport and entertainment, and all aspects of transportation. The natural and built environment, including national parks and historic towns, are vital to its success. Tourism is therefore encouraged by central government in response to market pressures, but subject to control in the interests of sustainable development. However, demand for new attractions is constantly changing (ibid.: §2 and §3) and it is fickle in that leisure is not as vital to life as are jobs and housing. The English Tourist Board has identified various tourist needs, including more and better-quality holiday villages and cottages, and much greater emphasis on design quality and respect for the environment in all tourist developments. The government for its part, in its support for tourism, wants to encourage a wider geographical and seasonal spread of tourism. These needs all have development control implications (ibid.: §5).

Tourism policies are key strategic topics in regional guidance, structure plans and local plans, dealing inter alia with the scale and distribution of tourist activity, the protection of tourism assets and tourism as a means of urban regeneration (ibid.: §4). Tourist development needs planning permission in the same way as other development and, in addition, caravan parks need site licences (ibid.: §5). Most tourist development is small scale and can be dealt with in the normal way. Special and large-scale development, such as ski-lifts, marinas and holiday villages, are likely to need environmental impact assessment. PPG21 draws attention (ibid.: para. 5.12 ff) to the principles of development control in specific types of location. Areas of high landscape quality, such as national parks and historic sites, have an intrinsic attraction for development which could damage them; control policies for tourism should be no less rigorous than for any other form of development. Indeed, most tourist needs for shops and accommodation can be met within existing development or outside sensitive areas. In sensitive areas it is a matter of controlling numbers, location and extent. Tourists visit historic towns not only for set-piece attractions such as cathedrals but also to enjoy historic environments. These are often covered by conservation areas and subject to tight development control, reported earlier in this chapter.

Seaside resorts present peculiar problems. Many were built before the First World War, have suffered from overseas competition and have been in decline. Nonetheless, they still comprise a very significant segment of the holiday market. Seafront architecture is increasingly appreciated and needs to be retained to help regeneration. The conversion of the hotel stock to other uses weakens a town's attraction as a tourist destination. Both of these problems are subject to development control. PPG21 also draws attention to the need for good design (see Ch. 6) and to outdoor advertising for tourist-related development. Outdoor advertisements may be acceptable in urban areas and, albeit muted, in rural areas, historic cities and conservation areas. More problematic are advance highway signs for tourist attractions remote from main roads but which are needed to attract passing traffic.

PPG21 ends with three development control annexes on hotels, caravans and planning conditions. Let us consider development control of holiday- and touring-caravan sites (ibid.: annex B). They are an important part of tourism: 13 million people a year have caravan holidays in Britain. Caravan sites can be particularly visually intrusive, especially on the coast. Tent camping enjoys permitted development rights for up to 28 days a year and a few tents on an existing caravan site would probably not constitute a change of use. The PPG suggests that LPAs think in terms of the number of "touring units", that is tents or caravans, in considering the use of local roads and access to a proposed site, within an overall limit on the number of pitches. The number of pitches can be controlled by planning conditions, as can seasonality of occupation (ibid.: annex C). Members of named caravan organizations may occupy up to five pitches on small sites in sensitive areas where larger sites would be intrusive. Basic decision-rules for larger caravan sites are screening, not visually intrusive, not by the sea but a short distance back, where they are not visible from the sea or the coast and are not floodable. Other PPGs (2, 7, 9 and 20) draw attention to green belt restrictions, the sensitivity of the coast and nature reserves, and specially designated areas such as national parks. The need to improve the layout and landscape quality of existing sites may involve site expansion. Model standards for caravan sites are given in Circular 23/83, *Caravan Sites and Control of Development Act* 1960 (DoE 1983).

The overall impression one gets of the growth of tourism and recreation is that many developments are small and are dealt with in the normal way through the development control system. Adverse environmental impacts arise because much activity does not involve development. The Environment Committee (House of Commons Environment Committee 1995: vol. I, xxvii) concluded that, compared with other activities, leisure and tourism do not cause significant widespread ecological damage to the countryside. The important issues to address are transport, rural culture and leisure management. Inter alia they recommended that design standards be strictly enforced through the planning system to ensure that development is of a form and in a material appropriate for the local environment (ibid.: para. 64) and that overall PPGs did not call for major changes, apart from an update of PPG17 to include sustainability (ibid.: para. 90). The Committee (ibid.: para. 102) urged LPAs to identify sites for noisy and obtrusive activities. They endorsed existing coastal zone policies but said progress was too slow (ibid.: para. 111). Permitted development rights for temporary activities such as clay pigeon shooting came under scrutiny and it was suggested the issue should be re-examined (ibid.: para. 168). The Committee (ibid.: para. 179) drew attention to the RTPI's principles of sustainability from its report, *Rural planning in the 1990s*, which are very germane to development control, albeit at a high level of generalization; we should:

- adopt the precautionary approach
- consider the ability of the countryside to absorb development without detriment to the social and physical environment
- preserve the integrity of environmental systems
- promote a self-sustaining rural economy
- maintain the character of rural communities
- ensure that the countryside has its own integrity and is not simply a façade for the amusement of visitors.

See also the RTPI evidence to the Committee (House of Commons Environment Committee 1995: vol. III, 319 ff)

Outdoor advertisements

Outdoor advertisements are, arguably, a necessary adjunct of commercial life: PPG19 says they are essential (DoE 1992f: para. 3). Uncontrolled proliferation is a self-defeating eyesore. In appropriate locations they can be used to mask ugly views and enliven otherwise subdued environments. The demand for hoardings (poster panels) can frequently outstrip supply (Trimbos 1996: 10). Outdoor advertisements must not harm amenity and they must be safe. As a generality they are not normally allowed in the open countryside or in residential areas. They are subject to their own development control legislation and guidance, and they form a comprehensive and self-contained regime: the *Town and Country Planning (Control of Advertisements) Regulations 1992*, DOE Circular 5/92 with the same title (DOE 1992e), PPG19, *Outdoor advertisement control* (DOE 1992f) with a popular version, *Outdoor advertisements and signs – a guide for advertisers* (DOE & WO 1995). Advertisement control constitutes about 6 per cent of the development control workload of an average LPA (Holt continuing: para. 30.03).

Advertisements are defined in the Town and Country Planning Act 1990 §220 ff and include posters and notices, placards and boards, fascia and projecting signs, pole and canopy signs, models and devices, directional name and traffic signs, estate agents' boards, captive balloons and flags, and price markers and displays. Such a wide definition invites an enormous development control workload. To circumvent this, advertisements are divided into three classes which limit the workload:

- "Excepted" advertisements, which may be displayed without consent as long as they keep to the rules. They include advertisements the public cannot normally see from a public place because they are enclosed, and those on vehicles. Notices relating to elections, official traffic signs and national flags come into this category. But there are complexities; for example, an advertisement incorporated in the fabric of a building is in this category, but not one that is painted on a building or which is a hoarding for the display of advertisements (DOE 1992h: Schedule 2).

- "Deemed consent" advertisements, which may be displayed without consent. Advertisements in this group, which has 14 classes with further subclasses, include functional advertisements related to local authorities and transport undertakings, advertisements related to the premises on which they are displayed, including business plates, temporary advertisements (e.g. "for sale" signs), charity posters, advertisements on business premises (including forecourts), flags, advertisements on hoardings around commercial building sites for which planning permission has been obtained, neighbourhood watch signs and directional advertisements (DOE 1992h: Schedule 3). But all categories are subject to conditions and limitations. A frequent condition is that they should not be illuminated. Frequent limitations are on size (e.g. not larger than $0.3\,m^2$) and on their position on buildings (e.g. no more than 4.6m above ground level).

- The final category of advertisements need "express consent" from the LPA. In practice they include the majority of illuminated signs, specialized structures such as hoardings, those more than 4.6m above the ground and gable-end advertisements (Holt, continuing: para. 30.03).

Making an application for express consent is somewhat like that for a normal application. The application form contains the name and address of the applicant and/or agent and the location of the proposal. Unlike normal applications, advertisement applications must receive the consent of the owner of the site before display: to do otherwise is an offence open to immediate prosecution. The LPA needs to know about the current use of the site and the type of proposed advertisement (e.g. a projecting box sign) and whether it is illuminated and whether intermittently. The normal display period is five years, but applicants may seek other periods. This differs from planning permission, which is normally in perpetuity as long as development starts within five years. A fee is payable. Plans are required to accompany the application, showing the proposed location, the size, the position on a building (say), the highest point above the ground, the materials and colours. Advertisements may relate to advertising sites, which take up an area of ground, or may be related to a site in another use (e.g. a fascia on a shop) (DoE 1992f: para. 24).

Advertisements have very positive uses. Hoardings can hide eyesores, particularly around building sites; they can enliven otherwise dull commercial streets and industrial estates, particularly by being illuminated at night, and can provide direction signs (e.g. new homes for sale). They can also help to provide site security. Most importantly, they promote business by displaying the names of the firms and products. This is particularly so in the case of shop fascia boards and hanging signs. Substantial changes to shop fronts need separate planning permission. The UK does not have "commercial strips" along main roads such as are common in the USA, where advertisement control is considerably relaxed to promote a lively mixture of shops, hotels, open-air displays and service workshops.

In considering advertisement applications, LPAs have two main concerns: safety and amenity. Safety refers to the structural soundness of hoardings and hanging signs, so that they are not a danger to the public who might physically walk or drive into them. Consider, perhaps unusually, captive balloons near airports. Other safety issues relate to the distraction of drivers by the various modes – water, rail, air and road. Advertisements are by their nature designed to distract. LPAs must ensure that, when they are illuminated or reflect they do not dazzle drivers, especially in wet conditions, or have written messages that move or flash intermittently. Advertisements must be so designed and sited that they are in no way confused with traffic signs and signals. Particular care must be taken that advertisements do not obstruct drivers' sight lines, especially at junctions (DoE 1992f: §27 ff).

The other concern is amenity; this is largely an aesthetic problem, discussed in Chapter 6 (see pp. 141–7), under the external appearance of development. The key consideration is the impact of a proposal on the building concerned or on the visual amenity of the immediate neighbourhood. LPAs consider scale, illumination and reflectivity, colour, type of material and overall design (DoE 1992f: para. 11 ff). It would be inappropriate to have a 5m × 5m bright internally illuminated yellow plastic box sign in a commercial conservation area in a small county town where there are listed buildings. It may be appropriate in a new retail warehouse park. As aesthetic judgements are subjective, it is important that LPAs are consistent across their districts. When considering applications, an LPA can consider the cumulative effect of existing advertisements, so that clutter can be avoided (ibid.). But as Morgan & Nott (1995: 221) pointed out, there is often quite a clutter of excepted and deemed consent advertisements in any event. In this general context, Holt (continuing: 30.033) drew attention to aggressive retail corporations who nationally try to insist on a specific house signage by way of colour, design, materials and illumination. Negotiation can bend this insistence to modify scale and the other elements to make the signage blend with the surroundings.

There are three categories of geographical area where advertisements are quite strictly controlled. First, it is thought that advertisements are not appropriate to residential areas. Small hotels in them may be allowed modest illuminated signage for use at night. Secondly, advertisements are not normally allowed in the open countryside, although a firm there may be allowed signage to indicate its presence. Thirdly, there are Areas of Special Control of Advertisements (ASCA) covering 45 per cent of the area of England and Wales. They are designated by the LPAs and approved by the Secretary of State for the Environment, and include National Parks, Areas of Outstanding Natural Beauty and Conservation Areas (DOE 1996a). Not all conservation areas are in ASCAs: some are thriving commercial centres where advertisements are to be expected. Control is much stricter than elsewhere. Hoardings may not be allowed and advertisements with "deemed consent" elsewhere have stricter siting and size limits (DOE 1992f).

To provide a background to application decisions, LPAs often include policies in development plans related to cognate concerns. For example, shop-front design policy, amplified by design guidance, may suggest that where one shop occupies two adjacent buildings there must be two separate fascia boards, one for each shop. Retailers may want one larger continuous board to attract attention; this interrupts the rhythm of the street frontage. Before an LPA makes its decision, it may consult other parties. If an LPA is mindful of granting planning permission for the display of advertisements, it must impose five standard conditions (DOE 1992h: Schedule 1). Advertisements must:

- be kept clean and tidy
- be maintained safely
- be removed to the satisfaction of the LPA when the applicant is required to do so
- not be displayed without the consent of the owner of the site
- not obscure traffic signs or render hazardous any transport mode.

If an applicant is aggrieved by a refusal of permission or by onerous conditions, he may appeal to the Secretary of State for the Environment, as for other forms of development (DOE 1992f: para. 31). Holt reported (Holt, continuing: para. 30.036) that the dismissal rate was 94 per cent. The Annex to PPG19 (ibid.) contained guidance on appeals involving poster sites. It gives an insight into the problems of this particular form of advertising. Apart from safety, poster panels are a matter of scale. In pedestrian streets they should be in scale with the street furniture and should not overwhelm walkers. On the other hand, freestanding units along highways can be larger in scale and accompanied by hard and soft landscaping which helps the display to blend with its surroundings. In villages, posters are thought to be out of place, but small displays may be appropriate. The same is true of residential areas, but posters may be allowed where there is a mixture of commercial uses.

An LPA may wish to ask an advertiser with deemed consent or with a time-expired express consent to discontinue displaying it by issuing a "discontinuance notice". Deemed consent applies to many classes of advertisements, for example notices on commercial premises such as window stickers. They are displayed without express permission, but once displayed may offend amenity considerations or be unsafe (Holt, continuing: para. 30.051; DoE 1992f: para. 17 ff). The LPA must give clear reasons for issuing the notice, which is appealable.

Finally, we come to the problem of unauthorized advertisements. Flyposting, if unchecked, is very unsightly (DoE 1992f: para. 51 ff) Clearly, the site owner, the fly poster and those whose goods and activities are displayed could all be beneficiaries. But those, other than billstickers, are not guilty of an offence if it is done without their knowledge or consent. LPAs constantly monitor and photograph the situation, write to offenders asking them to remove posters, and eventually pursue them in the courts. Highway authorities have power to remove and obliterate displays after notice has been given.

The content of advertisements cannot be controlled unless it affects amenity or public safety. Express consent cannot be refused because the LPA considers the content to be misleading, unnecessary or offensive to public morals (DoE 1992f: annex, para. 3).

Advertisement control was reviewed in 1985 (DoE 1985c) in the light of changing perceptions of what was acceptable at that time and with the aim of simplification. The report came to the conclusion that the statutory framework of "exclusions" and "deemed consents" did not need radical change as long as it commanded public confidence. The report recommended incremental change (ibid.: para. 1.9). Matters discussed were the display as advertisements of national flags at hotels and the use and size of bed and breakfast signs. The use of "house colours", for example on petrol filling stations, was more contentious. Should they constitute advertisements for the purpose of control? This was particularly sensitive in rural areas, where nationally uniform designs might not fit the surroundings. The forest of estate agents' boards in some London boroughs was particularly contentious at the time. The Secretary of State can now make a Regulation 7 Direction, which controls this problem in specified conservation areas, such as in Bath and Westminster (DoE 1992f: para. 28). From the postwar period the illumination of "deemed consent" advertisements was not normally allowed for, in the interests of safety. By the 1980s it was reported that much greater concern was expressed over their effect in conservation areas. The report suggested following Scottish practice then current, namely allowing them, subject to size and positioning limitations. The report also considered establishing a special regime for conservation areas but rejected it because of the work involved. It was felt that Areas of Special Control of Advertisements (ASCAs; see above) worked reasonably well (DoE 1985c: para. 5.6), as did "discontinuance powers" and the methods of dealing with illegal advertisements and flyposting (ibid.: para. 7.4). However, the issue of ASCAs, almost unchanged in concept since 1948, was reopened in a review in the mid-1990s (DoE 1995i, 1996a). It was argued that research had shown "that the ASCA system was inconsistent, inefficient and quite widely misunderstood" (DoE 1996a: 2). ASCAs should be reviewed regularly in the light of changing circumstances, but are not. Dismantling the system would bring fears of the proliferation of advertisements in sensitive environments.

Minerals

Minerals are extremely important to economic prosperity. Minerals can be worked only where they are found. Workings may last a long time and be large scale. Unlike many other forms of development, operations may be continuous or intermittent, and are irreversible. They have many considerable environmental impacts. For these and other reasons development control of mineral working poses problems rather different from those of building development and changes of use. As a result, mineral working is subject to separate development control guidance, namely Minerals Planning Guidance (MPG) 1 to 14. Most are specialist in nature, such as MPG10 on raw material for the cement industry, but MPG1 (DoE 1988g, DoE 1996e) and MPG2 (DoE 1988a) deal with the generalities of mineral plans and development control. Although now very dated, the "Stevens Report", *Planning control over mineral working* (Stevens 1976) is probably the best analysis of mineral working control. These sources are used extensively below. Mineral planning authorities are shire counties in England, where they have structure plan powers, but districts/London boroughs elsewhere in Britain (see Ch. 2).

Minerals embrace a wide variety of materials and uses, particularly fuels, such as gas, oil and coal; building materials, such as clay for bricks, sand for glass, cement and steel for major structures and aggregates for general building purposes; metals of all kinds for engineering uses; fertilizers for agriculture; and raw materials for chemical industries. Some are common, such as coal and aggregates; some are relatively rare and localized, such as kaolin. Some have high transport costs in relation to their market value, such as aggregates, and are therefore worked and used relatively locally. On the other hand, Britain is not well endowed with indigenous non-ferrous metals and these have to be imported. However, other British minerals are exported, especially oil. The discovery and exploitation of indigenous resources helps Britain's balance of payments position.

Mineral working not only creates jobs on site by extraction and mineral preparation, but also results in downstream industry, for example limestone extraction, cement making and concrete manufacture. Jobs in minerals and associated industries are particularly important in rural areas, where alternatives are few.

Minerals occur extensively under good-quality agricultural land, such as aggregates along river terraces and in areas of natural beauty such as green belts and national parks. Pressure to work minerals therefore results in conflicts of interest. There is also the historical spectre of mineral working being associated with dereliction. It is only since the end of the Second World War that mineral working has been subject to planning control, and only weakly at first at that. As mineral workings have a long life, some are operating today with only rudimentary control (Stevens 1976: 69).

Mineral working itself poses a range of issues. Some workings are on the surface, some underground; in both cases, waste has to be disposed of. In some cases the waste (or overburden) is of considerable bulk in relation to the mineral extracted, for example open-cast coal. Sometimes it can be stored underground or used to refill workings; otherwise it has to be tipped on the surface.

Ideally, mineral working should be planned ahead for decades, so that reserves can be safeguarded and not built over or otherwise sterilized. This is not easy, as the market for minerals fluctuates both with the trade cycle and because of long-term, often unforeseeable, secular influences, for example when one mineral is essentially superseded or replaced by another. New techniques and exploration may well alter our understanding of workable reserves. LPAs are anxious to confine mineral working so that its environmental impact is minimized, but operators want long-term certainty in planning permission so that they have commercial flexibility. Plant may be expensive and they may want decades of working life to make it pay.

Stevens (1976: 12) usefully drew attention to two interrelated strands in the control of mineral working. First, there is plan-making, which tries to look forward perhaps 20 years to safeguard and manage output. Secondly, there is development control, through which mining operations are recognized in the Town and Country Planning Act 1990 §55 as a specific category of development deserving special mention, like material changes of use. This division is reflected in the content of MPG1 dealing with plans (DoE 1996e), and MPG2 dealing with development control (DoE 1988a).

Stevens felt that earlier in the history of mineral development control, minerals were treated rather like any other form of development. However, he drew attention to three fundamental differences. First, with most development there is a flurry of construction activity between two successive land uses, say agriculture and housing. Mineral operations, although transitional, are much longer; they may be suspended for market reasons and be restarted. Working does not fit land for another use in the way construction does, but makes it unfit for another use. When finished, mineral workings have frequently to be repaired before re-use. Secondly, mineral working actually destroys land: ores, once extracted and processed, and fuels, once extracted and burnt, cannot be replaced. No other operation does this. It follows that enforcement procedures ought to be orientated towards stopping unlawful operations at the outset. Thirdly, there is a reasonably wide range of geographical locations in which much development can be carried on. Minerals can only be worked where they have been found. From these basic characteristics Stevens argued (1976: 13) that four planning consequences follow. In the first place, when an LPA allows, say, housing to be built, it is a permanent use, in the common sense meaning of the term. Of course, at some future date it may be changed, but that is not normally envisaged. In the case of minerals, the use is transitory. However long it takes, the LPA must look forward to the ultimate need for restoration. In the second place, the scope of conditions attached for mineral working is much wider than is usual, and regular monitoring is necessary. Once normal development operations are complete, say for housing or industry, LPAs rarely exercise any detailed supervision over development. LPAs do not normally need planning officers who are knowledgeable about the details of factory production processes to frame conditions or to monitor operations. In the case of minerals, Stevens argued, LPA officers need to know about the processes of mineral working to assess alternative methods of working, to frame practical and effective conditions, and to monitor working. In the third place, normal development operations take a short period in which society's values are unlikely to change. In the case of minerals, public views may alter; for example, they may become more noise conscious, or new extraction techniques may need to be considered. These needs are not normally found with other types of development. Finally, in normal development, an LPA has a good idea of the ultimate size of a proposal at the outset (e.g. so many thousands of square metres of floorspace). In mineral working this is not likely to be the case. Although initially it may be envisaged that 200000 tonnes a year might be extracted for 50 years, the operator may change his intentions and extract a million tonnes a year for 10 years. It may be necessary, by the use of conditions, to control the rate at which operations proceed.

Stevens listened to a wide-ranging debate on the control of mineral working, including tangles over ownership, the possibilities of nationalization, annual licences and the centralization of the control of mineral working in a new national body (ibid.: 14–15). Further issues explored were the range of skills needed by minerals planning officers, continuity of control, continuity of experience in LPAs, and the need for long-term development planning at national level to safeguard supplies (ibid.: ch. 5). He considered (ibid.: ch. 7) the imposition of conditions on the grant of planning permission of prime importance; they should be practical as far as the operator is concerned and soundly conceived on a long-term basis, so that all parties know what is expected of them. But because of the long-term nature of mineral working, there should be the possibility of a review of conditions from time to time (ibid.: chs 8 and 12). Normally, conditions once imposed are not altered and conditions cannot be added once planning permission has been granted. The fear was expressed that the review of planning conditions would lead to claims for compensation from LPAs. He suggested a review every five years and that operators bear the reasonable costs of new planning conditions in spite of practical and operational difficulties (ibid.: 69). Reviews of mineral working sites are now carried out by LPAs in accordance with MPG4 (DoE 1988c) at such intervals as they think fit (ibid.: para. 3.4). The purpose of the review is to improve environmental quality and to take account of technical changes, with the expectation that the minerals industry should accept any reasonable additional costs arising (ibid.: para. 1). LPAs have a range of legal devices at their disposal, such as modification, discontinuance and suspension orders, and also enforcement and stop notices. Which order is used depends on the circumstances of the case and the working status of the site (ibid.: paras 21, 41 ff). Compensation may be payable to operators.

Another issue explored was the problem of dereliction and restoration or after-use and aftercare. For example, Stevens (1976: ch. 9) cited the situation where a quarrying company takes over another quarrying company but then concentrates production at selected sites, leaving the others with their planning permissions as reserves for the future but in an untidy state (ibid.: ch. 10). After-use is very much related to whether surface tips and lagoons, deep opencast workings or shallower opencast workings are being considered. The use of waste as fill or elsewhere, for example for road construction, is economically and technically problematical. Planning policy must be mindful of the need to repair mineral damage as promptly as possible, to assure the public that restoration will in fact be carried out, to ensure that restoration is normal practice and to ensure that after-use is planned on an area basis, for example by creating a range of recreational uses. Stevens also explored the possibility of restoration funds and performance bonds to guard against wilful evasion and the bankruptcy of mineral operators. He rejected them, arguing that this problem was not that significant and could be tackled by amending planning law.

Stevens investigated the problems of enforcement and permitted development rights (ibid.: chs 11 and 13). There have been changes in law and practice in these subjects since he reported, but the peculiar substance of concern remains. A major problem with enforcement is unauthorized working. It can be very profitable to extract minerals without permission or by breaching conditions before detection and after enforcement proceedings have started. Arup Economics & Planning (1995a: 48), reporting generally on enforcement, said that there were still a few persistent contraveners playing the system. It is usually practically impossible to replace what has been unlawfully taken. Certain mining operations may have permitted development rights; planning permission is not necessary for them to be carried out (see DOE 1988e). Two important ones are mineral exploration and the tipping of waste (see Fig. 3.1). Much exploration activity is *de minimis* (trivial), in the context of development control, because it is very small in scale (e.g. taking small samples) or temporary (e.g. trenching). On the other hand, deep drilling may take some time and have an impact on its surroundings, in which case planning permission may be necessary. Stevens felt that there were three types of exploration: so trivial as not to constitute development (e.g. aerial surveying); that which should be classed as permitted development; and that which should be subject to planning permission. A more fraught argument runs as follows (ibid.: 142). Most LPAs take the view that exploration is quite separate from exploitation.

210

Conservationists take the view that to grant planning permission for expensive exploration may put subsequent pressure on LPAs to grant planning permission, if exploitable minerals are found, when they should refuse it (e.g. in a national park).

As development plans are the most important material consideration in development control, it is useful at this stage to consider plans in relation to mineral extraction. MPG1 (DoE 1996e) reiterated concerns raised by the Stevens Report, for example the conflict between economic growth and environmental protection. The aims of plans are to (ibid.: para. 35):

- cater for the needs of society for minerals with due regard for sustainability
- minimize environmental damage, waste production and transport
- ensure after-use and protect designated landscapes
- prevent unnecessary sterilization.

These aims can be implemented through plans, development control, enforcement and planning obligations (1996e: para. 9). In drawing up structure, local and unitary plans, LPAs must consider an assessment of reserves and the significance, both locally and nationally, of mineral working in their areas, taking account of demand, distribution and production of each type of mineral while safeguarding the confidentiality of individual operators' interests (ibid.: para. 24). Although minerals policies may be found in structure, local and unitary plans, they may also be found in minerals local plans, which deal in a comprehensive way with a broad geographical area (ibid.: para. 16). Policy strategies are likely to take into account the safeguarding of deposits, proposals to ensure extraction while minimizing environmental harm, and proposals to ensure reclamation and after-use. Minerals plans show the relationship with other plans, such as waste disposal plans (ibid.: para. 74 ff). Because of long lead times in mineral working, central government advised that LPAs should have landbanks of reserves with planning permission, so that operators can readily respond to market fluctuations (ibid.: para. 41). Plans contain guidance on where working may or may not be allowed, dividing areas into "specific sites", "preferred areas" (where geological knowledge is comprehensive and extraction is likely to be favoured), and "areas of search" (where extraction might be pemitted) (ibid.: para. 45). Pressure of demand for particular minerals and pressure from competing land uses may bear on whether planning permission is granted in a particular case. The purpose of plans is to provide a framework for development control (ibid.: para. 21). To that end they should include a checklist relevant to assessing applications, which may often be reflected in planning conditions. These conditions include the following: the impact of extraction, processing and distribution on local employment, landscape and residential areas, the quality and extent of deposits, the local and national economy, agriculture and reclamation (DoE 1988g; 1996e: para. 58).

MPG1 (DoE 1996e: para. 47 ff) drew particular attention to conflicts with other land-use policies, particularly the need to protect the best agricultural land, national parks, green belts, areas of outstanding natural beauty and sites of special scientific interest. Extensions to existing workings may be preferable to allowing workings on new greenfield sites. MPG1 (1996e: Annex B) also contains more detailed guidance on particular minerals such as coal, aggregates and brick clay. It drew attention to points such as the large amounts of waste in some mining (e.g. slate), and the reworking of old mine dumps as a source of minerals. It also included an exhortation to the industry to keep its own house in order, for example by better environmental management (ibid.: para. 77).

Of more importance from a development control point of view is MPG2, *Applications, permissions and conditions* (DoE 1988a). Much of MPG2 deals with matters that apply to all planning applications. Consultations between authorities over mineral working are very important (ibid.: para. 21 ff). They may be between counties acting as mineral planning authorities and districts acting as LPAs (which deal with the bulk of development control work). Minerals applications may affect other land uses adversely (e.g. by noise), and run-of-the-mill applications may adversely affect mineral working (e.g. by sterilization). LPAs may need to consult coal authorities over subsidence. Mineral planning authorities may need to consult water authorities over mining and tipping, as surface and underground water may lead to silting and pollution. The Ministry of Agriculture is concerned both with taking irreplaceable agricultural land and the restoration of land to agriculture (see DoE 1989b). Likewise, the Forestry Commission is consulted where forestry is suggested as an after-use. Other relevant consultees are involved where SSSIs, national parks, AONBs and nature reserves may be affected, as mining can have adverse effects over a wide area. Other consultations are involved regarding ancient monuments, archaeological remains, listed buildings and conservation areas, and yet others over pipelines, railway embankments, and so on, where, because of the destructive nature of mining, for example by destabilizing the ground, special measures may be necessary. Much of MPG2 is concerned with the imposition of planning conditions peculiar to mineral working (ibid.: para. 52 ff); they are subject to the same basic rules as other conditions mentioned in Chapters 3 and 5. The government advised that the mineral planning authority discuss with the applicant the proposed terms under which permission be granted, to ensure that they are practicable and to obviate the need for appeals. It also drew attention to the importance of clearly defining on a plan which areas were to be worked, for the avoidance of doubt in enforcement. It is possible to grant planning permission for parts of application sites and refuse it for others, especially where they are made up of separate and divisible elements. As with other applications, an LPA can grant permission subject to further approvals, so that, for example, the operator can get on and develop the site before screening is decided upon. However, LPAs are warned that planning conditions should relate to land-use considerations and must not cover matters that are subject to other legislation or common law (e.g. provision of support for other property). Duplication is *ultra vires* and unreasonable (ibid.: para. 61). But later (ibid.: para. 62), LPAs are advised that they ought not to decline to exercise planning powers solely on the grounds that other powers are available (for example, in ensuring waste tip stability and hence public safety). Planning conditions can be preventive; other legislation may be corrective only after the event.

MPG2 continues with advice on the types of condition particularly appropriate to mineral working (ibid.: para. 71 ff). For example, mineral workings are normally time limited to 60 years, or a shorter period if the LPA decides; some permissions are still extant without time limits. This is designed to curb very long-term amenity problems. Because heavy traffic is involved, new accesses and the improvement of old ones are controlled by conditions to improve safety. Operators may also have to carry out road improvement works in rural areas, where roads are inadequate for the traffic likely to be generated. Vehicle wheel-washing conditions can prevent mud being carried onto the highway. It is not normally possible to frame conditions requiring vehicles coming from mineral working sites to take specific routes, say avoiding quiet villages. Such highway restrictions would apply to all vehicles, which may not be the intention. Planning permission in such cases is perhaps best refused. It is normal to impose working hours limits to meet objections about plant and vehicle noise. Phasing conditions can steer and confine working to specific parts of a mineral site, so that farmers can use the land and large areas are not left unreclaimed for a long period. Depth conditions can safeguard groundwater and production can be limited to control heavy traffic flow. Conditions can ensure the storage of topsoil for restoration purposes. Normally, dust and noise are subject to control by conditions. MPG11 was specifically concerned with noise (DoE 1993d) and recommended, inter alia, acoustic fencing to control it.

The disposal of waste is a problem at most workings; conditions are imposed to control it. They should aim to prevent disfigurement, sterilization of deposits and good agricultural land, and water pollution. Sometimes conditions can turn waste to good use, particularly as fill to facilitate after-use, or for flood prevention or road construction. Conditions can control tip contouring and revegetation. Tip safety and imported waste for infill are controlled by separate legislation.

Blasting can cause vibration and flying rock, and is subject to control. The erection of plant and machinery are normally permitted development under the GPDO, but in sensitive locations conditions can limit permitted development rights, for example to improve siting. Conditions should be imposed to preserve existing trees as screens wherever possible; new trees in the context of the scale of mineral working may take a long time to grow. Among the most important conditions are those requiring reclamation and aftercare, including planting, cultivation, irrigation and drainage (see DoE 1989b). The effectiveness of restoration conditions for mineral working was reviewed in 1993 (DoE 1993e).

Besides MPGs there are DoE Circulars dealing with specialist aspects such as on minerals and high water tables (DoE 1985e), onshore oil and gas (DoE 1985a) and silica sand (DoE 1985d).

Hazardous development

Introduction

One of the mainsprings of town and country planning legislation in the twentieth century has been the desire to secure and improve amenity. The problems of noise, dust, dirt, grit, vibration, smell and glare are arguably merely irritating. The problems of fire, explosion, toxicity, biological and radiological hazards can be very dangerous. The control and regulation of these problems is divided between agencies at local and national government level. For example, the LPA deals with local land-use issues; local environmental health officers are concerned with air pollution and noise and the central government Environment Agency and the Scottish Environmental Protection Agency bring together the work of agencies, such as the former National Rivers Authority and HM Inspectorate of Pollution. It is the purpose of this section to highlight the development control issues related to these fraught amenity problems. Planning application forms ask specific questions about the type of development, the processes to be used, the nature, volume and methods of waste disposal and the substances to be stored at proposed industrial and commercial developments. Planning application forms also enquire about traffic but vehicle emissions as a hazard are not addressed here.

The boundaries of responsibility between the controlling agencies are not altogether clear (DoE 1994e: para. 1.34). However, these need not concern us as the core areas for development control purposes are laid out in Circulars and PPGs. The administrative arrangements, effective from 1996, with a critique were given by Barnes (1996: 14). It is important that the bodies involved consult and liaise. LPAs are enjoined (DoE 1994e: para. 1.34) to assume that other regulatory agencies will do their jobs properly and enforce their regulations and not to substitute their own judgement. Where LPAs do not have the powers to regulate problems, other agencies may do so. However, Griffiths (1995: 12) reported cases involving the processing of animal matter which highlighted the reluctance of local authorities to have confidence in other pollution controllers.

At this stage it is useful to describe a typical potentially hazardous development. At the core of the development is the hazardous element itself. It may be a process and/or material in store. This lies within the curtilage or site itself. The element may be surrounded by special containment such as tanking and the site may have substantial fencing and other security devices. Around the site may be a buffer zone within which there will not normally be development. Around the buffer zone is a consultation zone (see the pollution section below). The hazards, such as toxic waste or noise, are listed above. Apart from the safety of persons and property on site, there are offsite problems. Gases, dust, smell, smoke, etc. may drift through the air offsite, which may cause fire, explosion, poisoning or nuisance to neighbours. Water and liquid-borne pollutants may leak into the soil and contaminate underground water, which may flow away from the source. Apart from unintended offsite problems further issues may arise from materials in transit. The development will have inputs and probably outputs. Materials may be transported in and out by road, rail, air, water or pipeline. Each of these may pose hazards in itself, with the possibility of transit accidents. Raw materials and finished products may pose hazards, as may the disposal of wastes by stock piling, burial and the dispersion of cooling and contaminated water by pipe and contaminated air by chimney discharge. Highly pertinent are prevailing wind direction, the nature of the underlying soil and geology and topography, especially if there is the possibility of temperature inversion. The extent of risk is a common thread – How large? How often? And so what? Can mitigating measures be put in place? (Crossthwaite & Bichard 1990: 9–10). Planning policies for these problems are to be found particularly in Halton Local Plan (Halton Borough Council 1993). Case-studies are to be found in Miller & Fricker (1993).

For the purposes of explanation, the subject matter of this section is divided into pollution, noise, contaminated and unstable land, waste management and hazardous substances generally.

Pollution

The principal central government guidance on pollution and development control is given in PPG23, *Planning and pollution control* (DoE 1994e).

With regard to air or water pollution, the planning system can play a role in determining the location of development that may give rise to pollution. It can control development that may be near a polluting source and it can focus on the appropriateness of the proposed land use itself, as distinct from the control of polluting processes and substances (DoE 1994e: paras 1.31–1.33). The main material considerations in planning applications are given in Figure 7.3.

One problem an LPA has is the adequacy of the technical information provided and whether it can interpret it for the purposes of development control. This can be overcome by consulting with the Environment Agency. Normally, preapplication discussions, running in parallel with the processing of other consents, such as hazardous substances consent, help the LPA with buildings layout and with considerations such as chimney height (chimneys may be high to ensure dispersal, but then they may be visually intrusive). In some cases, environmental statements (Ch. 5) may be necessary so that a fuller technical appraisal can be made.

PPG23 advises consultation with the pollution control authorities where certain proposed development is within 500 m (or in some cases 250 m) of a potentially polluting source. These developments include homes for the young or old, which will attract people on a regular basis (e.g. shopping centres) and developments that in themselves may pollute, tall buildings near tall chimneys and development involving open space, which attracts many people on a regular basis. There may also be problems related to the cumulative impact that an additional polluting development may have on existing polluting developments. Thus, there is a difference in kind between consulting neighbours when a potentially polluting

215

Figure 7.3 Material considerations taken into account when considering a planning application for a potentially polluting development (DoE 1994e: para. 3.2).

- Availability of suitable land for potentially polluting developments. Development plans may show such land isolated from other uses.
- Sensitivity of the area, for example, the proximity of agricultural land or SSSIs which may be adversely affected by pollution.
- Loss of amenity which the pollution would cause.
- Benefits to be gained from the development, for example, the use of derelict land.
- The visual impact of the development.
- The impact on the road network.
- The condition of the site, especially if it is contaminated, which may be overcome by remedial works.
- Proposed after-use of the site.
- In the case of mineral extraction, whether the excavation can be used for landfill by waste.
- The hours of working of the development and how nearby development may be affected.
- The possibility/risk of nuisance and danger caused by the release of gases, noise, etc., where they are not subject to other regulation.
- In the case of waste facilities, the problem of birds, vermin and wind-borne litter.
- The transport of potentially polluting substances to and/or from the site.
- Economic advantages such as employment.
- Land contamination, including leaching outside the site.

---

development is proposed (which might prompt a NIMBY response) and consulting pollution control authorities when a benign proposal is placed near a potentially polluting development. O'Hara & Allen (1996: 13) reported fundamental differences in the way planners and the public viewed hazardous chemical facilities, for example over cost versus non-cost factors.

PPG23 warns that delay in granting authorization or licences by the pollution control authority may justify delaying the decision on a planning application until the LPA is satisfied the potential pollution problem can be overcome. It is possible that the pollution control authority may make changes to the authorization for a plant (e.g. a taller chimney), which may lead to the refusal of planning permission. Normally, applicants do not have to prove the need for development or consider alternative sites. However, in the case of potentially polluting development, national or regional need may have to be demonstrated and alternative sites considered (ibid.: para. 3.15).

When a potentially polluting development is proposed, the question of the extent of the risk of an incident immediately comes to mind. And if there is a risk, what is it? Is there likely to be danger to human health or pollution of an aquifer? PPG23 advises that LPAs should not carry out detailed risk assessment but rely on pollution control authorities. In these circumstances outline planning applications are not normally acceptable to LPAs, as details may be vital in coming to a reasoned decision. It is quite likely that a proposed development may come within the scope of environmental impact assessment and an environmental statement will be needed.

Traditionally, amenity and other problems occasioned by proposed development can be overcome by planning conditions and planning obligations, which accompany the grant of planning permission. However, in the case of potentially polluting development, these are usually overcome by separate pollution control regulations. Planning conditions and obligations are therefore limited to land-use considerations, for example reinstatement of the land after the activity has finished. Annexes 1–4 of PPG23 deal with the situations in which the pollution control authorities can impose conditions on the operation of plant and facilities. **Integrated pollution control** (IPC) operated by pollution control agencies imposes high pollution control standards on operators, who must use the best available techniques not entailing excessive cost (BATNEEC) to minimize pollution. The kinds of installations covered are smelting works, a wide range of chemical processes and the storage of chemicals in bulk. Pollution control authorities have enforcement powers.

Noise

The main guidance on noise in the environment from a planning point of view is given in PPG24, *Planning and noise* (DoE 1994h). Generally speaking, the environment is becoming more noisy, much of the noise coming from road traffic. Potentially noisy development can be controlled by planning conditions, and proposed development likely to be adversely affected by noise can be so located and designed as to minimize noise impact. Noise policies are likely to be found in development plans. Housing, hospitals and schools, as well as amenity areas, are thought to be particularly noise sensitive. Noise can be intrusive because of its loudness, its high or low pitch, whether or not it is intermittent and unexpected, its timing (whether in the day or night), and its relationship to ambient or existing background noise. Human reaction to noise is to some extent subjective. Noise may come from sources such as factories, construction work, mineral working, recreation and transport facilities.

Noise is often measured in decibels on the dB(A) scale, 0dB(A) being the threshold of hearing and 60–65dB(A) normal conversational speech. As noise levels double every 10dB(A), noise over 100dB(A) is pretty unbearable. The (A) scale incorporates a pitch component. For the purpose of proposed new residential development near existing noise sources four exposure categories are suggested to LPAs (ibid.): (a) noise need not be a factor considered; (b) noise should be taken into account and conditions imposed to ensure adequate protection against it; (c) planning permission should not normally be granted, but where there is little alternative conditions should be imposed to ensure commensurate levels of protection against noise; and (d) planning permission should normally be refused. Situations and sources of noise may vary, but noise in the open at night on proposed sites in category (a) should be less than about 45dB in terms of equivalent continuous sound level and greater then 66dB in category (d). Much noisy development is concerned with the creation of jobs, including night-time recreation and construction. LPAs are enjoined not to put obstacles in the way, but they must ensure that development does not cause an unacceptable degree of disturbance.

There are three approaches to the mitigation of noise:

- where essentially engineering noises are concerned, quieter machines, containment by insulated buildings and sound barriers, and/or insulation of adjacent buildings can be carried out
- interposing distance between the sound source and affected buildings and/ or putting noise-insensitive rooms or buildings closest to the source when laying out the site (Ch. 6)
- making administrative arrangements to restrict activities on the site, specifying operating times and noise limits.

The three approaches can be discussed during preapplication negotiation and implemented by the imposition of planning conditions on the grant of planning permission. Annex 5 (ibid.) gives advice on planning conditions, such as requiring that a new building will be constructed to attenuate external noise by a specified number of decibels. It usefully draws attention to two types of noise condition. First, there are conditions that require that noise shall not exceed a particular level at specified times; the advantages are that the operator can meet the requirement in the most cost-effective way and it operates over the long term; the disadvantage is that it needs monitoring, which may not be easy. Secondly, conditions may state which activities may take place at specified times; these are easier to check, but there is less control on noise levels. A combination of conditions may be also be considered.

PPG24 also draws attention to the special problems of noise in designated areas such as national parks, to the possible need for environmental assessment and to other statutory controls on noise, for example the power of local authorities to serve noise abatement notices.

Contaminated and unstable land

For historical reasons, the UK has a large area of contaminated land. The principle of sustainability means that, where practicable, brownfield sites rather than greenfield sites should be developed. Such brownfield sites may be contaminated. The government's approach in PPG23 (DoE 1994e: §4 and annex 10) is not necessarily to return a contaminated site to its original pristine condition but to make it "suitable for use". Contamination is a material consideration in development control. Very few sites are so contaminated that they cannot be re-used. Typically, contaminated sites may be old gas and sewerage works, landfill sites and land previously used for industry where hazardous substances may have been left behind. It is for the LPA to be aware that land may be contaminated, but the responsibility for providing information rests primarily with the developer. A new and improved regime was mooted in 1996 (Denton 1996: 12). It is then for the LPA to consider whether a development proposal takes proper account of contamination. Site investigation may be necessary before an application is decided, or investigation and remedial measures may be conditions imposed on the grant of planning permission, or they may be the subject of reserved matters (see Ch. 6). If planning permission is granted, it is advised that the developer is responsible for the safe development and occupancy of the site.

Circular 17/89, *Landfill sites: development control* (DoE 1989a), draws attention to gas from landfill sites. It may be toxic and explosive. It is a material consideration when considering development nearby or the redevelopment of the site itself.

Land instability or potential instability is also a material consideration in development control. Instability may be the result of underground cavities, possibly as a result of mining, unstable slopes and ground compression of unconsolidated material such as peat or landfill. Guidance is given in PPG14, *Development on unstable land* (DoE 1990b). The development control approach is similar to that for contaminated land. The developer is responsible for safe development and it is for him to make investigations so that remedial measures to safeguard the development can be undertaken. It is not the responsibility of the LPA to carry out investigations and it is not liable for loss if planning permission is granted. As with contaminated land, more information may be necessary, or conditions specifying remedial measures may be imposed. Ultimately, the LPA may refuse planning permission on grounds of land instability.

Waste management
Waste is the unwanted by-product of industrial, commercial and domestic activities, which has been discarded; it may be solid, liquid or gas. Its volume has grown dramatically in the past 50 years. It amounts to about 400 million tonnes a year in UK, much of it related to agriculture, mining and construction. Reduction at source, recycling, energy production and disposal are the key issues. Treatment should be safe, sustainable, environmentally acceptable and not burdensome to industry (SODD 1996a: 5). This section is based on Scottish and English guidance (DoE 1994e: annex 4; DoE 1994d, SODD 1996a). The planning system plays a part in the disposal of wastes and from April 1996 the Environment Agency (EA) and the Scottish Environmental Protection Agency (SEPA) coordinate and regulate a single waste disposal strategy (SODD 1996a, Environment Agency 1996). Five principles are involved:

- proximity, that is disposal closest to source, to encourage communities to take care of their own waste and minimize transportation
- regional self-sufficiency, which may entail consideration of neighbouring authorities' disposal facilities
- the precautionary principle, that is, don't dispose unless you know what the outcomes are
- the polluter pays, through a landfill tax and by the imposition of conditions, rather than neighbours or later generations
- the "best practical environmental option" (BPEO), which is not normally a planning matter.

Wastes may be of two legal types: from agriculture, mines and quarries and radioactive and explosive wastes, which are subject to special regulations; and so-called "controlled wastes", being mainly household, commercial, industrial and "special wastes", which are more difficult to dispose of. And there are three waste management functions: collection, including recycling; disposal, which involves waste management licensing; and regulation, carried out by the EA and SEPA, which involves strategic arrangements for the disposal of controlled waste, waste management licensing, the supervision of a duty of care, the supervision of licensed sites and the inspection of closed landfills. As a generality, waste collection and disposal are the responsibility of the local authorities. Development plans and the waste strategy interact and implement the European Union Framework Directive on Waste.

The line between planning and pollution control is not clear, but the planning system is involved in focusing on whether a particular development is an acceptable land use for a site (rather than the control of processes or substances), regulating the location and control of operations to mitigate effects on the environment and securing after-use by the use of conditions. Licensing is a material consideration in development control and it is recommended that LPAs work closely with the EA and SEPA to secure local amenity. Planning policies for waste disposal are found in development plans. At a basic level, waste disposal is just one more type of development not dissimilar from, say, changes of use or mineral working. The same considerations, such as appearance, traffic generation and so on, have to be taken into account, and care must be taken of amenity and amenity designations such as green belts. Special problems arise when waste is annoying, for example malodorous. It may result in gas emissions and leaching outside a site. Closed landfill sites may be unsuitable for building development because of instability. SODD (1996a: 29–31) usefully draws attention to the matters that may be controlled by planning conditions, for example: character of the area, hours of operation, noise levels, timescale and phasing, vehicle wheel cleansing, public road cleansing, area involved, storage of topsoil, fencing to control windblown litter, aftercare, specification for final contouring, and removal of buildings at the end of operations. It differentiates restoration conditions and aftercare conditions. LPAs must be mindful of conserving potential landfill sites, using waste to upgrade derelict sites, the possibility of raising land by the use of waste and the safe afteruse of sites. The EA and SEPA may object to proposed developments that adversely affect groundwater (ibid.: 24–5).

But development control can help with waste control obliquely, for example by resisting demolition and encouraging the re-use of buildings, by facilitating the setting up of scrapyards and by encouraging the use of second-hand building materials. In the case of some installations, for example incinerators, environmental impact analysis may be necessary (ibid.: 18).

Hazardous substances generally

In 1996 there was a reorganization of the administration of the controls over pollution, with the setting up of the Environment Agency and the Scottish Environmental Protection Agency, with statutory controls and standards largely unchanged (Barnes 1996: 14–15). However, it will facilitate a single overview of the state of the environment for the first time (Anonymous 1996e: 28). There is concern that controls may not be working well. Technical processes can change and materials in store can change in nature and quantity, without regulating authorities knowing. Some insight into effectiveness, in the early 1990s, can be seen through the operation of hazardous substances consent (HSC) operated by LPAs as Hazardous Substances Authorities (HSA).

HSC legislation was introduced in 1992. It was designed to control the presence of hazardous substances above specified quantitative thresholds, where by accident they might have consequences for people in the surrounding area (DOE 1992g). An example would be the liquefied petroleum gas limit at 25 tonnes or hydrogen at 2 tonnes (Thomas, continuing: ch. 10). There are exemptions (e.g. explosives and substances in transit). LPAs were designated as the HSC control authorities as they are particularly concerned with the offsite impact of any development in making development control decisions. The presence of hazardous substances in themselves did not constitute development amenable to planning control. Planning permission and HSC are necessary where a new building may be needed to store hazardous substances. Other control authorities advise the local authority on the technical nature of the risks involved.

Walker (1994) reported on the effectiveness of these particular controls by survey. Accidents rarely happen, but they did at Flixborough in 1974 and Seveso in 1976, which prompted renewed concern about the problem in the UK and Europe. The types of installation are very diverse, many LPAs (as HSAs) do not receive HSC applications and those that do receive them receive fewer than ten a year. It was found on balance that the legislation had closed a loophole in the law over the introduction and intensification of hazards, although there was concern about substances in transit. Some planners suggested turning the decision on HSC over to expert as opposed to elected bodies, but it is elected bodies that have to balance the risks against wider planning considerations. Most HSAs felt confident in their operation of HSCs, but the Health and Safety Executive (HSE, part of the Environment Agency, with effect from 1996) and industrialists were not impressed by HSAs because of the lack of understanding.

So-called "deemed consents" formed part of transitional arrangements from no control to full control to enable existing operators to continue. Records showed that there were "missing deemed consents" and there was non-compliance with HSC legislation. One controversial aspect of the administration of HSCs was specifying quantities when stocks fluctuated and operators wanted headroom in specifying maximum inventory levels. Quantities stored may involve an increased risk and thus have a knock-on effect on consultation distances. In built-up areas

221

particularly this can arguably and erroneously have a constricting effect on proposed new development nearby (ibid.: 38). At the time of the research, the express consent system for new storage (as opposed to existing storage) had been operating for less than a year. However, it was found that conditions were attached to permission for HSC in only half the cases. This meant that, although quantities were controlled, location, pressure, temperature and maximum tank size might be changed by the operator. This appeared to be a loophole. Where conditions were imposed, they were sometimes problematic because the roles of the HSE and the HSA were not clear. HSAs experienced few problems where substances were in transit, often because they were exempt from control. HSAs are responsible for enforcement action, but none had apparently been taken. This was partly because of lack of knowledge of controlled substances and partly because monitoring and enforcement simply did not take place (ibid.: 57). There is a parallel here with planning control generally. In view of the problem of "missing deemed consents" above, industrial applicants expressed concern about "cowboy operators" who were not being picked up.

As development plans are the most important consideration in determining planning applications, Walker (ibid.: ch. 10) investigated the inclusion of relevant hazardous installation policies in them. He found that 58 per cent of LPAs that contained HSC sites did not have such policies. For example, policies may identify new land away from inappropriate neighbours, to which new hazards could be guided, or may seek to control development near existing hazards.

Walker concluded (ibid.: ch. 11) that the HSC legislation had enhanced control over hazardous substances. He ended interestingly by commenting that many operators revealed that they could never envisage increasing their storage inventories and were trying to reduce them, which boded well for the future. An omission from Walker's report was an analysis of the recent history of significant accidents relating to hazardous substances. It is difficult therefore to appreciate the scale of the problem.

Conclusion

This wide-ranging chapter has illustrated the many and varied types of development proposals in different contexts faced by LPAs, which defy a general conclusion. It has concentrated on conveying largely technical considerations. The next chapter deals with much more controversial aspects of development control.

CHAPTER 8
Conflict and controversy

Introduction

This book has touched on many of the principles and practices of town and country planning in the UK. The emphasis has been on conveying mainline technical considerations. Controversy and polemic have not been avoided. Indeed, the author has endeavoured to intersperse a technical text with critical commentary drawn from research and other sources. The environment and planning practice are in a constant state of change. Pressures come from outside the planning system and there are endeavours to improve it from within. Figure 1.1 tabulates the many fields of incipient conflict.

The purpose of this chapter is to concentrate on some controversial issues *per se*, rather than on technical issues that may have controversial aspects. So-called technical aspects, such as legal procedures for processing planning applications or the consideration of appropriate carparking standards for a development proposal, may have a mystique for the layman, but for the town planning insider, used to the jargon, they have no mystique. Insiders know that underlying technical considerations, which purport an arm's-length unbiased immutable quality, are ordinary human values. Values change over time and technical considerations change. One change is the growing importance of public participation in development control in the processing of applications over the decades. Another is the realization that to insist on generous carparking at a proposed development, as LPAs may have done in the 1960s and 1970s, can lead to overloading the road network and to pollution. It would be an advantage to all involved in development to be able to rely on tried and trusted techniques to solve problems. However, such is the nature of town planning as a discipline that values and techniques evolve and change over time.

As the current development control system was conceived in 1947, it was seen as a facet of a democratic socialist welfare state. The lot of the bulk of citizens after two world wars and an unprecedented economic depression was austere; they had had enough of high unemployment, bomb damage and poor housing. Moreover, the beauty of the countryside was being spoilt by speculative developers and good food-growing land was wantonly taken. Clearly, there was a failure of the free market system. Nationalization of key industries was one answer to the problems, the creation of the National Health Service another. In the built environment, government agencies built houses and new towns. The nationalization of development rights in land, development charges and development control, usually without benefit of compensation, were other answers to the same set of problems. Apart from changes to development charges, there was apparent consensus between the main political parties that the shortcomings of the capitalist system manifest in the environment should be mitigated. This consensus ended with the election of a Conservative government in 1979. Development charges (Development Land Tax) were abolished, new towns were wound down, wound up and sold off, and planning-free Enterprise Zones set up, government housebuilding was greatly reduced and nearly all central government planning guidance replaced in the course of time. Far from being an arm of the welfare state, the planning system became the handmaiden of privileged capitalist property interests, helping to reduce economic uncertainty and to enhance property values. By the mid-1990s the rising importance of green environmental issues had challenged this view of planning. It is into this cauldron of controversy that we will now dip.

To help the reader to focus on conflict in development control it is worth recalling McAuslan's three competing and potentially conflicting ideologies in the legal history of planning (McAuslan 1980). First, there is the need to protect *private property interests*, which pre-dates the nineteenth century. Second is the need to overcome the shortcomings of the early emphasis by the state taking powers to control and regulate the use of property in the *public interest*. Thirdly, there is the desire by the public to participate in the land-use decision process as a matter of *democracy and justice*. The incipient conflict between these three interests underlies this chapter. Sometimes the arguments pull in one direction, sometimes in another, and the conflicts are not always resolved.

Two property issues will be discussed, whether development control works and land values. This is followed by political issues: public participation, Thatcherism and the relationship between members and officers. The chapter ends with a discussion of equality and some ethical dilemmas.

Does development control work?

Much effort is put into development control activities. A legitimate question is therefore : does it work? This depends on in whose eyes and by what criteria. A happy householder is granted permission for a house extension into his garden. His neighbour is furious because of perceived loss of privacy. It works for some and not for others. This section looks at some case studies of this question. PIEDA (1992) researched the effectiveness of the land-use planning system for the Department of the Environment. The report was very wide-ranging: development control was but part of the evaluation. It was concluded that the outcome of such an evaluation depended crucially on the weight applied to the interests involved.

Public attitudes to planning

A wide-ranging review of public attitudes to planning found that it was a worthwhile activity, especially development control (McCarthy et al. 1995). But different user groups had different perspectives. To the general public the term "planning application" was well known, with planning being perceived as dealing with transport infrastructure, new building design and protecting historic building environments (ibid.: 13). Property developers and businesses were seen as benefiting most, whereas the general public and individual householders got short shrift (ibid.: 14). As for the delivery of the planning service, they looked on it with suspicion, as not being fair to all users, but over half of the respondents in the review felt planning was a valuable public service. Private applicants had different concerns. For example, about a third thought that dealing with their applications was a slow business, but over three-quarters were satisfied with the way their particular development control applications had been handled (ibid.: 24–5). As with other interest groups, business users were more critical in general terms of the planning services' delivery than of their dealing with their own applications, although the results of planning were seen positively by most businesses. Taking another group on another subject, half of developers thought enforcement was reasonable and sufficiently used, about a third thought it was sufficient and overused, and a fifth thought it sufficient but under-used. As for improving the development control process, the most common comment was greater speed and "less political influence". In spite of considerable criticism of the operation of the system, virtually all developers and landowners quizzed valued planning, arguing it was essential in "a small crowded island with intense pressure on land", valuing the protection that planning gave to third parties. Chaotic consequences were thought to ensue without it (ibid.: 51). Local authorities – the deliverers rather than the recipients – thought that through their officers development control was essentially regulatory. Good results were achieved by default and bad applications were simply ameliorated (ibid.: 72). These few extracts give the flavour of the complex answers to a simple question.

A series of case studies of development control, in contrast to studies of different stakeholders in the process, demonstrated that each case was very different (ibid.: ch. 9). It was found that (ibid.: 81 ff), although the minds of participants were focused on the need for planning permission for development, development control was seen as a mechanism for solving all dimensions of a problem (e.g. energy or health issues). Planning problems were seen in terms of conflict, win-or-lose situations and an adversarial approach to problem-solving. Although participants in the case studies all recognized the need for planning as a system for solving complex problems, members of the public had difficulty accepting (or even understanding) where land-use considerations stopped and others started. Which brings us to the question of trade-off (ibid.: 87 ff), for example the provision of good housing and job-related development and the need for environmental protection. Stakeholders in a decision become frustrated when they see their (self-)interest not being safeguarded against the interests of others and, to boot, not being compensated in some way. Clearly, if this happens, development control does not work – at least for them.

Customer care

McCarthy et al. (1995) reported on a wide-ranging review of the attitudes of different segments of the public to town and country planning. This section focuses on customer care in development control. It considers development control both at LPA and Planning Inspectorate level.

Joyce (1994: 61–3) drew attention to two levels of care in LPAs, first the cosmetic "have a nice day" approach and secondly the deeper professional approach to the real issues involved. He regarded the customers as not only the applicants but the public, amenity bodies, councillors, consultees and others. The quality of service – often trying to satisfy conflicting demands – depends on responsive, even-handed staff, which in turn depends on good conditions of service and the feeling of being valued. He itemized the following barriers to giving good customer care: poor organization, poor attitudes (e.g. lack of mutual trust), poor communications (e.g. constant interruptions) and poor resources. An RTPI study (Elsworth Sykes Planning 1991: 19) highlighted particularly lack of staff and poor budgets and resources as the largest single constraint on an effective planning service. Joyce felt harnessing the ideas of development control staff, and understanding the perception of customers were crucial. Masochistically encouraging complaints improves the service. In Leeds, on which Joyce was reporting, the development control section within the planning department was given top priority for customer-care training as it came into contact with the public most frequently. Among other things, the "Planning Shop" was given a central role in customer care, seven area offices were opened, changes were made in the enforcement service and a code for preapplication discussions was drawn up. The need to publicize planning applications and the introduction of the Citizen's Charter have given a higher profile to customer care and the need to monitor performance.

The Citizen's Charter has arguably focused the LPA's attention on "watching its back". The Audit Commission (1992b: 44–5) laid down performance indicators for planning, including applications per 1000 of the population, the percentage of household applications decided within eight weeks, the appeal decision success rate, the number of application departures decided against the development plan and development control costs. However, Beattie (1995: 20) argued that such indicators are standardized and organization orientated rather than customer orientated. He actively set out in Tower Hamlets to find out, by questionnaire,

Table 8.1 Qualities perceived by customers of the planning service as being important in Tower Hamlets (Beattie 1995: 20).

Quality parameters ranked in order of importance	
Parameter	Mean value
Desired outcome	2.3
Communication	2.6
Access to information	2.7
Agreement and consensus	2.9
Trust	2.9
Speed and time	3.0

Value scale 1–6, highest value 1

Perceived value of employee attributes and skills	
Attribute	Mean value
Clarity of communication	6.70
Ability to find solutions	6.17
Consistency	6.15
Willingness to help	6.14
Politeness	6.00
Sensitivity to customer needs	5.98
Patience	5.20
Local knowledge	5.19
Ability to work fast	5.17
Friendliness	4.57

Value scale 1–7, highest value 7

Employee attributes and skills – by ranking	
Attribute	Mean value
Ability to find solutions	2.82
Clarity of communication	3.10
Consistency	3.49
Willingness to help	3.76
Sensitivity to customer needs	3.88
Politeness	4.10
Ability to work fast	4.80
Patience	4.96
Local knowledge	5.23
Friendliness	5.40

Value scale 1–10, highest value 1

what customers really wanted of the planning service. The results are tabulated in Table 8.1 and mirror the points made by Joyce in Leeds.

Speed of decision, although important to customers, was not of prime importance: many felt that the importance of meeting the government deadlines for speed of response depended on the circumstances. Ability to find solutions was highly prized. Quality is clearly a complex issue not readily measured.

To see how its customer care was faring, Mid-Sussex District Council (1993) quizzed a sample of agents who had submitted planning applications on behalf of clients and third parties who had made representations. Among the findings were that its development control service was perceived as quite good and that it was better than that of other authorities. Staff were very good in terms of courtesy and availability. Space for inspecting documents was poor: as a result it had been improved. However, although Mid-Sussex had one of the best records in the country for speed of determining applications, many agents regarded it only as "adequate". This rather paradoxical finding parallels that of McCarthy, who found that business users were more critical of the planning service than they were of the way their particular applications were handled (see above).

The Citizen's Charter is a central government initiative to improve customer satisfaction at the local level. But how do central government agencies, such as the Planning Inspectorate, measure up? Three research reports by W. S. Atkins Planning Consultants (1993a, 1993b, 1994) throw light on customer satisfaction with the development control appeals system. Most appellants choose to appeal by written representations, 84 per cent of cases (1993a: iii). In this type of appeal, there was a high level of satisfaction with the procedure, but this understandably was coloured by an appeal's outcome. About two-thirds had their appeals dismissed. Overall appellants thought well of the clarity of letters, courtesy and helpfulness of Inspectorate staff (ibid: 3.7). Timetabling of the appeal arrangements was well regarded. However, with regard to the time taken to issue a decision letter and regarding satisfaction with the reasons for decisions, there was a wide divergence of views between those appellants who won and those who lost their appeals. For example, of those who won their appeals, 82 per cent were satisfied with the reasons for the decision, but, of those who lost 78 per cent were dissatisfied (ibid.: 3.11). Irrespective of the outcome, there was on balance satisfaction with the overall service of the Inspectorate (53 per cent of appellants) (ibid.: 3.12–13). About 13 per cent of appellants had made formal complaints about their written appeals and the majority of these were dissatisfied with the way the complaints were handled. Where appellants were represented by agents, the overall pattern of response was broadly similar, but those who lost and won were not differentiated. Overall, appellants and agents expressed a high level of satisfaction with the procedure and the service provided by the Planning Inspectorate (ibid: 6.1).

The Atkins survey of the inquiry method of examining planning appeals also showed a fairly high level of satisfaction with the procedure and service provided (1994: iv). In this research appellants, agents and LPAs were surveyed. The quality of submissions was often criticized and it was felt that inspectors could intervene more in cross-examination that was lengthy and repetitious. Levels of dissatisfaction with the decision letters were coloured, as for written representations, by the outcome of the appeal. Chapter 7 of the 1994 report usefully compared customer perceptions of the three methods of appeal; findings were broadly the same.

Development control and the evaluation of policy

Development plan policies have long been the background to development control decisions. A good deal of effort is put into their compilation. Development control is a method of implementing plans. Development pressures, as evinced by the planning applications received, feed into policy formulation. An analysis of planning applications refused, granted and implemented is a way of testing the efficacy of policy in development plans in terms of the end result on the ground. In this section, the Cotswold Area of Outstanding Natural Beauty (AONB) is taken as a case study to illustrate how effectively development plan policies were implemented by development control (Preece 1981). The methodological problems were described by Preece (1990). The case study does not claim to be representative. Indeed, such case studies are few and far between (see Gilg & Kelly 1996: 203–28).

Preece examined a 10 per cent sample of planning applications in the southern part of the Cotswold District Council area for the years 1959–76, partly in the AONB and partly outside, to provide comparability. The development control authority at the time was the then Gloucestershire County Council. The local authorities were Tetbury Rural District and Cirencester Rural District. Cirencester Urban District lay on the boundary of the AONB and was excluded. Designation took place in 1966 and local government reorganization in 1974. The main purpose of the AONB was to conserve the characteristic natural beauty of the area. The inside and outside areas had similar population sizes, but the inside area had fewer "key settlements". To provide a common basis of comparison, planning applications were expressed per thousand of the population by parish. Since in conservation terms even minor extensions are important, all types and scales of application were considered. A particular criticism of AONB designation was and is that conservation policies discriminate against normal development. Some of the findings were as follows. Over time, the fluctuations in the number of applications was similar to national trends, although more exaggerated. Planning application refusal rates – nationally, locally, inside and outside the AONB – were similar whether before or after designation. Using this indicator, it would not appear that designated area status made it more difficult to obtain planning permission. The number of planning applications per 1000 population was higher outside the AONB before designation, but afterwards there was little difference. Moreover, just taking the census years 1961 and 1971, there was a much greater increase in absolute numbers of applications inside than outside the AONB. Thus, it would not appear that designation was a deterrent to applications.

It should be noted that parishes inside the AONB have fewer key settlements than outside. Thus, the two areas were different in terms of the nature of the policies that existed for their settlements. It was found that the AONB received significantly more applications than might be expected from the relatively few key settlements, which might be expected to have had a restrictive effect. Disaggregating applications into residential (single and multiple house applications) and other, and new development and extensions or similar, did not basically alter the general validity of this finding. There was the possibility that AONB designation might attract applications from non-residents living outside the study area, but an analysis of addresses of applicants showed that this was not significant.

A major way of securing visual amenity in an AONB (as elsewhere) is to attach traditional design and materials conditions to planning permission for houses. This is thought to be onerous in AONBs. In the study period, this imposition was greatly increased in the AONB. However, it was estimated that it added only about 1 per cent to housing construction costs. Surveyors pointed out that it saved on maintenance over the years and was preferred by purchasers.

Comparing job-related planning applications inside and outside the AONB, it could not be concluded that AONB designation *per se* resulted in lower levels of activity inside than outside. Indeed, the number of business permissions substantially increased inside.

Preece concluded that AONB status as such did not have a burdensome effect, but the problems of rural areas often stem from intrinsic characteristics, especially dispersed population and few key settlements. The administration of AONBs seeks a balance or compromise between conservation and development. The Cotswold AONB case study showed that, although there was a lower level of overall development activity in the AONB than in the control area outside it, it appeared that it was allowed and encouraged to increase faster inside than outside. It was also found that differentiation between inside and outside was decreasing over time, AONB designation notwithstanding. Such differentiation as existed was the result of pre-designation characteristics.

Preece's work (1981, 1990) illustrates the considerable complexity of analyzing the efficacy of policy *ex post facto*. He postulated that policy analysis should be logically rigorous to be scientifically and commercially acceptable, should address itself to hypothesis formulation and to the "operationalization" of planning policies, and be positive, rather than defensive, with regard to policy objectives (1990: 73). How easy it is to come to quick and ill researched judgements in a discipline that is forward looking, Utopian and beset by the demands of legal and administrative procedures.

The costs of development control

The costs of the development control system can be interpreted as the costs of determining planning applications and the costs of delay – time is money to the developer.

Costs of determining planning applications

Before 1981, there were no fees payable by applicants on submission of planning applications. Since then, fees have been charged, with a view to covering the costs of the development control service (DoE 1994o). Fees vary from time to time and relate roughly to the size of development proposed; for example, alterations to existing dwellings: £60 per dwelling house; but for new dwellings: £120 per house, with a maximum of £6000 (DoE 1992t: Appendix 5).

The arguments *for* fees are that it is not unreasonable to recover the costs of a service; they may discourage frivolous applications; fees could improve the quality of the service; punitive fees could be imposed on those trying to avoid seeking planning permission; and for retrospective approvals fees could be made to match the work involved.

The arguments *against* fees are that there will be an expectation of approval in return for the fee; in cases of refusal, fees are non-returnable; development control is a public service from which the public benefits, so it is inequitable to charge a fee; fees as set by central government do not bear much relationship to the costs incurred; fees, especially higher fees, could increase evasion and the need for enforcement; and listed buildings impose enough of a burden on applicants without fees.

A further view is that fees should relate to the value of the proposal, which would reflect local cost structures, and that they should be set locally. Currently, large-scale developments with large fees effectively cross-subsidize householder applications (DoE 1994o: 52).

The DoE survey of 25 LPAs relating to 1992–3 found that fee income to LPAs covered on average 66 per cent of the costs of determining applications, but varied between 23 and 143 per cent (DoE 1994o). Fees averaged 31 per cent of the total costs of the development control service, again with wide variations. These wide variations were attributed to type and size of authority, case mix and local cost structures. Fee income also varied quite a bit from year to year, with the number of applications made and the trade cycle. Costs of the development control service were found to be split into: 50 per cent dealing with applications, 16 per cent enforcement, 15 per cent advisory work, 6 per cent appeals, 5 per cent conservation work and, surprisingly, development plan work less than 1 per cent, with other costs at 7 per cent (ibid.: annex 3). In 1992–3 the median cost per application was £233 but with a very wide range. Inter alia the study suggested that fees should be set locally.

A survey of firms operating widely in western Europe found that in England and Wales administrative fees charged by local authorities were very reasonable, compared well with other countries and were a very small percentage of overall project costs. Professional support costs were also reasonable (GMA Planning 1993: 61).

The costs of delay

The Department of the Environment has for some time published development control statistics showing the proportion of planning applications dealt with by LPAs within an eight-week target period. The purpose of the statistics is to highlight progress in reducing delay in decision-making. The Department of the Environment wants 80 per cent of applications dealt with within the eight-week period. In practice there is considerable variation from year to year and from LPA to LPA (Anonymous 1994c: 5). The problems of defining statistical categories were discussed by Blackman (1996: 10). Delay, it is suggested, adds unacceptable costs to development. The purpose of this section is to examine the arguments that surround this issue.

Henneberry (1982: 72) analyzed constituent costs and revenues for an industrial development project with reference to the costs of delay. He argued that many of the factors in the cost–revenue equation could vary quite considerably during the development period, for example building costs and interest rates. He showed that by far the largest influences on the cost–revenue equation were rental income and building costs. Changes in land costs, developers' profit and interest rates had considerably less effect on rates of return. The economic viability of a scheme was least sensitive to changes in the development period, which included the period occasioned by planning delay. Planning delay, of itself, had little effect on the return from development schemes. Why then, Henneberry asked, has delay attracted so much attention? He argued further that the other variables could vary in a delay period, thus threatening the viability of a scheme. However, building delay costs could be shifted to the builder, but planning delay costs were beyond the developer's control. On the other hand, elimination of planning delay would not of itself significantly affect the number of successful schemes. Other factors were significant, particularly the market demand for new development and rental levels. Reporting Durham County Council for 1981, he drew attention to the fact that the Northern Region was the fastest region in terms of dealing with planning applications at that time, but had the lowest rate of housing starts. The South West, one of the slowest regions for dealing with applications, had the second highest level of housebuilding in the country. "Planning delay does add to developers' costs but let us see it in perspective" (ibid.: 95).

A cognate concern is the failure of developers to implement planning permission once granted or at least to delay in doing so. No comprehensive statistics are available on this subject. Procter (1996: 2) commented that his experience in the early 1980s in Surrey, when the Confederation of British Industry was concerned about delay, was that thousands of square metres of approved office and industrial development had not been taken up.

"Delay" in itself may be a pejorative expression, better replaced by "decision-making time". It is part of the development process. Its causes are various. Applications may be submitted incomplete, consultations may need to be carried out and planning agreements and conditions negotiated. Some delay is occasioned by the planning committee cycle. Development control workloads vary quite noticeably with the trade cycle (see Appendix III). Large and complex applications cannot necessarily be satisfactorily resolved in an eight-week period. There may be delay by the developer between the approval of an outline application and the resolution of reserved matters. Differences between LPAs in the preparation of applications dealt with in the eight-week period may be accounted for by the degree of delegation to officers and the proportion of more time-consuming applications in designated areas, such as conservation areas. (See Larkham 1992: 101–107; Glasson & Booth 1992: 63 ff.)

Underlying arguments about the speed of decisions are those about the quality of decisions and the quality of outcomes on the ground. The management of the development control process can be improved by more rapid committee cycles, drafting in more staff from other sections at times of overload, the use of information technology, separating minor from major applications and improving staff morale (Anonymous 1996a: 25). A controversial proposal mooted in 1994 was that there should be a fast-track system for some applications, with developers paying a higher fee for it. On the one hand this would look like paying for planning permission but on the other it would bring extra fee income (Fair 1994b: 6).

Development control and land values

The granting of planning permission can considerably increase the value of land and buildings. For example, in spring 1996 agricultural land in the South East Region with vacant possession was worth just over £6000 per hectare, but housing land £844000 to £969000 per hectare (Valuation Office 1996: 11, 21). Lees (1993: 33), for example, reported that in North Cornwall the grant of planning permission for an average dwelling in the countryside without onerous conditions would result in a financial gain of £50000 solely attributable to the permission. Arguably, the most important single determinant of land value in this context is its planning status. Increases in value are created by the community at large by the LPA granting planning permission, but the enhancement in value accrues to the developer. In the 1990s this enhancement was subject to ordinary income, capital and corporation taxes (Greenwood 1995: xxiii). Planning gain (see Ch. 5) is seen as a method by an LPA of clawing back for the community some of the increased value brought about by the grant of planning permission.

The purpose of this section is to ventilate some of the arguments surrounding this subject. It has a long and fraught history on which the last word has not been said. It puts the finger on the distributive effects of development control. Who wins and who loses by the grant of planning permission and to what extent in money and other terms? The matter is shrouded in mystery because the financial results are not in the public domain and the distributive effects can be very diffuse. Consider, for example, a superstore operator who has built on a derelict site. The

233

financial outcome (profit) will depend on how much was paid for the land, the cost of shop construction and the running costs of the building. Quite separately the trading results will depend on management skill, trends in the grocery trade, the cost of buying stock and employing labour, the size of the population and purchasing power in the catchment area, transport facilities and the degree of competition. More diffuse effects include the possible closure of supermarkets nearby, the improved quantity and quality of the shopping experience for shoppers, increased traffic congestion and pollution, the clearance of a derelict site, and so on. The planning gain may involve improved site access and landscaping, which the developer may have carried out in any event.

It is useful at this stage to define terms in the argument: betterment, worsement, compensation, recoupment, floating value and planning blight.

Betterment is the enhancement of land and building values, brought about by no or little effort on the part of the owner himself. This might arise in at least two ways: the specific grant of planning permission for a higher-order use (e.g. turning agricultural land into housing land) and improvements in the local or national economy or improvement in local amenities (e.g. the building of a new road or shops by another party near a property where planning permission may or may not be involved). Worsement is the decline in land values *mutatis mutandis*. The refusal of planning permission is the extinguishment of "hope value": a speculator may buy land he does not want (for his own use) with money he does not have (he may borrow it) in order to sell it later with planning permission (which he may not get) at a higher value. Worsement may occur through a decline in the local economy (e.g. through industrial change) or because amenity is damaged by the activities of other parties (e.g. the building of a noisy motorway nearby), which may or may not involve planning permission.

Compensation is money paid to landowners whose interests have been adversely affected. This may come about, for example, because an LPA has decided to consolidate complex landownership patterns in a town centre site in order to redevelop it in an orderly way. Some land may be bought by agreement with owners, but compulsory purchase may eventually be necessary for which compensation is payable. Compensation may also be payable by an LPA to owners whose permitted development rights are restricted by Article 4 Directions (see Ch. 4). Compensation may also be paid by other parties to those aggrieved by their actions, for example a contribution for noise insulation to households because of increased noise by airport use (Denyer-Green 1994: 295). The valuation of compensation payments is also fraught and is subject to statute.

Recoupment is an attempt to balance compensation and betterment within a redevelopment scheme. Consider a slum area ripe for redevelopment but in respect of which individual owners and developers do not have the powers and resources. An LPA may compulsorily purchase the sites and compensate the owners by granting planning permission for higher-order uses (betterment) sufficient to cover compensation.

Floating value is a term used in the Uthwatt Report (Uthwatt 1942). Where

234

there is a free market in land and buildings, it is argued that there is enough putative development in the pipeline to satisfy the demand for buildings on the one hand and the desire of developers to profit from development on the other. The problem is that one is not sure where or when the development will take place and settle geographically; hence, the term "floating value". Land allocations in development plans and the operation of development control ensure that development settles in specific locations to the benefit of specific landowners but to the anguish of others unspecified. The latter are not normally compensated for their ill luck.

Planning blight is a depression in land and building values brought about by the uncertainty engendered by development proposals, which may or may not materialize. There may be a road proposal in a development plan or a NIMBY proposal by a developer, which may not get planning permission. This heady mixture of problems has been the subject of various solutions since the Second World War.

The first solution came immediately after the Second World War, when development control, as practised in the late twentieth century, was initiated. It was "solved" by a Labour Government nationalizing development rights and the imposition of a development charge. One way to solve the interlocking problems mentioned above would be to nationalize all land at existing use value and to compensate the owners by collecting betterment from them on the granting of planning permission when they sought to develop it. This was thought too expensive and politically unacceptable. In the upshot a Central Land Board was set up to levy a development charge (at a rate of 100 per cent on betterment) on the grant of planning permission. A fund of £300 million was set aside to compensate for the hardship that owners of nationalized development rights suffered as a result of the provisions of the Town and Country Planning Act 1947 (Cullingworth 1980: 37). The land itself was not nationalized. The Central Land Board had compulsory purchase powers to buy land at existing use value without planning permission and dispose of it with planning permission, collecting betterment on the way. The result of these provisions was that the sale of bare building land "dwindled to negligible proportions" (ibid.: 41).

A Conservative government was returned to power in 1951. To cut through the complexities and frustration of the Labour "solution", the Conservative government abolished the development charge and repealed the provision for the disbursement from the £300 million fund (ibid.: 139). The 1954 Act was complex and it facilitated payments to certain owners who had claimed on the £300 million fund. Essentially, there was a return to free market values in land and buildings. However, it was strongly felt that development control as we now understand it should be kept. Land prices rose rapidly in the 1950s and there were calls for some kind of betterment charge (ibid.: 217–18).

Labour returned to power in 1964 and set up the Land Commission. It bought land, managed it, disposed of it on a commercial basis and also charged a betterment levy on sales and leases at 40 per cent (ibid.: 390). The levy was linked to a land fund, so the Land Commission could operate (ibid.: 356). It was hoped

235

to make land available for builders, forestall rising land prices and prevent land hoarding (ibid.: 380).

The Conservatives returned to power in 1970, abolished the Land Commission, before it had hardly started, and the betterment levy. This was replaced by the taxation of profits and capital gains (ibid.: 405).

Labour returned again in 1974 and introduced the Development Land Tax and the Community Land Act. This empowered local authorities to bring development land into public ownership, net of development land tax otherwise payable by vendors. In this way it was intended that local authorities could steer development to secure the planning aims of their areas by land management, and collect betterment. When payable by a private developer, the tax was collected by central government. In Wales, a Land Authority for Wales was set up to carry out the functions of local authorities elsewhere (Boisot Waters Cohen Partnership 1976).

The Conservatives returned to power in 1979, predictably abolished Labour's arrangements and reinstalled corporation and capital gains tax.

Since the Second World War, probably the major gain to society at large, but not to aggrieved landowners, has been that compensation is not payable from the public purse on the refusal of planning permission or when land is zoned contrary to owners' wishes in development plans. This means that planning activity is not threatened by fears of compensation. Compensation of course is still payable for compulsory purchase by LPAs. At this point the views of Left and Right political parties diverge. The Right will argue that the free market will bring forward development without much bureaucracy and the interference of local authorities; betterment can be collected through taxes already in place. The Left will argue that speculators will hoard land and drive up the price. It is therefore necessary for either central or local government to intervene directly in the land market and to manage it, using compulsory purchase if necessary, to bring about the aims of development plans. Betterment needs to be collected on behalf of the community without its being buried in other business transactions.

History shows that betterment, although created locally, is usually creamed off by central government. One advantage of planning gain is that it is created and accrues locally. Solutions to the problem are legally and technically complex and have foundered as a result. Where the Left has tried a particular solution, it has been defeated politically before its solutions have had a good run.

As far as the author is aware no studies have been carried out on the effects of the trade cycle, generally falling property values and geographical variations in the phenomenon. It is also difficult to gauge the magnitude of the financial sums involved. The Uthwatt Committee, for example, estimated that hope value or floating value was possibly two or three times as great as the probable value, should it actually be realized (Cullingworth 1980: 5). Moreover, the £300 million set aside in the 1940s was to deal with hardship and "certainly did not purport to be a 'global' sum representing the total development value of all land covered by the scheme" (ibid.: 408).

This development control issue has been a major political battleground over the decades. It has visceral overtones of land hoarding, speculation, landowner-ship, power, the free market, bureaucracy and technical complexity. Perhaps we do not really know enough about the detailed workings of property markets for a consensus to be established. We only think we know. Perhaps we should look abroad to see how others have solved the problem.

Public participation in development control

The concept of public participation in development control immediately raises the questions of who the public are and what they are participating in. In short, there are many publics and they participate in many things in the context of planning. Two writers averred that there is a blur between principles, outcomes, benefits and objectives on the one hand and between the different publics on the other (Bishop et al. 1994: 6; Thomas 1996: 184). Skeffington (1969: 1) saw the public as groups and individuals in the community apparently without limit. Par-ticipation was defined as the act of sharing in the formulation of policies and proposals.

The major purposes of participation are as follows. As development control decisions are taken by democratically elected councillors, public participation improves democratic involvement by commenting and lobbying in respect of pro-posals. However, it can be argued that this is mere political theatre and, once an unwelcome decision has been made, objectors can be fobbed off by saying, "You have had your say; you have lost; bad luck!" The invitation to comment may also give greater legitimacy to the decision itself. On the other hand, participants take great satisfaction in making comments when it is felt that the decision has really been influenced by them, for example, imposition of conditions on the grant of planning permission which a participant has suggested. Community involvement is thereby enhanced and public support gained by openness in decision-making. Apart from democratic involvement, better technical decisions may be made by involving as many parties as is possible. Statutory consultees, non-statutory con-sultees and local people may facilitate better decisions because of their expert and detailed knowledge. For example, improved traffic circulation and more visually acceptable development may result. Finally, where proposals are controversial and fraught with conflict, participation brings the issues into the public arena, where they can be tested and weighed in a structured rational way.

A major opportunity for the public to influence development control policy lies in development plan preparation. Once plan-making has been set in motion by the publication of a draft plan, the public (Chs 2, 3; see definition below) may make written representations, complete questionnaires for the LPA eliciting infor-mation, appear at public inquiries, and lobby councillors, MPs and so on, to put their point of view. There are opportunities to do this before a plan is finally adopted. As development plans are the major consideration in development control deci-sions, what is eventually decided as development plan policy is crucially important.

The other major opportunity for the public to participate is in development control procedures *per se*. Current central government guidance for public involvement in development control is Circular 15/92, *Publicity for planning applications* (DoE 1992i), and the General Development Procedure Order 1995 Article 8 (DoE 1995l). "Consultations" invite the views of specialist bodies: "notification" requires developers to notify owners and tenants of agricultural land (DoE 1992i: 1). Mandatory responsibility for publicizing applications in England and Wales lies with the LPAs. Three types of publicity are advocated: notification in a local newspaper, site notices visible to the public, and neighbour notification. Neighbours are defined by reference to Scottish practice (ibid.: annex); briefly, they are those having coterminous boundaries, including above and below and within 4m of the boundary. Site notices may reach an audience wider than immediate neighbours but may be vandalized. LPAs may also put lists of applications in libraries and elsewhere. Parish councils and community councils, where they exist and have an intimate knowledge of their areas, comment on applications. It is for an LPA to decide, on the merits of a case, whether site notices and neighbour notification are necessary. Major developments requiring site notices and neighbour notification may include those that cause all sorts of nuisances such as noise, introduce significant change (e.g. tall buildings) or affect privacy, and those where environmental impact assessments are necessary (see Ch. 5). As mentioned above, central government is particularly concerned about delay in development control. It advocates two or three weeks for those affected by a proposal to put in comments to the LPA, otherwise they may lose their opportunity. The LPA must take representations into account. It is up to the LPA whether it further publicizes changes in an application once it has been made, for example between outline approval and the approval of reserved matters (see Ch. 2). These can be substantial and very worrying to neighbours. Notification of LPA decisions to affected third parties is up to the courtesy of the LPA. Where applications are being handled by appeal, call-in, are on Crown land or are covered by some permitted development rights (e.g. agriculture) (Ch. 4), these also have to be notified to the public. Apart from mechanisms advocated by Circular 15/92, LPAs may choose to hold public meetings, send leaflets to households and run exhibitions. The Citizen's Charter invites citizens to complain when they are dissatisfied (Thomas 1996: 177).

Participation is about power – the power to decide an outcome and what the content of an agenda will be. The public to which reference has been made is made up of:

- Statutory consultees who are normally asked for comments on applications by LPAs; they are listed in the GDPO (Article 10 ff) and include:
  - the Department of Transport in respect of trunk roads
  - the local highway authority in respect of volume and access
  - the Historic Buildings and Monuments Commission in respect of listed buildings
  - the Environment Agency related to various sewerage and river matters.
- Non-statutory consultees mentioned in Circular 9/95 Appendix B, which

include the Ministry of Agriculture, where agricultural land quality is in question, and the police, in relation to crime prevention.

- Others, especially neighbours to a proposed development and residents' associations, civic societies, chambers of commerce, transport user groups and pressure groups such as the Council for the Protection of Rural England.

District councils and county councils mutually consult, for instance on issues concerning them at structure plan level. Parish and community councils are consulted on applications affecting their areas.

Many planning applications are from occupiers for minor development who can readily look after their own interests. The ultimate owners and occupiers of speculatively built houses, shops and factories and the generations to come are conspicuously absent participants. It is the task of LPAs to safeguard their interests when all the current parties to a proposed development are dead and gone.

Bishop et al. (1994) drew attention to Arnstein's so-called ladder of citizen participation, ranging from the power to make decisions (citizen control, delegated power and partnership) through tokenism (placation, consultation and informing) to non-participation (mere therapy and manipulation). It would appear from this characterization that the public at large has delegated its power to make development control decisions to LPAs through elected councillors and professional officers, but retains some influence on decisions through consultation. Sections of the public such as developers can be involved in partnership. Regrettably, Bishop's work was not directly concerned with planning applications but with community involvement with wider planning and development processes, illustrated by ten case studies. Some of the studies would have involved development control issues. They concluded (ibid.: 56) that community involvement has been shown to make a positive contribution to planning and development processes where, at its best, it led to speed, more effective use of resources, product quality, feelings of local ownership, added value, the increased confidence of participants and the more ready resolution of conflict. "You can't just do things to people; you have to provide what they want; community involvement is to everybody's benefit" (ibid.). The general chracteristics of these findings were borne out by other studies of neighbour notification in Scotland and of the planning service by LPAs.

Since 1981, in the context of development control in Scotland, rather more stringent neighbour notification requirements have been in place than in the rest of the UK. In England, LPAs have a statutory responsibility to publicize planning applications but have discretion. In Northern Ireland the Department of the Environment operates a non-statutory system of notification to neighbours against a list provided by the applicant (School of Planning & Housing et al. 1995: 11). In Scotland an applicant informs neighbours (owners, occupiers and tenants) who share a common boundary with the application site, or are within 4m of the boundary, and those on the opposite side of the road. The notification must contain a location plan and some details of the proposal. Comments from neighbours

239

need to be returned in 14 days (ibid.: appendix v). A review (ibid.) sought to see how practice balanced efficiency, effectiveness and economy in neighbour notification. The main finding was that notification was widely supported by LPAs, applicants and neighbours, the principal requirement being the simplification of procedures. Among recommendations were simplifying definitions of neighbouring land (ibid.: 5).

Spawforth, in a survey of LPAs and public participation in plan-making (1995: 16–17), found that nearly all LPAs went beyond statutory minimum requirements. With regard to development control, in contrast to development plan consultation, he found that, apart from statutory consultees, the most commonly notified groups were civic societies, chambers of commerce, archaeological/historical societies and professional groups. Of much less importance were religious groups, trade unions, political parties, charities and voluntary aid groups (ibid.: fig. 2). Overall, LPAs were quite satisfied with the public consultation measures they used.

Public participation is not without its problems. It may be argued that it politicizes planning, ranging one group of interests against another to the detriment of society at large. But this is to misunderstand the nature of development control: it is a political process. Planning applications are not decided by a local bishop or the managing director of the largest firm in the locality. Participation may lead to delay, as neighbours and consultees fail to respond in the limited time set for them. On the other hand, delay may facilitate better decisions as more information becomes available. Undoubtedly, articulate and powerful pressure groups such as large-scale housebuilders and retailers backed by money and expertise have a great influence, as compared with isolated householders. The middle classes, used to bureaucratic processes, are better at putting their case, than those who do not have the training and experience. Regrettably too, there is a lack of public interest in strategic issues, such as the location of a superstore, unless their own property is fairly directly involved, usually by its proximity. They may also be deterred by the technical complexity of issues related, say, to traffic or trading area calculations, especially where experts disagree among themselves. Wingate reported a case where a putative commercial applicant made enquiries of an LPA "in total confidence" so that employees at other sites, and neighbours, did not get wind of proposals that might have adversely affected them (Wingate 1996: 9; Coon 1996: 10).

An unresolved issue in development control public participation is the position of aggrieved third parties when planning permission has been granted. Applicants can appeal against the refusal of planning permission. Currently, neighbours likely to be adversely affected by proposed development for which planning permission has been granted have no right of appeal.

Thatcherism and after

Thatcherism

Circular 22/80, *Development control – policy and practice* (DoE 1980), was the major development control Circular to be issued by the 1979 Conservative government, which was still extant in the mid-1990s. However, paragraphs 1–4 on speed, efficiency and a positive attitude by LPAs plus a commitment to conservation, paragraphs 11–16 on the need to encourage small businesses, paragraphs 18–21 on aesthetic control, Annex A on planning permission for private sector housebuilding and Annex B on enforcement against small businesses – were all withdrawn by 1995 (DoE 1995f). Arguably, much of this was replaced by later Circulars and PPGs. What guidance remains? Paragraphs 5 to 10 are concerned, as were paragraphs 1 to 4, with speed and efficiency in decision-making. They urge preapplication consultation, delegation of powers, short committee cycles, efficient consultation with and notification to applicants, and the publication of details of planning application handling times. The Circular exhorts LPAs not to use delay to apply pressure to an applicant who is resisting changes to the application. However, on the other hand, the Circular urges applicants to complete their application forms correctly. Paragraph 17 on alternative uses for historic buildings stands in lonely isolation. The Secretary of State will not be prepared to grant listed building consent for the demolition of a listed building until every possible effort has been made to find an alternative use. Before consent will be given, evidence is needed that every effort has been exerted to market the building's freehold, and applicants are warned not to impose burdensome covenants to make it unmarketable. If it is possible to summarize the Circular, one can say it is business driven but seeks to continue to protect the more attractive places. It used to contain (in my view) contentious and irritating overstatement. For example, "But the [planning] system has a price, and when it works slowly or badly, the price can be very high and out of all proportion to the benefits" (ibid.: para. 2); or again, "LPAs should be sensitive to the many jobs and the large quantity of economic activity which is locked up in planning applications and should settle their priorities accordingly" (ibid.: para. 11).

A characteristic of Conservative central government guidance is its insistence that planning is concerned primarily with land-use issues and not with people issues – uses and not users. Socially orientated aims have been rejected on the grounds that social issues would be dealt with by the trickle-down (or treacle-down) resulting from a more buoyant deregulated economy (Thornley 1996: 191).

Conservative attitudes to town and country planning and to development control are based on their views of the free market and on local democracy. Until about 1990 they espoused deregulation, but after that there seems to have been a sea change with the onset of growing environmental concerns. The Conservative approach has been one of incremental and perhaps experimental change, rather than root and branch change, such as the purchaser/provider split in the

241

National Health Service or the outright privatization of strategic industries. This section draws freely on the work of Thornley (1993, 1996).

Although development rights in land were effectively nationalized after the Second World War, land and buildings have remained largely in private ownership and subject to free market transactions. Compulsory purchase by government agencies has been used sparingly, for example in the new towns, and in city centres, to facilitate both public and private development. Planning and development control have been concerned with two elements: democratically elected accountable government and an asset-owning private sector. The extent to which government has regulated the private sector has depended on the stance of both local and central government, when both have sought to mitigate incidental externality effects of untrammelled private enterprise. Parallel to this relationship has been the attitude of central government to local government. Since 1979 many LPAs have been abolished: the metropolitan counties and the GLC in England, the counties of Wales and the regions in Scotland. Local authorities have seen their expenditure restricted, the revenue from business premises rates transferred to central government and property assets sold, and compulsory competitive tendering to the private sector has moved them from a provider to a facilitator role. In the context of development control, Enterprise Zones and Simplified Planning Zones are free of the customary planning controls (Ch. 4) and the UCO and the GPDO have been modified to relax planning restrictions in favour of business (Ch. 4). The free market has been unable to solve the problems of the inner city because individual owners acting alone cannot readily overcome so-called "neighbour effects". If an individual in a run-down area redevelops his property, he may not cover his costs because development (or market) value is largely determined by the value of neighbouring property in the same location. To overcome this type of problem, urban development corporations (UDCs) were set up in London and elsewhere with considerable finance and powers to carry out (re)development on a large and comprehensive scale. Normally, development control powers were transferred from the LPAs, in which they found themselves, to the UDCs. UDCs were set up on business lines and were not democratically accountable at the local level; board members were appointed by central government. As a generality, areas of high amenity – national parks, AONBs, green belts and conservation areas – were excluded from deregulation.

It appears that, by the late 1980s, new pressures were emerging which persuaded the central government to alter tack. In 1989, the Secretary of State was faced with appeals over proposals for new settlements in the countryside, particularly near London. LPAs had rejected them and central government was exposed in a very public manner. Free enterprise housebuilders wanted them and natural Conservative supporters in the shires did not. This might be termed "appeal-led planning". At that time there was a substantial green vote in the European elections. The idea of "local choice" allowed difficult decisions to be shifted to local level (Thornley 1996: 196). Whereas development plans had been one material consideration in development control decisions, development plans became the key consideration unless material considerations indicated otherwise. Development control became plan led (Town and Country Planning Act 1990: new §54A). Plans are largely a local matter. There is a good deal of debate as to the interpretation of §54 A and what it means for development control practice. It is for the planning decision-maker to weigh the importance of "otherwise" (Gatenby & Williams 1996: 137 ff).

Development plans and development control have multiple objectives. This raises the issue of the planning/market relationship in another way and prompts the question: what is the proper role of planning? In the Thatcherite context the planning system may be: (a) merely regulatory, mitigating the effects of the free market in land and buildings, (b) a major facilitator in areas and times of economic buoyancy – so-called "trend planning" or (c) an advocate of development in times and places of economic depression. Thatcherism leans towards (b) and (c), as both promoting places in competition with each other, and leans away from (a) through deregulation. Arguably, the purpose of planning is the creation, enhancement and preservation of property values. An advantage of development plans and planning permission, once granted, is increased certainty. The developer has considerable uncertainty to cope with as it is, with fluctuating demand for the output and with changes in building costs between tendering and out-turn. Largely gone are the problems of "floating value" examined by Uthwatt in the 1940s (Uthwatt 1942). The situation is not a new one; it dates back to the 1920s.

Two other aspects of Thatcherism need to be explored: the contracting out of planning services, referred to above as compulsory competitive tendering (CCT), and the Citizen's Charter. CCT – engaging private contractors to do more efficiently and profitably what public authorities have done in house – relies on competition between contractors to drive down costs. Higgins has summarized the situation (Higgins 1996: 18 reporting the RTPI). It was established by a survey of LPAs that 82 per cent of them had contracted out work in the two-year survey period, usually one-off specialist pieces, because of lack of expertise or workload pressure. In "some cases, large parts" of the planning service had been contracted out. Much of the specialist work related to appeals, plan preparation topics and environmental assessments. Most frequent subjects were retail studies, design/conservation/landscape, and environmental issues and transport. The reasons were independent advice, outside funding requirements, appeals where the members had overturned officer advice, competitive bidding for resources and political will. Benefits included technical expertise, workload management, potential cost savings, time control and innovative and independent advice. Problems mentioned were breach of confidentiality, conflicts of interest, lack of quality and budget control, lack of local knowledge, inconsistency, doubtful cost effectiveness, loss of control and lack of accountability. However, only a minority (14 per cent) thought that development control work would be contracted out. There was uncertainty about the future of CCT, particularly as a result of local government reorganization.

The Citizen's Charter initiative is a device promulgated by the Conservative government to improve public services to the public in a situation where customary market forces do not apply because it is not a competitive one and market prices are not used. This is the case in the development control service. The customers are applicants, neighbours and the general public. The charter for planning was issued in two documents, *Development control: a charter guide* (National Planning Forum et al. 1993) for LPAs and *Planning: charter standards* [England and Wales] (DoE et al. 1994: 13 ff) for the public. The Citizen's Charter lays down six general principles (ibid.: 3):

- setting and checking standards
- providing information
- choice and consultation
- politeness and helpfulness
- putting things right
- giving value for money.

In the context of development control there are too many details to be recounted here. Some of the standards suggested inter alia are as follows. When responding to a written request for advice, LPAs should reply within five working days and make a decision on 80 per cent of planning applications within eight weeks. With regard to providing information, the LPA should tell the public what documents they have the right to see. On consultation, the charter suggests that LPAs publish lists of applications and consult amenity societies. As for putting things right, if a member of the public complains that possibly unauthorized development has been carried out, the LPA should respond within 15 working days as to what action it is going to take (e.g. enforcement). In the case of planning appeals, the English Inspectorate set itself the target in 1993–4 of deciding 80 per cent of written representation appeals within 19 weeks of receiving them. Attention is drawn to recourse by the public to the local ombudsman in the case of maladministration. Of course, much of this is not new and LPAs are aware of good practice.

And after

This book was completed in 1996 and one could only speculate on what changes might be made to the planning system if there were a change of central government. Some informal pointers can be found in Hobson et al. (1996: 214 ff), a book to which Tony Blair, the Labour Party leader, wrote the foreword. The well established plan-led system of development control operated by democratically elected LPAs was endorsed by the authors. However, the traditional "presumption in favour of planning permission" in PPG1 (DoE 1992c: para. 5) was queried. Town and Country Planning Act §54A, plan-led development, has been construed as favouring proposed development in accord with the plan. The converse is not necessarily true. It was suggested that there should be a presumption against development that does not conform to the plan, to be overridden only by demonstrating that the development would cause no harm or if there were overriding need. This is virtually identical to the procedure in green belts. It was also suggested that development should be more socially responsible, with an emphasis on sustainability. The availability of alternative sites was said to be a proper reason for refusing planning permission where, for example, greenfield sites might have been taken. Permitted development rights should be reviewed and possibly a class of affordable housing created within the UCO; express planning permission would be needed for a change to other use classes. It was also argued that the combination of light industry and offices into Class B1 had resulted in a loss of light industrial land and a surplus of offices, with a consequent mismatch of employment needs and land availability. The fear of capitalist speculators reared its ugly head. It is possible to obtain planning permission for development, merely start the development process and then hold the land for speculative purposes. It was held that the law should be altered to enforce the completion of development in the public interest or for the LPA to revoke planning permission without the longstanding fear of compensation. The writers also turned to the hoary chestnut of betterment and planning gain. Earlier solutions by the Labour Party were relegated to history and attention focused on how developers could be required to contribute to the needs of the community. As in the early 1990s, LPAs should be free to seek planning gain, but the concept broadened so that wider benefits can be obtained. Under the Conservative regime, LPAs could seek planning gain only if a planning application would be refused without it. The Labour authors said that this should be relaxed. However, they turned their face against benefits unconnected with a proposed development, as this would be tantamount to "buying" planning permissions, and LPAs may be improperly influenced. The writers then drew attention to two sources of inequalities in the development control system. First, there is the problem of the very great resources that major developers, such as superstore operators, have *vis-à-vis* LPAs, who may be forced into expensive planning inquiries. Indeed, the outcome of such appeals may be dependent on the balance of the resources, rather than on the balance of planning arguments. Secondly, although aggrieved applicants for planning permission may appeal against the refusal of planning permission, aggrieved third parties such as neighbours cannot appeal against the grant of planning permission. To overcome these two problems, some kind of independent review procedure was mooted to filter out appeals where the LPA has refused planning permission in line with the development plan and to consider the grant of planning permission where a review is initiated by aggrieved third parties. A proposed review body could possibly be at regional level and have local knowledge. It would endeavour to decide whether issues should be dealt with by full public inquiry or some form of abbreviated/informal procedure. This still left the problem of inequality of resources between parties to a planning inquiry. Legal aid was dismissed as expensive and difficult to administer. Partly to overcome all-round concern about mammoth inquiries, such as a major airport expansion, it was suggested that the inquiry itself should commission independent reports and have the power to cross-examine on issues that (impoverished) third parties wanted raised. But this may raise many NIMBY spectres and undermine local democracy. The reader will note that these changes deal with procedural matters, as one might expect in a book on law reform (Hobson et al. 1996), and not with substantive matters such as transport policy. The authors did not advocate root and branch change, such as the widespread use of the Simplified Planning Zone regime or the municipal ownership of developable land.

Another Labour group, the Labour Planning and Environment Group, reported by Burton (1996a: 6), advocated inter alia a regional tier of government to take strategic decisions on planning, that local plans should take in community structure and that explicit housing tenure should be built into local plans.

Members, officers and little local difficulties

Development control decisions are made by locally elected unpaid councillors on the advice of paid technical officers who are normally members of the Royal Town Planning Institute or other chartered professional bodies. Councillors are accountable to their electorate, chartered planners to their Institute, but central government has an overall controlling interest through parliament. The political colour of LPAs and central government may be quite different and councillors may choose not to follow professional advice. These ingredients in the development control process may lead to what one might call "little local difficulties".

Essex (1996: ch. 10) has drawn attention to this situation; at least five reports in the public domain deal with the problems in detail (George 1991 on Brent, House of Commons Welsh Affairs Committee 1993 on Ceredigion, Lees 1993 on North Cornwall, Barrow 1994 on Warwick, and Phelps 1996 on Bassetlaw). This section summarizes some of the conflicts involved, first by reviewing some of Essex's points and secondly by giving a flavour of the more detailed reports.

Essex quoted the National Local Government Code (para. 23): "Both councillors and officers are servants of the public and they are indispensable to one another. But these responsibilities are distinct. Councillors are responsible to the electorate and serve only as long as their term of office lasts. Officers are responsible to the council. Their job is to give advice to councillors and the council, and to carry out the council's work under the direction and control of the council, their committees and subcommittees." On the other hand the Royal Town Planning Institute's Code of Professional Conduct says: "Members shall not make or subscribe to any statements or reports which are contrary to their own bona fide professional opinions and shall not knowingly enter into any contract or agreement which requires them to do so" (RTPI 1994: 2). Sincere councillors will want sincere advice from sincere officers, even if they do not like what they hear. To want otherwise could mean that councillors would be prepared to receive poor advice, resulting in poor decisions. Difficulties arise, for example, where an officer recommends granting a planning application, possibly because it will not stand up on appeal if it is refused. But this advice is rejected by councillors and the application is refused. The applicant appeals and the officer may be faced with defending a council decision which cannot be supported professionally. In these cases another employee or outside consultants may represent the council. Clearly, it is an embarrassing situation for the personnel involved and the LPA is sending out a mixed message to the applicant. Ideally, members and officers should develop beneficial partnerships each respecting the other's role. However, development control is a highly political activity. Crawley, reporting experiences in Conservative-controlled Wandsworth, said that "Some councillors made clear their belief that planners, by their nature, were considered to be socialists whose advice was politically motivated and therefore easily dismissed" and speaking of the economic section of the planning department "Semantics and presentation became paramount. 'Cooperatives' were out but 'common ownership enterprises' were in" (Crawley 1991: 107–108).

There is wide variation in practice between LPAs, often reflecting the strength of personalities, political style and the social and economic characteristics of the area (Essex 1996: 157). Further conflicts arise when central government guidance advises one policy but the LPA is opposed to it. This was so in the 1980s when PPG6 (on retailing) advocated a free market approach to superstore development but LPAs feared for the future of their existing shopping centres. This particular advice has now changed. As central government guidance and development plans are only guidance and not strictly binding legally, an LPA may wish quite correctly to override them when considering particular applications, especially in response to lobbying by constituents.

The source of decision-making can also become confused by the use of delegation. The full council of an LPA normally delegates its planning powers to its planning committee (or development or environment committee) to cope with the flood of detail on site-specific issues. In turn, the planning committee may delegate its powers to small subgroups of members, possibly on a small-area basis, in order to speed decision-making. Planning committees may also delegate their powers over minor development to paid technical officers for the same reason. "Schemes of delegation" lay down the powers delegated and allow for contentious decisions to be referred back to higher levels, to the full council of an LPA for example. Of course full delegation inhibits local councillors' ability to represent their constituents; there is a trade-off between speed and efficiency and democratic representation. Drawing on the Ceredigion and North Cornwall experiences, Essex (ibid: 165) stressed the importance of clear and up-to-date development plans, also put together by democratic process, so that councillors can respond to the demands of their constituents in individual planning application cases. There can well be a conflict between overall planning objectives and the immediate concerns of local residents. But unfortunately members, as much as the general public, find it difficult to get involved with strategic plan-making. Two added difficulties are that plan preparation, including the wait for the outcome of the plan inquiry, can take quite a long time and central government policy guidance can frustrate locally formulated policy (ibid.: 166).

Essex (ibid.: 161) reported the House of Commons Welsh Affairs Committee's (1993) concern in Ceredigion about the economic and social future of local communities and the Welsh language and culture, by quoting "Where a planning committee approves significant numbers of planning applications against the advice of their planning officers (and on occasions their legal officers too) the relationship between officers and members is bound to be put under some strain." It was found that "excessive weight was being given to the views of local ward members". Or again, "some councils [in Wales] are making decisions not on the basis of adopted plans, but on an arbitrary basis, not infrequently based on the untested assertions of individual councillors, most commonly representing the ward where the development takes place". Local councillors are in a real dilemma where they have known many local people over a long period of time.

The report by Lees (1993) is possibly the best known recent national inquiry into the granting of planning permission locally. She wrote, "the crux of the problem in North Cornwall District is that the Council had granted planning permission for development in the open countryside, on an inconsistent basis, and contrary to national planning guidance and approved policies in the County Structure Plan. It seems that in contributing to decision-making, some councillors favoured certain applicants, often local people, because of their personal circumstances rather than material planning considerations" (ibid.: ix). Lees received many assertions that "there must be some corruption" to account for certain decisions of the Council but she made it clear that she received no specific evidence about criminal corruption of any kind during the Enquiry (*sic*), nor was there any evidence of conspiracy (ibid.: 9). Some respondents to the Enquiry felt that the increase in the value of land resulting from a planning application was so great that district councillors should not be vested with the power to make people's fortunes without external checks, for example by the County Council (ibid.: 10). Lees balanced this reporting of apparent criticism with positive planning achievements, for example conservation and helping rural businesses (ibid.: 11). In the early 1990s, improvements in procedures were made and she reported that "the planning system has therefore by no means collapsed in North Cornwall" (ibid.: 12).

It is difficult to summarize a report that ended with 64 recommendations (ibid.: 73 ff). Among the issues and allegations were the following (ibid.: ch. 4): that preference was given to particular groups, particularly "Cornish" people, and that councillors arranged "pacts" to support each other's applications, and that there was unfairness and inconsistencies. While the Enquiry was under way, the district council altered its procedures, whereby proposals by the planning committee to grant planning permission contrary to policy or officers' advice were referred to the full council for decision and minutes were more fully recorded. Lees drew attention to the problem of hardship and the personal circumstances of applicants, which generally do not weigh heavily in planning matters, saying "Personal preferences have no place in this system. However, personal circumstances of applicants have a place in this system, albeit very exceptionally" (ibid.: 16). The theme of helping local people was taken up further (ibid.: ch. 5), for example helping elderly farming couples find a house locally which they could afford. In this type of case, Lees felt it was necessary to have development plan policies in place for affordable housing and agricultural workers' dwellings. She reported that "by far the most common concern of respondents to the Enquiry was that North Cornwall DC was 'destroying the countryside' by allowing sporadic development" (ibid.: ch. 6). She agreed there was a problem which sprang from housing demand by locals, second-home owners and the holiday industry, but in a relatively weak economy in need of jobs. Traditional housing tended to be sheltered in valleys, but new housing was scattered pepper-pot fashion in more prominent sites in beautiful countryside (ibid.: 32). Lees recommended firmer development plan policies safeguarding the countryside and controlling extensions to settlements (ibid.: 34–6).

It was also reported that the District was in need of design guides, did not have professionally qualified staff to advise on design issues (although this was brought in from outside), and that the majority of applications were made without design advice. A further problem reported was a housing policy in the structure plan that sought to confine much new development to villages that had village shops and other basic facilities (ibid.: ch. 7). As such facilities were declining and many hamlets did not have them, this had a very limiting effect on where development could be allowed in the District. Moreover, the District had, in the past, been reluctant to adopt a formal local plan because it was "not the most appropriate planning concept to be adopted in a disadvantaged area . . . where development opportunities need positive encouragement . . ." (ibid.: 40). Lees urged councillors and parish councils to be more closely involved in plan preparation necessary under the 1991 Act. Chapter 8 of the Lees report urged greater publicity and notification of planning applications.

She also put her finger on the delicate relationship between officers and members (ibid.: ch. 9) and reported the tag that "a good planning officer is a weak one", meaning that members can easily sway officers. Very often a chief planning officer is the subject of criticism, because the work of the planning department is carried out in his name. But in this case, Lees reported that "I have no criticism of the basic substance of the current advice being given" (ibid.: 50).

As for planning procedures (ibid.: ch. 10), they were found "to be broadly in line with the average local authority of this type and size and being run in a competent manner . . ." (ibid.: 53), although Lees recommended improvements (e.g. monitoring planning conditions) and drew attention to the relationship between the extent of delegation to officers, which had been subject to complaint, and speed of decision (ibid.: 56). Complainants also felt that the South West regional office of the DOE was too remote and unaware of the situation in North Cornwall, was not responsive enough to complaints, and did not call in applications that warranted such treatment (ibid.: ch. 11). Lees reported: "Confidence in the planning system will be difficult to restore, however, until the prospects of call-in, or the revocation of inconsistent decisions, are seen to be more likely, or at least understandable" (ibid.: 62). The problem here, however, is that call-in undermines an LPA's independence. The situation is complicated by the fact that a few inconsistent local decisions may not matter, but cumulatively they do raise national issues, as in North Cornwall. As a reserve power, the Secretary of State may also direct that local plans be modified or may call them in for his own decision if he is not satisfied that policies are adequate, for example to protect designated areas (ibid.: 64).

Finally, Lees drew attention to sanctions available (ibid.: ch. 12). These included, inter alia, the local government ombudsman on maladministration, the judicial review of planning decisions, the Secretary of State exercising call-in powers, the revocation or modification of planning permission once granted, the removal of buildings once built, the council's monitoring officer reporting to the full council on a range of matters and the district auditor ensuring value for money, for example when costs have to be paid by the LPA.

The Barrow report (1994) on the administration of the planning system in Warwick District Council, like the Lees report on North Cornwall, was set up to investigate matters of concern:

> The circumstances of several major planning applications seemed to be suspicious, allegations were made about some Councillors who appeared to have strong associations with particular developers and some planning proposals had been actively promoted by serving or former Councillors. Reference was made to Police investigations in the late 1980s although no charges had been preferred (ibid.: 4).

A report so sensitive is best read in the original. The author quotes here from Barrow's executive summary, to give the reader the flavour of the issues involved.

> I have concluded that many of the criticisms about previous activities and practices – some now supplanted – of the District Council are justified. This applies especially in the perception of how Councillors performed in the process of dealing with planning applications and in making decisions; about preapplication contacts with applicants and developers; about the acceptance of lobbying; on expressing opinions amounting to commitments; on the conduct and operation of site visits; on the absence of reasons for decisions, especially approvals. I find shortcomings in the previous form and contents of reports by officers, and in the keeping of records and files. These are areas where significant changes have recently been or are being introduced and provide a basis for future improvement.

Evidence was taken in strictest confidence and normally no reference is made to individual planning applications (ibid.: 2). As in the Lees report, Barrow made a point of recording the District Council's planning achievements, especially in this case in the conservation of town centres (ibid.: 11).

The George report (1991) on development control in the London Borough of

Brent differed from those of Lees and Barrow, in that sites, applicants, councillors and officers are clearly identified. It was concerned inter alia with whether there was any evidence that other than proper planning considerations were taken into account by the development control subcommittee in deciding applications between 1986 and 1990 and whether there were particular patterns of community groups, applicants or agents gaining approvals. George investigated decisions only where permission was granted contrary to officers' recommendations to refuse (ibid.: 10), which was a narrow range of matters; to review all decisions would have been impracticable. Reasons for granting permission are not normally recorded (ibid.: 12).

George examined 122 planning decisions in the period (ibid.: 31), when applications were running at 2500–3000 per year, of which 60–70 per cent were delegated to officers (ibid.: 14), but concentrated on 27 (ibid.: 33). It was found that decision delay was a problem caused by a surge of applications and planning posts being frozen (ibid.: 41 ff) In controversial cases, plan revision also caused delay (ibid.: 170). Within the 120 or so applications in ten categories, four categories stood out: bed and breakfast for the homeless, unrestricted hotel permission, residential conversions and extensions, and new blocks of flats (ibid.: 37). George used individual planning application files and interviews with personnel involved to disentangle, in reported detail, what had transpired. As in many contentious cases, the details are somewhat labyrinthine and impossible to report here. A separate section of the report (ibid.: chs 23–25) is devoted to relations between officers, members and applicants. This highlighted the problems involved where members disagree with officers over decisions, where officers help applicants with applications but where there may be delay or fresh issues raised, where officers are perceived as having negative attitudes and where applicants lobby committee members, expecting their applications to be granted. A further dimension is the unease felt by third parties (e.g. objectors), when third parties perceive the appearance of the relationship between officers, members and applicants. As for investigating patterns of approvals, George found that disentangling patterns of agents and applicants was extremely difficult (ibid.: 212 ff). The roles of individual applicants and agents and of corporate bodies with directors changed from case to case and over time, as properties sometimes changed hands between application and decision. The ethnic origin of applicants was considered, as there were disproportionate numbers of Irish and Asian people in Brent. George also explored the possibility that some planning decisions were legally flawed or perverse. The report ended (ibid.: ch. 29) with 24 reasoned recommendations. Regrettably, the report contained neither an executive summary nor a specific section drawing together findings and conclusions. For those not conversant with the interplay of politics, personalities and planning, George reported the very human side of the development control process, whereas the Lees and Barrow reports tended to be somewhat more at arm's length.

This section may be drawn together by reporting research commissioned by the Royal Town Planning Institute on member–officer relationships in the context

251

of development control (Zetter et al. 1996: 1–6). It was carried out by questionnaire and interview surveys of elected members and officers. Some of the findings were as follows. Chairs of planning committees saw their role as serving the public interest in the LPA as a whole, whereas other councillors placed greater emphasis on ward issues. The majority of councillors serving on planning committees felt that relationships with officers should be informal and friendly, in the form of a partnership. But when pressed about the most important aspects of the relationship, the chairpeople often mentioned the employer to employee relationship with officers. On the other hand, chief officers preferred a partnership relationship with the chair. With regard to delegation of development control decisions to officers, it was commonly felt by members that most cases could be left to officers. Lobbying by applicants and the public was a key issue. The most likely response by councillors was to listen but to make no commitment prior to committee meetings where relevant applications were discussed. Councillors considered that delay in granting planning permission could be reduced partly by more frequent meetings and greater delegation to officers. Decisions taken against officers' advice were common, but such decisions were very few considering the number of applications received. Job creation was often cited by members as a reason for taking decisions against existing planning policy and officer advice. Where members had suspicions or had direct approaches from fellow councillors which could entail non-planning considerations or impropriety they preferred to deal with it privately. Backbench planning committee members usually did this with the chair and the chair with the chief executive or solicitor. Generally, the majority of members and officers felt they needed further national guidance. The most frequently mentioned subjects were departures from established planning policy and "all matters relating to town planning". The report ended with 15 recommendations.

Lees (1993: appendix B) usefully drew attention to the National Code of Local Government Conduct (see also DOE 1990a, Widdicombe 1986) with which this section may be usefully concluded. It provided guidance to LPA council members and officers on their conduct and applied to Great Britain. Councillors are enjoined to act within the law and for the whole community. When personal private interests are involved, these must normally be disclosed and councillors may not normally speak or vote. This may well apply to councillors and their friends and associates when they apply for planning permission. Officers are responsible to the council; their job is to advise councillors and the council and to work under the direction of the council. Mutual respect is essential between councillors and officers; personal familiarity can damage this relationship. When officers are being appointed, involved councillors are expected to consider which candidate would best serve the whole council and not let political or personal preferences influence their judgement. Councillors acquiring confidential information are advised not to betray trust and to treat with extreme caution any favours shown to them, such as hospitality.

Equality

The grant or refusal of planning permission is an exercise of political power. Planning applications are made by propertied interests; those who are not propertied are largely disenfranchised from the process. For historical and cultural reasons the following are well represented in the planning and property nexus in UK: Whites, males, the fit, the relatively well off and the car-borne. Conversely, the following are underrepresented: the poor, elderly, female, disabled, ethnic minorities, children and the car-less. There are more of the latter group than the former, but separately they each have specific needs that are difficult to articulate in the planning process because they are largely absent from it. At best they are inadvertently overlooked or they are treated as "a problem" to be coped with, or at worst there is direct discrimination against them. Parliament has recognized this by passing the Disabled Persons Act 1970, the Race Relations Act 1976 and the Sex Discrimination Act 1975, designed to combat the difficulties (Davies 1996b: 215). An unequal society is a divided society in which those who are marginalized cannot contribute fully to it, nor can they lead full and satisfying lives.

The literature shows concern with the following particular needs of this underrepresented heterogeneous group and of course not all of them apply to all subgroups: access (including parking and public transport), shopping, personal safety, facilities for small businesses and self-employment, and specific facilities (e.g. places of worship). These concerns can be addressed by explicit policies in development plans, conditions attached to planning permission and planning agreements. Greed (1994: 176) argued that if you plan well for minorities then the majority groups also benefit from the higher level of provision. Indeed, planning for women (52 per cent of the population) means altering planning for men.

Planning for women

Greed (1994: ch. 11) in particular has drawn attention to women's perception of the built environment and how it might be improved. Davies (1996a: ch. 17) reported on research into planning policies found in development plans. Davies, quoting PPG12, *Development plans and regional planning guidance*, drew attention to the advice to LPAs to "consider the relationship of planning policies and proposals to social needs and problems, including their likely impact on different groups in the population" (Davies 1996a: 228). However, apparently the DoE prefers integration of women's policies into other policies, the separation of minority issues not being considered good practice (ibid.). One advantage of integration is that policies are less likely to be eliminated in any cost-cutting exercise. But if planning agreements are to be entered into, for example to ensure crèches are included in shopping developments, they need to be included in development plans. Davies (ibid.) quoting Calder et al. (1993) listed the following areas of particular concern:

- housing, especially affordable housing, designed sensitively to the needs of women

- retailing, especially with easy access to local and town centre shopping
- employment, especially ease of access, and childcare facilities
- personal mobility, especially within and between buildings, and access to safe public transport
- recreation, especially easy access for women and children
- community facilities, especially those needed by women
- crime prevention, fear and safety, which overlap other issues, including sensitive design.

Of these, Davies found in her research that these concerns were reflected in unitary development plans, especially policies for shopping, employment, transport, recreation and environment. Under retailing, policies embraced childcare facilities, crèches, toilets, baby changing and feeding areas. But where quotas were laid down (e.g. nursery provision related to retail or employment space), the DOE tended to alter provision. On mobility some LPAs mounted policies to avoid the construction of subways and poorly lit footways. Policies to deter crime in the environment included mixed use areas and improving security by arranging for the overlooking of public areas, although such policies might have been seen as protecting property rather than people. Recreational policies for women were found to be largely ignored. It was found that funding to cater for women's special needs came partly from public funds, partly through planning agreements and partly from other sources.

Greed (1994: ch. 11) took a macro- rather than a micro-view of the environment, arguing that women use a set of classifications different from those used by men in organizing environmental problems. She stressed caring, housing, jobs and skills, the protection of local shopping centres, safety from violence, and mobility. Workplace and shopping nurseries, public conveniences, safe parking and good lighting figure as key improvements needed in the built environment. She also advocated de-zoning, that is, restructuring and integrating land uses at city level to bring home and work closer together. The RTPI (1995b) made the point that in women's caring capacity for young and old and their propensity for part-time employment, they are tied more than men to the home environment. Planning for local services (e.g. for parents with children) that support local communities is therefore of key importance. Greed drew attention to the fact that childcare facilities are D1(b) non-residential uses within the UCO and need planning permission, although arguably they are integral to the enjoyment of a residential area. As she rightly wrote, childcare facilities are totally inadequate in the UK. She also advocated crèche standards for workplaces – one carparking space per $200\,m^2$ of offices, so why not one crèche space per $50\,m^2$? She also argued for working from home and thought that Thomas (1988b) took a negative view of this, which he does, when dangerous and exploitative outworking takes place out of sight. Men are interested in sport and, as a result, open space standards elide the distinction between sport and leisure open space to the disadvantage of women and children. She advocated new-style Victorian parks. Returning to shopping and crèches, one telling argument reported was that mothers spend more when unencumbered by children. The nub of Greed's argument was that what women want is a caring city and a caring environment.

In the context of development control, implementation is by the imposition of conditions, the use of agreements and mandatory standards. Greed cited cases where crèches, toilets and baby changing facilities were obtained in this way. The RTPI (1995b) stressed the importance of good design details, for example the avoidance of dead frontages and high walls, the encouragement of safe landscaping, level access and wide doors to buildings. Walking is the most common form of travel for women (and children), as they are less likely than men to have a driving licence and may not have the use of a car. Transport facilities need to be designed with this in mind, for example bus stops at appropriate intervals and with seating.

Greed felt there was a long way to go. It is noteworthy that there is no PPG on planning and women or planning and the family. The RTPI (1995b) argued for implementation, monitoring, review and research.

Planning for disabled people

Over six million people in the UK suffer from disabilities or limitations, including people who are blind, deaf, wheelchair bound, those who lack physical coordination, those who suffer from painful conditions such as arthritis and those who are pregnant. As the population ages, the situation will worsen. Many of these people are denied ready access to jobs, houses and services (Davies 1996b: ch. 17). Development Control Policy Note 16 (DoE 1985g) and Circular 10/82 (DoE 1982) constitute the principal guidance on disabled people in the context of development control. They are complemented by the Building Regulations. Much literature focuses on the problem of access to buildings. Access improvements appear difficult to implement and effectively apply only to new buildings or where redevelopment takes place (e.g. new shop fronts). Access for the disabled is a material consideration in development control.

> The arrangement for access to buildings can be a planning matter and the arrangements for use by the public, which includes disabled people, raises issues of public amenity which . . . can be material in a planning application . . . conditions may be attached to a grant of planning permission to deal with the matter . . . in the case of any appeals . . . it is the [Secretary of State's] intention . . . to take account of the considerations set out above in deciding whether to allow or dismiss the appeals. (DoE 1982)

> Where appropriate the planning authority may impose conditions requiring access provision for disabled people. (DoE 1985g)

Development plans and **development briefs** may make explicit reference to disabled people in a wide range of policy topics, for example transport, housing, shopping, employment and leisure. Specifically appointed access officers in local authorities look after this particular need. Local access groups, comprising disabled people and those who design for them, should have relevant planning applications referred to them for comment (RTPI 1988b).

RTPI guidance (ibid.) advised that ensuring that the planning system takes cognizance of disability starts with a thoughtful attitude of mind with constant awareness of differing needs. Key external factors are: parking, paths, kerbs and street furniture, as well as entrances, including ramps, doors and lobbies. Internal features may also be subject to planning control.

Planning for ethnic minorities

The UK is a multiracial country. In 1991 just over 5.5 per cent of the population were classified as non-White, involving a variety of cultures and national backgrounds. Many are concentrated in specific geographical areas. Historically they have suffered social and economic disadvantage, such as poor housing and high unemployment. Part of this is attributable to discrimination (Thomas & Krishnarayan 1994: 2). They are poorly represented in the town planning profession (ibid.: 15), tend not to get involved with planning issues (ibid.: ch. 6) and may be excluded from making representations because of language difficulties (ibid.: 6). Davies (1996b: 217) drew attention to PPG12 (DoE 1992b: para. 5.48), which gave the following guidance ". . . in preparing detailed plans too, authorities will wish to consider the relationship of planning policies and proposals to social needs and problems, including their likely impact on different groups in the population such as ethnic minorities".

The Housing and Planning Act 1986 §19A states that: "It is unlawful for a planning authority to discriminate against a person in carrying out their planning functions" (Thomas & Krishnarayan 1994: 6). The Act identifies two kinds of discrimination: direct and indirect. An example of direct discrimination was quoted by Thomas & Krishnarayan in the case of an applicant of Indian origin who applied to open an English restaurant in a detached house in a village in North Yorkshire:

> Some members of the local Planning Committee visited residents in the area urging them to object to the proposal on the grounds that "it would bring Indians into the village and residents would be forced to suffer the smell of Indian food". The Planning Department had no objection to the proposal on planning grounds and recommended that permission be granted. Despite a positive recommendation the application was rejected twice by the Planning Committee and was finally approved at the third attempt. (ibid.)

Indirect or institutional discrimination consists in applying a requirement that is applied equally to all racial groups but where the requirement cannot be justified. For example, if an LPA required that all third-party representations about a proposal must be in writing, this would discriminate against those who felt uneasy writing in English. The requirement is unjustified because representations could be made orally or could be translated from another written language. The perpetrators of indirect discrimination may just be unaware. On the policy side Thomas & Krishnarayan quoted the situation in Waltham Forest: "In some cases,

256

established planning policies can have a disproportionately negative effect on ethnic minority communities. For example, for historical and economic reasons, many black businesses operate in non-retail service uses (mini-cab hire, restaurants, takeaways, etc.). Policies which are devised to retain a high proportion of shops in shopping centres may prevent black businesses gaining access to prime trading locations. Such conflicts underline the need to review the effects of planning policies." (ibid.: 5).

This may happen also where refusal rates for planning permission show wide differences between ethnic groups of applicants. Thomas & Krishnarayan advocated two anti-discrimination approaches: first, a positive strategy to sensitize planning policies and procedures, rather than cope with issues on a fire-fighting basis, and secondly monitoring the impact of planning decisions on ethnic groups with a view to exposing discrimination and improving the situation (ibid.: ch. 2).

In a survey of LPA policies which referred to the needs of ethnic minorities, they found (ibid.: 14) the following topics in order of frequency: places of worship, community facilities, housing, general issues, employment, safety and security in design, leisure, and the retention of specialized and local shops. On the development control side, it was found in Sheffield (ibid.: 78) that a race adviser was able to assist in two ways; first, overcoming language or cultural barriers in completing applications and, secondly, explaining the particular aspects of applications with a cultural dimension. The difficulties of imposing an hours-of-use condition on a mosque in a residential area were cited.

Thomas & Krishnarayan reported three case studies of the relationship between development control activity and ethnic minorities. One such study, commissioned by the RTPI, was on hot-food takeaways. About 9 per cent of the ethnic minority workforce in the UK are employed in hotels and catering, that is, over twice the proportion of White employees. As self-employment is more common among ethnic minorities, hot-food takeaways are an important source of employment. Hot-food takeaways, in Class A3 of the UCO, need planning permission when converted from other classes of shop. Particular planning characteristics are smell, fumes, litter, long working hours, noise from cars and customers, and possibly parking in roadways contrary to traffic regulations. These problems excite considerable public opposition, especially when they are near living accommodation. The applicants themselves may not be used to dealing with bureaucracy. Studies have shown that LPAs are inclined to refuse takeaway applications, whoever makes them, more than other types of applications, and the outcome, it seems, is not easy to predict. Councillors, faced with many public objections, may go against the recommendation of their officers. Where the outcome of an application may be uncertain, planning officers normally encourage preapplication discussions so that difficulties can be overcome. However, some ethnic minorities choose to minimize their contact with officialdom, as their experience may have been unpleasant or unfruitful. An added problem is that of planning jargon. But sometimes it is a matter of cultural perceptions. It was found, for example, that Asians in Kirklees acknowledged the need for government regulation. They were far less likely to object to hot-food takeaways than non-Asian residents. Their views of nuisance related solely to late night rowdiness and, in particular, the possibility of outsiders being attracted to the area. Non-Asian groups seemed to define nuisance as the LPA would do – noise, smell, litter and general nuisance (ibid., reporting Woulds).

Then there is the problem of direct discrimination by council officials. They concluded that a combination of factors make for severe difficulties in ethnic minorities obtaining planning permission for hot-food outlets. To overcome this, sustained political pressure by ethnic groups is probably needed to bring about meaningful change. Meanwhile, more explicit criteria are needed, it is argued, replacing vague references to nuisance or amenity, which would help applicants understand the ways their applications are likely to be judged.

The limitations of market mechanisms
I am well aware that I have only addressed some aspects of the equality problem. Many but not all of the environmental problems of particular groups in society spring from gross inequalities in wealth and income, which have become worse in the last decades of the twentieth century. Those disadvantaged by low income may be in more than one disadvantaged group, for example the older, partly disabled worker who may be unemployed. Town planning and development control address only some aspects of the issue. Some argue that the free market is the most efficient way of running an economy. It may result in gross inequality, but that is the price we must pay. But the espousal of planning as a free market modifier, rather than its rejection, is a source of hope.

It is noteworthy that government Circulars and PPGs normally direct their attention in their titles to property, procedures and activities and not to particular groups of people, for example town centres and retail development rather than shoppers (PPG6) and transport rather than travellers (PPG13). The few exceptions are disabled people (DCPN 16, Circular 10/82), travelling show people (Circular 22/91) and gypsy sites (Circular 18/94).

Ethical dilemmas

Both politicians and moralists address the question: How shall we live? Questions about what is "right" and what is "wrong" by way of thought and action have been asked for millennia. Ultimately, we are led, or driven, by our moral stance on issues. Currently, we do not believe it is right to discriminate between applicants because of their gender or creed, but we do know that discrimination does take place in society. Is it right that an owner cannot do as he wishes with his property but is constrained by the planning system? Development control is a political activity and therefore a moral activity. When a planning application is decided we hope that there is a win–win situation and all parties are satisfied. But we know that some win and some lose, for example, if family or business networks are disrupted in a redevelopment scheme. As an aside, it is said that when, say, an application to change a shop to an amusement arcade is made, no credence is given to those who say gambling is a bad thing, as moral issues are not relevant to planning (DOE & WO 1996a: 36). Perhaps they should be.

Ethics, a major branch of philosophy, cannot be condensed readily to a few paragraphs, nor can ethical questions necessarily be resolved, although we face them all the time. The Royal Town Planning Institute's Code of Conduct for its members is an ethical statement. Just to explain the sources of morality will give the reader food for thought. Cook (1994: ch. 2) argued that morality springs from three different sources: reason, experience and the will. To argue from reason leads in two directions. First, one can reason that, by observing the world, goodness and badness are just features of nature. Secondly, one can take the intuitive approach: everyone knows the difference between right and wrong. It is self-evident: we all have consciences. The problem is that we know what is right but sometimes do the opposite. Consciences also tell us to do contradictory things. But are we all reasonable? And what is natural? The second source of morality is feeling and experience. Subjectivists say that morality is a matter of personal taste and preference: it is just what we feel about things. Morality is to do with our emotions, derived from our experience – abortion, right or wrong? As moral judgements depend on different people at different times and places, in different societies, there can really be no moral absolutes. This is moral relativism: let us be tolerant. On the other hand, it is argued that there are common themes running through many societies, for example the importance of truth-telling and promise-keeping. Maybe there are objective elements in morality after all. Moral argument presupposes an objective arena to which we may refer and in which moral arguments can be resolved. A major variant of the feeling and experience theme is the utilitarian view, which seeks to promulgate laws that lead to the greatest happiness for the greatest number. But what of those made unhappy by the outcome? This can be countered by the principles of justice and equality, each person counting equally. But can we measure happiness? This idea is still at the heart of government today. Finally, the will is a source of morality. The world is meaningless, argues the existentialist, but we create our own morality because we choose and will it. Morality is created by facing moral dilemmas. But these in themselves need reason and emotion to resolve them. Moreover, we are constrained in our choices by others around us. Anyway what is the will?

However, Cook continued by opening up fresh sources of morality, namely the sciences, very widely defined. In the biological sciences, morality may derive from the need for the survival of the species. For the psychoanalyst, morality comes from infantile experience, whereas Marx argued that morality springs from socio-economic conditioning. These sources of morality, one might say, are paralleled by the light that religious thought and practice throw on moral issues, especially Judaeo-Christian perspectives in the UK – now a multi-faith society.

To help solve moral dilemmas Cook (ibid.: ch. 4) advocated the following approaches:
- consider all the factors involved

259

- identify the important principles involved and prioritize them
- classify aims, goals and objectives relevant to the situation
- consider alternatives, possibilities and choices
- understand and integrate other people's viewpoints.

Although Cook is a philosopher, this approach will be very familiar to plan-makers and development controllers. If you find this diversion into ethics confusing, do not be surprised. Morality and development control are about choices. For an earlier wide-ranging discussion of ethics and planning, see McConnell (1981: chs 5 and 6).

Thomas & Healey (1991) have usefully drawn together some of the dilemmas facing planners. Dilemmas – that is the difficulties of choice between unpalatable alternatives – of course may never be satisfactorily resolved. It appears that these concerns can be grouped into the general role of the planner in bringing about the just society and the problems that face professionals and politicians personally in their everyday development control work.

First Healey and then Thomas (ibid.: chs 2 and 3), dealing with the role of the planner, put forward the following ideas, which I have has modified. The planner is a land manager and urban designer; this derives from an earlier stage in the formation of the planning profession. Until about 1950 it was dominated by those already trained in architecture, civil engineering and surveying, arguably concerned with "technical" solutions to "technical" problems, as if devoid of moral content. After this date, economists, sociologists and geographers joined the profession, with views of how wealth and power are and should be distributed in society. The second role of the planner is that of the public bureaucrat, performing duties in a professional way but defined by politicians. This reflects a legalistic view of planning, springing from the fourth founding profession of planning – the law. The reader will be very aware that development control is very legally bounded, as reflected, for example, by development control application processes and the definition of permitted development rights (PDR). Another role is that of the public policy analyst and formulator. Development plans, based on survey and analysis, reflect many of society's values, for example housing and transportation policies. These are further reflected in implementation through development control. This is referred to as the rational decision model. The rational planner's values are a key to understanding this approach; in the UK they are concerned with the promotion of democracy and social justice. A fifth role of the planner is that of mediator or referee trying to ensure that developers can build without too much harm to neighbours. Conditions, legal agreements and ultimately refusal of planning permission are the tools. Finally, planners have a role as social reformers. Planning has always had a strong dose of idealism and evangelism. What we build is but a reflection of our social values; by building we can bring about social reform.

Thomas (ibid.: ch. 3) has cut the ethical cake in another direction – professional values, the validation of professional knowledge and professional legitimation. The professions, such as law, medicine and planning, claim to be acting in the public interest, whatever that may be. The values that professional codes of conduct may promulgate (e.g. the RTPI code: RTPI 1994), involve personal stances. Members shall act with competence, honesty, integrity, impartial exercise of judgement, due care and diligence, non-discrimination on grounds of sex, and so on, and they shall not bring the profession into disrepute. The problem, as Cook pointed out, is putting them into practice when faced with professional dilemmas. Individual professions lay claim to unique bodies of knowledge through professional examinations and admission requirements for membership. But it is up to the members what shall be examined and who shall be admitted. In examining these privileges there is an implicit claim that the exercise of knowledge is in the public interest. Underlying this is a value judgement that the knowledge is valid. As new professions struggle to emerge – in the case of planning from law, surveying, architecture and civil engineering – there is a value judgement made that the profession has something to offer society. Is serving customers giving them what they want, or what is good or right (Thomas & Healey 1991: 41)? Professional action is legitimized and sanctioned by government through the grant of charters. The government of the day is in itself a reflection of the values of society or only the powerful and articulate part of it.

The heart of the Thomas & Healey book (1991) reported the dilemmas faced by planners in their day-to day work. This is a small selection of what they wrote. Nicholson (ibid.: ch. 4), who moved from an academic research environment to local government practice, wrote that he found that local government was hierarchical and he was somewhat anonymous; little weight was given to research activity. The use of precedent, policy, consultations, negotiations and technical tests in deciding applications required a mixture of knowledge, skills and values. Swinbourne (ibid.: ch. 5) found that knowing how to plan for ethnic minorities was important, partly absorbed by learning that "this is the way we [planners] do things here". Management was important for setting the context in which ethical issues could be resolved. An obvious personal conflict was between speed and quality in working in development control. Tibbs (ibid.: ch. 9), involved with the possibility of steering resources to socially stressed areas of a city, found that writing about them can lead to unwanted public stigmatization. Essex (ibid.: ch. 7) recalled being at the receiving end of a clearance area policy in inner London at a time when residents had little say, but planners acted out of the highest motives. Yet public participation was seen as undermining the role of elected representatives. Pell, from the private sector (ibid.: ch. 8), was taught by his colleagues to appreciate different styles of professional behaviour. "We have many instances (in our practice) where persistence wins but others where compromise is the essence of a solution . . . The lack of respect between those involved is, I believe, at the core of many disagreements but I must now admit to a growing belief that compromise and negotiation may be a recipe for mediocrity and pastiche". Crawley (ibid.: ch. 9) summed up his contribution by saying: "Planners must know their politicians!" and, almost as an aside, that hung councils[1] in some areas have given officers far greater power than hitherto. Finally, Kitchen (ibid.:

ch. 10) felt that "perhaps the most awkward ethical problem that a negotiating approach to development control gives rise to is the tension between being piggy in the middle on the one hand and on the other hand being sufficiently detached from what is going on to be able to make a recommendation to elected members at the end of the day".

The author could not possibly do justice to the second half of Thomas & Healey (1991), which reworks and discusses the paragraph above and much more. One can but clutch at a few salient points. First, there is a lack of a tradition of, and perhaps a forum for, discussing ethical issues. Secondly, two dominant themes emerged: whether professionals of any kind should be value neutral or should forcefully advocate certain values in their work (ibid.: 176). Thirdly, (ibid.: 178 ff) individuals develop coping strategies, for example discussion with others, changing jobs or compartmentalization, that is mentally shutting out moral reservations about one's work. Underwood (ibid.: 180) argued explicitly for a central guiding principle for planners: care for the Earth. That is a value all can subscribe to.

In addition, ethical issues are raised in day-to-day development control over applications for particular land uses, for example amusement arcades, betting shops, the sale of alcohol, and unwelcome neighbours. Some of these uses are subject to other regulatory regimes. Sturt (1995), reporting his survey of moral dilemmas in planning, showed that about 80 per cent of officers and members had faced moral dilemmas in their work for LPAs. Of councillors, 75 per cent said moral issues were material considerations, but 69 per cent of officers said they were not. By far the most important issue he found was where people's homes and jobs were at risk of enforcement action. Should we not, he concluded, be concerned not only with "the character of the area" but also with "the interest of the community?" Readers might like to ponder on whether casinos should play a part in town centre regeneration (Smith et al. 1996); whether a planning condition can restrict the class of person who might use a shop (Laxton 1993, Condron 1994); how affordable housing can be provided (Irlam 1994); how the LPA should cope with "unwelcome neighbours" such as a house for the treatment of offenders (Minton 1993: 13), or a club for "adult babies" (Anonymous 1996g), or a house used for immoral purposes (Millichap 1994).

Conclusion

This chapter on conflict and confusion opened by drawing attention to McAuslan's threefold characterization of that which may lead to conflict and confusion – private interests, the public interest and the need for public participation in the cause of democracy and justice. It was shown, at least to some extent, that these

---

1. That is, where no one party has overall political control.

interests are not necessarily in conflict. Confusion arises because different interests may be irreconcilable and there seems to be no obvious way out of an impasse. The participants may be bewildered, as the reader probably will be, or the situation may be disordered.

The final chapter will consider some development control issues likely to be of increasing importance in the future: the concepts of quality and sustainability and a consideration of the international dimension.

CHAPTER 9
The future

Introduction

The final chapter of this book will deal with three issues that have come to the top of the town and country planning agenda in the last decade of the twentieth century. By its nature the future is uncertain. It will be easy at some future date to look back and prove whether matters that concern us at the end of the twentieth century will turn out to concern us in the twenty-first. Abercrombie, in his plans for London, prepared during the Second World War, failed to foresee the considerable growth in car ownership and office employment. He assumed there would be full employment, of which there must have been little hope at the time considering the inter-war experience. He assumed that London docks would continue to be a hive of water-related activity. He also assumed that there would be strong statutory powers to control development and the location of industry. Readers may muse on the success or otherwise of this visionary for London.

I have chosen quality, sustainability and the international dimension. Other issues could have been chosen, for example the implications of increasing car use or an ageing population (Moor 1996).

Quality

What is quality?

As society becomes more affluent and the daily struggle for existence rises above subsistence, we look for better quality in our lives. A better-quality environment is an aspect of this. Another aspect also in the context of development control is a good quality development control system.

But what is quality? Pfeffer & Coote (1991) defined quality in four different ways. First, it can be the best goods or services that money can buy; no expense is spared. They said that this is part of the aristocratic tradition, when in the nineteenth century aristocrats were known as "the quality". Secondly, there is what might be termed the expert or scientific approach, where emphasis is on fitness for purpose. Quality is enforced by setting standards and monitoring. BS5750 *Quality assurance for planners* (RTPI 1993: 9), made the point: "Which is the quality car – the Rolls–Royce or the Mini?" For people requiring a small economical runabout, is it not the Mini that best meets their requirements? Thirdly, there is total-quality management, which involves the whole of the organization in quality, based on the argument that the way to maximize profit is to give customers what they want. Fourthly, there is the consumerist approach, in which standards are set by pressure groups for the good of consumers. It is clearly important to know which definition of quality is being used in any particular context.

Quality assurance for planners

BS 5750 *Quality assurance for planners* (ibid.) was concerned with improving the quality of services provided by RTPI members, whether working in the public or the private sector. This is the second group above. Quality assurance is becoming increasingly important as the public sector is becoming commercialized in its outlook and the private sector is being driven by clients' desire to see proper quality assurance when they employ consultants. Several stages are postulated in obtaining the certificated quality assurance accolade (ibid.: 10):

- reviewing and clarifying the contract between the provider and the client
- drawing up a quality plan for the guidance of those involved
- design control, setting out the procedures for the work to be undertaken
- controlling documentation
- auditing quality to ensure that activities are carried out according to the quality plan
- training staff to ensure they can do the job properly
- other procedures such as inspection.

Certification of a scheme of quality assurance is carried out by several bodies, for example BSI Quality Assurance (ibid.: appendix 2).

Quality assurance is not without its problems (ibid.: 11 ff). It does not ensure a good quality of service, because only minimum standards may be specified, much of the literature relates to manufacturing, and it may be expensive to introduce, unwieldy and pedantic. Benefits include marketing image, a quality culture in an organization, the elimination of errors by staff, improved office practice, improved staff morale, and cost savings. In conclusion it was said that "Quality assurance is only common sense written down in an organized way. . . . Plan what you do. Do what you plan. Write down what you did." (ibid.: 59).

Building in quality

The Audit Commission (1992a: 1), in its report *Building in quality*, was concerned with the quality of the development control process and the quality of the outcome of the process. As such it was not primarily concerned with the quality of the environment *per se*. It did not give a clear definition of quality. The implication is (ibid.: 26) that it was concerned with quality indicators at each of eight stages in the development control process, from setting process objectives (e.g. reasonable expectations for customers) to, for example, preprinted decision notices, which can be modified if necessary, at decision notification stage. Indeed, it admitted that "because of the absence of objective measures of quality it is not possible to demonstrate that the current availability of resources is creating an improvement in the quality of decisions" (ibid.: 47). Looking to the future it drew attention to safeguarding future generations, the need to cope with new legislation (e.g. from Europe), increasing public interest and involvement with planning issues, and the constant pressure of applications, especially during boom times (ibid.: 1).

What is striking is that the Audit Commission's investigation of a variety of quantitative indicators, which might shed light on, say, speed of decision, as a quality indicator of the development control process, showed little rhyme or reason. For example, one might expect the proportion of applications dealt with within an eight-week period to increase as the caseload (in number of applications dealt with per planning officer) declined over a range of LPAs. This was not so; indeed, there were very wide differences in performance between LPAs (ibid.: 9). Many variables are involved, such as the mix of applications by type (e.g. major, minor, change of use and listed buildings) and the weight of other duties to perform besides processing applications (e.g. enforcement and appeals). Surprisingly too, the degree of delegation to officers appeared to have little effect on the proportion of decisions made within eight weeks (ibid.: 12).

The Audit Commission admitted: "As a measure of quality of the development control service, the eight week figures have grave weaknesses." For example, it listed that it did not measure the value added to applications through negotiation, LPAs may deem an application withdrawn while they seek extra information, returns are not rigorously checked, it discourages negotiation and may divert time and resources to LPA league tables rather than focus on service quality.

Taking an exemplary pleasant suburban LPA area (ibid.: 28), the Audit Commission suggested a list of development objectives as a way forward. The first list included customary local plan policies but added "ensure all developments [are] satisfactorily completed" and "rectify all contraventions". The second list of service objectives included general objectives such as "ensure high quality design" and "review quality of all decisions" and much more specific objectives such as "examine all complaints within two weeks" and "delegation to officers 70 per cent [of applications]". The quality of the outcome of the development control process can be looked at in two ways. First, there is implementation on which the Commission commented (ibid.: 40): "In practice most authorities lack systems to ensure that their decisions are faithfully implemented. They rely on the integrity of applicants to build according to approved plans. . . . There is scope for improvement in most planning departments in this respect. . . . Development control has traditionally been viewed as the poor relation within the planning profession. . . . And within development control, enforcement has itself been seen as the ever poorer relation". The Commission (ibid.: 48) reported "a profound mismatch between the degree of attention given by authorities to planning decisions and the degree of attention given to ensuring that those decisions are properly implemented". New legislation as a result of the Carnwath Report (see Ch. 3) will, it is hoped, bring improvement in the quality of the environment. Secondly, there is the quality of the overall management of the development control process itself (ibid.: 42 ff). It was suggested that this could be improved by training, peer review, a review of a sample of applications, the adoption of BS 5750, surveys of customers/applicants, more accurate identification of the costs within the development control system, checklists of performance indicators (ibid.: 44), including appeal results, development permitted and housing targets achieved, members visiting sites to see how their decisions have turned out on the ground, and many others. The usefulness of the Audit Commission's approach is that it provided a series of checklists so that good practice could be disseminated.

Quality in the environment

A major purpose of development control is to create, enhance and maintain an environment of quality. However, as Pfeffer & Coote showed, quality is an elusive thing to define (see pp. 265–6). This book has described the culmination of at least half a century of endeavour to produce an environment of quality through the development control system. There is much to be thankful for as a result of planning initiatives. One could highlight city-centre redevelopment and pedestrianization, new and expanded towns, the protection of the countryside from urbanization, the separation of unpleasant industry from residential areas into industrial estates, improvements in housing standards through slum clearance and relocation and improvements brought about through planning gain. Unsung and largely unnoticed are environmental problems forestalled by the need for planning permission. The development control system filters out unacceptable proposals by refusal; it makes unacceptable proposals acceptable by negotiation and the imposition of conditions.

However, as living standards are raised and the built environment becomes run down and obsolescent in the face of economic, social and technical change, there is a constant need to revisit issues.

To stimulate debate, the Department of the Environment issued a consultation paper, *Quality in town and country* (DoE 1994f), and invited responses on how the environment could be improved. A reworked version occurs in the UK

Figure 9.1 Department of the Environment consultation paper on Quality in Town and Country 1994 (DoE 1994f).

- Town and country – growing population and economic and technical changes mean that our environment is constantly evolving. Sustainable development is vital.
- Towns as villages – recognizable village communities within our towns may suggest a mechanism for improving the quality of urban life.
- Vital and viable town centres – "A city without a heart has no hope of life".
- Our local environment – a "whole approach" is necessary to architecture, open space, pollution and maintenance.
- Heritage – there is a need to protect the historic environment.
- Better-quality building – preservation is not enough; to build ought to be to improve.
- Traffic and travel – managing mobility to improve the environment.
- Housing – "the creation of a home is one of the most central experiences in many people's lives".
- Quality and investment – "a high-quality environment attracts inward investment and this investment helps the environment further".
- Taking decisions in the round – the life of the city is more than the sum of its parts. Improvement in quality depends on inputs from us all.

---

national report for the Habitat Conference II 1996 (DoE 1996d: ch. 8). Figure 9.1 paraphrases the principal concerns in 1994.

These were reformed into six objectives in 1996 (ibid.: 74) for the improvement of the quality of life:

- maintain and enhance the built environment and encourage high standards of design
- protect and enhance the vitality and viability of town centres
- protect the heritage and re-use old buildings
- create and maintain safe and secure living environments
- protect and enhance the community, cultural and social life of settlements
- meet needs for open space and recreation in urban areas.

Some themes are common to both documents, for example the town centre and the heritage. The latter document stressed fresh themes, giving equal prominence to crime and security and the need for recreation and open space.

Both documents sought to stimulate debate. *Quality in town and country* posed a series of questions inviting replies, such as:

- How can we involve local communities effectively in the broad design decisions that determine the outline development of an area without slowing the planning process?
- Could local authorities be more responsive to ideas from business about how the revenues from the business rate should be spent (on town centres)?
- Should urban design statements accompany major planning applications?
- What more can be done to enable homeowners and tenants to work together to improve the quality of their local environment?

The Habitat II report advanced contentious viewpoints with similar intent; for example, some in the professions are reluctant to debate and justify proposals to planning committees and the public, or to recognize the right of others to comment on design matters (ibid.: 73). Moreover, the lasting benefits of initiatives to reduce crime in any particular area have yet to be established and they may displace crime from one area to another (ibid.: 74).

Noticeable by their almost complete absence are explicit references to quality in the work environment and to development control as a mechanism for ensuring a quality environment. Using the fourfold activity classification of land uses postulated in Figure 4.1 – jobs, living, leisure and transport – housing, leisure and transport received an airing in one or other of the documents but the quality of the work environment did not. (Local economic development and the enhancement of job prospects occurs in the Habitat II Conference Report, Ch. 5.) Arguably, this may be covered by reference to town centres and quality and investment (Fig. 9.1) but the tone is one of concern for shoppers and those engaged in leisure or doing business. At any one time about half the population have jobs, as do most of us at some time. Views on the qualities required of the work environment, whether factories, warehouses, offices, shops or other places, have to be inferred from other statements, for example on better-quality building. Likewise, there are usually only oblique references to development control through mention of the planning system, PPGs and good practice guidance. More particularly, it is argued that the qualities inherent in listed buildings and conservation areas can be safeguarded by care with change-of-use applications and by the withdrawal of permitted development rights (DoE 1994f: 13; see Ch. 4). Explicit reference to development control is found in discussion on better-quality building. "Development control can prevent only the worst abuses of urban design. The promotion of what is good is substantially in the hands of architects, designers and property owners. It is largely for the professional bodies to inspire good practice. . . . The planning system should give confidence to building design professionals. Planning refusal should be seen as a costly and time-consuming failure in the partnership between public and private sectors. The challenge of paying more attention to design is shared between developers, designers and planners and it need not, and should not, founder in delayed decisions or refusals. Indeed, there is scope for improved dialogue to increase the efficiency of the planning system." (ibid.: 15–16). Surprisingly, in an admittedly short document, no mention is made of the value of negotiations, conditions and planning obligations as a route to better quality. The Habitat II report drew attention to Tibbald's approach to urban design (see Table 6.10), feeling that a relative consensus on the principles of good design had emerged (DoE 1996d: 74). But again development control as an activity aiming for quality in the environment is scarcely mentioned other than obliquely.

The proof of the pudding is in the eating. Stevenson (1996: 24–5) reported occupiers' perceptions of quality in recently built housing in London. Residents raised issues outside the control of planning, for example management. Key matters of concern to planning were: external appearance (which demonstrated a liking for traditional designs and materials), internal standards (relating to sunlight and daylight), proximity to other uses (e.g. noisy uses), communal space and facilities (e.g. a perceived failure to provide play-space) and safety (including location and design of parking with open access to the street). There was far more reported than this but it gives the flavour of what may be involved.

Clearly, as with the issue of sustainability, we are edging our way forwards. The results of the Department of the Environment consultation document, *Quality in town and country*, were awaited in 1996.

Sustainability

The more things change, the more they remain the same. The concept of sustainable development in the context of development control has taken on new dimensions in the last decade of the twentieth century. This section will discuss the concept from a high level of generalization to practical day-to-day application.

> The government therefore supports the principle of sustainable development. This means living on the Earth's income rather than eroding its capital. It means keeping the consumption of renewable natural resources within the limits of their replenishment. It means handing down to successive generations not only man-made wealth (such as buildings, roads and railways) but also natural wealth, such as clean and adequate water supplies, good arable land, a wealth of wildlife and ample forests. (DOE 1994m: 28)

One of the mainsprings of town and country planning in the UK after the Second World War was the desire to conserve resources. This found expression particularly in green belts, the special regard given to good-quality agricultural land in development control, safeguarding aggregate supplies in our major river valleys near large cities, the work of the Forestry Commission, and preventing urban sprawl. Efforts were made to bring jobs and homes within easy travel distances, for example in new and expanded towns.

At that time, the war blockade on imported food and fuel was fresh in everyone's mind. This old theme has taken a new turn at the end of the century. Many of the ideas floated below have already found their way into current practice and are a reworking of traditional ideas with a fresh emphasis.

Rowan-Robinson et al. (1995: 269 ff) felt that the development control system as it was constituted in the 1990s already took sustainability into account through a consideration of environmental impact analyses, the use of conditions, and planning obligations. They did not envisage a dramatic shift in the practice of development control to accommodate sustainability considerations. They admitted that development control was not always "precautionary" as the principle was to allow development unless it harmed interests of acknowledged importance. They questioned, as others have done, whether there should be a presumption in

271

favour of development. They drew attention to the once-and-for-all nature of a development control decision, which made review difficult if circumstances changed in future.

Various ideas about sustainability are found elsewhere in this book, but are gathered here for convenience. Since the Earth Summit in Rio in 1992, we are now feeling our way forwards in sustainable development control. Bishop (1996: ch. 13) has provided a general description of the situation, touching on international reports such as the "Brundtland Report", *Our common future* (1987), and national reports such as *Sustainable development: the UK strategy* (DoE 1994m). He then drew attention to planning policy guidelines and local plans, which deal with local scales. Some, he argued, saw the greening of planning as a new paradigm for planning practice; others saw environmental stewardship as involving little shift from longstanding development control concerns.

The concept of sustainability embraces a very wide range of concerns and accompanying regulations. Much agricultural, forestry and industrial practice is beyond the reach of development control. Building regulations and integrated pollution control, for example, are within the remit of other regulations. Perforce, the influence of development control is likely to be slow in effect as annual additions to the building stock are small, as is the number of planning applications refused. However, the imposition of conditions involving land restoration, after mineral working in particular, is a way in which development control can be made effective. In particularly sensitive developments, environmental impact analysis (Ch. 5) should facilitate better decisions.

The UK Environmental Law Association, in its evidence to the House of Lords Select Committee (House of Lords 1995: III, 159–62), countered the slow incremental influence by suggesting action against current unsustainable uses using existing legislation. They had in mind compulsory purchase and discontinuance orders applied to uses that conflict with the aims of sustainable development. Compensation may well be involved, which could be offset in part by granting planning permission on a sustainable site (Town & Country Planning Act 1990 §102). The situation could be secured by planning agreements (§106 Agreements). They also argued that as "amenity" is a material consideration in development control, why not "sustainability"? Amenity was a woolly term but is now acceptable; sustainable development could similarly be deployed. They drew attention to the special considerations already given to listed buildings and conservation areas in development plan policies and development control.

It is telling that development control as an instrument of regulation is not explicitly mentioned in the House of Lords Select Committee Report on Sustainability (ibid.: I, 36) or in the Royal Town Planning Institute's evidence to it (ibid.: II, 447). The Committee concluded: "Nonetheless it was generally recognised that, on its own, the role of the land-use planning system was limited and that it is a necessary but not sufficient means of delivering sustainable development." They reported three reasons for this: first, planning deals only with land-use changes at the rate of 1 to 2 per cent of the built environment per annum;

secondly, without clear national policies for transport, planning decisions are taken in a vacuum; and thirdly, as local environmental targets were absent, planners had little firm guidance for their decisions or how to evaluate their success (House of Lords 1995: I, 36).

Barton et al. (1995) have probably gone furthest in exploring and summarizing issues and implementation in detail. Only an outline of their approach can be given here. Rather than start from war blockade, they start from the threats posed by increasingly decentralized car-dependent land-use patterns, more particularly the need to maintain global ecological systems, husband natural resources and improve the quality of the local human environment (ibid.: 19). Their theme is one of scale, from individual building to world level, applied to the *natural environment, travel and locational patterns* and *individual sites and buildings*.

They see an interdependence of one scale of activity on another. The design of the individual building has effects on its neighbourhood and in turn on its city and region, its country and finally on the world biosphere. And of course the reverse is true: changes in the biosphere affect individual buildings. This established, they then enunciate three principles in the context of development control: the home, the neighbourhood and the town should be seen as ecosystems (with inputs, e.g. rain and food, and outputs, e.g. wastes) that we should endeavour to make self-sufficient, for example by siting buildings to minimize fuel use, which implies greater local diversity; we should have concern for human social and economic needs (e.g. economic development and choice); and the need to design a robust and adaptable environment, which keeps present and future options open, for example houses that can adapt to changing family needs (ibid.: 12 ff).

They further drew attention to the well established principles of environmental standards and targets that help define the capacity of an area or site to take new development or population. However, thresholds may be reached that require considerable further action for further development to take place. To facilitate further consideration of development proposals, three categories of environment may be differentiated: first, "critical stock", which should not be sacrificed to development (e.g. SSSIs); secondly, "constant stock", where, for example, the felling of one woodland may be replaced by another of equivalent area in the context of overall woodland conservation (this is termed "transferability"); and thirdly, "negotiable stock", where "mitigation" and "trade-offs" are possible, for example using north-facing slopes for well insulated housing. These three categories may be looked on as various degrees of constraint on development. Over-arching these is the need to minimize transport energy use; sites that are well located so as to minimize the need for travel represent a critical environmental asset (ibid.: 17–18).

Let us return now to the earlier concerns of the natural environment, travel and locational patterns, site layout and individual buildings. The general significance of the natural environment for development control is that there is a need to conserve, protect and enhance it. With regard to the hydrological cycle, development increases the rapidity of water runoff, which may be polluted, for example by vehicle oils. To ameliorate potentially adverse effects, the catchment area needs

273

to be considered as a whole. Soakaways and ponds are needed to recharge aquifers, and floodplains need to be protected from development. Natural vegetation and landscaping should help control water runoff and should not need to be irrigated. Foul water should if possible be treated on site, for example by oil traps. Air pollution, for example dust or noise, can be mitigated by landscaping (ibid.: 33).

With regard to land as a resource, brownfield sites should be used for development wherever possible, so that good agricultural land can be kept to foster local sustainability. In the event of development, soils should be preserved *in situ*. Barton et al. (ibid.: 38) opined that government had no guidelines for mineral conservation at local level, as minerals are freely traded between regions on the basis of "national need" (a euphemism for "commercial demand"). National and local policy should maintain an effective level of proven reserves in relation to the consumption rate. In the context of development control, transport should be minimized, land reclaimed after working and groundwater should not be polluted or depleted.

Ultimately, we are dependent on nature as the ultimate source of our commercial crops and stock. Wildlife is an indicator of environmental change and as much a part of our heritage as listed buildings are. It behoves us not to abuse it. Simmons & Barker (1988: 9–11, quoting Graf & Barker) identified 22 fundamental principles, to which Barton et al. (1995: 31) drew attention. In the context of development control the following considerations are the most important: environmental factors underlie town and country planning; wildlife needs recognition, both in plans and when considering proposals for development; avoid pollution; maintain groundwater; value historical continuity of habitats, corridors and islands, and larger sites rather than smaller ones; maintain local variety and create diversity; buildings themselves are a resource for wildlife; native species should be used in landscaping; avoid disturbing existing green spaces and enhance existing open spaces; and, as far as possible, streams and ponds should have soft sloping edges.

Transport uses 33 per cent of energy delivered in the UK. Vehicle use is rising and is responsible for many worrying emissions, which we are seeking to control. Because of dispersed settlement patterns, road improvements and low fuel costs, trips are becoming longer and more frequent. More sustainable development control would seek to localize and cluster facilities, possibly along linear public transport routes, increase development densities, mix land uses, avoid expanding dormitory settlements and restrict parking provision at major traffic generators (e.g. town centres) (Barton et al. 1995: 21–4). It should also encourage walking, cycling and public transport, for example by promoting permeable environments (see p. 172) and locating facilities and jobs within walking distance of home (say up to 400m). Barton et al. (ibid.: 77 ff) drew attention to four major decision areas. First, they differentiated net and gross density of development, advocating higher net densities using as little space as possible to minimize journeys to work, and so on, but giving good solar access in housing. Lower gross densities, it was argued, would encompass the parks and allotments that sustainable development demands. Secondly, as for housing location, they advocated many small brown-field sites in and around built-up areas, rather than fewer larger greenfield sites. Thirdly, drawing on PPG13 (DoE 1994c), jobs and facilities were seen in a hier-archy with low-order facilities such as primary schools being provided at a neigh-bourhood level at walking distance and higher-order facilities such as technical colleges being provided in town centres served by public transport nodes. Finally, they argued for a comprehensive movement strategy tied to land use, giving high-level accessibility with priority for energy-efficient modes. Complementary pol-icies, for example, would include a better cycling environment, improving the effectiveness of public transport, parking restrictions, orientating new develop-ment around public transport and limiting edge-of-town park-and-ride schemes. They postulated three types of locational pattern through which these policies could be implemented: the compact city with its hinterland, for example York; the polycentric city system, for example West Yorkshire, and the corridor or linear settlement, such as the valleys of South Wales.

Ever mindful of the problems of implementation, they drew attention to the problems of the B1 Use Class (Ch. 4) and the need for inspectors to back sus-tainability policies on appeal.

Let us now turn to issues of site layout and individual buildings as the third main area of concern in sustainable development. Barton et al. (1995: ch. 6) stressed the sustainability importance of site appraisal, drawing particular attention to:

- the context of a proposed development, for example accessibility and local character
- conditions below ground, for example waterthe quality and quantity, and topography with regard to slope and aspect
- conditions above ground, for example shelter from the wind, pollution, day-light and solar heating
- existing structures, for example the re-use of local materials and existing buildings.

They then approached site layout in four sections: movement, services, land-scape and built forms (ibid.: ch. 7). Under movement, for example, they advocated moving away from tree-like cul-de-sac access in residential areas to loops and circuits as advocated by Design Bulletin 32 (DoE & Department of Transport 1992). More use should be made of shared surfaces constructed to lower speci-fications, and pedestrian and cycle movement should be improved. Services should be laid so as to facilitate district heating in future. Landscape design, inter alia, should facilitate food production in back gardens of dwellings, with a variety of garden sizes available, and external surfaces should be planted rather than paved to reduce site runoff. However, they felt that there was no single prescription for built forms in the context of sustainability, whether detached, terraced or court-yard. For example, a detached building may be suitable for an awkwardly shaped site or on a south-facing slope of a north–south road to maximize solar gain. Terracing of building units reduces heat loss and land take, but may be visually monotonous. Courtyard forms are probably more efficient than detached buildings of the same floor area, reducing heat loss and providing shelter from the wind, but natural light in corners is often poor.

At the level of the individual building they took dwellings as an example and considered building elements, services and materials (Barton et al. 1995: ch. 8). Considerable emphasis is placed on energy efficiency and internal layout and construction methods, which are not normally matters for development control. However, the size of windows, roof pitch, future extensions in roofs and, at ground level, the use of local stone, which are considered in the light of energy efficiency and adaptable buildings, may involve development control considerations.

To help councillors to make development control decisions on a day-to-day basis, Woking Borough Council devised a specific environmental checklist which included sustainability items, to be used by planning officers when they considered planning applications (Woking Borough Council, quoted by David Tyldesley & Associates 1994: case study K). Examples from the list include the following:

- If hard surface parking is involved, will it be porous and allow natural drainage to surrounding vegetation?
- Does the proposal include re-use of land or buildings?
- Does the landscape encourage wildlife?
- Do the proposals facilitate walking and cycling?
- What is the orientation of the development – do the principal rooms face south?

It is at this level of detail that sustainable development will be implemented.

The international dimension

The purpose of this section is to look at some international dimensions of development control. It is a commonplace to say we live in a global economy and in a global village. As environmental concerns do not recognize international boundaries, the Rio Summit made it incumbent on governments to regulate the manmade environment more closely. Likewise, UK membership of the European Union has fed through into the development control system, for example through the need for environmental impact analysis in the case of some proposals. Conversely, where a country like the UK has internal problems, it may look elsewhere to find solutions, for example, the enterprise zone philosophy from Hong Kong and the USA. The UK in its turn provided a model to the world through the development of its new towns after the Second World War. In this context, this section will consider development control systems elsewhere and the impact of European legislation on the UK development control system.

Davies (1996: 220–38) has provided a very useful summary of the planning systems of Europe and he drew out the differences between the UK and the rest of the European Union. One question he raised was whether the UK would eventually line up with other European countries in their approaches or whether each country would still control development based on its individual traditions. It was only in 1992 that a mandate was given for town and country planning.

European and UK planning systems started early in the twentieth century and had in common a focus on land use and development, legally binding planning schemes, decentralization to local authorities without any higher-level plans, and plans that dealt with town expansion and that were not comprehensive. All evolved similarly until 1947, when the UK adopted somewhat different principles: it had a nationwide definition of "development"; it imposed a duty on LPAs to prepare comprehensive development plans; there was a requirement to obtain planning permission for development; the system included a right of appeal against refusal of planning consent; and an enforcement system was instigated. The current UK system, which developed in the late 1940s, is characterized by a high degree of administrative discretion in the grant of planning permission and appeal to the Minister, and not to the courts, as long as the decision is in itself legal. In Europe, plans are legally binding at local level with recourse to the courts and not to ministers. European countries have also a formal system of national, regional and local planning in place, promulgated by elected bodies accountable to their areas. Davies postulated a spectrum of planning systems. At one end is the Netherlands, where the plan is regulatory and legally binding; at the other is the UK where the plan constitutes discretionary guidance. The Netherlands has a decentralized system and the UK a centralized one. Some systems are proactive, as in the Netherlands, where plan preparation and so on is done by the municipalities (compare the UK in the post-war period with its slum clearance, new town building and town centre redevelopment), whereas other systems are reactive, as in the UK, where funding and initiatives come from the private sector. Most systems have evolved gradually, but in Spain, with the demise of Franco, the system was changed radically to a federal structure.

A major concern of the European Union has been regional disparities in prosperity. Funds are available to member states to combat this through infrastructural and industrial projects. Cognate with this initiative is the thought being given to the urban development of Europe in the twenty-first century, which transcends national boundaries, and is driven by the economic implications of a single market. Development control activity will ultimately be dependent on development pressure, which will be influenced by funding policies. These factors have development control implications through the spatial distribution of physical development on the one hand and of individual site development on the other, which are largely dealt with locally. Subsidiarity – that is, making decisions at an appropriate level on development proposals, whether national, regional or local in scale – is an issue which occupies the European Union Committee of the Regions (Silvester 1996: 20).

A second prong of European concern is the campaign to combat pollution, improve the quality of life and protect the environment. So far, these have been made manifest in the UK development control practice through environmental impact assessment (Ch. 5), nature conservation through SSSIs (Ch. 7) and sustainability as a concept underlying development control practice (Ch. 9). A comparison of planning permission procedures in Europe showed that applicants' perceptions of the UK system did not show it to be noticeably burdensome (GMA Planning 1994: 48). However, a noticeable difference between the UK and Europe to which Davies (1996: 236) drew attention was that the UK has a coherent and well established professional association. Planners elsewhere tend to be urban designers, engineers, geographers or economists, each with a particular perspective rather than a synoptic one (Rodriguez-Bachiller 1988). The real challenge for Europe is juggling so many scales of planning – international, transnational, national, regional, local and site – with tensions between cooperating nations, self-conscious regions, competing cities and economies, and with so much of the overall outcome depending on myriads of individual site developments. No doubt the upshot will be convergence, as Europeans learn from one another through technical exchanges and the promulgation of Europe-wide regulations which are framed to combat problems common throughout the Union.

The countries of Europe have had long and diverse planning and development histories, now converging because of shared environmental problems. On the other hand, the USA has had a unified federal government with an overriding planning and development theme, namely the settlement of what for Europeans was an empty land. Many migrated to new worlds, new lives and Utopia. What has been the development control result?

Wakeford (1990), for the whole of the USA, and Thomas (1988c, 1991), for the state of Oregon, have usefully compared British and US development control. Oregon is not typical and may have the best developed land-use control system in the USA. Wakeford (ibid.: 6 and 166 ff) described it as "much vaunted". Summarized quickly, the US system is rather like the Simplified Planning Zone system in the UK. That is to say, there is a zoning scheme with regulations: developers may develop without specific permission as long as they keep within the regulations for their schemes. If developers wish to do otherwise, express permission may be necessary. Arguably, it is an augmented version of British permitted development rights under the GPDO. As an aside at this point, the grid plan that characterizes so many US cities is very familiar. This pattern was promulgated, largely ignoring urban design, transport considerations and topography, so that roads run up hill and down dale, with dramatic results if you drive in hilly San Francisco. Surveying was basic, with the aim of readily identifying plots for legal ownership purposes. The grid must have provided orderly relief for early settlers from the chaotic, organic cities of Europe from which they came. The advent of cars has altered all subsequent layouts.

The USA is a federation of 50 states, many matching the UK in size. As a generality, the Federal government is not concerned with the details of land use. This is the concern of states jealous of the rights protected in a written constitution. This contrasts strongly with the UK, where central government, through Circulars, PPGs and the planning appeal system, concerns itself with development control details. Planning powers largely lie with the cities, many of which are small by British standards, and with counties, which are thos residual parts of states that are not cities. As in the UK, planning is operated by democratically elected councillors advised by professional staff (Thomas 1988c: 11 ff). Plans drawn up at local level are marked with land-use zones. In Lane County in the City of Eugene, Oregon, for example, there is a metropolitan plan rather like a structure plan, and refinement plans rather like local plans and action area plans. The metropolitan plan categorizes about twenty such zones, four of which are industrial. The characteristics of each are described in detailed land-use regulations or ordinances, which in the case of the industrialized zones specified dozens of industries appropriate to each zone (ibid.: 101 ff). Zoning regulations can be as complex as the GPDO in Britain, and each LPA has a set. Wakeford estimated there were 10000 LPAs in the USA (ibid.: 84). This stands in contrast with the UK, where zoning and the classes in the UCO are much simpler. In Oregon, which is perhaps unique, there is a state plan to which all subsidiary plans must conform (ibid.: 9). There is a parallel here with English Regional Planning Guidance, but of course by the mid-1990s England had no democratically elected local assemblies promulgating them. Wakeford (1990: 6) made the interesting point that the historical genesis of US zoning was the desire of individuals to protect their private land against the injury that neighbours may do by their activities, resulting in falling land values. Owners normally have the right to be heard by the local planning committee if neighbours intend to carry out development that might affect their property. In the UK, almost the converse is the case: planning operates to protect the public interest, and aggrieved private owners have no right to be heard, but of course may make written representations.

Although development can take place without explicit planning permission as long as the regulations are observed, many other permits may be required, for example for building near streams and wetland. Both Wakeford (1990: ch. 4) and Thomas (1988c: 120) found the system surprisingly bureaucratic. There is a ladder of appeal. Just as the UK has different types of permission (e.g. outline and listed building consent), so do the Americans (e.g. variances and conditional use permits; Thomas 1988c: 74). Variances (perhaps "waiver" would be an equivalent word in the UK) need to be obtained where proposed development departs in minor ways from the ordinances. For example, perhaps the slope of the ground necessitates bringing a proposed building in front of a set back (building line) (Thomas 1988c: 25 ff; Wakeford 1990: 57). An explicit control that does not have a close UK equivalent is subdivision control, which is the process of creating legally defined plots. The original purpose was to clarify ownership; just as important now is ensuring adequate plot size and utility services for the zone (Thomas 1988c: 27; Wakeford 1990: 59).

There are many other planning devices in the USA that are unknown in Britain, one worthy of mention being performance zoning, as it brings plans and development control closely together (Kendig 1980). Historically the zones merely indicated the use to which plots could be put. With the passage of time it was found necessary to control noise, aesthetic appearance, parking, building lines and many other variables. Standards for these are incorporated in zoning ordinances, and developers must conform. They may be negotiated downwards, but there is in-built pressure for high standards. In the UK all standards are negotiable and may be varied by the use of planning conditions. The US equivalent of planning gain is impact fees and exactions, which provide for social and physical infrastructure (Wakeford 1990: ch. 9).

Whether the US development control system is better than that of the UK is an impossible question to answer, as there are so many jurisdictions and so many variables (Thomas 1988c: ch. 6). The two countries also start from different points. In the USA private interests are the prime consideration; in the UK the public interest is. The US system evolved from simple zoning to complex regulations and ordinances and is quasi-judicial. The UK system depends on political discretion, and efforts were made after 1979 to simplify it. The US system is said to be more certain (i.e. regulated) for the developer. The UK system is flexible but uncertain. UK Enterprise Zones and Simplified Planning Zones were modelled on US experience but have not been widely adopted (see Ch. 4). The overall impression is that the US and UK systems of development control are converging.

Signposts to the future

This book has been reliant on Planning Policy Guidance notes (PPGs), among other sources. The advantages of this source of information are that they summarize many of the substantive issues faced in the day-to-day exercise of development control powers and describe central government policy in relation to the issues. The disadvantages are that not all relevant and important topics are covered, although they may be found in government Circulars, and the policies are the product of a particular political view of development control. A government of another political hue is likely to identify different issues for their subject matter to promulgate other policies. How different is a matter for speculation.

A way of looking to the future is to consider the first 23 PPGs issued since 1988 and how the stakeholders in the development process view them. A research review was carried out for the Department of the Environment by Land Use Consultants on *The effectiveness of Planning Policy Guidance notes* (1995) with this in mind, for England and Wales only. It excluded mineral planning guidance and regional planning guidance. Some PPGs dealt with different types of development (e.g. housing); others were topic based (e.g. development on unstable land).

The report's overall conclusions were (ibid.: i–ix):

- PPGs have greatly assisted a more consistent approach to the determination of planning applications and appeals in England and to a lesser extent in Wales.
- Taking account of the discretionary powers of local authorities, this approach reflects closely the government's planning policy priorities in so far as they are set out in PPGs.

- PPGs have been remarkably effective as a means of disseminating national policy.
- As yet PPGs have not made clear in practical terms how the planning system can help secure sustainable development.
- There is scope to increase the operational effectiveness of PPGs, for example by improving the formulation and the consultation process, providing clearer guidance on sustainable development, and better integration with other government policies, including PPGs.

With special reference to development control (ibid.: 41–3), it was argued that, if the plan-led system was working correctly, it would be difficult to trace development control decisions directly to PPGs, since they would have been decided on the basis of development plans. The research confirmed this to be the case and that PPGs had an influence "on the ground", although this was implicit rather than direct. Where outdated development plans were superseded by later PPGs or development proposals were contrary to development plans, PPGs were drawn on directly. An analysis of appeals against refusal of planning permission showed that PPGs were rarely the critical issue in deciding an appeal.

Three-quarters of LPAs and planning inspectors in the survey felt that the PPG series was "comprehensive in its coverage of current planning issues" (ibid.: 14). Those who felt there was a lack suggested PPGs in the following topics, some of which are covered in Circulars:

- water issues: flooding, water resources and groundwater protection
- landscape issues: designated and undesignated landscapes
- urban issues: regeneration, urban design, trees and landscaping, urban fringe, open space, crime prevention and disabled access
- sustainable development.

However, this is a rather narrow view of our future and our environment. The Association of Metropolitan Authorities and others (AMA et al. 1996) in *The future of the planning system: a consultation paper* took a broad view to stimulate debate. It was felt that planning needed to recapture the visionary qualities of the immediate post-war years, which led to the Town and Country Planning Act 1947. They advocated not root and branch changes but major running repairs to the present system. The two central purposes of planning, worthy of restatement, were seen to be the regulation of land use in the public interest and the achievement of sustainable development (ibid.: 9).

For the purpose of explanation, the paper was divided into the processes and the substance (termed "the end product") of planning (see Ch. 1). As for process, it was argued that it should be holistic, proactive, transparent and locally owned. That it is to say, it should be all-embracing, forward looking, open to public scrutiny and based in local communities. Eight key issues were raised about process, of which the flavour is as follows (ibid.: 13 ff):

- *Fragmentation of structures* There was felt to be a fragmentation of administrative structures (e.g. urban development corporations and English Partnerships dealing with regeneration). This could be overcome by regional assemblies producing regional strategic plans and by a national planning framework to include "disparate" PPGs and other national strategies (e.g. waste, which already exists, and energy and transport, which do not).

- *Fragmentation of processes*   Processes were thought to be fragmented and best brought together by widening the remit of land-use planning by broadening the concept of material considerations (see Ch. 5) to include sustainability issues, for example, and the use of finite resources.
- *Funding*   The inadequacy of funding may be approached by the inclusion of allocations in regional plans and by revisiting the issue of betterment taxes (see Ch. 8).
- *Implementation*   To improve implementation through development control, the introduction of a "presumption in favour of the development plan" (compare "presumption in favour of development" in PPG1) and speedier land assembly powers were advocated.
- *Plan preparation*   Plan preparation needed to be speeded up, for example by making it less "adversarial" and more "round table".
- *Enforcement*   Enforcement needs to be improved by making the flouting of planning law a criminal offence.
- *Development control complexity*   Development control has become too complex (e.g. by the prior notification procedures needed in agriculture and telecommunications (see Ch. 4); the work requires planning permission or it is permitted development) and too weak (e.g. the B1 Class, which it was suggested should be split into offices and light industry (see Ch. 4)). However, new third-party rights of appeal were advocated.
- *Sustainable development*   Currently, it was argued that the development control system could not deal with sustainability issues satisfactorily but could be helped to do so: by widening material considerations (for example to include public health and energy), by preparing local State of the Environment reports, by setting targets (e.g. on air quality) and by strengthening environmental assessment procedures.

The AMA (ibid.: 20 ff) targeted five substantive areas for special consideration so that shelter, employment and habitable environments could be provided on a sustainable basis:

- *Town centres*   Neglected town centres needed funds (possibly via a local levy), stronger powers of land assembly and the encouragement of effective public–private partnerships.
- *Transport*   Greater integration of planning and transport at the strategic level was needed through the mooted national planning framework. Interlocking issues of pollution, energy, parking, shopping provision and investment in transport modes could thus be addressed.
- *Housing*   The integration of housing and planning could be addressed in regional strategic plans and by developing brownfield sites. Despite the contribution of PPG3 in suggesting exceptions sites for affordable housing, there was no substitute for a proper level of public funding.

- *Regeneration*   Regeneration can be facilitated through the planning system by bringing under-used land into productive use.
- *Environmental quality*   Finally the quality of the physical environment was addressed. It was suggested that planning control could be extended over street furniture and streetscape, (e.g. in conservation areas), and end-user surveys and peer group reviews could be introduced.

These two reviews have ranged from the vision of a national planning framework to detailed design guidance. They continue to reflect the theme of the book, which has illustrated the tensions between central government guidance and local implementation. It is the task of both government and developers to consider these issues and to seek a balance between the conflicting demands of national coherence and local initiative.

Without vision, the people perish – but – the devil lies in the detail.

Appendix I
Planning in Celtic lands

Introduction

The purpose of this appendix is to alert readers to development control practice in the Celtic parts of the UK. What does he know of England who only England knows? It does not purport to be comprehensive. The general principles of development control are the same throughout the UK, but there are differences between England and the Celtic parts of the UK. Development control in the Republic of Ireland is not considered here.

Each of the four parts of the UK has a separate Secretary of State responsible for the environment (which includes town and country planning): the Secretary of State for the Environment, the Secretary of State for Wales, the Secretary of State for Scotland and the Secretary of State for Northern Ireland.

Wales

England and Wales generally have the same legislation. Circulars are usually issued jointly by the Department of the Environment and the Welsh Office, but have different numbering systems. Planning Policy Guidance notes were assumed to apply to both countries and they were issued jointly. In 1996 a separate PPG was issued for Wales (WO 1996). It contains a table showing which English guidance was cancelled, as it applied to Wales, and those parts of English PPGs which remain in force in Wales (ibid.: paras 222–3). Separate technical advice notes (TANs) were published in late 1996. The planning appeals system in Wales is run separately.

Northern Ireland

The town and country planning service in Northern Ireland is significantly different from that of Great Britain in that, since 1973, central, not local, government is the local planning authority. The Department of the Environment for Northern Ireland has powers derived from the Planning (Northern Ireland) Order 1991. About 19000 planning applications are received a year. In 1994–5 the development control service cost £6.3 million, of which £4.4 million was covered by fees (Northern Ireland Audit Office 1995: 7).

The Department of the Environment for Northern Ireland both prepares plans and administers development control, which it does through six divisional offices and two subdivisions (ibid.).

Planning applications are processed in a way similar to those in Britain but the

Divisional Planning Office takes the lead, and, after the customary consultations and discussions the District Development Control Group for the relevant district discusses and "decides on a recommended opinion on each application" (ibid.: 44). The final decision on an application is made by the Planning Service. The District Development Control Group is made up of elected councillors. The Planning Service consists of appointed professional officers. Appeals may be made to the Planning Appeals Commission (ibid.: 16), an independent body but funded by the Department of the Environment (ibid.: 11). There is therefore a democratic deficit. The extent of community involvement in planning depends on the peace process and negotiations over wider political structures (Singleton 1995: 7). Particular concerns noted by the Comptroller and Auditor General for Northern Ireland were that: development control decisions were slower than in Great Britain (ibid.: 9), consultation with some district councils was problematic (ibid.), enforcement was reactive rather than proactive, and no inspection was carried out to see if conditions were complied with (ibid.: 32). Singleton (ibid., quoting House of Commons Environment Committee 1990) drew attention to two other problems in Northern Ireland: the approval of up to 3000 houses per year in the countryside (more than in the whole of Great Britain) and the absence of strategic planning guidance, such as PPGs, which informs the development control process.

For further information on Northern Ireland, see Department of the Environment for Northern Ireland (1993), House of Commons Environment Committee (1990), House of Commons Northern Ireland Affairs Committee (1996) and Department of the Environment for Northern Ireland (1996).

Scotland

"Scotland is not a northern extension of England" (Hayton 1996: 78) but a very separate and distinctive part of the UK. The key Scottish statute is the Town and Country Planning (Scotland) Act 1972 as amended. Inter alia it sets out the framework for the administration of the development control system. The Planning and Compensation Act 1991 indicates the weight that should be attached to development plans and other material considerations in the development control process (SOED 1994a: 24). The Scottish Office administers the planning system. There is a separate set of central planning policy guidance: National Planning Policy Guidelines (NPPG), Circulars, National Planning Guidelines (NPGs) and Planning Advice Notes (PANs) comparable with Planning Policy Guidance (PPG) in England, separate development control appeals and call-in powers. It has its own research unit producing reports on development control (e.g. see Brand et al. 1994). The GPD(S)O (1992) and the UC(S)O (1989) are numbered differently from those in England. Inspectors at appeals are called reporters.

Core advice on development control is contained in NPPG1 *The planning system* (SOED 1994a: 14 ff), and is very similar to that followed in England. Further advice is given in PAN40 *Development control* (SOED 1993). It is primarily concerned inter alia with quality, monitoring, the responsibilities of councillors and officers, delay, efficient procedure and value for money, and it includes a quality control checklist. Informatively, it suggested (ibid.: 9–10) that good development control decisions should always meet three tests: accord with the development plan unless material considerations indicate otherwise; they are made only after statutory consultations have been fulfilled; and the legal test of

286

reasonableness. Neither NPPG1 nor PAN40 contains an explicit list of the purposes of development control. For those outside Scotland who want a short summary of Scottish planning legislation, see *Green's guide to environmental law in Scotland* (Reid 1992: ch. 6); for a fuller guide, see *Green's concise Scots law - planning* (Collar 1994).

Until local government reorganization in 1996, Scotland was divided into regions (comparable with English counties) with districts within them, and island authorities (Western Isles, Orkney and Shetland), which because of their distinctiveness had plan-making and development control powers. Three regions, Dumfries and Galloway, Highland and Borders, were termed general planning authorities in which districts had no development control powers (Hayton 1996: 81). This arrangement apparently worked very well, especially its strategic dimension (ibid.: 92). It was based on the understanding that urban and rural areas have functional interaction. From 1996, regions were abolished (compare the abolition of metropolitan counties in England as LPAs in the 1980s and counties in Wales in the 1990s) and district boundaries were redrawn. The cities of Dundee, Edinburgh, Glasgow and Aberdeen were politically separated from their hinterlands. It is envisaged that structure plans or strategic plans will be produced by the voluntary cooperation of districts in joint bodies (ibid.: 94). Changing boundaries and powers at the same time appeared a recipe for rivalry and lack of coordination; "If it works why fix it?" It remains to be seen whether the Scottish Office will act as a strategic planning authority, as well as a central government agency.

Scottish National Planning Guidelines (NPGs) and National Planning Policy Guidelines (NPPGs) were subject to a critique by Hayton (ibid.: 82 ff) comparable to that for PPGs in England (Land Use Consultants 1995). NPGs are being phased out and are being replaced by NPPGs (compare PPGs and Development Control Policy Notes in England.) Hayton felt that NPGs were idiosyncratic in coverage, in that they did not cover transport and urban renewal; they had a rural bias; review was idiosyncratic and it was unclear whether they were mandatory or advisory. Overall it was felt by Hayton that their status and purpose were unclear.

NPPGs and PANs were designed to replace NPGs and PINs (Planning Information Notes), so that there are three types of guidance: NPPGs which are the equivalent of English PPGs in that they state government policy of national importance; Circulars designed to describe legislation comparable to English Circulars; Planning Advice Notes (PANs), which disseminate good practice and for which there is no English equivalent. Planners outside Scotland would do well to read them. NPPGs and Circulars are material considerations in development control.

The Scottish Office Environment Department itself carried out a review of planning in Scotland (SOED 1994b). It was felt that "The planning system in Scotland has served us well" (ibid.: i) but further improvement was sought. It opined particularly that "it is in the area of development control that the greatest tensions and frustrations with the planning system arise" (ibid.: 7). A series of questions were raised (ibid.: 24). For example, can measures improve the efficiency of procedures? Should some minor developments be taken out of control or into control? And how can the quality of decisions be improved and measured? The document circulated for response (ibid.) elicited 172 responses with 4000 comments. The number of comments on development control applications outstripped all others, with the problem of balancing development and conservation some way behind (SOED 1995: 3). Comments about taking minor development out of or into control were roughly balanced in number. There was widespread support for the main elements of the current system (cf. similar findings by McCarthy et al. (1995) on attitudes to planning in England and Wales). But there is a need for a consolidating planning act (ibid.). Among the more interesting comments were those from the Scottish Conservative and Unionist Association, which advocated "Areas of Restricted Development Opportunity" in which there would be a presumption against development (ibid.: 6; compare green belts) and from many commentators who were concerned about the need to safeguard third-party rights and the possible need for third-party appeals (against the grant of planning permission; ibid.: 7, 17). Most respondents felt that the level of involvement of the Secretary of State in development control matters was "about right" (ibid.: 11). With regard to delay in making decisions on applications, the following points were made: the problem of incomplete applications, limited staff resources, the complexity of the system and consultation delays. Appeal delays were thought to be worse than in England and Wales, with applicants forced into negotiating unpalatable terms with LPAs (ibid.: 17). As south of the border, the issues of speed, efficiency and quality were recurring themes (ibid.: 21).

Figure AI.1 Planning policy in Scotland (in addition, there are many Circulars too numerous to list here).

National Planning Guidelines (NPGs), current late 1995

Guideline	Date	Status
Coastal planning	1974	Current in part
Aggregate working	1977	Replaced by NPPG4
Priorities for development planning	1981	Parts replaced by NPPGs 2, 3 & 4
Skiing developments	1984	Current
High technology	1985	Replaced by NPPG2
Location of major retail developments	1986	Current
Agricultural land	1987	Current

Source: Hayton (1996: table 6.1).

National Planning Policy Guidelines in Scotland (NPPGs), current August 1995, updated

1. The planning system	Jan. 1994
2. Business and industry	Oct. 1993
3. Land for housing	Jul. 1993
4. Land for mineral working	Apr. 1994
5. Archaeology and planning	Jan. 1994
6. Renewable energy	Aug. 1994
7. Planning and flooding	Sep. 1995
8. Retailing	1996
9. The provision of roadside facilities	1996
10. Planning and waste management	1996
Sport and physical recreation	Aug. 1995 draft
Skiing developments	Feb. 1996 draft
Transport and planning	May 1996 draft

Source: SODD (1996d).

Planning Advice Notes (PANs): advice on good planning practice in Scotland

PAN33	Development of contaminated land, 1988
PAN35	Town centre improvement, 1989
PAN36	Siting and design of new housing in the countryside, 1991
PAN37	Structure planning, 1992
PAN38	Structure plans: housing land requirements, 1993
PAN39	Farm and forestry buildings, 1993
PAN40	Development control, 1993
PAN41	Development plan departures, 1994
PAN42	Archaeology, 1994
PAN43	Golf courses and associated developments, 1994
PAN44	Fitting new housing development into the landscape, 1994
PAN45	Renewable energy technologies, 1994
PAN46	Planning for crime prevention, 1994
PAN47	Community councils and planning, 1996
PAN48	Local planning, 1996

Source: SODD (1996d).

Appendix II
Development control case studies

The purpose of this appendix is to list development control case studies in which the reader may be interested. Case studies show how the development control system works in practice. The studies sometimes relate to individual sites and sometimes to sites that group themselves together because they show a common theme. They are not a representative cross-section of the many types of application:

- Greed, C. (ed.) 1995. *Implementing town planning*. Harlow: Longman.
  This book includes a series of case studies in the Bristol area: York Gate and Canon's Marsh, two mixed sites in central Bristol, and the redevelopment of two hospital sites. King's Cross, London, constitutes a separate study.
- House of Commons Environment Committee 1995. *The environmental impact of leisure activities*, 4th Report [HC 246]. London: HMSO.
  The Cleveland Four Lakes development proposal covers 635 acres of old mineral workings in North Wiltshire for water recreation. The case covers many aspects of management and development control (ibid.: vol. III 55 ff, and Appendix 17). Evidence submitted by English Nature gives site-specific examples of how permitted development rights affect SSSIs through noise, excavation, etc. (ibid.: vol. III, 130–32).
- Chapter 8 itemizes and summarizes four inquiry reports into development control in Ceredigion (House of Commons Welsh Affairs Committee 1993), Warwick (Barrow 1994), North Cornwall (Lees 1993) and Brent (George 1991). These are case studies of situations where there was cause for concern about day-to-day operations. They deal with both the substance and procedure of development control.
- Glasson, J., R. Therivel, A. Chadwick 1994. *Introduction to environmental impact assessment*. London: UCL Press.
  This book contains case studies of environmental impact assessment of new settlements (Ch. 9) in Nottinghamshire and Cambridgeshire.
- Casely-Hayford, M. 1995. *Practical planning: permission and application*. London: FT Law and Tax.
  This book is written from a legal point of view. Chapter 11, "Samples and Examples", contains useful model letters which may be used by applicants in a range of planning application situations, for example change of use and listed building consent. It also describes hypothetical proposals, for example development with permitted development rights from a legal perspective.
- Speer, R. & M. Dade 1995. *How to get planning permission*. London: Dent.
  This is a practical book for householders who want to obtain planning permission for new homes or extensions. It contains illustrated case studies of applications for planning permission, with arguments.
- Miller, C. & C. Fricker 1993. *Planning and hazard*. Oxford: Pergamon Press.
  This book contains three detailed development control case studies of the problems

of new development near hazardous installations and of new hazardous installations in the Greater Manchester area.

- Barrett, G., G. Russell, C. Athey 1994. *Toyota impact study*. Birmingham: Department of the Environment.

  The wide-ranging study of the impact of a large car plant near Derby, including land-use matters.

- Ratcliffe, J. & M. Stubbs 1996. *Urban planning and real estate development*. London: UCL Press.

  This companion volume contains boxed case studies, for example on aesthetic and urban design control in the Paternoster Square redevelopment in London.

Appendix III
Selected development control statistics

Table AIII.1 Planning applications, numbers and percentages granted, England (thousands).

	Applications received	All decisions	Granted	Percentage granted
1986/7	534	493	406	84
1987/8	598	542	446	84
1988/9	683	620	498	82
1989/90	628	596	464	80
1990/1	532	518	401	80
1991/2	512	483	383	83
1992/3	464	441	363	85
1993/4	478	448	376	87

Source: DoE annual (1995: table 7.1).

Table AIII.2 Numbers of planning application decisions by type, England, 1993/4 (thousands).

	Major developments	Minor developments
Dwellings	8.4	51.1
Offices/light industry	0.9	8.1
Heavy industry/warehousing	1.5	7.9
Retail distribution & servicing	1.4	17.0
All other major developments	3.5	57.2
All major/minor	15.7	141.3
Change of use	–	39.1
Householder developments	–	169.2
Minerals	–	0.3
Advertisements	30.2	
Listed building consent	26.8	
Conservation area	5.8	
All development	428.3	

Source: Ibid.: table 7.3.

Table AIII.3   Planning appeals, numbers, percentages, types, England.

Numbers of appeals, England

	Received
1989/90	32281
1990/91	26692
1991/2	22121
1992/3	17959
1993/4	14979

Source: Planning Inspectorate Executive Agency (1994: table 1).

Number of appeals decided by type of appeal, England, 1993/4

	Decided	Allowed	% allowed
Written representations	11237	3794	33.8
Inquiries	1176	495	42.1
Hearings	1705	688	40.4

Source: Ibid.: table 3.

Appeals decided 1993/4 by development type, England, numbers and % allowed

	Decided	% allowed
Major dwellings (more than 10 units)	389	31.1
Minor dwellings (less than 10 units)	4225	24.7
Householder development	2629	38.5
Major manufacturing & warehousing	34	58.8
Minor manufacturing & warehousing	99	31.3
Major offices	28	60.7
Minor offices	49	42.9
Major retail	115	46.1
Minor retail	151	46.4
Mineral	22	36.4
Other major	276	40.6
Other minor	3980	40.1
Change of use	2116	41.0
Total	14113	35.2

Source: Ibid.: table 10.

293

Glossary and short notes

architectural liaison officer   A member of the police who can advise on security and crime prevention aspects of development.

blight   Blight or planning blight is a depression in a local property market brought about by a development proposal. Such a proposal may or may not be in a development plan or be the subject of a planning application (Uzzell 1995: 18; Burton 1996b: 10).

brownfield/greenfield   Brownfield sites are those previously developed which may be redeveloped in preference to greenfield sites (in agricultural use) in the interests of sustainability.

Certificate of Lawful Existing Use or Development (CLEUD)   Physical development that should have planning permission but which does not is immune from enforcement action after four years and change of use after ten years. For the avoidance of doubt, the purpose of CLEUD is to establish that a development or use is lawful. Application is by the applicant to the LPA, which may or may not refuse the application. Appeal to the Secretary of State is possible (Mason 1996: 89).

Certificate of Lawfulness of Proposed Use or Development (CLOPUD)   Where there is doubt as to whether a proposed use or development is lawful, application can be made to the LPA to establish whether it is so or not. Appeal to the Secretary of State is possible if there is a refusal (Mason 1996: 41).

computers and development control   Computers may be used particularly for operating development control packages. Working from a property database, inputs from planning application forms, development plans and other sources can facilitate the output of decision letters, monitor development and the development control process, produce statistical returns, etc. (Stothers & Shaw 1992: 5–12; Hepburn 1994).

conservation area   An area of special architectural or historic interest, the character or appearance of which it is desirable to preserve or enhance. There are about 8000 in England (DoE 1994g: para. 4.1).

curtilage   The area of enclosed land next to a building, usually a dwelling house.

departure   Planning applications may be made which are granted but are a substantial departure from the development plan in force.

design brief   See **planning brief**.

design guide   Informal advisory document produced by LPAs to help applicants for development improve their applications. Typically they cover house improvements such as roof extensions and porches, shop fronts and signs. They may well include guidance in permitted development rights, such as parking in front gardens. Where they are formally adopted by LPAs, note may be taken of them in appeals.

developers' brief   See **planning brief**.

development brief   See **planning brief**.

Discontinuance Order   LPAs have the power if they think it expedient in the interests of the proper planning and amenity of an area to order that a land use be discontinued or a building altered or removed. Conditions may be imposed on continuance. Orders need to be confirmed by the Secretary of State (Town and Country Planning Act 1990 §102–4).

English Heritage   An English central government body that, inter alia, secures the preservation, etc. of historic buildings and conservation areas through giving advice to LPAs. Involved with "listing" buildings, grants and loans and archaeological investigations (DoE 1994g: 39)

environmental capacity   The ability of a natural or built resource to contain, absorb or hold a use or development, for example the ability of infrastructure to cope with housing development (Anonymous 1995: 3).

estoppel   Estoppel arises where a person, encouraged by another, acts to his detriment in the expectation of acquired rights from another. This may happen, for example, when a planning officer mistakenly states that a development does not need planning permission when it may, and enforcement ensues (Ward 1994: 16).

expert systems in development control   Expert systems are computer programmes that assist in decision-making activities, using expertise that has already been formalized. They may be used in development control. Where, as in making a development control decision, there are many factors to be taken into account and discretion may be exercised, expert systems can be used as a tool to aid decision-making (Leary & Rodriguez-Bachiller 1988).

greenfield   See **brownfield/greenfield**.

gypsies and development control   The development control of gypsy sites is covered by *Gypsy sites policy and unauthorised camping* (DoE Circular 18/94). Some of the issues involved are the definition of the client group, the servicing of sites, the location of development in the countryside, NIMBY attitudes, inclusion in development plans, and the use of planning conditions (Home 1994).

housing and development control   Housing has been mentioned in several places in this book. Current central government guidance is given in PPG3, *Housing* (DoE 1992d). The key features are:
- Use guidance such as *Design Bulletin 32* and PPG1 Annex A (see Ch. 6).
- LPAs should ensure adequate land supply looking five years ahead. The choice of sites is led by market demand.
- Use brownfield sites if possible. Infill is acceptable as long as it does not result in town cramming.
- Allow for affordable housing (i.e. low cost) but no tenure control.
- Land availability studies are a material consideration.

Annexes: affordable housing in rural areas, land availability studies, land supply methodology.

industry and development control   Planning for industry has been mentioned in several places in this book. Current government guidance is given in PPG4, *Industrial and commercial development* (DoE 1992p).

296

The key features are:

- Encourage economic growth and jobs compatible with environmental objectives.
- Primacy is given to development plans, which must include policies for industrial and commercial users.
- Refuse a proposal only if it would "cause harm to interests of acknowledged importance".
- Small firms should be guided through the planning system.
- Encourage mixed uses. "The fact that an activity differs from the predominant land use in any locality is not a sufficient reason in itself for refusing planning permission."
- Encourage re-use of old buildings, but care is to be taken in conservation areas, countryside, etc.
- Conditions can be used to control problems, but PDR and UCO classes should not normally be restricted.
- Enforcement against small businesses – great care to be taken.

integrated pollution control (IPC)   A system of control of releases from the potentially most polluting industrial processes, enforced by the Environment Agency. The Agency considers releases into land, water and air in the context of their effects on the environment as a whole (DoE 1996d: 125).

intensification of use   A situation where a land use increases within a plot, for example a factory which adopts double-shift working or where mezzanine floors are inserted in the building. This may cause amenity and traffic problems.

listed building   An historic building listed by the Secretary of State for the Environment under the Planning (Listed Buildings and Conservation Areas) Act 1990 §1. In England there are about half a million listed buildings in Grades I, II* and II. Those listed I and II* are of particular importance to the nation's heritage, but statutory controls apply equally to all. Listing depends on architectural interest, historic interest, historic association and group value. Age and rarity are important criteria. The Department of the Environment may use "spot listing" to save buildings under threat. Building preservation notices can be used by LPAs similarly (DoE 1994g: paras 3.0 and 6.0).

material consideration   A consideration taken into account when making a decision on a planning application (see Ch. 5).

National Planning Forum (formerly National Development Control Forum)   The forum for the discussion of planning issues led by the Association of Metropolitan Authorities. Members include local authorities, central government agencies, professional associations, environmental pressure groups and trade associations. It produces reports in considerable depth on development control issues (National Planning Forum 16 June 1995: Agenda Item 5).

NIMBY   "Not in my back yard": the public reaction to proposals for unwanted and unwelcome developments, such as unpleasant industrial plants near housing and other areas where amenity is important.

non-conforming use   A land use not compatible with surrounding land uses (e.g. heavy industry in a residential area, often pre-dating planning control. Where non-conforming uses exist, LPAs usually have a policy of removal and/or relocation by fortuitous acquisition.

ombudsman (Commission for Local Administration)   The ombudsman receives many complaints on planning matters. The usual reason for a complaint is a contentious proposal, the handling of which causes grievance to neighbours and/or applicants. "The way in which a planner arrives at his planning advice is within the scope of the ombudsman but malad-ministration will not be found if the advice has been properly and reasonably given." (RTPI 1989a). Good office practice, consultation over deemed consent, established procedures, marshalling relevant facts for councillors, revealing personal interests and interdepart-mental liaison with LPAs are advised in the interests of good administration. The accuracy of submitted plans is the responsibility of the applicant. But LPAs should check for gross errors (ibid.: para. 6). For a discussion of natural justice and development control, see Walsh (1988) and Hammersley (1980).

Planning Aid   Unpaid voluntary service run by planners to help those who are unable to pay for professional advice (Cowan 1995).

planning brief, development brief, developers' brief, design brief   A brief is a are summary statement of what the author's policy position is on development matters on a site and/or premises. The author may be an LPA or an owner. More particularly a planning brief deals with planning and land-use matters. A development brief may be of two kinds: a developers' brief that deals with finance and land management, or a design brief that deals with townscape, design and aesthetics. A development brief normally states the kind of development required, desired, proposed or likely to be permitted on a site, for the guidance of interested parties. It has no legal status unless agreed between the parties. Briefs are likely to contain inter alia a description of a site's physical potential and constraints and planning policies related to it. Briefs may be used to promote a site and indicate what may be allowed in development control terms, should a planning application be made. Draft briefs may be used for public consultation (RTPI 1990)

planning gain, planning obligation, unilateral undertaking, planning agreement   Planning gain is a popular term covering planning obligation (a promise by a developer to do or not to do something, usually to overcome objections preventing planning permission being granted), unilateral undertaking (ditto, often at appeal) and planning agreement (an agreement between an LPA and a developer covering planning gain – so-called §106 agreements (see Ch. 5)).

planning standard   A standard is an accepted or approved example of something against which others are judged or measured. The term planning standard is somewhat ambiguous. It may indicate a mandatory environmental standard on which LPAs insist, possibly by way of a planning condition when they grant planning permission. For example, to control noise levels at an industrial site, they may specify that noise levels at the site boundary shall not exceed 50dBa (see DoE 1994h). Standards may be targets that in an ideal world it would be desirable to achieve, for example sunlight and daylight standards for housing (as in Ch. 6). They may be benchmarks against which a development can be compared. For exam-ple, houses built at about 12 houses per acre (30 per hectare) immediately suggest semi-detached houses in the suburbs, of which there are many millions in the UK; they represent a certain standard. The standards involved may be guidelines for good practice, such as road dimensions in Design Bulletin 32 (DoE & Department of Transport 1992), mentioned in Chapter 6.

   The derivation of particular standards is not clear. Some are derived from function and common sense; for example, road widths on industrial estates need to be wide enough for large vehicles to pass (Ch. 6). Others appear to be intuitive or derived from day-to-day practice, for example, the rule-of-thumb that 21 m between facing windows in houses should ensure reasonable privacy for the occupants. Some may be researched in a more objective way, for example daylight standards for housing.

Surprisingly PPGs do not normally contain planning standards, but see PPG13, *Transport* (DoE 1994c: annex), which contains standards for visibility splays at road junctions. Equally surprising, as far as I am aware there is no handbook of planning standards that can be referred to readily. Standards and quality in the environment are to some extent synonymous. But standards also conjure up ideas of monotony, regimentation and unthinking application.

See Keeble (1985: ch. 14) for a discussion of planning standards, especially space about buildings, traffic and parking and the appearance of development (Tutt & Adler 1979, Hilton 1981, Bentley et al. 1985, Milton Keynes Development Corporation 1993, Barton et al. 1995).

planning unit The planning unit is a concept that has evolved as a means of determining the most appropriate physical area against which to assess the materiality of change of use, to ensure consistency in applying the formula of material change of use. It is suggested that there are three categories which help to identify the planning unit:

- If it is possible to identify a single main purpose to which other activities are ancillary (e.g. house and swimming pool) then there is one planning unit.
- It is usually appropriate to treat mixed development where no use predominates as one planning unit (e.g. a leisure centre with a pool, a gym, etc.).
- Where a unit is in single occupation but with physically distinct and separate activities, then each activity is likely to be a planning unit (Casely-Hayford 1995: 55–6).

protected building The GPDO specifies that, when certain agricultural buildings are proposed, they may have permitted development rights, and planning permission may not be necessary. However, if they are to be used for livestock or are slurry tanks, they may need planning permission if within 400 m of "protected buildings", so that the latter may be protected from smell, etc. "Protected buildings" are permanent buildings occupied by people, but the term does not include buildings on the agricultural unit or dwellings or buildings on another agricultural unit (DoE et al. 1992: 28).

revocation of planning permission It is possible for an LPA to revoke a planning permission already given, where it is in the public interest (Anonymous 1994b).

Royal Commission on Historical Monuments of England The national body of survey and record. It has responsibility to consider recording listed buildings threatened by demolition (DoE 1994g: 39).

Royal Fine Art Commission Advises LPAs in England and Wales on individual major development proposals which are submitted to it for scrutiny (DoE 1994g: 39).

shops and development control Shops and retailing have been mentioned in various places in the text. The main central government guidance is given in PPG6, *Town centres and retail development* (DoE 1996c). The key features are:

- Development control is plan led, to facilitate competition, employment, innovation and sustainability.
- Support is to be given to the strengthening of local centres.
- Where new retail development is envisaged, sites should be sought sequentially:

town centre, edge-of-centre, district or local centre, and out-of-centre with good transport.

- Town centres should be attractive, have mixed uses, key uses and a coherent parking policy, and be monitored.
- Retail proposals should be tested for impact on vitality and viability of town centres, accessibility by choice of mode and overall impact on car travel.

Annexes include a glossary of terms and advice on development plan policies, town centre management, amusement centres and traffic management (see Thomas 1990).

Site of Special Scientific Interest (SSSI) Sites of special scientific interest, which include plant and animal habitats, as well as geological and physiographical features of interest, are designated by English Nature (with the Countryside Council for Wales and Scottish Natural Heritage). Within this designation are sites of national and international importance such as National Nature Reserves. Designation criteria are to be found in Comptroller & Auditor General 1994: Appendix 4; DoE 1994j: 5–6 and annexes.

town cramming Infill development within existing settlements, which results in high densities. Such development is to the detriment of existing and future occupiers through loss of character and of privacy (Lowe 1996).

transport policies and programme (TPP) An annual bid by a highway authority to central government for funds for road building, maintenance, etc.

Tree Preservation Order (TPO) Specified trees, groups of trees and woodland may be subject to a TPO made by the LPA. The effect of this is that the consent of the LPA is necessary to lop, top or fell such trees. It is an offence to damage or destroy such trees wilfully. Trees in conservation areas (q.v.) have similar protection (DoE 1994i; see Ch. 6).

unilateral undertaking See **planning gain**.

white land Land safeguarded in development plans to allow for longer-term development needs. It often lies between an urban area and the green belt. Specific development control policies are usually found in development plans related to such land, for example recreation (Elson et al. 1993: 84, 89–91). It is so called because it is uncoloured on a development plan map and it may not be allocated for any purpose (Cullingworth 1980: 369).

Bibliography

Adams, C. D. 1994. *Urban planning and the development process*. London: UCL Press.

Alder, J. 1989. *Development control*, 2nd edn. London: Sweet & Maxwell.

Allmendinger, P. 1994. *Thatcherism and Simplified Planning Zones*. PhD thesis, School of Planning, Oxford Brookes University.

— 1996. Twilight zones. *Planning Week* **4**(29), 14–15.

AMA 1982. *Review of Article 4 Directions*. London: Association of Metropolitan Authorities.

AMA, ACC, ADC 1996. *The future of the planning system: a consultation paper*. London: Association of Metropolitan Authorities, Association of County Councils, Association of District Councils.

Anonymous 1991. Institute wants action on building demolition. *Planning* **911**, 4–5.

— 1993. Sproat intervention on hostels rallies Use Class campaigners. *Planning* **1028**, 4.

— 1994a. Marsham Street gives way on use changes to benefit hostels. *Planning* **1060**, 3.

— 1994b. Revocation hat-trick spells more trouble for authority. *Planning* **1081**, 24.

— 1994c. Planners warn higher processing speeds will compromise quality. *Planning Week* **2**(27), 5.

— 1995. Report calls for more rigour in environmental capacity field. *Planning* **1115**, 3.

— 1996a. Control performers start to get their act together. *Planning* **892**, 25.

— 1996b. Draft guidance seeks to bring planning benefit above board. *Planning* **1151**, 1.

— 1996c. Commission warns of threat to food supply from urbanization. *Planning* **1159**, 5.

— 1996d. Minister harassed by own side on planning control for masts. *Planning* **1159**, 28.

— 1996e. Agency aims to cure distorted views on the state of the environment. *Planning* **1163**, 28.

— 1996f. Listed building threat recedes as area designations fall back. *Planning* **1179**, 5.

— 1996g. Gillingham "adult babies" club has appeal upheld. *Planning Week* **4**(36), 4.

Arup Economics and Planning 1995a. *Evaluation of planning enforcement provisions*. Ruislip: Department of the Environment and Welsh Office.

— 1995b. *Derelict land prevention and the planning system*. London: HMSO.

Ashworth, W. 1954. *The genesis of modern British town planning*. London: Routledge & Kegan Paul.

Audit Commission 1992a. *Building in quality: a study of development control*. London: HMSO.

— 1992b. *Citizen's Charter performance indicators*. London: Audit Commission for Local Authorities in England and Wales.

Baber, P. 1996a. PPG6 to revive the High Street's heart. *Planning Week* **4**(26), 1.

— 1996b. PPG7's rural business use meets with mixed response. *Planning Week* **4**(32), 4.

Barnes, P. 1996. Working with the new regime. *Planning Week* **4**(8), 14–15.

301

Barrett, G., G. Russell, C. Athey 1994. *Toyota impact study*. Birmingham: Department of the Environment.

Barrow, J. F. 1994. *External enquiry into issues of concern about the administration of the planning system Warwick District Council*. Leamington Spa: Warwick District Council.

Barton, H., G. Davis, R. Guise 1995. *Sustainable settlements: a guide for planners, designers and developers*. Bristol & Luton: University of the West of England & Local Government Management Board.

Beattie, R. 1995. Human touch counts for users of service. *Planning* **1100**, 20–21.

Beddington, N. 1991. *Shopping centres, retail development design and management*. London: Butterworth.

Bell, S. 1992a. Change of use regime still out of order. *Planning* **994**, 14–15.

— 1992b. *Out of order: the 1987 Use Classes Order: problems and proposals*. London: London Boroughs Association.

Bell, S. 1993. *Elements of visual design in the landscape*. London: Spon.

Bentley, I., A. Alcock, P. Murrain, S. McGlynn, G. Smith 1985. *Responsive environments: a manual for designers*. London: Butterworth Architecture.

Bishop, J., I. Davison, J. Rose 1994. *Community involvement in planning and development processes*. London: HMSO.

Bishop, K. 1996. Planning to save the planet? Planning's green paradigm. See Tewdwr-Jones (1996), 205–219.

Blackman, T. 1996. Taking control of the numbers game. *Planning Week* **4**(17), 10.

Boisot Waters Cohen Partnership 1976. *The Community Land Act explained*. London: Architectural Press.

Booth, P. 1996. *Controlling development: certainty and discretion in Europe, the USA and Hong Kong*. London: UCL Press.

Brand, J., D. Bryce, N. McClure 1994. *A review of the Use Classes Order: a report to the Scottish Office*. Edinburgh: Scottish Office Central Review Unit.

Brenan, J. 1994. PPG16 and the restructuring of archaeological practice in Britain. *Planning Practice and Research* **9**(4), 395–405.

Bridger, A. 1987. *Development control: a manual. Unit 3 aesthetic issues*. London/Oxford: Royal Town Planning Institute/Oxford Polytechnic.

Brooke, C. E. 1996. *Natural conditions – a review of planning conditions and nature conservation*. Sandy: RSPB.

Brotherton, I. 1992. *Towards a theory of planning control*. Working paper, Department of Landscape, University of Sheffield.

Bruton, M. J. 1983. *Bargaining in development control*. Cardiff: UWIST.

Bruton, M. J. & D. Nicholson 1987. *Local planning in practice*. London: Hutchinson.

Buchanan, P. 1988. Facing up to facades. *Architects' Journal* **188**, 21–8.

Building Design Partnership 1990. *Time for design: monitoring the initiative*. London: HMSO.

BRE 1990. *Climate and site development*, parts I, II and III [BRE Digest 350]. Watford: Building Research Establishment.

Bunnel, G. 1995. Planning gain in theory and practice – negotiation of agreements in Cambridgeshire. *Progress in Planning* **44**(1) 6–113.

Burman, P., R. Pickard, S. Taylor (eds) 1995. *The economics of architectural conservation*. York: Institute for Advanced Architectural Studies.

Burton, I. 1996a. Labour planning group shoots for home goals. *Planning* **1161**, 6.

— 1996b. Group seeks answers to generalised blight. *Planning* **1175**, 10.

Burton, T., F. Reynolds, N. Sinder 1991. *The political dynamic of planning gain*. Working Paper 4, Department of Geography, Bristol University.

Calder, N., S. Cavanagh, C. Eckstein, J. Palmer, A. Stell 1993. *Women and development plans*. Working Paper 27, Department of Town and Country Planning, University of Newcastle upon Tyne.

Campbell, G. 1992. Telecommunications and the GDO. *Journal of Planning and Environment Law*, 222–6.

Carnwath, R. 1989. *Enforcing planning control*. London: HMSO.

Casely-Hayford, M. 1995. *Practical planning: permission and application*. London: FT Law and Tax.

Central Statistical Office 1996a. *Annual abstract of statistics*. London: HMSO.

— 1996b. *Social trends*. London: HMSO.

Cherry, G. E. 1974. *The evolution of British town planning*. Leighton Buzzard: Leonard Hill Books.

City of London Law Society 1995. *Inquiry procedures: another dose of reform?* London: City of London Law Society.

Collar, N. 1994. *Green's concise Scots law – planning*. Edinburgh: Green.

Comptroller & Auditor General 1994. *Protecting and managing sites of special scientific interest in England* [HC 379]. London: HMSO.

Condron, M. 1994. Class war over retail club. *Planning* **1056**, 23.

Cook, D. 1994. *The moral maze*. London: SPCK.

Cooke, P. 1983. *Theories of planning and spatial development*. London: Hutchinson.

Coon, A. 1996. When the cost of control gets out of hand [letter]. *Planning Week* **4**(35), 10.

Cormier, J. M. 1995. *Living with a listed building*. Newbury: Courtland Books.

Countryside Commission 1991. *Tourism in national parks: a guide to good practice*. Cheltenham: Countryside Commission.

— 1995. *Sustainable rural tourism opportunities for local action*. Cheltenham: Countryside Commission.

— 1996. *England's countryside: the role of the planning system* [consultation paper]. Cheltenham: Countryside Commission.

County Planning Officers' Society n.d. *The review of mineral working sites*. Matlock: Derbyshire County Council.

Cowan, R. 1983. The case for demolition control. *Town and Country Planning* **31**(3), 71.

— 1995. Coming to the aid of the people. *Planning Week* **3**(8), 12.

CPRE 1991. *Building responsibilities: the case for extending planning control over agricultural and forestry buildings*. London: Council for the Protection of Rural England.

— 1993. *Protection of conservation areas*. London: Council for the Protection of Rural England.

— 1994. *Historic buildings and conservation areas*. London: Council for the Protection of Rural England.

Crawley, I. 1991. Some reflections on planning and politics in Inner London. See Thomas & Healey (1991), 101–114.

Cronin, A. 1993. The elusive quality of certainty. *Planning Week* **1**(4), 16.

Cross, D. & C. Whitehead (eds) 1994. *Development and planning*. Cambridge: Granta (for the Department of Land Economy, University of Cambridge).

Crossthwaite, P. J. & E. M. Bichard 1990. Risk assessment – a tool for planners. *The*

Planner **76**(9), 9–10.

Cullingworth, J. B. 1980. *Environmental planning 1939–1969: land values, compensation and betterment*, vol. IV. London: HMSO.

David Tyldesley & Associates 1994. *Sustainability in practice: a report prepared for English Nature*. Peterborough: English Nature.

Davies H. W. E. 1994. *The impact of the EC on land-use planning in the UK* [2 volumes]. London: RTPI.

— 1996. Planning and the European question. See Tewdwr-Jones (1996), 220–238.

Davies, H. W. E., D. Edwards, A. R. Rowley 1986. The relationship between development plans, development control and appeals. *The Planner* **72**(10), 11–15.

— 1989. *The approval of reserved matters following outline planning permission*. London: HMSO.

Davies H. W. E., D. Edwards, A. J. Hooper, J. V. Punter 1989. *Planning control in western Europe*. London: HMSO.

Davies, L. 1996a. Equality and planning: gender and disability. See Greed (1996: 227–37).

— 1996b. Equality and planning: race. See Greed (1996: 215–26).

Delafons, J. 1994. Aesthetic control in British land-use planning. See Cross & Whitehead (1994: 85–8).

Denton, L. 1996. Whose turn to do the cleaning? *Planning Week* **4**(25), 12.

Denyer-Green B. 1994. *Compulsory purchase and compensation*. London: Estates Gazette.

Department of the Environment for Northern Ireland 1993. *A planning strategy for rural Northern Ireland*. London: HMSO.

— 1996. *The Planning (Northern Ireland) Order 1991* [SI 1991, 1220 (NI 11)]. Belfast: HMSO.

Department of National Heritage and Cadw 1994. *The ecclesiastical exemption: what it is and how it works*. London: Department of National Heritage.

Dijksman, K. 1992. *Planning permission: the essential guide for homeowners*. Newbury: Courtland Books.

Dobry, G. 1974. *Control of demolition*. London: HMSO.

— 1975. *Review of the development control system: final report*. London: HMSO.

DOE [Department of the Environment] annual. *Development control statistics: England 1992/93*. London: Government Statistical Service.

— 1969. *Town and Country Planning (Tree Preservation Order) Regulations* [SI 1969, no. 17]. London: HMSO.

— 1978. *Trees and forestry* [Circular 36/78 WO 64/78]. London: HMSO.

— 1980. *Development control – policy and practice* [Circular 22/80 WO 40/80]. London: HMSO.

— 1982. *Disabled Persons Act 1981* [Circular 10/82]. London: HMSO.

— 1983. *Caravan Sites and Control of Development Act 1960* [Circular 23/83 WO 32/83]. London: HMSO.

— 1985a. *Planning control over oil and gas operations* [Circular 2/85 WO 3/85]. London: HMSO.

— 1985b. *Development and employment* [Circular 14/85 WO 38/85]. London: HMSO.

— 1985c. *Control of advertisements: the report of the working party*. London: Department of the Environment.

— 1985d. *Guidelines for the provision of silica sand in England and Wales* [Circular 24/85 WO 58/85]. London: HMSO.

— 1985e. *Mineral workings – legal aspects relating to restoration of sites with high water tables* [Circular 25/85 WO 60/85]. London: HMSO.

— 1985f. *Service uses in shopping areas* [Development Control Policy Note 11]. London: HMSO.

— 1985g. *Access for the disabled* [Development Control Policy Note 16]. London: HMSO.

— 1986. *Proposals to modernize the Town and Country (Use Classes) Order 1972* [consultation paper]. London: DOE.

— 1987a. *The town and country planning (appeals) written representations procedure* [Circular 11/87 WO 21/87]. London: HMSO.

— 1987b. *Town and Country Planning (Use Classes) Order* [SI 1987, 764]. London: HMSO.

— 1987c. *Town and Country Planning (Use Classes) Order 1987* [Circular 13/87 WO 24/87]. London: HMSO.

— 1988a. *Applications, permissions and conditions* [MPG2]. London: HMSO.

— 1988b. *Environmental assessment* [Circular 15/88 WO 23/88]. London: HMSO.

— 1988c. *The review of mineral working sites* [MPG4]. London: HMSO.

— 1988d. *Simplified Planning Zones* [PPG5]. London: HMSO.

— 1988e. *Minerals planning and the General Development Order* [MPG5]. London: HMSO.

— 1988f. *Town and country planning (applications) regulations* [SI 1988, 1812]. London: HMSO.

— 1988g. *General considerations and the development plan system* [MPG1]. London: HMSO.

— 1988h. *Green belts* [PPG2]. London: HMSO.

— 1989a. *Landfill sites: development control* [Circular 17/89 WO 38/89]. London: HMSO.

— 1989b. *The reclamation of mineral workings* [MPG7]. London: HMSO.

— 1989c. *Town and Country Planning (Use Classes) Order 1987: review of special industrial use classes, B3–B7* [consultation paper]. London: DOE.

— 1989d. *Environmental assessment – a guide to the procedures*. London: HMSO.

— 1990a. *National code of local government conduct: annex B* [Circular 8/90 WO 23/90]. London: HMSO.

— 1990b. *Development on unstable land* [PPG14]. London: HMSO.

— 1990c. *Archaeology and planning* [PPG16]. London: HMSO.

— 1990d. *This common inheritance: Britain's environmental strategy* [Cmnd 1200]. London: HMSO.

— 1990e. *Planning permission: demolition of houses* [consultation paper]. London: DOE.

— 1991a. *Planning and Compensation Act* [Circular 14/91 WO 44/91]. London: HMSO.

— 1991b. *Sport and recreation* [PPG17]. London: HMSO.

— 1991c. *Planning obligations* [Circular 16/91 WO 53/91]. London: HMSO.

— 1991d. *Strategic guidance for London 1989* [RPG 3 Annex] London: HMSO.

— 1991e. *Planning and Compensation Act 1991: implementation of the main enforcement provisions* [Circular 21/91 WO 76/91]. London: HMSO.

— 1991f. *Enforcement of planning control* [PPG18]. London: HMSO.

— 1991g. *Review of tree preservation policies* [consultation paper]. London: DOE.

— 1991h. *Simplified Planning Zones: progress and procedures*. London: HMSO.

— 1992a. *The countryside and the rural economy* [PPG7]. London: HMSO.

— 1992b. *Development plans and regional planning guidance* [PPG12]. London: HMSO.

— 1992c. *General policy and principles* [PPG1]. London: HMSO.

— 1992d. *Housing* [PPG3]. London: HMSO.
— 1992e. *Town and Country Planning (Control of Advertisements) Regulations* [Circular 5/92 WO 14/92]. London: HMSO.
— 1992f. *Outdoor advertisement control* [PPG19]. London: HMSO.
— 1992g. *Planning controls for hazardous substances, The Planning (Hazardous Substances) Act 1990, The Planning (Hazardous Substances) Regulations 1992* [SI 1992, no. 656, Circular 11/92 WO 20/92]. London: HMSO.
— 1992h. *The Town and Country Planning (Control of Advertisements) Regulations* [SI 1992, 666]. London: HMSO.
— 1992i. *Publicity for planning applications* [Circular 15/92 WO 32/92]. London: HMSO.
— 1992j. *Planning controls over demolition* [Circular 16/92 WO 33/92]. London: HMSO.
— 1992k. *Planning and Compensation Act 1991, implementation of remaining enforcement provisions* [Circular 17/92 WO 38/92]. London: HMSO.
— 1992l. *Town and country planning (inquiries procedure) rules 1992* [SI 1992, no. 2038], *the town and country planning appeals (determination by inspectors) (inquiries procedure) rules 1992* [SI 1992, no. 2039] [Circular 24/92 WO 47/92]. London: HMSO.
— 1992m. *Coastal planning* [PPG20]. London: HMSO.
— 1992o. *Planning controls over demolition* [Circular 26/92 WO 57/92]. London: HMSO.
— 1992p. *Industrial and commercial development and small firms* [PPG4]. London: HMSO.
— 1992q. *Tourism* [PPG21]. London: HMSO.
— 1992r. *Modification and discharge of planning obligations* [Circular 28/92 WO 66/92]. London: HMSO.
— 1992s. *Development and flood risk* [Circular 30/92 WO 68/92]. London: HMSO.
— 1992t. *The Town and Country Planning (Fees for Applications and Deemed Applications) (Amendment) (2) Regulation 1992* [Circular 31/92 WO 73/92]. London: HMSO.
— 1992u. *Telecommunications* [PPG8]. London: HMSO.
— 1992v. *Development plans: a good practice guide*. London: HMSO.
— 1993a. *Public rights of way* [Circular 2/93 WO 5/93]. London: HMSO.
— 1993b. *Renewable energy* [PPG22]. London: HMSO.
— 1993c. *Award of costs incurred in planning and other (including compulsory purchase) proceedings* [Circular 8/93 WO 23/93]. London: HMSO.
— 1993d. *The control of noise at surface mineral workings* [MPG11]. London: HMSO.
— 1993e. *Review of the effectiveness of restoration conditions for mineral workings and the need for bonds*. London: HMSO.
— 1994a. *Gypsy sites and planning* [Circular 1/94 WO 2/94]. London: HMSO.
— 1994b. *Planning out crime* [Circular 5/94 WO 16/94]. London: HMSO.
— 1994c. *Transport* [PPG13]. London: HMSO.
— 1994d. *Environmental Protection Act 1990, part II: waste management licensing, the framework directive on waste* [Circular 11/94, WO 26/94 SO 10/94]. London: HMSO.
— 1994e. *Planning and pollution control* [PPG23]. London: HMSO.
— 1994f. *Quality in town and country: a discussion document*. London: DoE.
— 1994g. *Planning and the historic environment* [PPG15]. London: HMSO.
— 1994h. *Planning and noise* [PPG24]. London: HMSO.
— 1994i. *Tree Preservation Orders: a guide to the law and good practice*. London: DoE.
— 1994j. *Nature conservation* [PPG9]. London: HMSO.
— 1994k. *Gypsy site policy and unauthorized camping* [Circular 18/94 WO 76/94]. London: HMSO.
— 1994l. *Planning permission: a guide for business*. London: DoE.

— 1994m. *Sustainable development: the UK strategy* [Cm 2426]. London: HMSO.

— 1994n. *Vital and viable town centres: meeting the challenge*. London: HMSO.

— 1994o. *The costs of determining planning applications and the development control service*. London: HMSO.

— 1994p. *Evaluation of environmental information for planning projects*. London: HMSO.

— 1995a. *Green belts* [PPG2]. London: HMSO.

— 1995b. *Digest of data for the construction industry*. London: Government Statistical Service, HMSO.

— 1995c. *Permitted development and environmental assessment* [Circular 3/95 WO 12/95]. London: HMSO.

— 1995d. *General Development Order 1995 Consolidation* [Circular 9/95 WO 29/95]. London: HMSO.

— 1995e. *Planning controls over demolition* [Circular 10/95 WO 31/95]. London: HMSO.

— 1995f. *Index of planning guidance*. London: HMSO.

— 1995g. *The use of conditions in planning permissions* [Circular 11/95 WO 35/95]. London: HMSO.

— 1995h. *Town and Country Planning (Environmental assessment and unauthorised development) Regulations 1995* [Circular 13/95 WO 30/95]. London: HMSO.

— 1995i. *Outdoor advertisement control in areas of special control of advertisements (ASCAs)*. London: DoE.

— 1995j. *Preparation of environmental statements for planning projects that require environmental assessment*. London: HMSO.

— 1995k. *Town and Country Planning (General Permitted Development) Order 1995* [SI 1995, 41]. London: HMSO.

— 1995l. *Town and Country Planning (General Development Procedure) Order* [SI 1995, 419]. London: HMSO.

— 1996a. *Outdoor advertisement control: areas of special control of advertisements* [consultation paper]. London: DoE.

— 1996b. *Local Government Act 1992 and the Town and Country Planning Act 1990 local government change and the planning system* [Circular 4/96 WO not applicable]. London: HMSO.

— 1996c. *Town centres and retail developments* [PPG6]. London: HMSO.

— 1996d. *Sustainable settlements and shelter: the United Kingdom National Report Habitat II*. London: HMSO.

— 1996e. *General considerations and the development plan system* [MPG1]. London: HMSO.

DoE & Department of Transport 1992. *Residential roads and footpaths: layout considerations* [Design Bulletin 32]. London: HMSO.

— 1995. *PPG13, a guide to better practice: reducing the need to travel through land-use and transport planning*. London: HMSO.

DoE & WO 1992. *A householder's planning guide for the installation of satellite television dishes*. London: DoE/WO.

— 1995. *Outdoor advertisments and signs: a guide for advertisers*. London: DoE and WO.

— 1996a. *Planning: a guide for householders*. London: HMSO.

— 1996b. *Telecommunications prior approval procedure, as applied to mast/tower development. Code of best practice*. London: DoE.

DoE, WO, Ministry of Agriculture and Food 1992. *A farmer's guide to the planning system*. London: DoE, WO, MAFF.

307

DOE, WO, National Planning Forum 1994. *Planning: charter standards*. London: DOE.

DOE, Scottish Office, Joint Nature Conservation Committee 1995. *The Habitat's directive: how it will apply to Great Britain*. London: HMSO.

Drury, J. (ed.) 1981. *Factories, planning, design and modernization*. London: Architectural Press.

EHTF 1991. *Townscape in trouble – seminar papers*. Hove: English Historic Towns Forum.

— 1992. *Townscape in trouble: conservation areas – the case for change*. London: Butterworth.

Elson, M. & D. Payne 1993. *Planning obligations for sport and recreation: a guide for negotiation and action*. London: Sports Council.

Elson, M. J., S. Walker, R. Macdonald 1993. *The effectiveness of green belts*. London: HMSO.

Elson, M., C. Steenberg, J. Wilkinson 1995a. *Planning for rural diversification: a good practice guide*. London: HMSO.

Elson, M., R. Macdonald, C. Steenberg 1995b. *Planning for rural diversification*. London: HMSO.

— 1996. Planning ways forward on diversified rural economy. *Planning* **1150**, 8–9.

Elsworth Sykes Planning 1991. *Planning – is it a service and how can it be effective?* London: RTPI.

English Estates, Scottish Development Agency, Welsh Development Agency, Industrial Development Board for Northern Ireland, Development Board for Rural Wales, Highlands & Islands Development Board 1986. *Industrial and commercial estates planning and site development*. London: Thomas Telford.

English Heritage 1993. *Conservation area practice*. London: English Heritage.

English Heritage & RICS 1993. *The investment performance of listed buildings*. London: RICS.

English Tourist Board 1991. *Tourism and the environment: monitoring the balance*. London: ETB.

Ennis, F., P. Healey, M. Purdue 1993. *Frameworks for negotiating development*. Project paper, Departments of Law and Town & Country Planning, University of Newcastle upon Tyne.

Environment Agency 1996. *Customer charter: our statement of service standards*. Bristol: Environment Agency.

Essex County Council 1975. *A design guide for residential areas*. Chelmsford: Essex County Council.

Essex, S. 1991. The nature of the job. See Thomas & Healey (1991: 86–91).

— 1996. Members and officers in the planning process. See Tewdwr-Jones (1996: 156–67).

Evans, A. 1988. *No room! No room! The costs of the British town and country planning system*. Occasional Paper 79, Institute of Economic Affairs, London.

Fair, J. 1994a. A permit to offer room at the inn. *Planning Week* **2**(12), 11.

— 1994b. On the fast-track to an elitist system. *Planning Week* **2**(22), 6.

— 1994c. Pragmatism versus purity in the conservation debate. *Planning Week* **2**(28), 10.

Flowers, Lord (Chair) 1986. *Town and country planning: the report of a committee of inquiry appointed by the Nuffield Foundation*. London: Nuffield Foundation.

Friend, B. 1996. Lichfield maladministration case highlights lack of resources. *Planning*

Week **4**(21), 7.

Fyson, A. 1991. Limiting the right to destroy. *The Planner* **77**(11), 3.

Gatenby, I. & C. Williams 1996. Interpreting planning law. See Tewdwr-Jones (1996: 137–54).

George, C. 1991. *Independent inquiry into planning decisions in the London Borough of Brent 1986–1990*. Wembley: London Borough of Brent.

Gilg, A. & M. Kelly 1996. The analysis of development control decisions. *Town Planning Review* **67**(2), 203–28.

Glasson, B. & P. Booth 1992. Negotiation and delay in the development control process: case studies in Yorkshire and Humberside. *Town Planning Review* **63**(1), 63.

Glasson, J., R. Therivel, A. Chadwick 1994. *Introduction to environmental impact assessment*. London: UCL Press.

GLC 1983. *An introduction to housing layout*. London: Architectural Press.

— 1985. *Traffic generation: user's guide and review of studies*, 2nd edn. London: Greater London Council.

GMA Planning 1994. *Integrated planning and granting of permits in the EC*. London: HMSO.

Grant, M. 1995. *Permitted development*. London: Sweet & Maxwell.

Grant, M. (ed.) continuing. *Encyclopedia of planning law* [6 volumes]. London: Sweet & Maxwell.

Greed, C. 1994. *Women and planning*. London: Routledge.

— (ed.) 1995. *Implementing town planning*. Harlow: Longman.

— (ed.) 1996. *Implementing town planning, the role of town planning in the development process*. Harlow: Longman.

Greenwood, B. (ed.) 1995. *Butterworth's planning law handbook*. London: Butterworth.

Griffiths, M. 1995. Cleaning the air. *Planning Week* **3**(49), 12.

Grimley J. R. Eve (in association with Thames Polytechnic) 1992. *The use of planning agreements*. London: HMSO.

Guy, C. 1994. *The retail development process*. London: Routledge.

Hague, C. 1984. *The development of planning thought: a critical perspective*. London: Hutchinson.

Hague, C. 1991. A review of planning theory in Britain. *Town Planning Review* **62**(3), 295–310.

Hall, T. 1995. Visual reality. *Planning Week* **3**(11), 16–17.

Halton Borough Council 1993. *Halton local plan*. Widnes: Halton Borough Council.

Hammersley, R. 1980. The local ombudsman and his impact on planning. *The Planner* **66**(1), 10.

Harrison, M. L. & R. Mordey (eds) 1987. *Planning control: philosophy, prospects and practice*. London: Croom Helm.

Hartop, S. 1993. *The effects of business class on the supply of business space and on the existing uses of office and industry in Edinburgh*. Research Paper 49, School of Planning and Housing, Edinburgh College of Art/Heriot–Watt University.

Hayton, K. 1996. Planning policy in Scotland. See Tewdwr-Jones (1996: 78–97).

Hayward, R. & S. McGlynn 1993. *Making better places: urban design now*. Oxford: Butterworth Architecture.

Healey, P., G. McDougall, M.J. Thomas (eds) 1982. *Planning theory – prospects for the 1980s*. Oxford: Pergamon.

309

Healey, P., M. Purdue, F. Ennis 1995. *Negotiating development: rationales and practice for development obligations and planning gain*. London: Spon.

Henneberry, J. 1982. Planning delay in perspective. *The Planner* **68**(3), 72–3, 95.

Hepburn, G. 1994. Empowering the enforcers. *Planning Week* **2**(45), 14–15.

Higgins, M. 1996. Contracting out of planning services: RTPI survey of planning authorities. *Planning Week* **4**(15), 18.

Hillman, J. 1990. *Planning for beauty*. London: Royal Fine Arts Commission, HMSO.

Hilton, I. C. (ed.) 1981. *Carparking standards in development control*. Manchester: UMIST.

Hirst, C. 1996a. Associations draw up 21st century planning agenda. *Planning Week* **4**(26), 3.

— 1996b. Street campaigners voice public concerns. *Planning Week* **4**(34), 4.

Hobson, J., S. Hockman, P. Stinchcombe 1996. The future of the planning system. In *Law reform for all*, D. Bean (ed.), 214–20. London: Blackstone Press.

Holt, G. (ed.) continuing. *Development control practice* [3 volumes]. Gloucester: Ambit.

Home, R. 1989. *Planning use classes: a guide to the Use Classes Orders*. Oxford: Blackwell Scientific (BSP Professional Books).

— 1994. The planner and the gypsy. In *Race, equality and planning*, H. Thomas & V. Krishnarayan (eds), 111–27. Aldershot: Avebury.

Hope, D. 1992. *The 1990–91 Planning Acts: a plain English guide with case law references*. London: RIBA.

House of Commons, Environment Committee 1990. *Environmental issues in Northern Ireland* [HC 39]. London: HMSO.

— 1995. *The environmental impact of leisure activities*, 4th Report, vols I & III [HC 246 – I & III]. London: HMSO.

House of Commons Northern Ireland Affairs Committee 1996. *The planning system in Northern Ireland* [HC 53-I]. London: HMSO.

House of Commons Welsh Affairs Committee 1993. *Third report on rural housing* [HC 621 – I, II, III]. London: HMSO.

House of Lords 1995. *Report of the Select Committee on Sustainable Development* [HL 72 – I, II, III]. London: HMSO.

HRH Prince of Wales 1989. *A vision of Britain: a personal view of architecture*. London: Doubleday.

Hubbard, P. 1994. Professional versus lay tastes in design control – an empirical investigation. *Planning Research and Practice* **9**(3), 271–87.

Hutchinson, M. & P. Fidler 1991. New RTPI/RIBA initiative on planning and design. *The Planner* **77**(16), 5.

Hutton, R. 1996. Keeping the neighbours happy lines up with the public interest. *Planning* **1168**, 9.

ILEX 1993a. *Town and country planning law*. Bedford: ILEX.

— 1993b. *Town and country planning law, book 2: cognate legislation*. Bedford: ILEX.

IHT (with the Department of Transport) 1987. *Roads and traffic in urban areas*. London: HMSO.

IHT 1994. *Guidelines for traffic impact assessment of development*. London: Institution of Highways and Transportation.

Irlam, R. 1994. Robbing rich is no solution [letter]. *Planning* **1067**, 2.

Institution of Civil Engineers 1993. *Land drainage and flood defence responsibilities*. London: Thomas Telford.

Jacobs, J. 1961. *The death and life of great American cities*. New York: Vintage Books.

Jarvis, B. 1980. Urban environments as visual art or as social settings. *Town Planning Review* **51**, 51–66.

Jones, A. & P. Larkham 1993. *The character of conservation areas*. London: RTPI.

Joyce, P. 1994. Customer care. In *Proceedings, Town and Country Planning Summer School 1991*, 61–3. London: Royal Town Planning Institute.

Keeble, L. 1985. *Fighting planning appeals*. London: Construction Press.

Kendig, L. 1980. *Performance zoning*. Chicago: American Planning Association.

Kitchen, T. 1991. A client-based view of the planning service. See Thomas & Healey (1991: 115–44).

Krishnarayan, V. & H. Thomas 1993. *Ethnic minorities and the planning system*. London: RTPI.

Land Use Consultants 1995. *The effectiveness of Planning Policy Guidance Notes*. London: DoE.

Land Use Consultants & Countryside Planning and Management 1995. *Planning controls over agricultural and forestry development and rural building conversions*. London: HMSO.

Larkham, P. J. 1990. *Development pressure and development delay*. Working Paper 56, School of Geography, University of Birmingham.

— 1992. The concept of delay in development control. *Planning Outlook* **33**(2), 101–7.

Larkham, P. J. & D. W. Chapman 1996. Article 4 Directions and development control: planning myths, present uses and future possibilities. *Journal of Environmental Planning and Management* **39**(1), 5–20.

Lavers, A. & B. Webster 1990. *A practice guide to planning appeals*. London: Estates Gazette.

Laxton, P. 1993. Costco offers rich pickings [letter]. *Planning* **1045**, 2.

Leary, M. & A. Rodriguez-Bachiller 1988. Expert systems in development control. *The Planner* **74**(10), 26–8.

Lee, M., C. Roberts, P. Hands 1987. *Retail warehouse appeals review*. London: Lee Donaldson Associates.

— 1988. *Superstore appeals review*. London: Lee Donaldson Associates.

Lee Donaldson Associates 1989. *The third wave breaks*. London: Lee Donaldson Associates.

Lees, A. M. 1993. *Enquiry into the planning system in North Cornwall District*. London: HMSO.

Little, A. J. 1992. *Planning controls and their enforcement*, 6th edn. Crayford: Shaw & Sons.

Littlefair, P. J. 1991. *Site layout planning for daylight and sunlight – a guide to good practice*. Watford: BRE.

Local Government Management Board and Royal Town Planning Institute 1992. *Planning staffs survey*. London: LGMB & RTPI.

Lowe, A. 1996. Balancing acts. *Planning Week* **4**(34), 11.

Lynch, K. 1960. *The image of the city*. Cambridge, Massachusetts: MIT Press.

— 1982. *A theory of good city form*. Cambridge, Massachusetts: MIT Press.

Macdonald, R. 1991. *The use of planning agreements by district councils*. Oxford: Oxford

Polytechnic and the Association of District Councils.

Manns, S. 1995. Communication breakdown over new demolition regime. *Planning* **1120**, 10.

Mason, R. 1996. *Planning law manual*. School of Planning, Oxford Brookes University.

McAuslan, P. 1980. *The ideologies of planning law*. Oxford: Pergamon.

McCarthy, P., Prism Research, T. Harrison 1995. *Attitudes to town and country planning*. London: HMSO.

McCluskey, J. 1992. *Road form and townscape*. Oxford: Butterworth–Heinemann.

McConnell, S. 1981. *Theories for planning*. London: Heinemann.

McLoughlin, J. B. 1973. *Control and urban planning*. London: Faber & Faber.

McNamara P. 1986. *Development control – a training manual. Unit 1: development control in action: a reader*. London/Oxford: Royal Town Planning Institute/Oxford Polytechnic.

McNamara, P., A. Jackson, S. Mithrani 1986. *Appellants' perceptions of the planning appeal system*. Working Paper 93, Department of Town Planning, Oxford Polytechnic.

Mid-Sussex District Council 1993. *Development control customer surveys*. Haywards Heath: Mid-Sussex District Council.

Miller, C. & C. Fricker 1993. Planning and hazard. *Progress in Planning* **40**(3), 169–260.

Millichap, D. 1994. Red light for planners caught in moral maze. *Planning* **1096**, 24–5.

— 1996. Keeping up appearances in defining development. *Planning* **1157**, 20.

Milne, R. 1991. Whitehall sees no sign of problem on demolition control. *Planning* **904**, 21.

Milton Keynes Development Corporation 1993. *The Milton Keynes planning manual*. Milton Keynes: Milton Keynes Development Corporation.

Minett, J. 1986. *Development control: a manual introduction*. London/Oxford: Royal Town Planning Institute/Oxford Polytechnic.

Ministry of Housing and Local Government 1970. *Development plans: a manual on form and content*. London: HMSO.

Minton, A. 1993. Birmingham faces sensitive issue of offenders' clinic. *Planning Week* **1**(12), 13.

Moor, N. 1996. Preparing for the dawn of the "Third Age". *Planning Week* **4**(12), 12–13.

Morgan, P. & S. Nott 1995. *Development control: law, policy and practice*. London: Butterworth.

Nathaniel Lichfield & Partners 1990. *Commuted carparking policy and practice*. London: Nathaniel Lichfield & Partners.

National Planning Forum, Department of the Environment, Welsh Office 1993. *Development control: a charter guide*. London: National Planning Forum.

Nicholson, D. 1991. Planners' skills and planning practice. See Thomas & Healey (1991: 53–62).

Northern Ireland Audit Office 1995. *Department of the Environment: town and country planning service*. London: HMSO.

O'Callaghan, D. 1996. Branches of communication. *Planning Week* **4**(31), 12–13.

O'Hara, L. & P. Allen 1996. Guardians of the peace? *Planning Week* **4**(1), 13.

Osborn, S. & H. Shaftoe 1995. *Safer neighbourhoods? Successes and failures in crime prevention*. London: Safe Neighbourhoods Unit.

PA Cambridge Economic Consultants 1987. *An evaluation of the Enterprise Zone experiment*. London: HMSO.

— 1995. *Final evaluation of Enterprise Zones*. London: HMSO.

Paris, C. 1982. *Critical readings in planning theory*. Oxford: Pergamon.

Payne, S. 1992. Development and planning permission. *New Law Journal* **24**, 1061–2.

Pell, B. 1991. From the public to the private sector. See Thomas & Healey (1991: 92–100).

Pfeffer, N. & N. Coote 1991. *Is quality good for you?* London: Institute of Public Policy Research.

Phelps, R. W. 1996. *Report of an independent inquiry into certain planning related issues in Bassetlaw to the Bassetlaw District Council*. Worksop: Bassetlaw District Council.

Philips, A. 1993a. *The best in industrial architecture*. London: Batsford.

— 1993b. *The best in science, office and business park design*. London: Batsford.

Philips, D. 1995. Flying in the face of reason [letter]. *Planning* **1138**, 2.

PIEDA 1992. *Evaluating the effectiveness of land-use planning: a study for the Department of the Environment*. London: HMSO.

Pinder, A. & A. Pinder 1990. *Beazley's design and detail of the space between buildings*. London: Spon.

Planning Advisory Group 1965. *The future of development plans*. London: HMSO.

Planning Inspectorate 1992. *Planning appeals – a guide*. Bristol: Planning Inspectorate.

Planning Inspectorate Executive Agency 1994. *Annual report and accounts for the year ending 31st March 1994*. Bristol & Cardiff: DOE & WO.

Preece, R. A. 1981. *Patterns of development control in the Cotswolds Area of Outstanding Natural Beauty*. Research Paper 27, School of Geography, University of Oxford.

— 1990. Development control studies: scientific method and policy analysis. *Town Planning Review* **61**(1), 59–73.

— 1991. *Designs on the landscape*. London: Pinter (Belhaven).

Procter, S. 1996. Assessing the truth on delay [letter]. *Planning* **1162**, 2.

Property Advisory Group 1985. *Town and Country Planning (Use Classes) Order 1972: Report*. London: DOE.

Punter, J. 1985. *Office development control in the Borough of Reading 1954–84: a case study of aesthetic control within the planning process*. Working Paper 6, Department of Land Management, University of Reading.

— 1990a. *Design control in Bristol 1940–90*. Bristol: Redcliffe Press.

— 1990b. The ten commandments of architecture and urban design. *The Planner* **76**(39), 10–14.

— 1994. Aesthetics in planning. See Thomas (1994: 38–67).

Raine, D. 1995. Resolution of design issues [letter]. *Planning* **1137**, 2.

Ratcliffe, J. & M. Stubbs 1996. *Urban planning and real estate development*. London: UCL Press.

Rawlinson, C. 1989. Design and development control: an analysis of conditions and refusals. *The Planner* **75**(19), 17–20.

Reade, E. 1987. *British town and country planning*. Milton Keynes: Open University.

Redman, M. 1989. *Planning uses and Use Classes*. London: Estates Gazette.

Reference Services, Central Office of Information 1992. *Aspects of Britain – planning*. London: HMSO.

Reid, T. C. (ed.) 1992. *Green's guide to environmental law in Scotland*. Edinburgh: Green.

Richards, R. *Conservation planning*. London: Planning Aid for London.

Roberts, M. 1974. *An introduction to town planning techniques*. London: Hutchinson.

Rodriguez-Bachiller A. 1988. *Town planning education: an international survey*. Aldershot: Avebury.

Roger Tym & Partners 1989a. *The effect on small firms of refusal of planning permission.* London: HMSO.

— 1989b. *The incidence and effect of planning conditions.* London: HMSO.

— 1995. *The use of Article 4 Directions: a report of the Department of the Environment.* London: HMSO.

Roger Tym & Partners & Pagoda Associates 1995. *Review of the implementation of PPG16: archaeology and planning.* London: English Heritage.

Ross, A. 1990. Getting the best from landscape conditions. *Planning* **884**, 24–5.

Ross, S. 1991. Planning in the public interest. *Proceedings Town and Country Planning Summer School 1991.* London: RTPI.

Rowan-Robinson, J., A. Ross, A. Walton 1995. Sustainable development and the development control process. *Town Planning Review* **66**(3), 269–86.

Royal Commission on Environmental Pollution 1996. *Sustainable use of soil* [Cm 3165]. London: HMSO.

Roy Waller & Associates 1989. *Study of special industrial Use Classes.* London: DOE.

RSPB 1992. *SSSIs in the 1990s: a check on the health of internationally important bird areas.* London: Royal Society for the Protection of Birds.

RTPI 1986. *Town and Country Planning (Use Classes) Order, memorandum of observations to the DoE on the Report of the Property Advisory Group.* London: Royal Town Planning Institute.

— 1988a. *Development control: handling planning applications* [PAN1]. London: Royal Town Planning Institute.

— 1988b. *Access for disabled people* [PAN3]. London: Royal Town Planning Institute.

— 1989a. *Professional practice and maladministration* [PAN7]. London: Royal Town Planning Institute.

— 1989b. *Chartered town planners at inquiries* [PAN4]. London: Royal Town Planning Institute.

— 1990. *Development briefs* [PAN8]. London: Royal Town Planning Institute.

— 1993. *BS 5750 Quality assurance for planners: guidelines and case studies.* London: Royal Town Planning Institute.

— 1994. *Code of professional conduct.* London: Royal Town Planning Institute.

— 1995a. *Development control – handling appeals* [PAN9]. London: Royal Town Planning Institute.

— 1995b. *Planning for women* [PAN12]. London: Royal Town Planning Institute.

— 1995c. *Environmental assessment* [PAN13]. London: Royal Town Planning Institute.

— 1996. *Enforcement of planning control* [PAN6]. London: Royal Town Planning Institute.

Salt, A. 1991. *Planning applications: the RMJM guide,* 2nd edn. Oxford: Blackwell Scientific (BSP Professional Books).

School of Planning & Housing, Edinburgh College of Art/Heriot–Watt University, Peter P. C. Allen (Chartered Town Planning Consultants) Ltd 1995. *Review of neighbour notification.* Edinburgh: Scottish Office Central Research Unit.

Scrase, A. 1988. Grounds for refusal. *The Planner* **74**(4), 20–23.

Sennitt, M. 1993. Tidy site notice shows metal. *Planning* **1013**, 17.

Short, J. R., S. Fleming, S. Witt 1986. *House building, planning and community action: the production and negotiation of the built environment.* London: Routledge.

Silvester, J. 1996. European spatial planning starts from the bottom up. *Planning* **1180**, 20–21.

Simmons, S. & A. Barker 1988. Nature conservation in towns and cities – principles for implementation. *The Planner* **74**(6), 9–11.

Singleton, D. 1995. Ulster town and country planning up for scrutiny. *Planning* **1146**, 7.

Skeffington, A. M. 1969. *People and planning: Report of the committee on public participation in planning*. London: HMSO.

Smith, A., P. Challen, S. Marsh, A. Hilton 1996. Should casinos play a part in the regeneration of town centres? [comment]. *Planning Week* **4**(10), 28.

SODD 1996a. *Planning and waste management* [NPPG 10]. Edinburgh: Scottish Office Development Department.

— 1996b. *Planning application forms* [PAN48]. Edinburgh: Scottish Office.

— 1996c. *Local planning* [PAN49]. Edinburgh: Scottish Office.

— 1996d. *Planning series publications*. Edinburgh: Scottish Office.

SOED 1993. *Development control* [PAN40]. Edinburgh: Scottish Office Environment Department.

— 1994a. *The planning system* [NPPG1]. Edinburgh: Scottish Office.

— 1994b. *Review of the town and country planning system in Scotland*. Edinburgh: Scottish Office.

— 1995. *Review of the town and country planning system in Scotland – summary of responses to consultation*. Edinburgh: Scottish Office.

Spawforth, P. 1995. Vox pop. *Planning Week* **3**(27), 16–17.

Speer, R. & M. Dade 1995. *How to get planning permission*. London: Dent.

Steel, J., V. Nadin, A. Cave, R. Daniels, T. Westlake 1994. *The efficiency and effectiveness of local plan inquiries*. London: HMSO.

Stevens, R. 1976. *Planning control over mineral working*. London: HMSO.

Stevenson, N. 1996. London boroughs build quality into decisions. *Planning* **1145**, 24–5.

Stothers, N. & C. Shaw 1992. Implementation of a development control package. *Planning Practice and Research* **7**(3), 5–12.

Sturt, D. 1995. Officers and members ready to take planning moral stand. *Planning* **1104**, 9.

Swinburn, R. 1991. Entering practice. See Thomas & Healey (1991: 63–72).

Taussik, J. 1991. *Preapplication enquiries, an examination of the practice (including charging) relating to this service by LPAs and developers*. Occasional paper, Faculty of Environmental Studies, Portsmouth Polytechnic.

— 1992. Preapplication enquiries. *The Planner* **78**(13), 14–15.

Taylor, N. 1994. Environmental issues and the public interest. See Thomas (1994: 87–115).

Telling, A. E. & R. M. C. Duxbury 1993. *Planning law and procedure*, 9th edn. London: Butterworth.

Tewdwr-Jones, M. (ed.) 1996. *British planning policy in transition*. London: UCL Press.

Thomas, H. 1993. Welsh planners voice some lingering doubts. *Planning* **1041**, 20–21.

— (ed.) 1994. *Values and planning*. Aldershot: Avebury.

— 1996. Public participation in planning. See Tewdwr-Jones (1996: 168–88).

Thomas, H. & P. Healey 1991. *Dilemmas of planning practice*. Aldershot: Avebury.

Thomas, H. & V. Krishnarayan 1994. *Race, equality and planning: practices and procedures*. Aldershot: Avebury.

Thomas, K. 1972. *Industry and employment in NW Kent 1945–1960*. PhD thesis, Department of Geography, London School of Economics.

— 1988a. *A survey of development control issues*. Working Paper 106, School of Planning, Oxford Polytechnic.

— 1988b. *Issues in development control: a manual. Unit 4: issues in development control*. London/Oxford: Royal Town Planning Institute/Oxford Polytechnic.

— 1988c. *American industrial planning*. Working Paper 110, School of Planning, Oxford Polytechnic.

— 1990. *Planning for shops*. London: Estates Gazette.

— 1991. *Planning for shopping in America*. Working Paper 135, School of Planning, Oxford Polytechnic.

— 1994. *An introduction to development control*. London: Estates Gazette.

— 1995. *The supply and demand for planners in Britain in the 1980s and 1990s*. Working Paper 155, School of Planning, Oxford Brookes University.

Thomas, P. (ed.) continuing. *The planning fact book*. London: Gee Publishing.

Thomas, R. & H. Thomas 1990. *Not an appropriate area: the consideration of planning applications for hot-food takeaways*. Working Paper 1, School of Hospitality Management, Leeds Polytechnic.

Thompsett, R. 1995. A breakdown in communication with ground control. *Planning Week* 3(41), 14.

Thornley, A. 1993. *Urban planning under Thatcherism: the challenge of the market*, 2nd edn. London: Routledge.

— 1996. Planning policy and the market. See Tewdwr-Jones (1996: 189–204).

Tibbalds, F. 1988. Urban design: Tibbalds offers the Prince his ten commandments. *The Planner* 74(12) [mid-month supplement], 1.

Tibbs, N. 1991. Sociology, planning and pragmatism in twenty short years. See Thomas & Healey (1991: 75–85).

Trafalgar House 1987. *Developing business success*. London: Trafalgar House.

Trimbos, J. 1996. Hoarding up positive benefit from outdoor advertising. *Planning* **1182**, 10.

Turner, T. 1987. *An introduction to landscape planning*. London: Hutchinson.

Tutt, P. & D. Adler (eds) 1979. *New metric handbook: planning and design data*. London: Butterworth.

Underwood, J. 1981. Development control: a review of research and current issues. *Progress in Planning* 16(3), 179–242.

— 1991. What is really material? Rising above interest group politics. See Thomas & Healey (1991: 147–55).

URPI 1981. *Shopper and service users* [Information Briefs 81/4, 81/7]. Reading: Unit for Retail Planning Information.

Uthwatt, L. J. 1942. *Final report of the expert committee on compensation and betterment* [Cmd 6386]. London: HMSO.

Uzzell, C. 1995. The price of tunnel vision. *Planning Week* 3(31), 18.

Valuation Office Spring 1996. *Property market report Spring 1996*. London: HMSO.

Wakeford, R. 1990. *American development control*. London: HMSO.

Walker, G. 1994. *Hazardous substances consents: a review of the operation of statutory planning controls over hazardous substances*. London: DOE.

Walsh, P. D. 1988. *Natural justice: influences on development control*. Occasional Paper

4, Department of Estate Management, Oxford Polytechnic.

Walsh, P. D., K. Thomas, J. Porter 1986. *Home based economic activity.* Working Paper 94, Department of Town Planning, Oxford Polytechnic.

Ward, C. 1994. False promises. *Planning Week* **2**(32), 16.

Wates, N. 1989. Ten green commandments. *Environment Now* (February), 10.

Wenban-Smith, A. & J. Beeston 1990. *Negotiating with planning authorities.* London: Estates Gazette.

Widdicombe, D. 1986. *The conduct of local authority business: Report of the Committee of Inquiry.* London: HMSO.

Willman, J. 1990. *The Which? guide to planning and conservation.* London: Consumers' Association.

Wingate, D. 1996. Developing the art of control. *Planning Week* **4**(33), 9.

WO 1993. *Development control – a guide to good practice.* Cardiff: Welsh Office.

— 1996. *Planning guidance (Wales) planning policy.* Cardiff: HMSO.

Wootton Jeffreys Consultants Ltd & Bernard Thorpe 1991. *An examination of the effects of the Use Classes Order 1987 and the General Development Order 1988.* London: HMSO.

Worthington, T. 1996. A sustainable land-use policy for agriculture? *Planning* **1159**, 20–22.

Wright, A. 1991. *Planning for householders.* London: Planning Aid.

W. S. Atkins Planning Consultants 1993a. *Customer survey: study of appellants' experience of the written representations appeals system.* Bristol: Planning Inspectorate.

— 1993b. *Customer survey: study of appellants' and local authorities' experience of the hearings system.* Bristol: Planning Inspectorate.

— 1994. *Customer survey: study of customers' experience of the inquiry procedure.* Bristol: Planning Inspectorate.

Zetter, R., R. Darke, R. Mason 1996. *The role of elected members in plan-making and development control.* London: Royal Town Planning Institute.

Index

Page numbers in **bold** indicate glossary items, reference to key terms, or substantial information, depending on the context.

Readers may find the following indexes particularly useful:

DOE, June 1995. *Index of planning guidance*. London: HMSO.
Council for the Protection of Rural England and Planning, July 1995 *Index of planning policy guidance notes*. London: CPRE.
Ware, P. (ed.) continuing. *Barbour index planning and environmental law microfile*. Windsor: Barbour Index.